久保帯人

...ybe it's because I've been so busy lately, but I constantly find myself thinking, "I wish I could draw without worrying about time." But in reality, when I do get some free time, I'll probably piddle around and do nothing. I guess you always want what you don't have.

Tite Kubo

BLEACH is author Tite Kubo's second title. Kubo made his debut with *ZOMBIE POWDER*, a four-volume series for *WEEKLY SHONEN JUMP*. To date, *BLEACH* has been translated into numerous languages and has also inspired an animated TV series that began airing in Japan in 2004. Beginning its serialization in 2001, *BLEACH* is still a mainstay in the pages of *WEEKLY SHONEN JUMP*. In 2005, *BLEACH* was awarded the prestigious Shogakukan Manga Award in the *shonen* (boys) category.

BLEACH
Vol. 11: A STAR AND A STRAY DOG
The SHONEN JUMP Manga Edition

STORY AND ART BY
TITE KUBO

English Adaptation/Lance Caselman
Translation/Joe Yamazaki
Touch-Up Art & Lettering/Andy Ristaino
Design/Sean Lee
Editor/Kit Fox

Managing Editor/Frances E. Wall
Editorial Director/Elizabeth Kawasaki
VP & Editor in Chief/Yumi Hoashi
Sr. Director of Acquisitions/Rika Inouye
Sr. VP of Marketing/Liza Coppola
Exec. VP of Sales & Marketing/John Easum
Publisher/Hyoe Narita

Printed in the U.S.A.

Published by VIZ Media, LLC
P.O. Box 77010
San Francisco, CA 94107

SHONEN JUMP Manga Edition
10 9 8 7 6 5 4 3 2
First printing, January 2006
Second printing, July 2006

www.viz.com

THE WORLD'S
MOST POPULAR MANGA

www.shonenjump.com

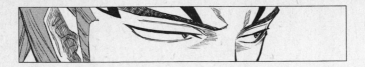

Light a fire to the fang that cannot be reached
So that I do not have to see that star
So that I do not slit this throat

BLEACH 11

A STAR AND A STRAY DOG

Shonen Jump Manga

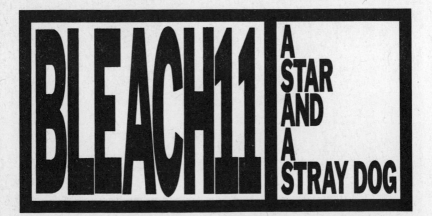

STARS AND

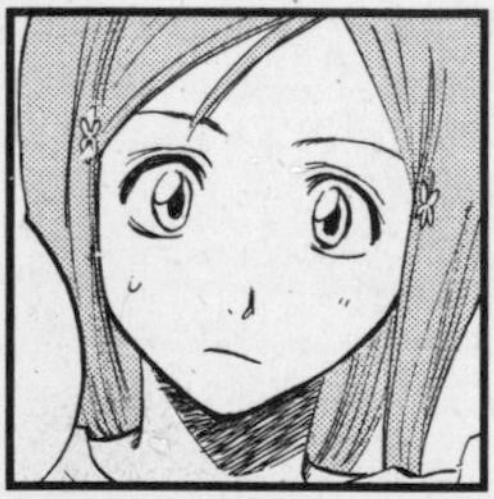

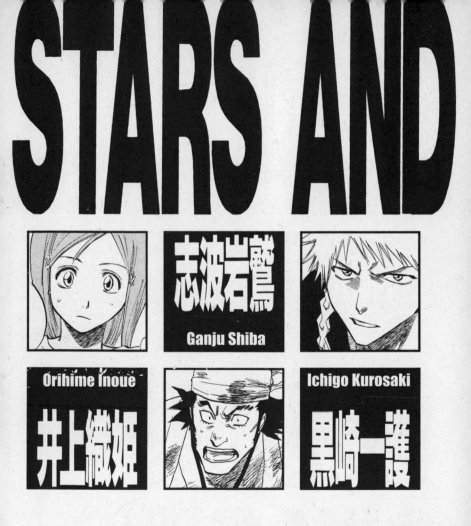

志波岩鷲
Ganju Shiba

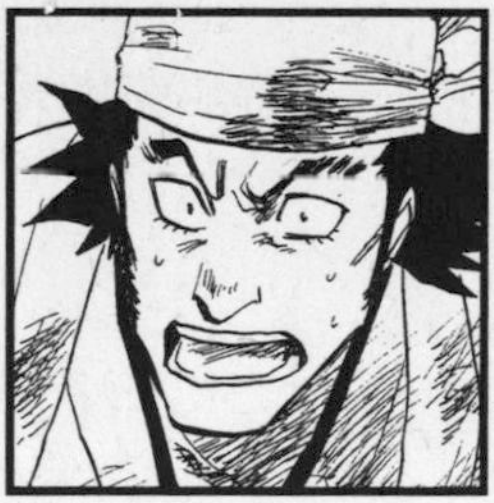

Orihime Inoue
井上織姫

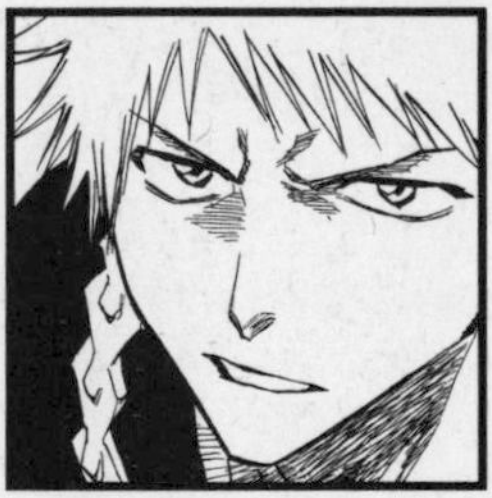

Ichigo Kurosaki
黒崎一護

plot

While Rukia awaits execution in a Soul Society cell, Ichigo and the others try to rescue her. They manage to penetrate the shield that protects the inner city of the Soul Reapers but are hurled in different directions by the impact. They find themselves scattered and hunted by an army of Soul Reapers. Ichigo fights and defeats Ikkaku Madarame, a Sansetsukon user! Meanwhile, Ganju faces off with a pursuer of his own...

BLEACH ALL

阿散井恋次

Renji Abarai

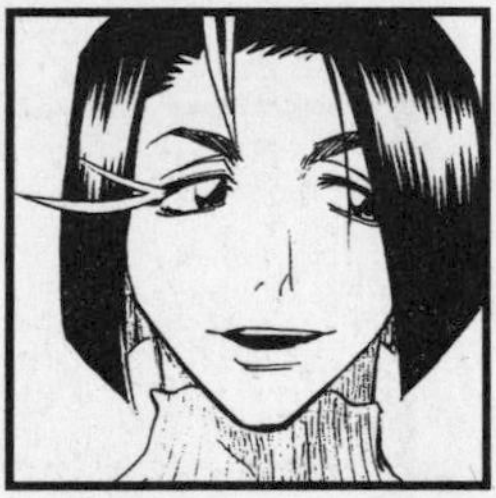

石田雨竜

Uryû Ishida

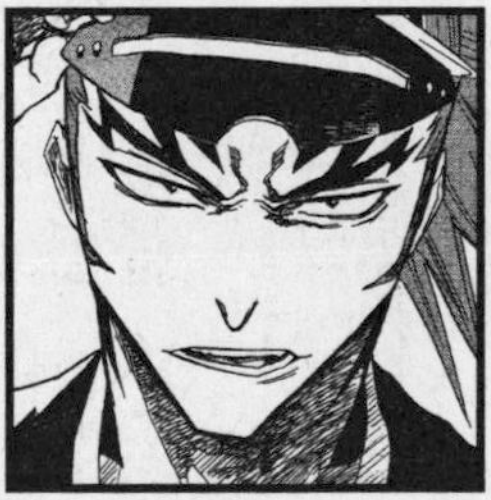

Yumichika Ayasegawa

綾瀬川弓親

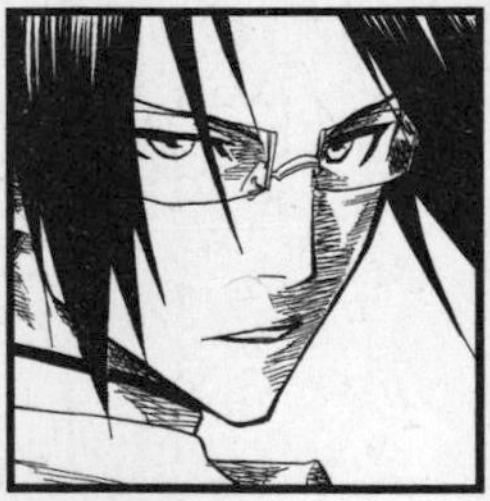

STORIES

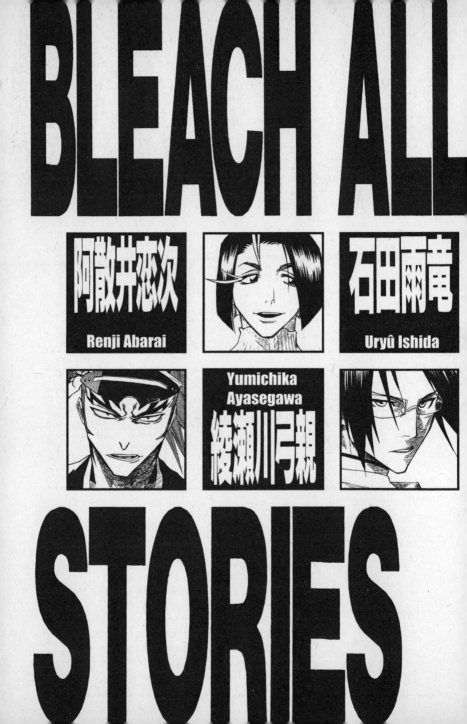

BLEACH11

A STAR AND A STRAY DOG

Contents

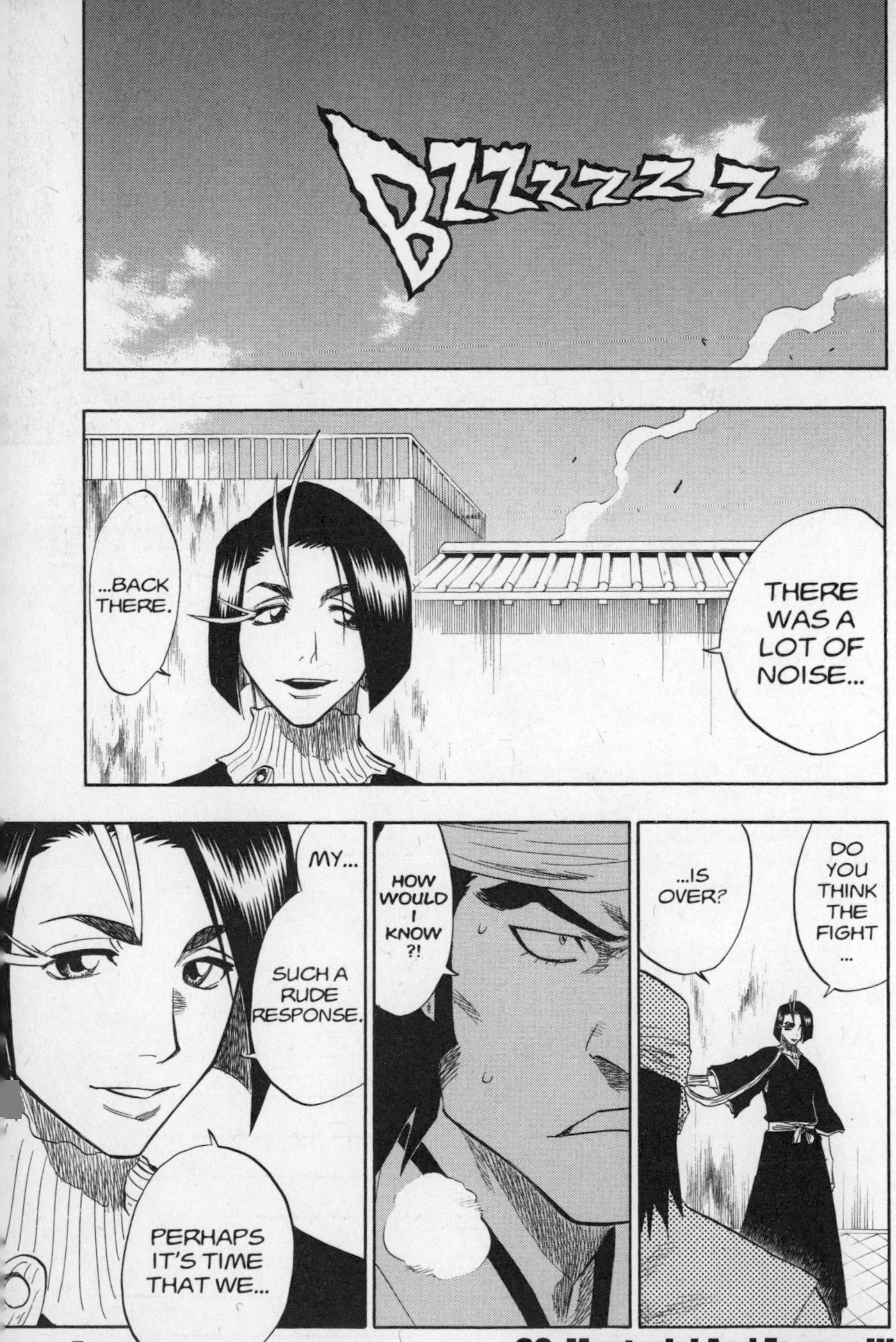
BZZZZZZ
THERE WAS A LOT OF NOISE...
...BACK THERE.
DO YOU THINK THE FIGHT ...
...IS OVER?
HOW WOULD I KNOW ?!
MY...
SUCH A RUDE RESPONSE.
PERHAPS IT'S TIME THAT WE...

89. Masterly! And Farewell!

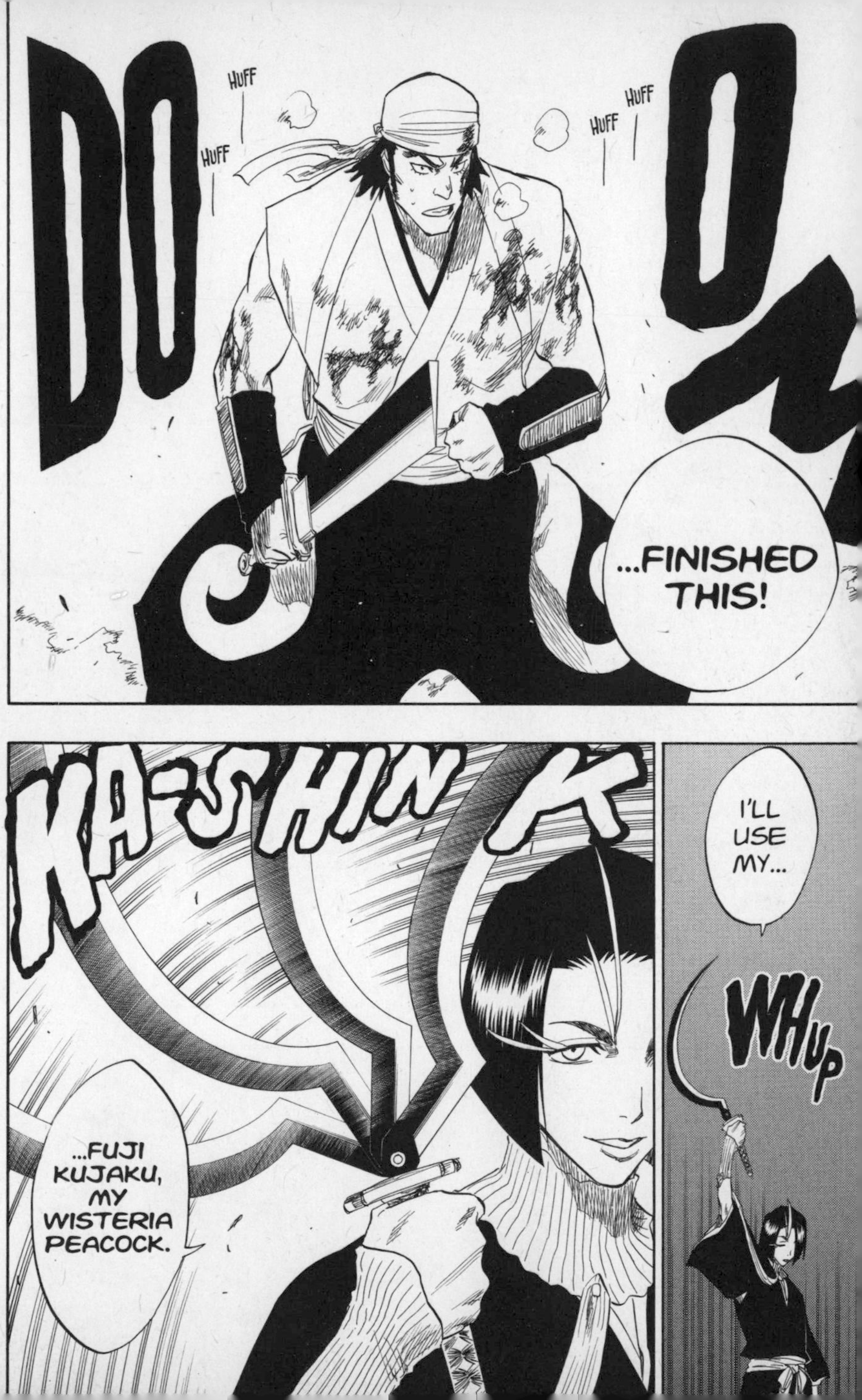
DOON
HUFF
HUFF
HUFF
HUFF
...FINISHED THIS!
I'LL USE MY...
WHUP
KA-SHIN K
...FUJI KUJAKU, MY WISTERIA PEACOCK.

READ THIS WAY

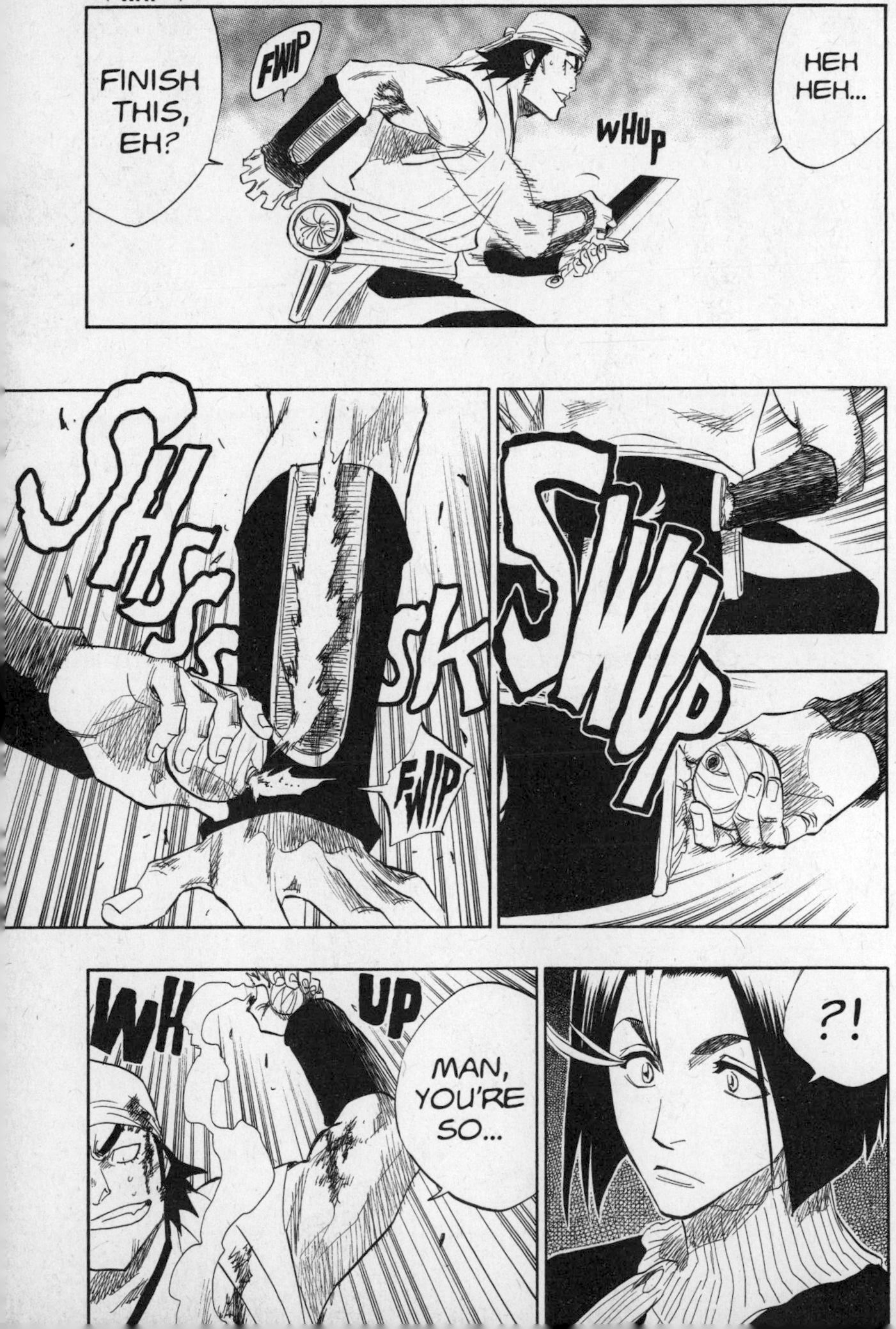
HEH HEH...
FWIP
WHUP
FINISH THIS, EH?
SWUP
SHSSSSK
FWIP
?!
UP
WH
MAN, YOU'RE SO...

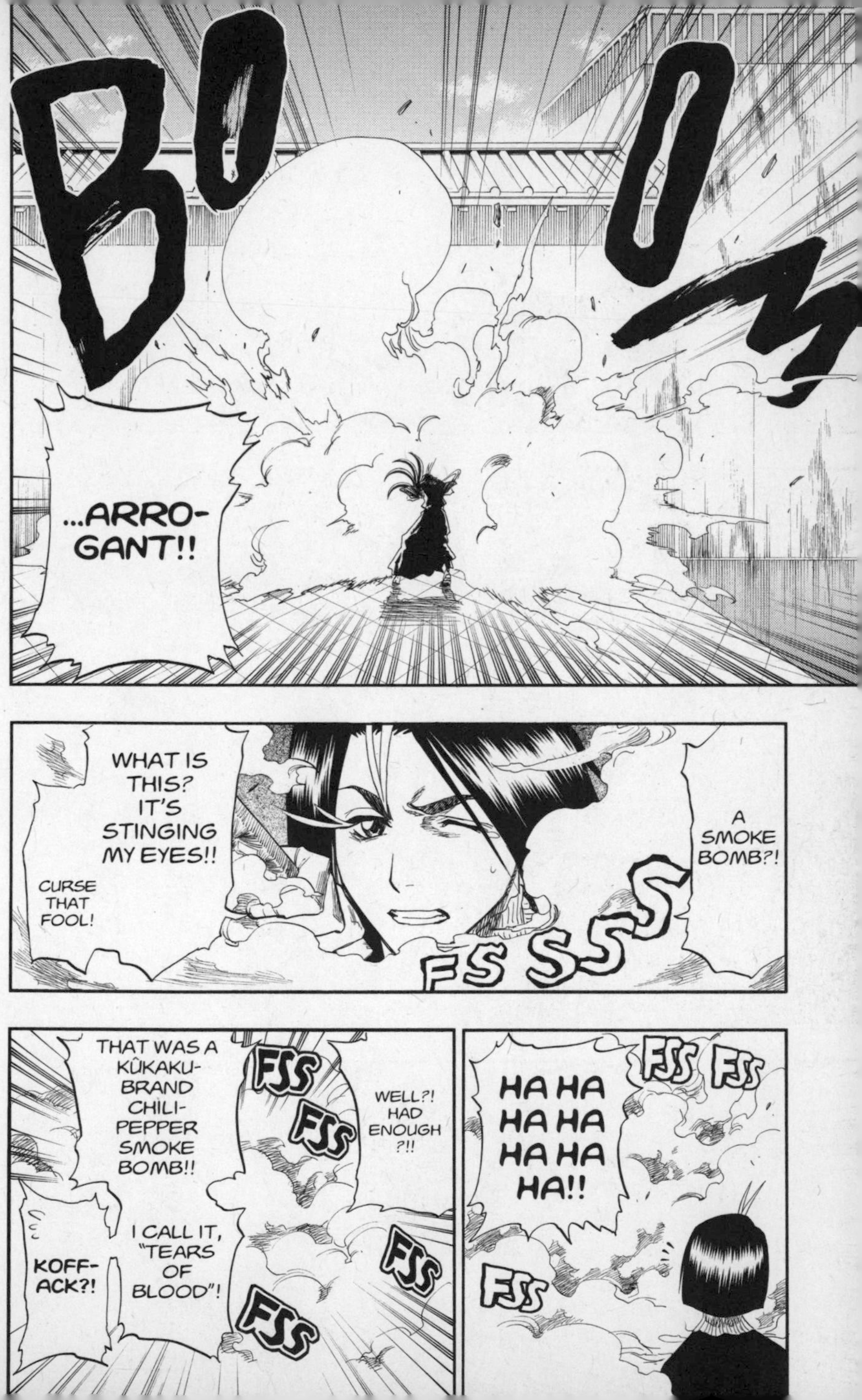
BOOM
...ARRO-
GANT!!
A
SMOKE
BOMB?!
WHAT IS
THIS?
IT'S
STINGING
MY EYES!!
CURSE
THAT
FOOL!
FSSSSS
FSS FSS
HA HA
HA HA
HA HA
HA!!
FSS
WELL?!
HAD
ENOUGH
?!!
FSS
FSS
THAT WAS A
KÛKAKU-
BRAND
CHILI-
PEPPER
SMOKE
BOMB!!
I CALL IT,
"TEARS
OF
BLOOD"!
FSS
KOFF-
ACK?!
FSS

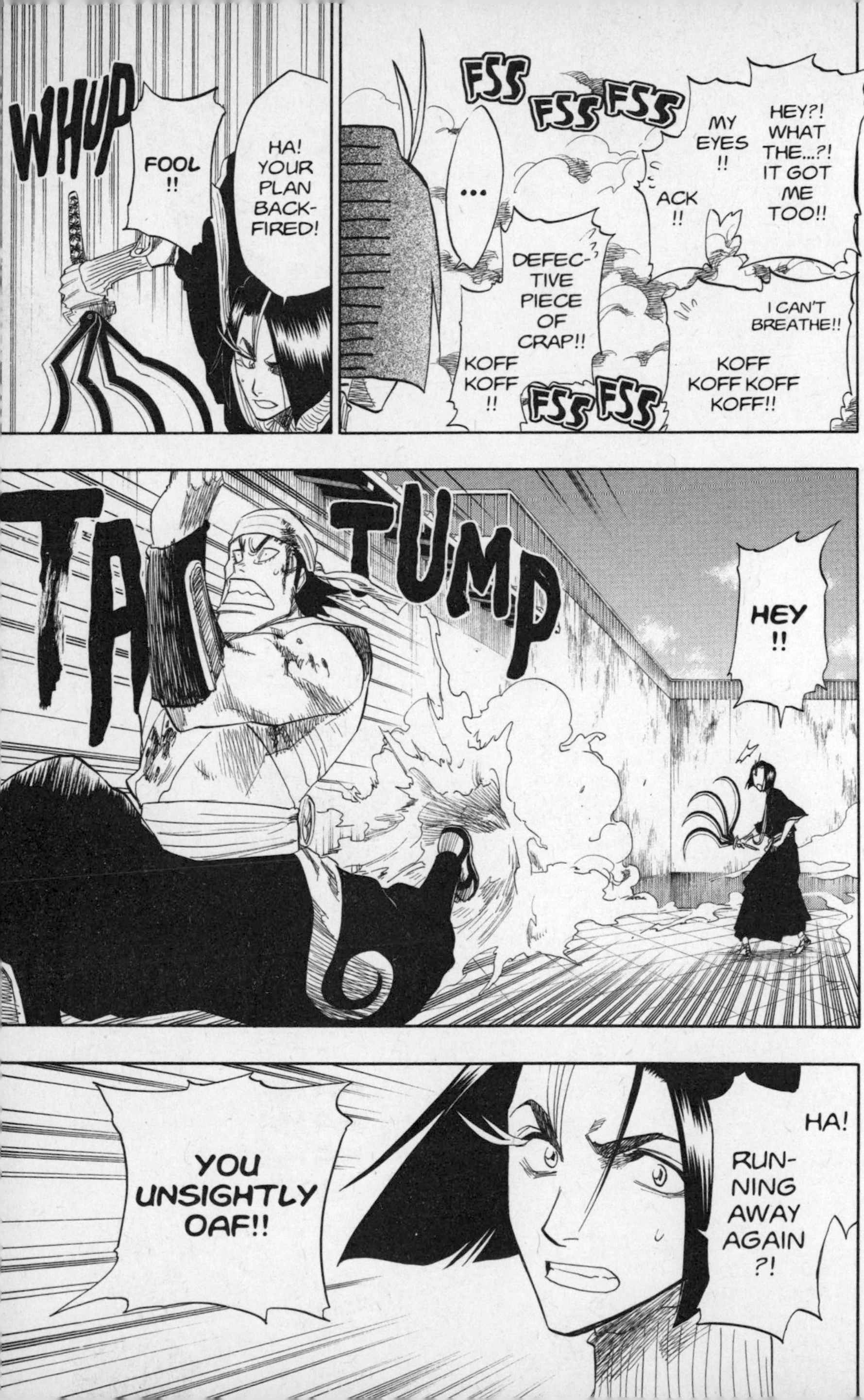
HEY?! WHAT THE...?! IT GOT ME TOO!!
MY EYES !!
ACK !!
FSS FSS FSS
I CAN'T BREATHE!!
...
DEFECTIVE PIECE OF CRAP!!
KOFF KOFF KOFF KOFF!!
FSS FSS
KOFF KOFF !!
HA! YOUR PLAN BACKFIRED!
FOOL !!
WHUP
HEY !!
TUMP
TA
HA! RUNNING AWAY AGAIN ?!
YOU UNSIGHTLY OAF!!

BLEACH
ブリーチ

89. Masterly! And Farewell!

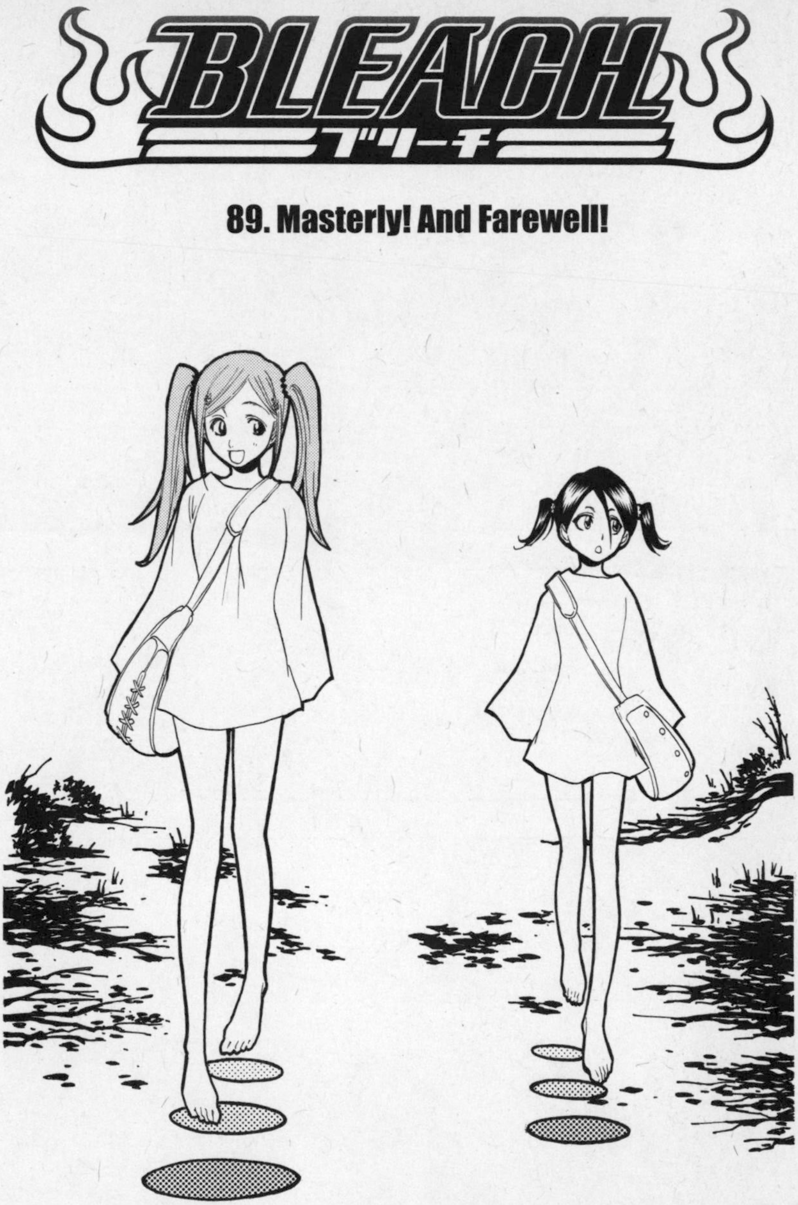

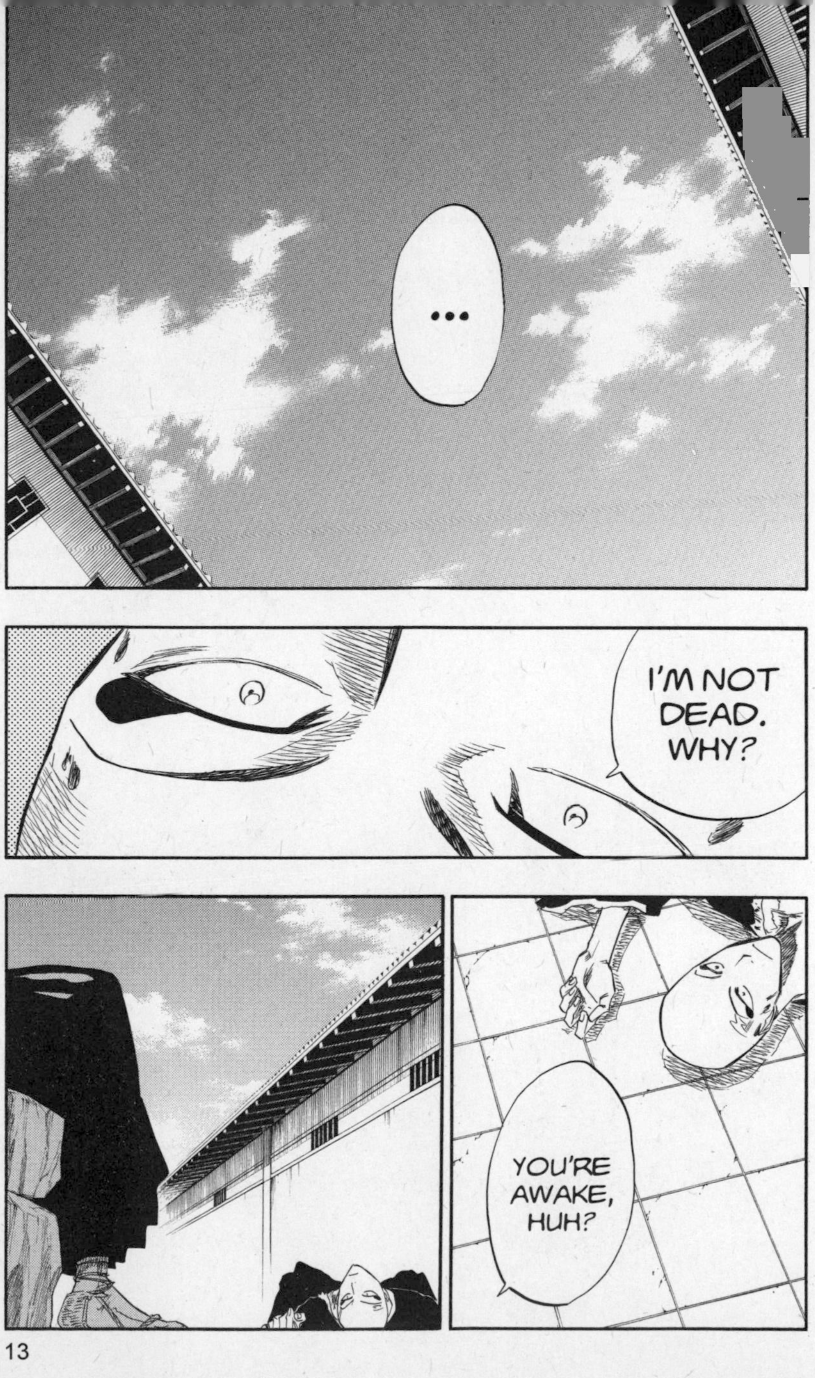
...
I'M NOT DEAD. WHY?
YOU'RE AWAKE, HUH?

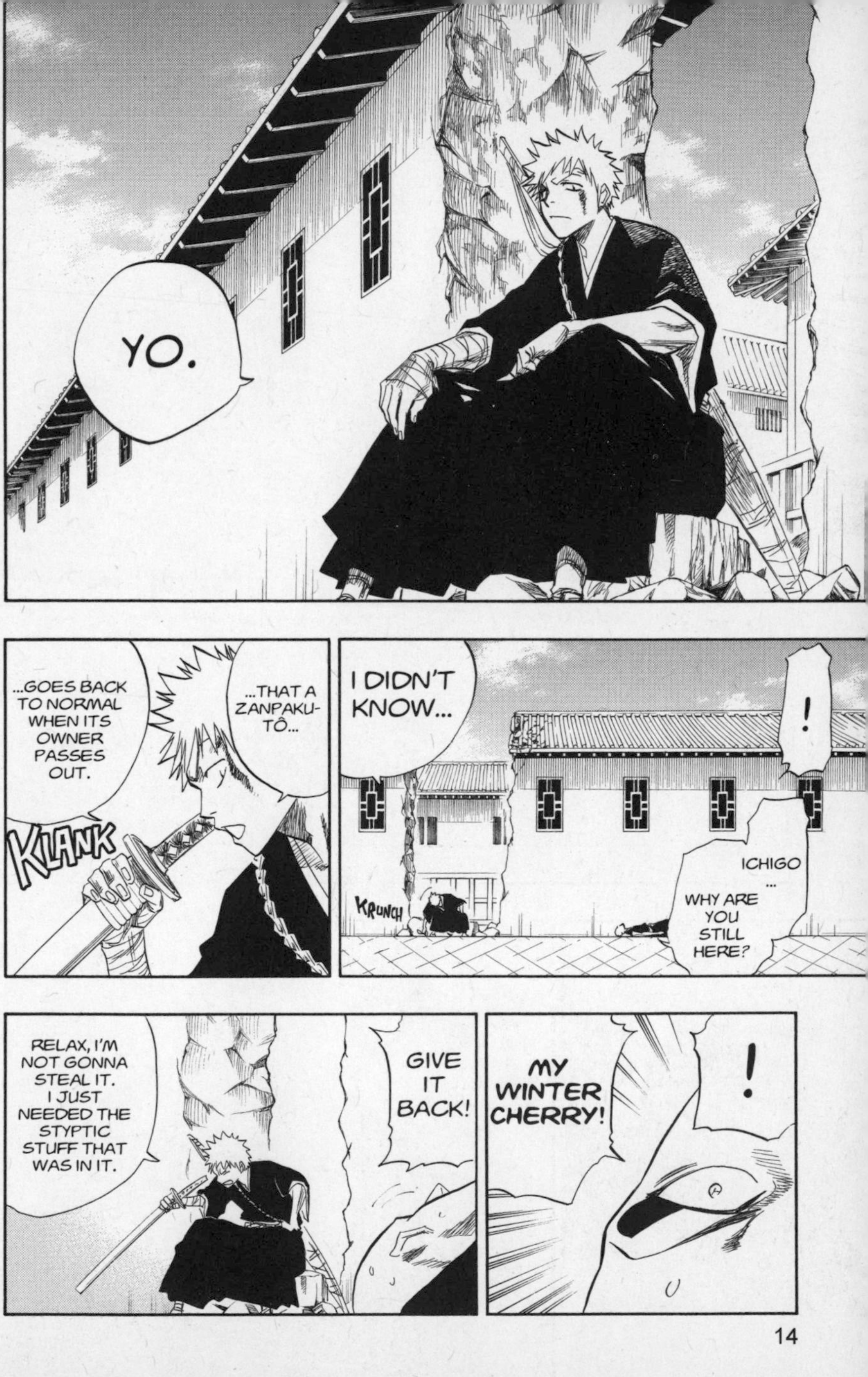
YO.
!
I DIDN'T KNOW...
ICHIGO ... WHY ARE YOU STILL HERE?
KRUNCH
...THAT A ZANPAKU-TÔ...
...GOES BACK TO NORMAL WHEN ITS OWNER PASSES OUT.
KLANK
!
MY WINTER CHERRY!
GIVE IT BACK!
RELAX, I'M NOT GONNA STEAL IT. I JUST NEEDED THE STYPTIC STUFF THAT WAS IN IT.

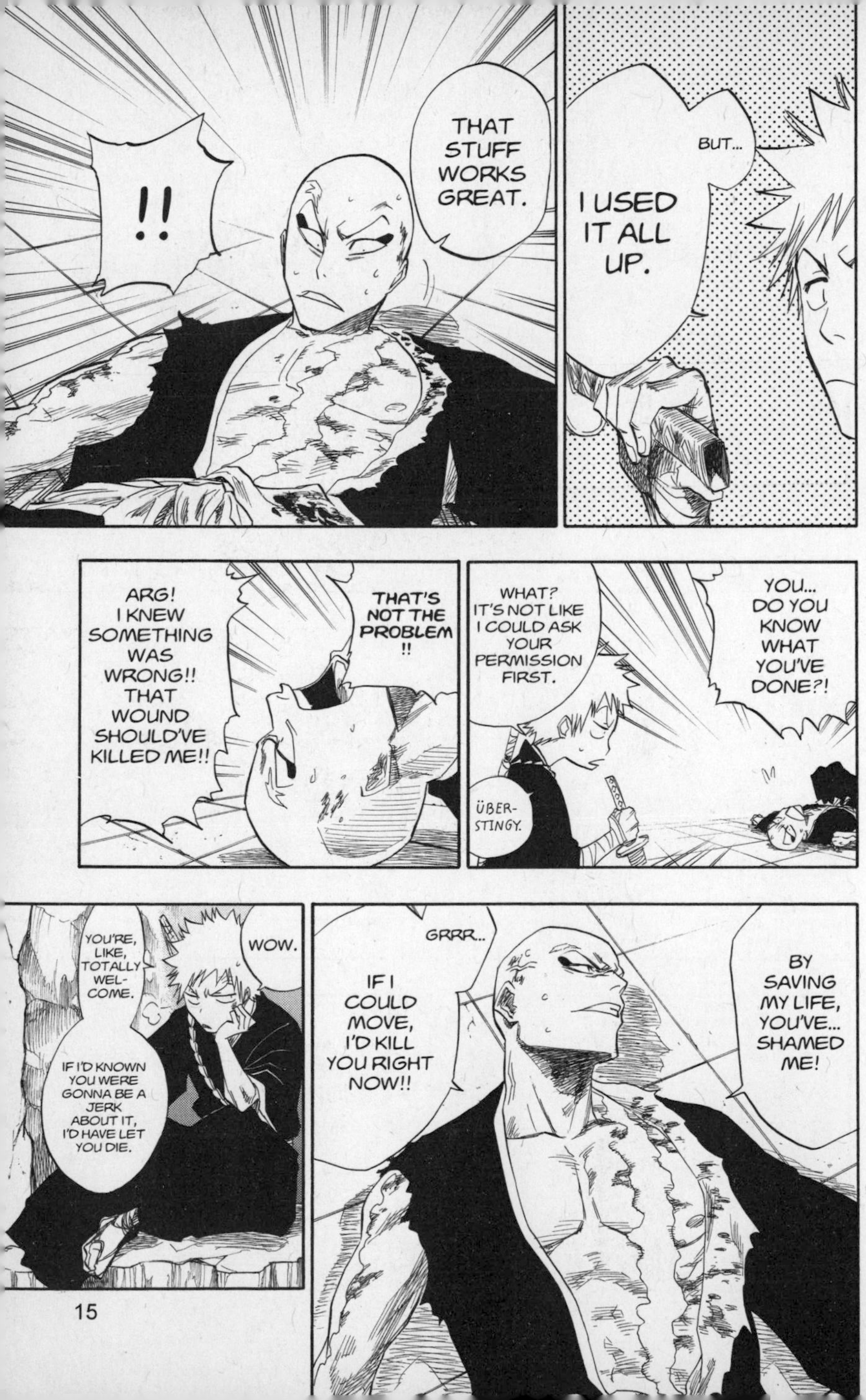
BUT...
I USED IT ALL UP.
THAT STUFF WORKS GREAT.
!!
YOU... DO YOU KNOW WHAT YOU'VE DONE?!
WHAT? IT'S NOT LIKE I COULD ASK YOUR PERMISSION FIRST.
ÜBER-STINGY.
THAT'S NOT THE PROBLEM!!
ARG! I KNEW SOMETHING WAS WRONG!! THAT WOUND SHOULD'VE KILLED ME!!
BY SAVING MY LIFE, YOU'VE... SHAMED ME!
GRRR...
IF I COULD MOVE, I'D KILL YOU RIGHT NOW!!
WOW.
YOU'RE, LIKE, TOTALLY WEL-COME.
IF I'D KNOWN YOU WERE GONNA BE A JERK ABOUT IT, I'D HAVE LET YOU DIE.

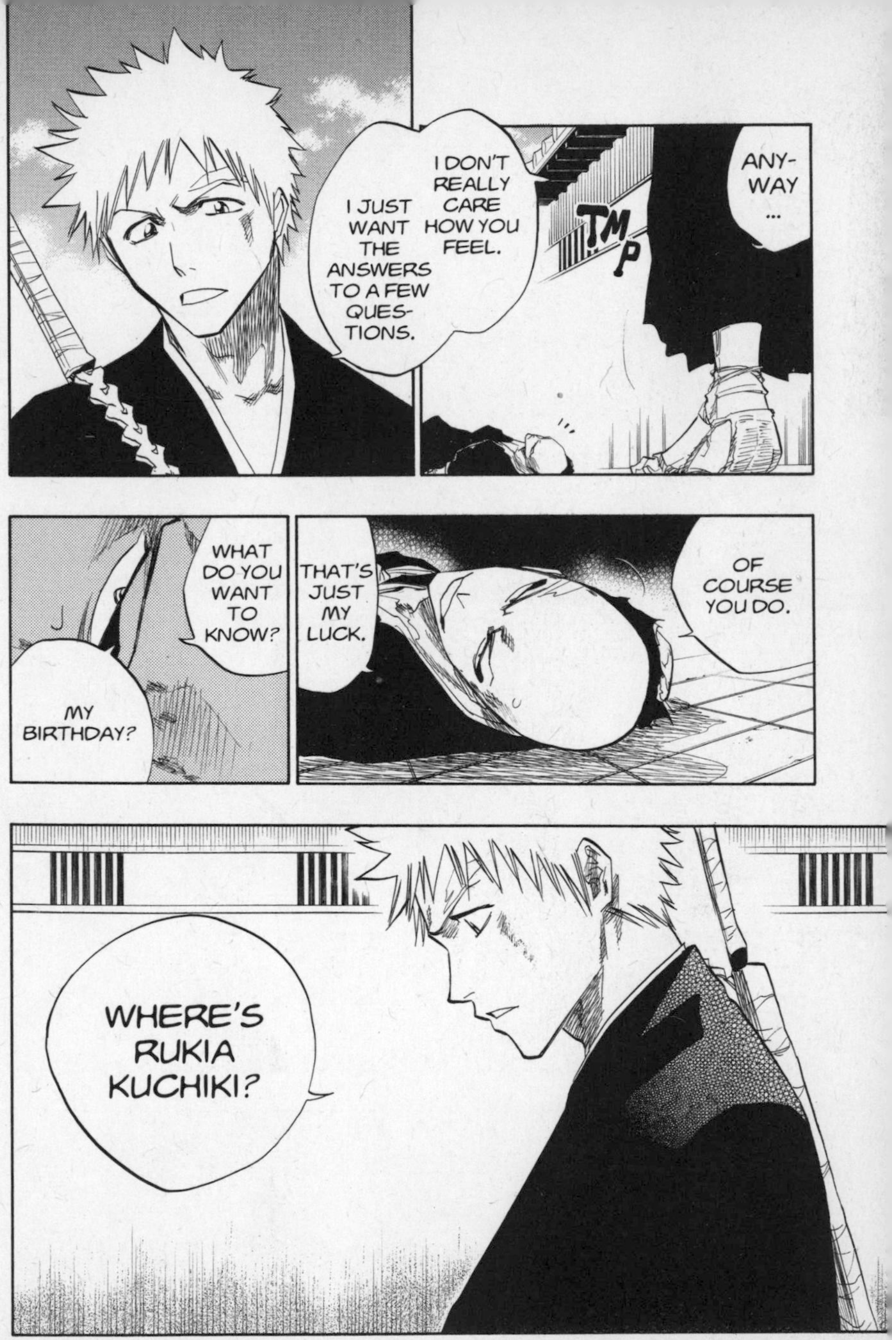
ANY-WAY ...
TMP
I DON'T REALLY CARE HOW YOU FEEL.
I JUST WANT THE ANSWERS TO A FEW QUES-TIONS.
OF COURSE YOU DO.
THAT'S JUST MY LUCK.
WHAT DO YOU WANT TO KNOW?
MY BIRTHDAY?
WHERE'S RUKIA KUCHIKI?

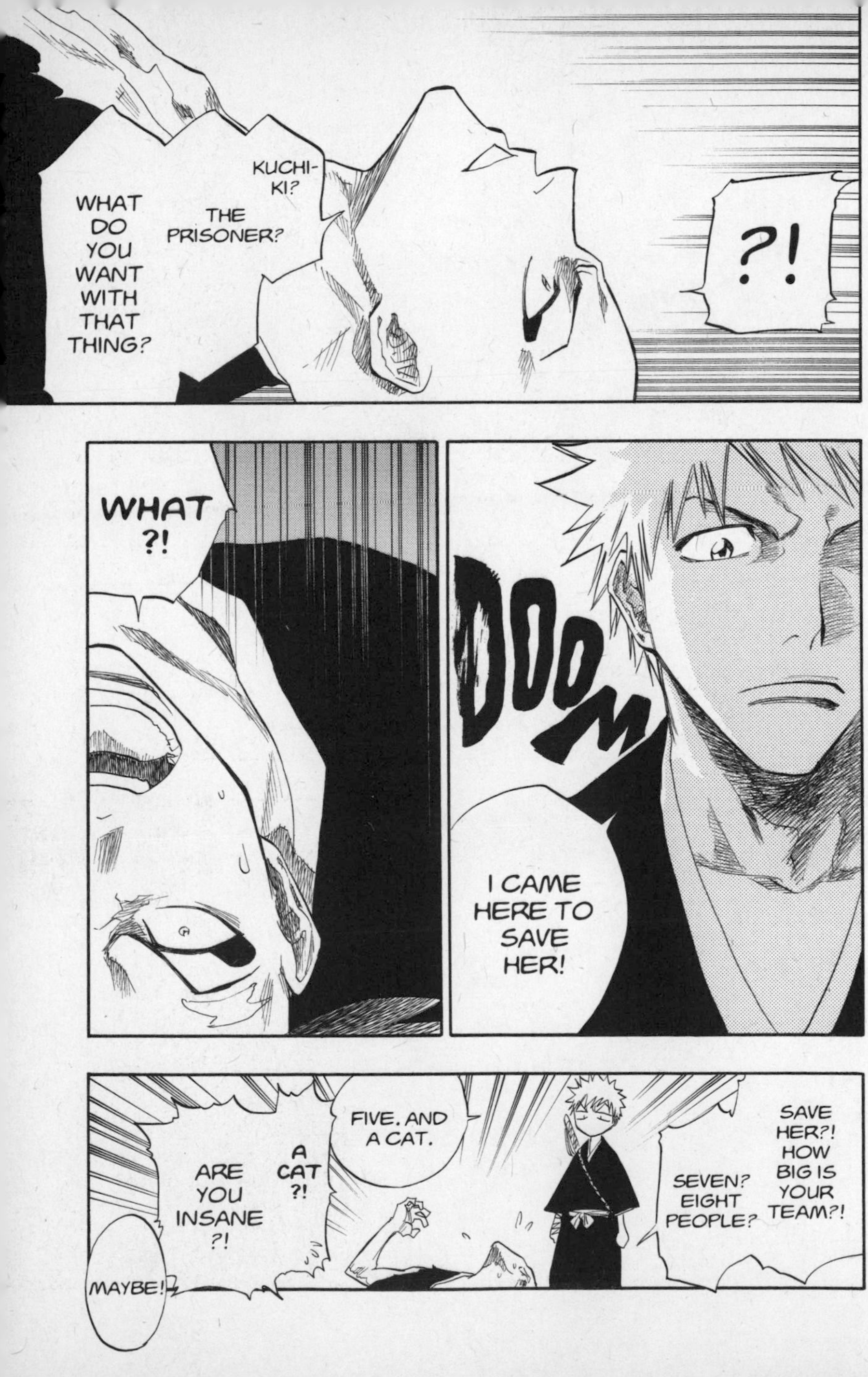
?!
KUCHI-KI?
THE PRISONER?
WHAT DO YOU WANT WITH THAT THING?
DOOM
I CAME HERE TO SAVE HER!
WHAT ?!
SAVE HER?! HOW BIG IS YOUR TEAM?!
SEVEN? EIGHT PEOPLE?
FIVE. AND A CAT.
A CAT ?!
ARE YOU INSANE ?!
MAYBE!

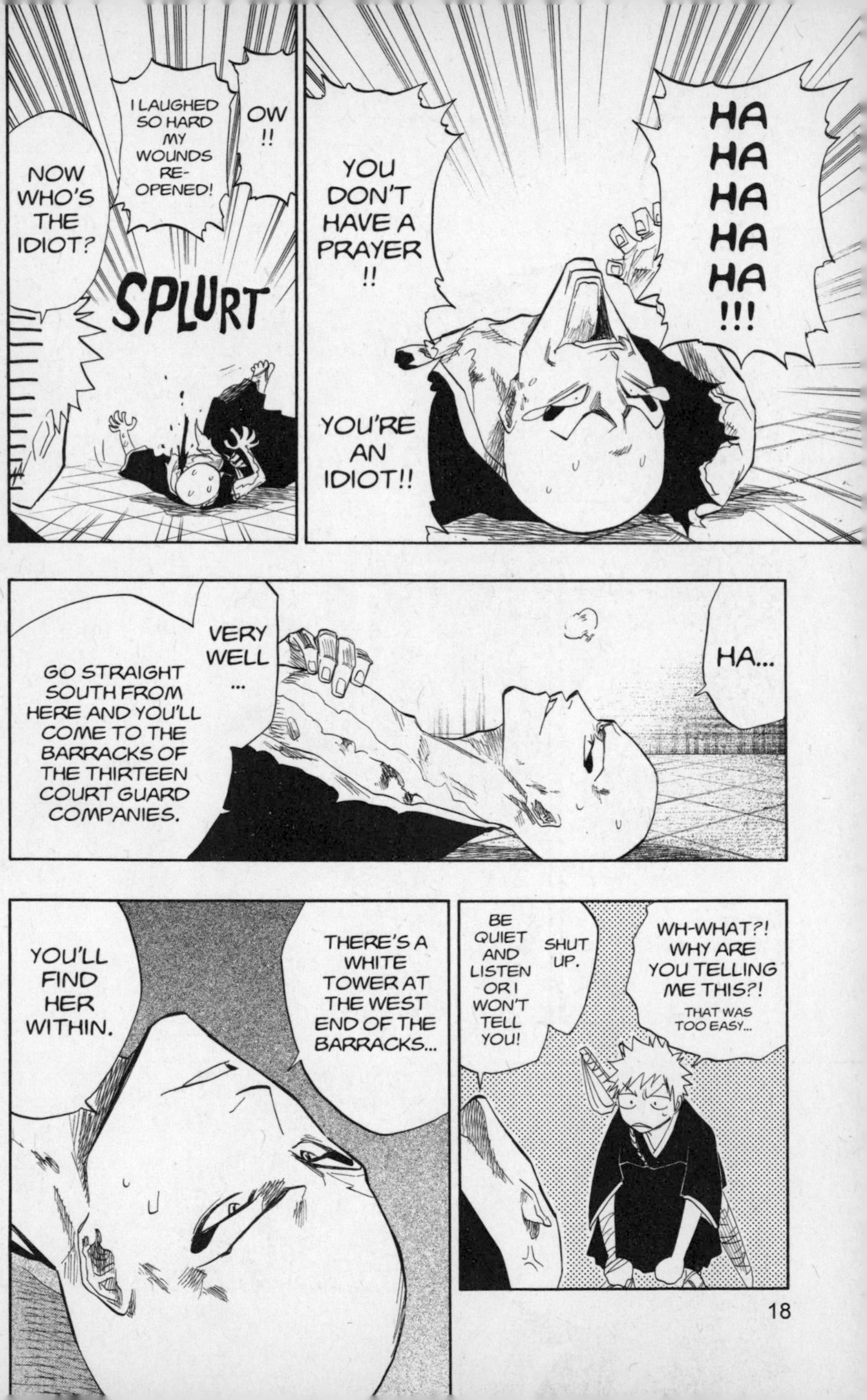
HA HA HA HA HA HA !!!
YOU DON'T HAVE A PRAYER !!
YOU'RE AN IDIOT!!
OW !!
I LAUGHED SO HARD MY WOUNDS RE-OPENED!
SPLURT
NOW WHO'S THE IDIOT?
HA...
VERY WELL ...
GO STRAIGHT SOUTH FROM HERE AND YOU'LL COME TO THE BARRACKS OF THE THIRTEEN COURT GUARD COMPANIES.
WH-WHAT?! WHY ARE YOU TELLING ME THIS?!
THAT WAS TOO EASY...
SHUT UP.
BE QUIET AND LISTEN OR I WON'T TELL YOU!
THERE'S A WHITE TOWER AT THE WEST END OF THE BARRACKS...
YOU'LL FIND HER WITHIN.

READ THIS WAY

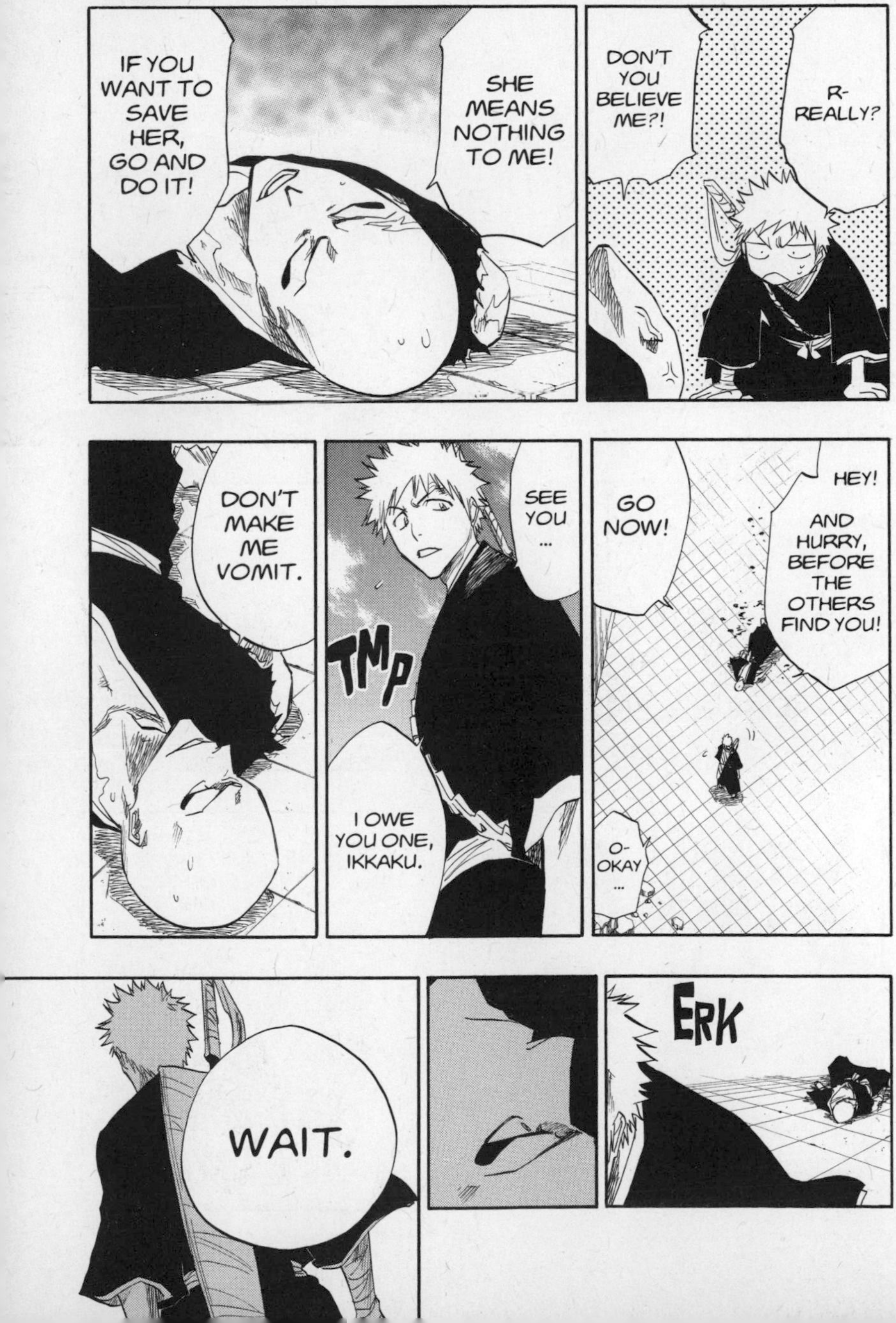
R-REALLY?
DON'T YOU BELIEVE ME?!
SHE MEANS NOTHING TO ME!
IF YOU WANT TO SAVE HER, GO AND DO IT!
HEY!
AND HURRY, BEFORE THE OTHERS FIND YOU!
GO NOW!
O-OKAY ...
SEE YOU ...
TMP
I OWE YOU ONE, IKKAKU.
DON'T MAKE ME VOMIT.
ERK
WAIT.

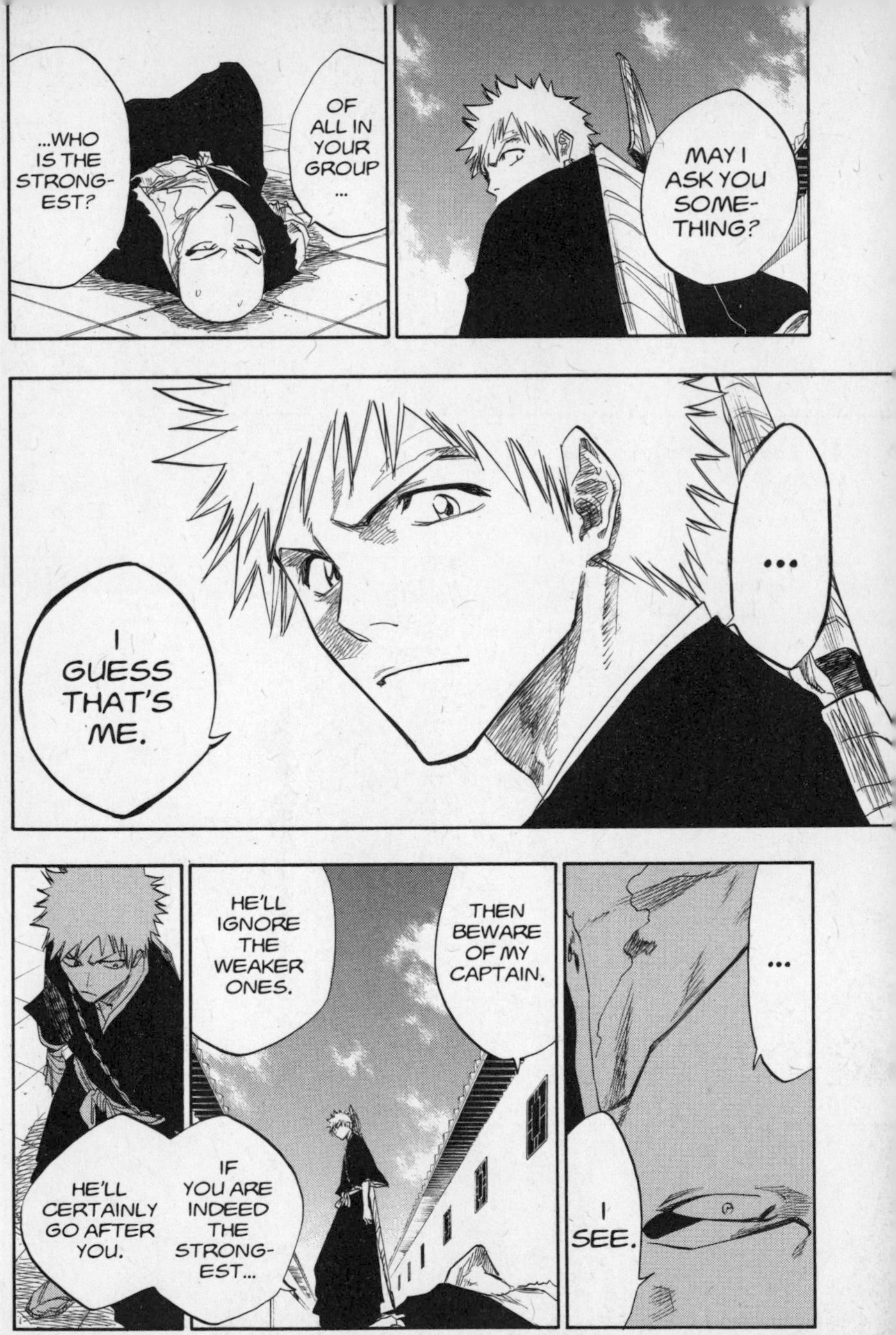
MAY I ASK YOU SOMETHING?
OF ALL IN YOUR GROUP ...
...WHO IS THE STRONGEST?
...
I GUESS THAT'S ME.
...
I SEE.
THEN BEWARE OF MY CAPTAIN.
HE'LL IGNORE THE WEAKER ONES.
IF YOU ARE INDEED THE STRONGEST...
HE'LL CERTAINLY GO AFTER YOU.

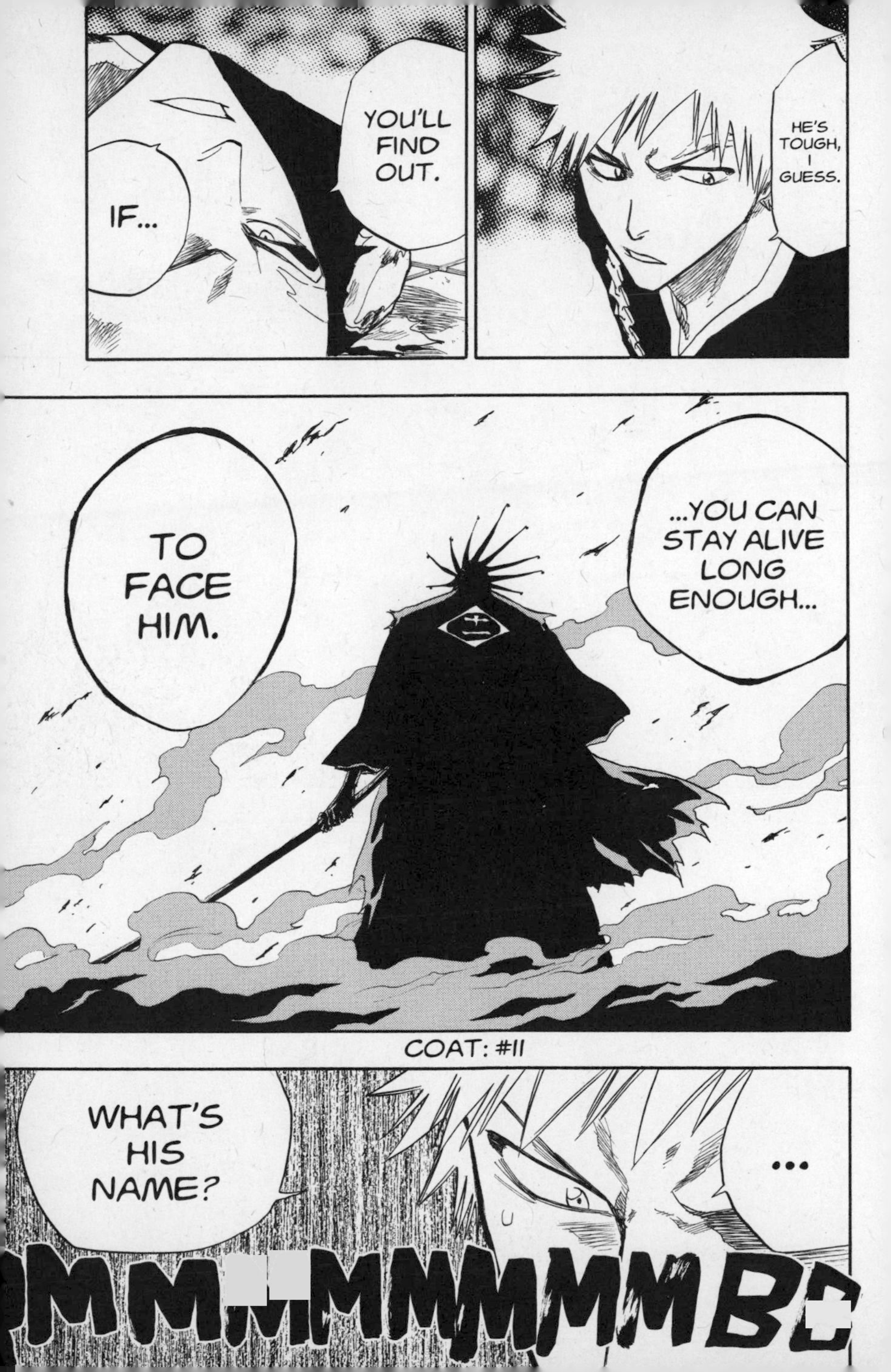
HE'S TOUGH, I GUESS.
YOU'LL FIND OUT.
IF...
...YOU CAN STAY ALIVE LONG ENOUGH...
TO FACE HIM.
COAT: #11
...
WHAT'S HIS NAME?

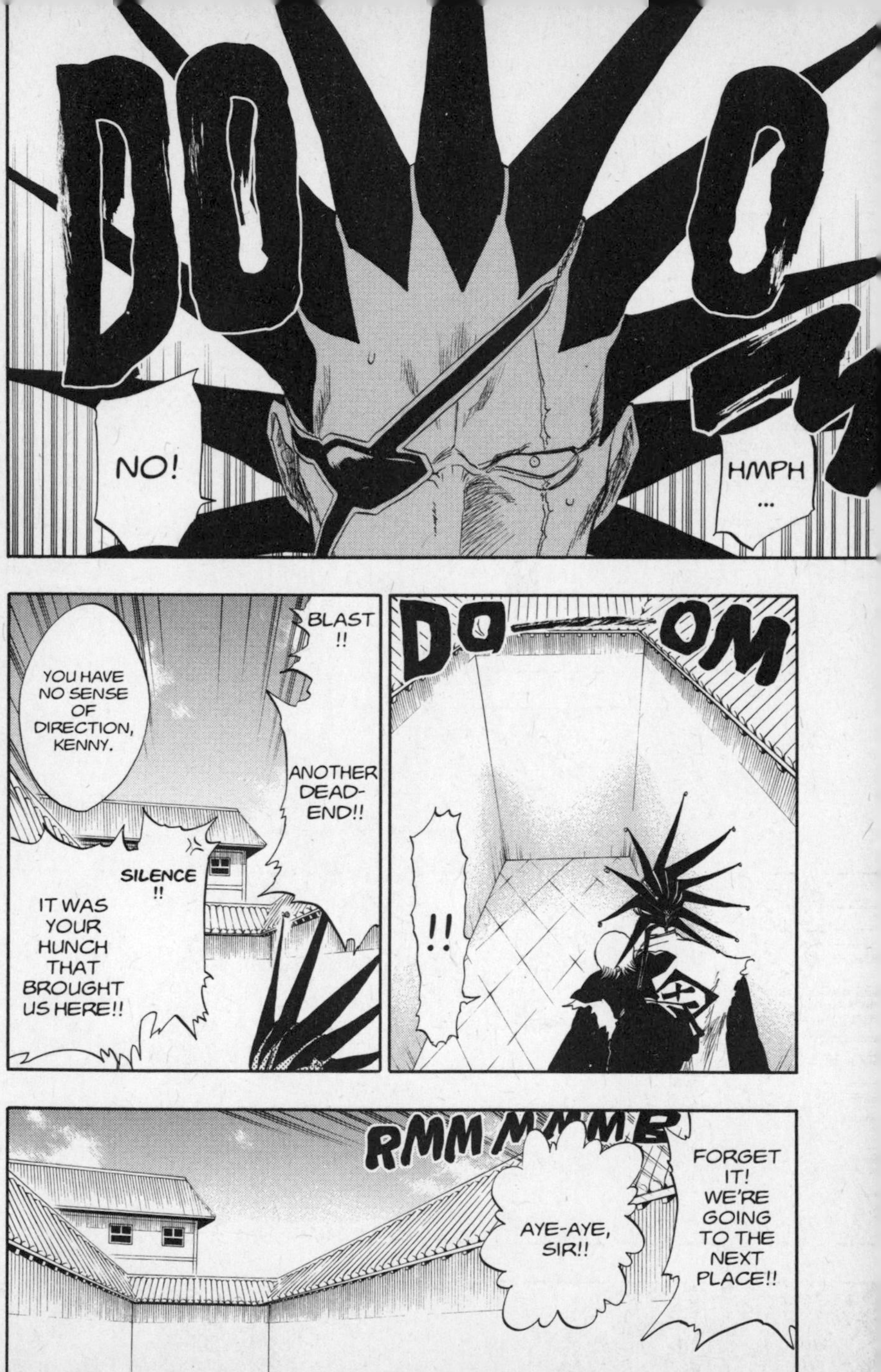
DOOOM
HMPH ...
NO!
DO——OM
!!
BLAST !!
ANOTHER DEAD-END!!
YOU HAVE NO SENSE OF DIRECTION, KENNY.
SILENCE !!
IT WAS YOUR HUNCH THAT BROUGHT US HERE!!
RMMMMMB
FORGET IT! WE'RE GOING TO THE NEXT PLACE!!
AYE-AYE, SIR!!

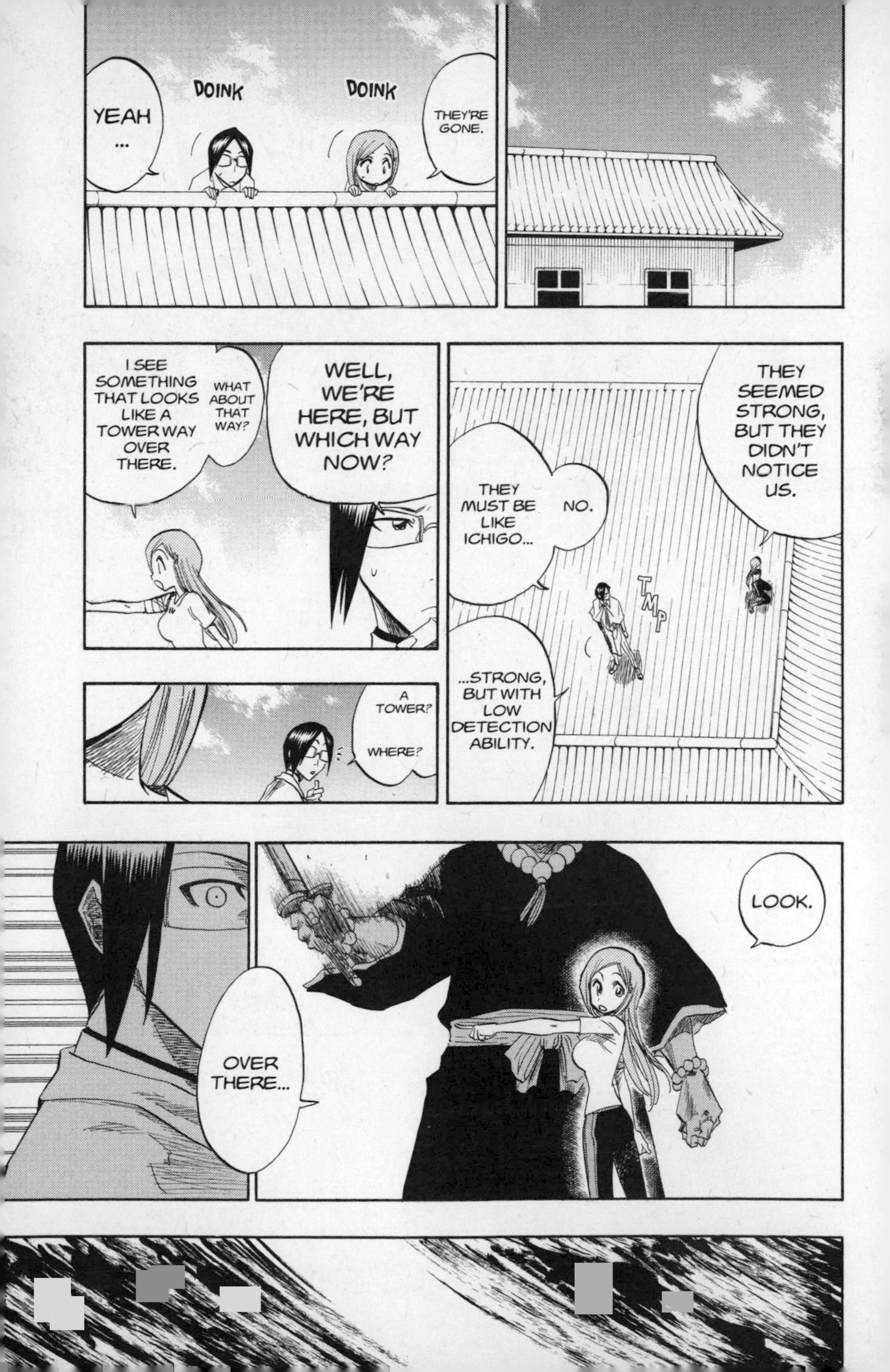
THEY'RE GONE.
DOINK
DOINK
YEAH ...
THEY SEEMED STRONG, BUT THEY DIDN'T NOTICE US.
NO.
THEY MUST BE LIKE ICHIGO...
TMP
...STRONG, BUT WITH LOW DETECTION ABILITY.
WELL, WE'RE HERE, BUT WHICH WAY NOW?
WHAT ABOUT THAT WAY?
I SEE SOMETHING THAT LOOKS LIKE A TOWER WAY OVER THERE.
A TOWER?
WHERE?
LOOK.
OVER THERE...

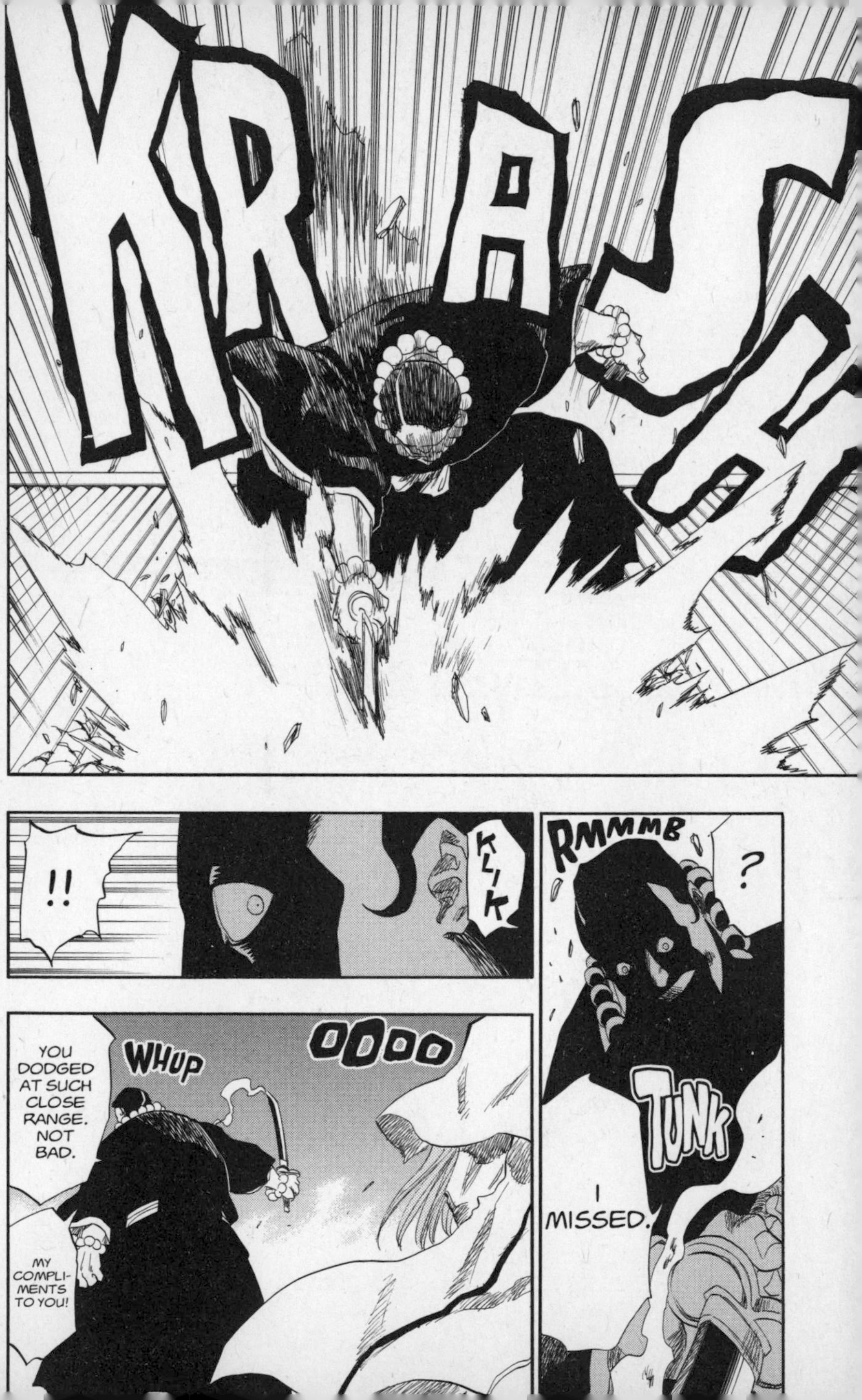
KRAS
RMMMB
?
TUNK
I MISSED.
KLIK
!!
OOOO
WHUP
YOU DODGED AT SUCH CLOSE RANGE. NOT BAD.
MY COMPLI- MENTS TO YOU!

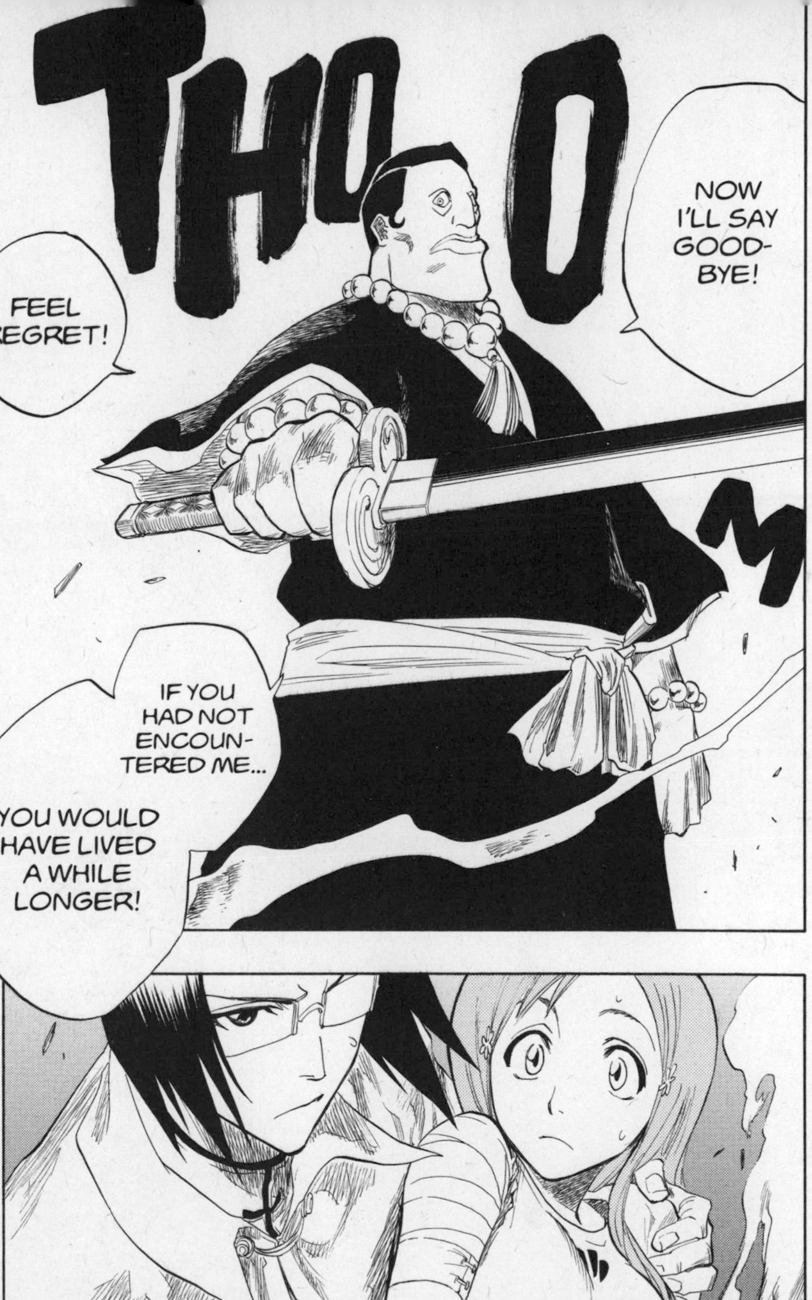
THOOM
NOW I'LL SAY GOOD-BYE!
FEEL REGRET!
IF YOU HAD NOT ENCOUN-TERED ME...
YOU WOULD HAVE LIVED A WHILE LONGER!

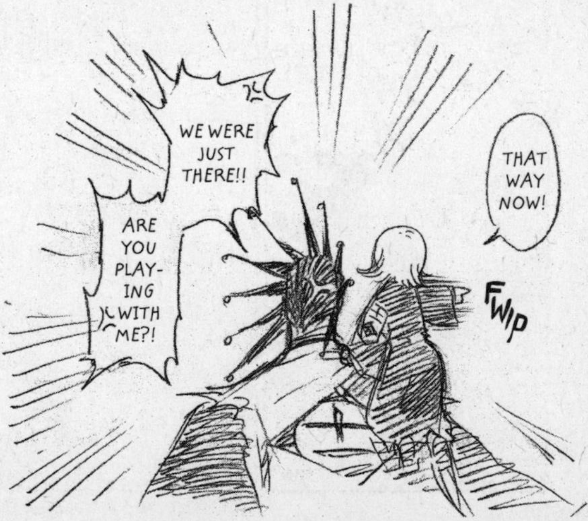
THAT WAY NOW!
FWIP
WE WERE JUST THERE!!
ARE YOU PLAY-ING WITH ME?!

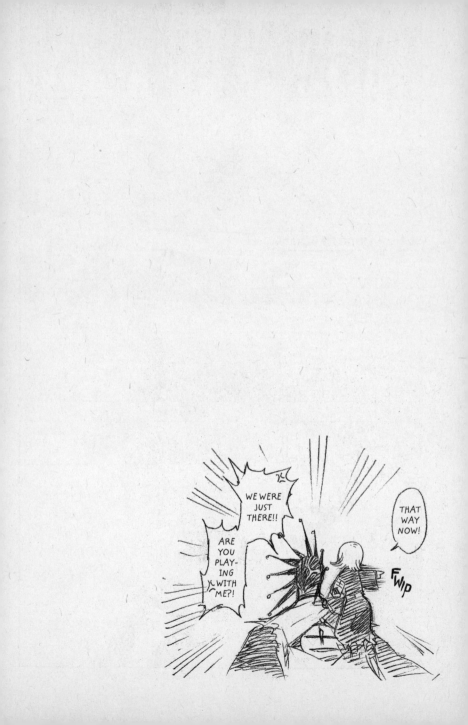

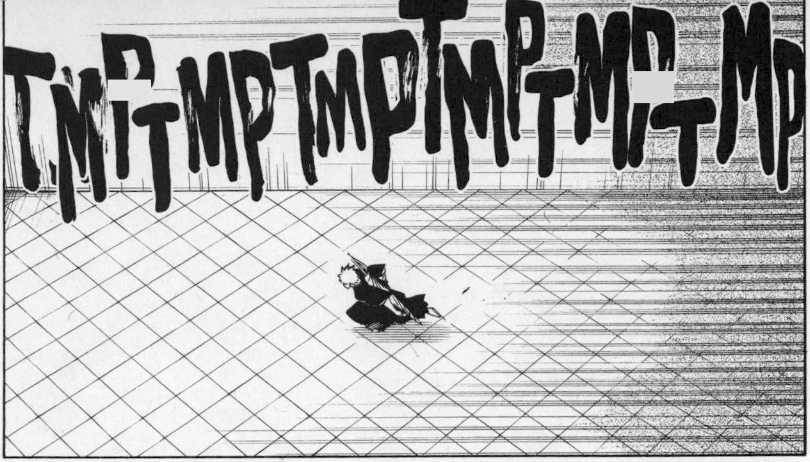
TMP TMP TMP TMP TMP TMP

90. See You Under the Fireworks

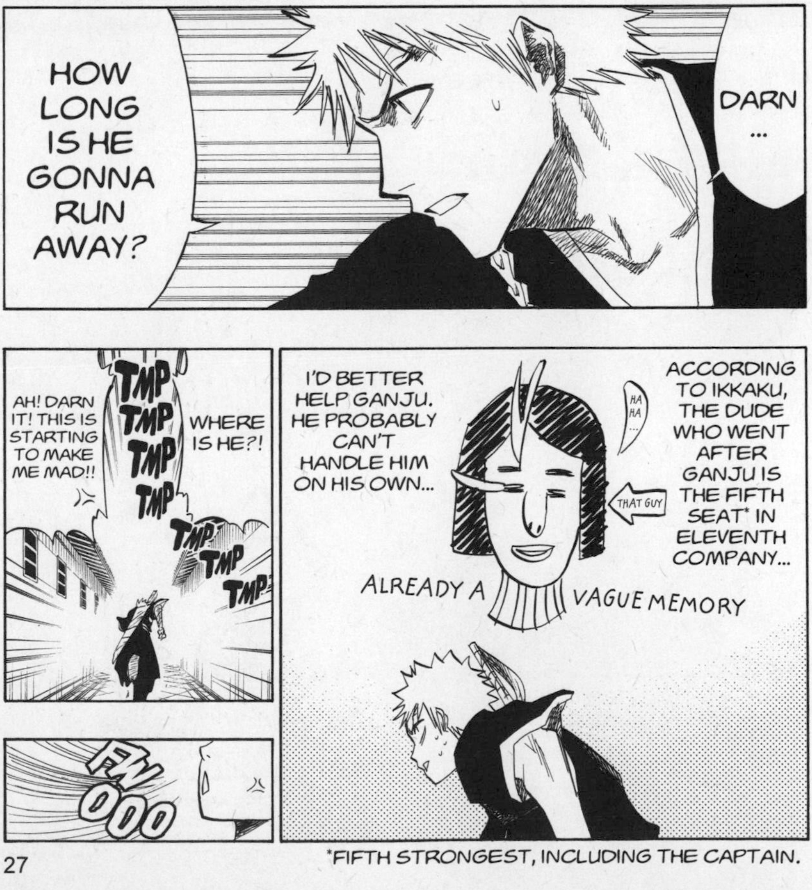
DARN ...
HOW LONG IS HE GONNA RUN AWAY?
ACCORDING TO IKKAKU, THE DUDE WHO WENT AFTER GANJU IS THE FIFTH SEAT* IN ELEVENTH COMPANY...
HA HA ...
THAT GUY
I'D BETTER HELP GANJU. HE PROBABLY CAN'T HANDLE HIM ON HIS OWN...
ALREADY A VAGUE MEMORY
WHERE IS HE?!
AH! DARN IT! THIS IS STARTING TO MAKE ME MAD!!
TMP TMP TMP TMP TMP TMP TMP
FWOOO

*FIFTH STRONGEST, INCLUDING THE CAPTAIN.

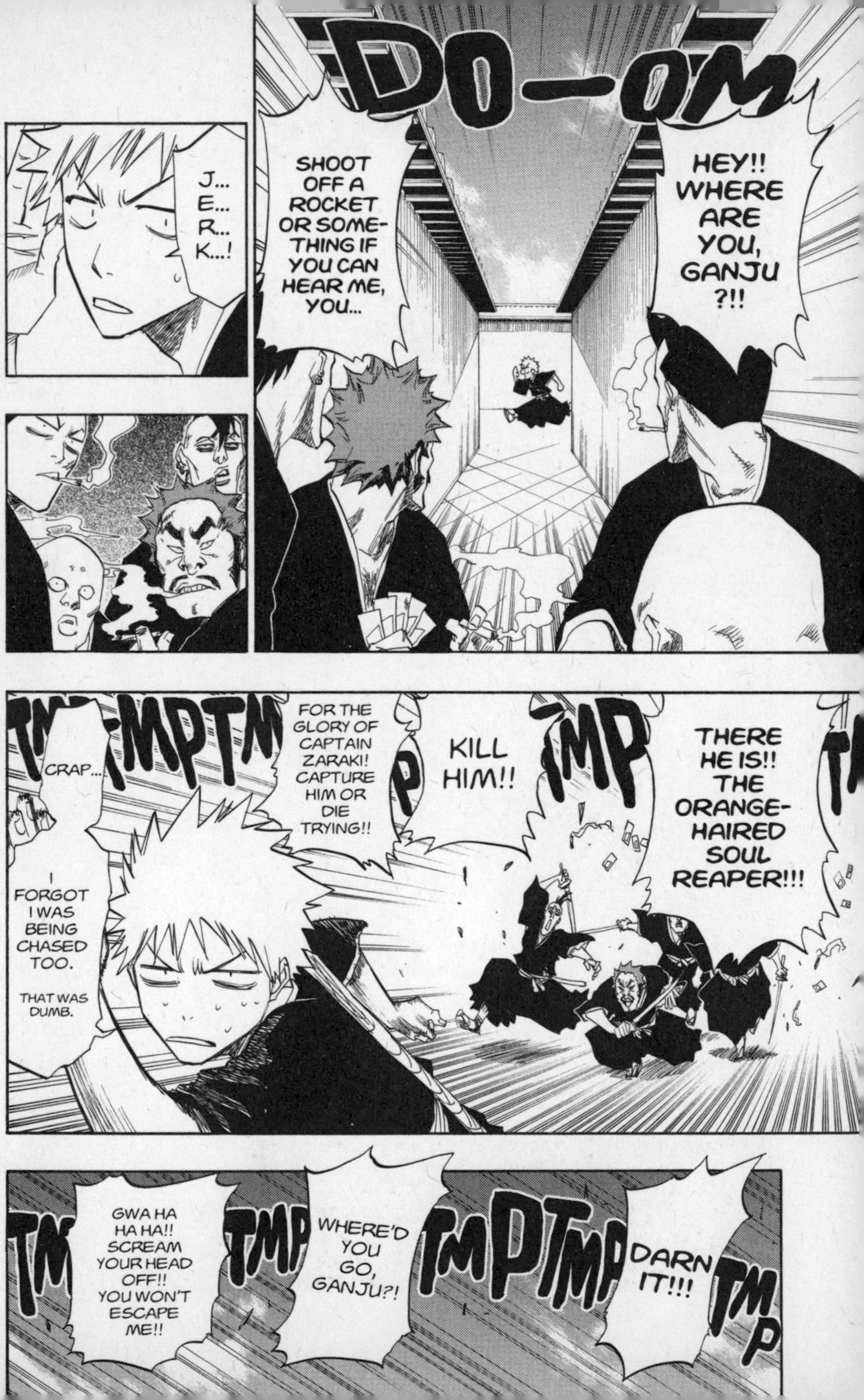
DO-OM
HEY!! WHERE ARE YOU, GANJU?!!
SHOOT OFF A ROCKET OR SOMETHING IF YOU CAN HEAR ME, YOU...
J... E... R... K...!
THERE HE IS!! THE ORANGE-HAIRED SOUL REAPER!!!
TMP
KILL HIM!!
FOR THE GLORY OF CAPTAIN ZARAKI! CAPTURE HIM OR DIE TRYING!!
TMPTM
CRAP...
I FORGOT I WAS BEING CHASED TOO.
THAT WAS DUMB.
TMP
DARN IT!!!
TMPTMP
WHERE'D YOU GO, GANJU?!
TMP
GWA HA HA HA!! SCREAM YOUR HEAD OFF!! YOU WON'T ESCAPE ME!!

90. See You Under the Fireworks

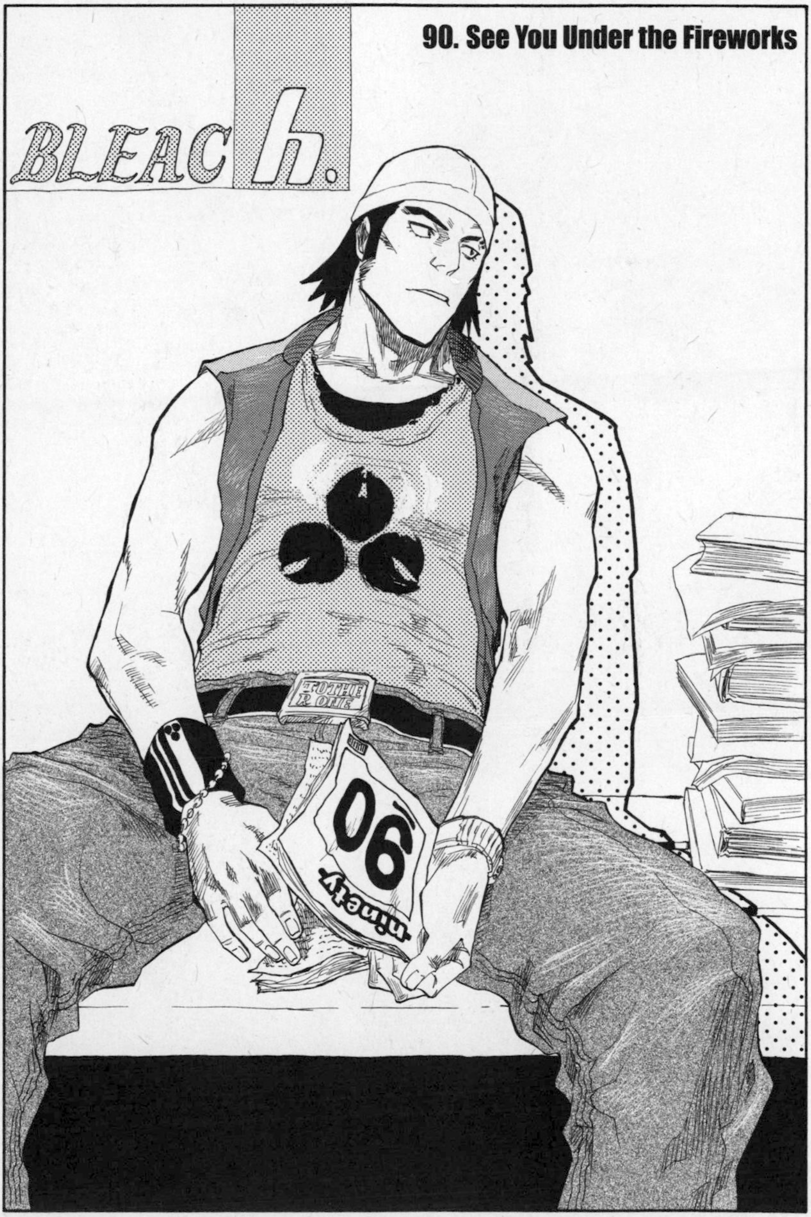
BLEACH.
90
ninety

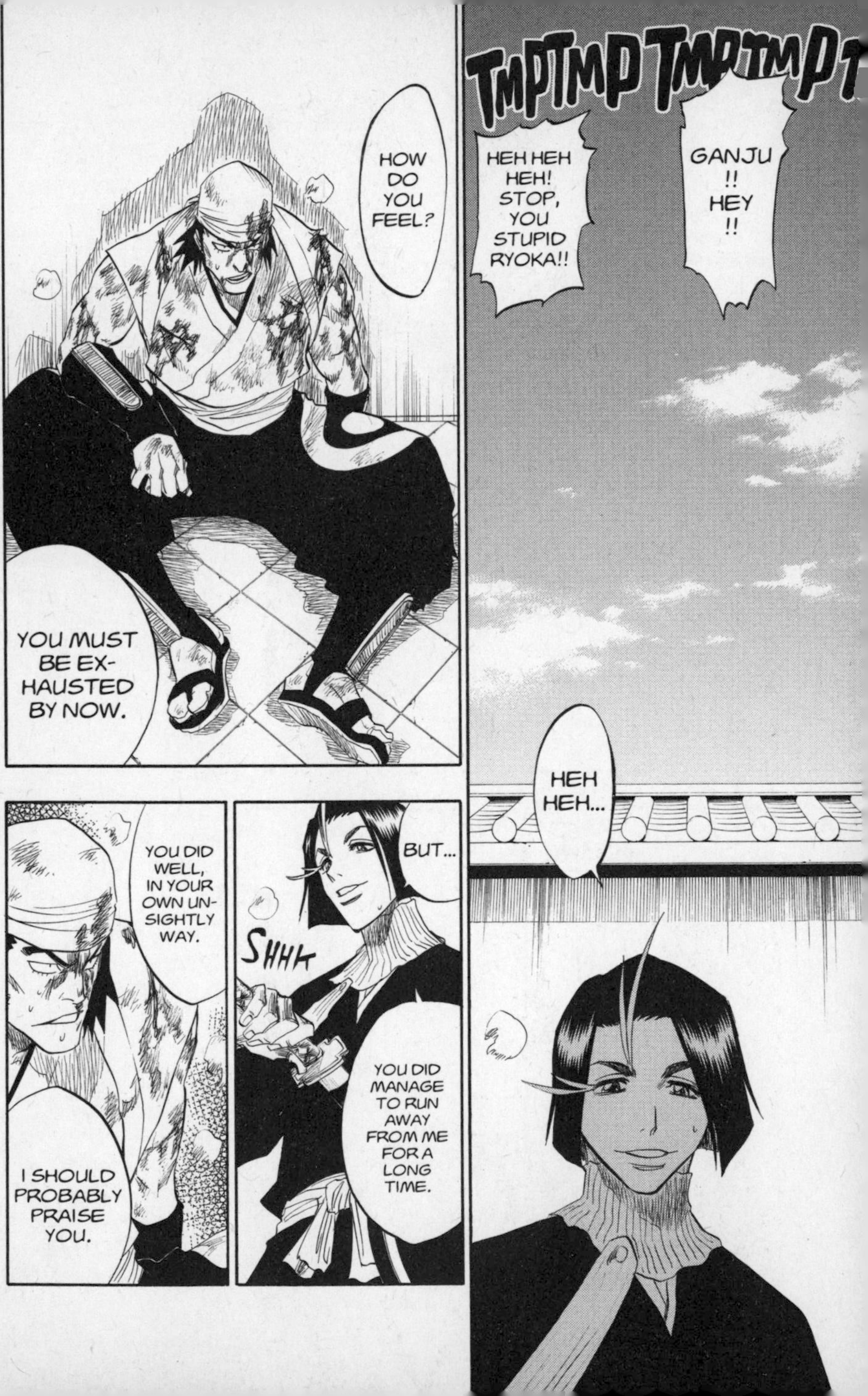
TMPTMP TMPTMP
GANJU!! HEY!!
HEH HEH HEH! STOP, YOU STUPID RYOKA!!
HEH HEH...
HOW DO YOU FEEL?
YOU MUST BE EX-HAUSTED BY NOW.
BUT...
SHHK
YOU DID MANAGE TO RUN AWAY FROM ME FOR A LONG TIME.
YOU DID WELL, IN YOUR OWN UN-SIGHTLY WAY.
I SHOULD PROBABLY PRAISE YOU.

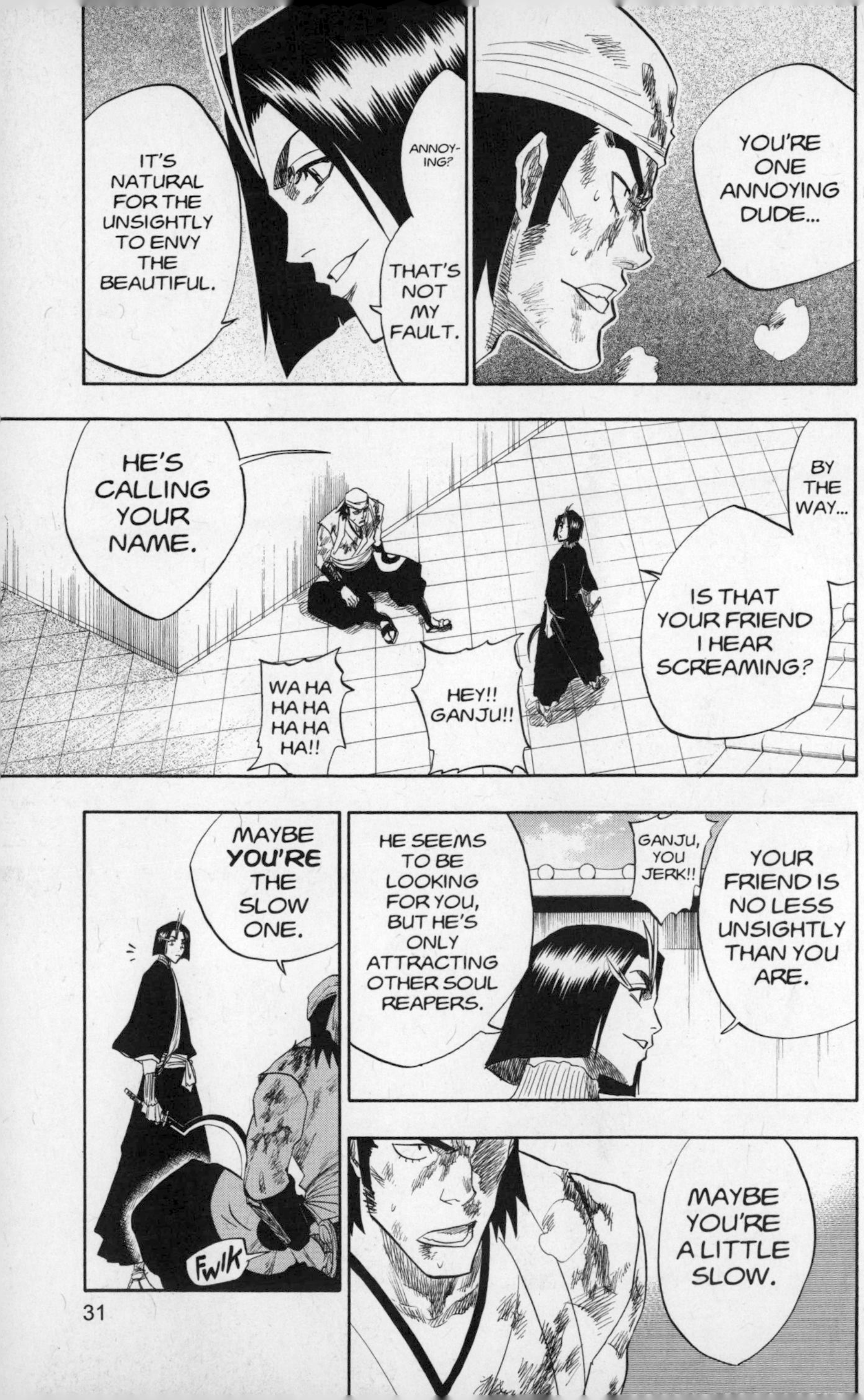
YOU'RE ONE ANNOYING DUDE...
ANNOYING?
THAT'S NOT MY FAULT.
IT'S NATURAL FOR THE UNSIGHTLY TO ENVY THE BEAUTIFUL.
BY THE WAY...
IS THAT YOUR FRIEND I HEAR SCREAMING?
HEY!! GANJU!!
WA HA HA HA HA HA HA!!
HE'S CALLING YOUR NAME.
GANJU, YOU JERK!!
YOUR FRIEND IS NO LESS UNSIGHTLY THAN YOU ARE.
HE SEEMS TO BE LOOKING FOR YOU, BUT HE'S ONLY ATTRACTING OTHER SOUL REAPERS.
MAYBE YOU'RE A LITTLE SLOW.
MAYBE YOU'RE THE SLOW ONE.
FWIK

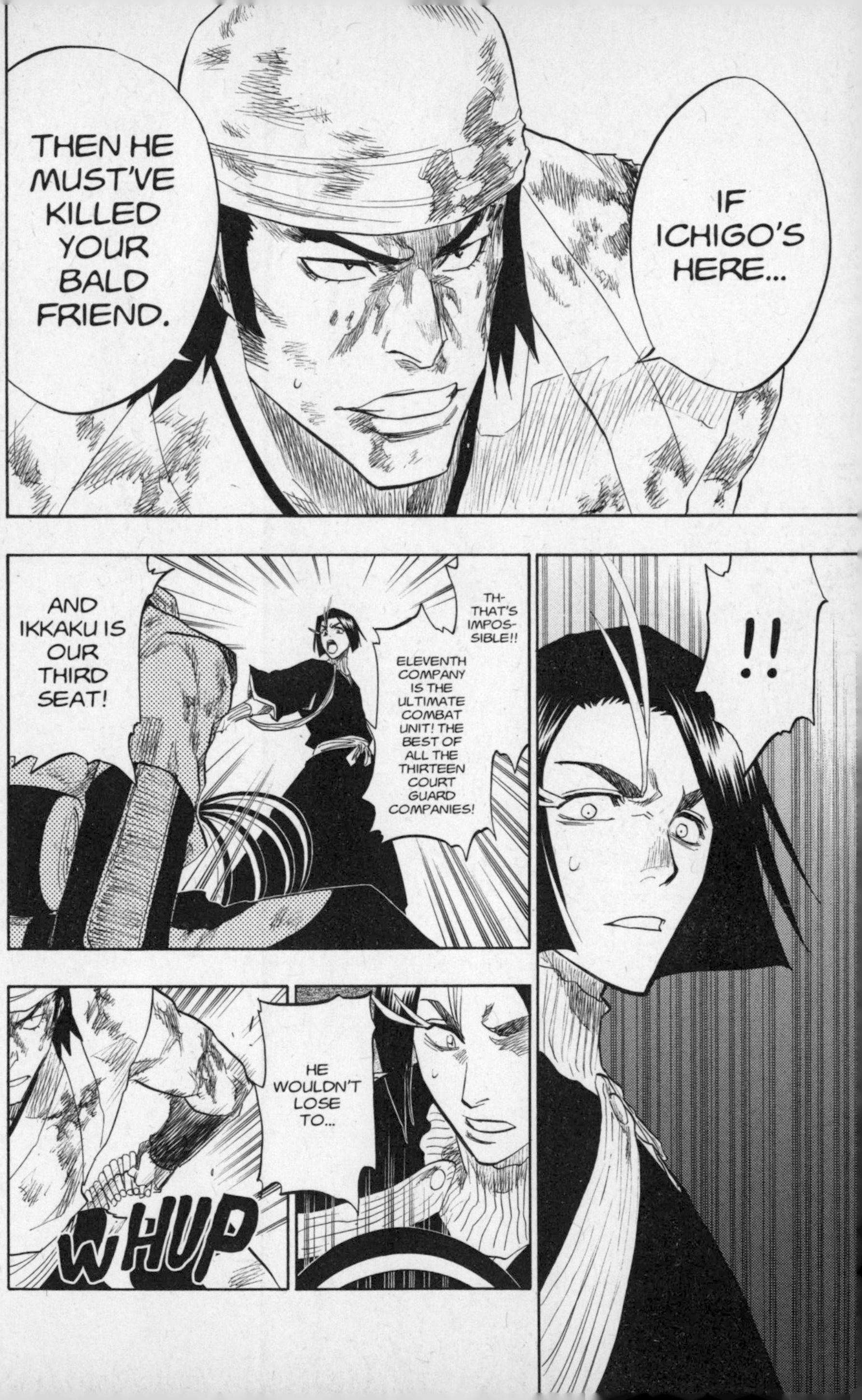
IF ICHIGO'S HERE...
THEN HE MUST'VE KILLED YOUR BALD FRIEND.
!!
TH-THAT'S IMPOSSIBLE!!
ELEVENTH COMPANY IS THE ULTIMATE COMBAT UNIT! THE BEST OF ALL THE THIRTEEN COURT GUARD COMPANIES!
AND IKKAKU IS OUR THIRD SEAT!
HE WOULDN'T LOSE TO...
WHUP

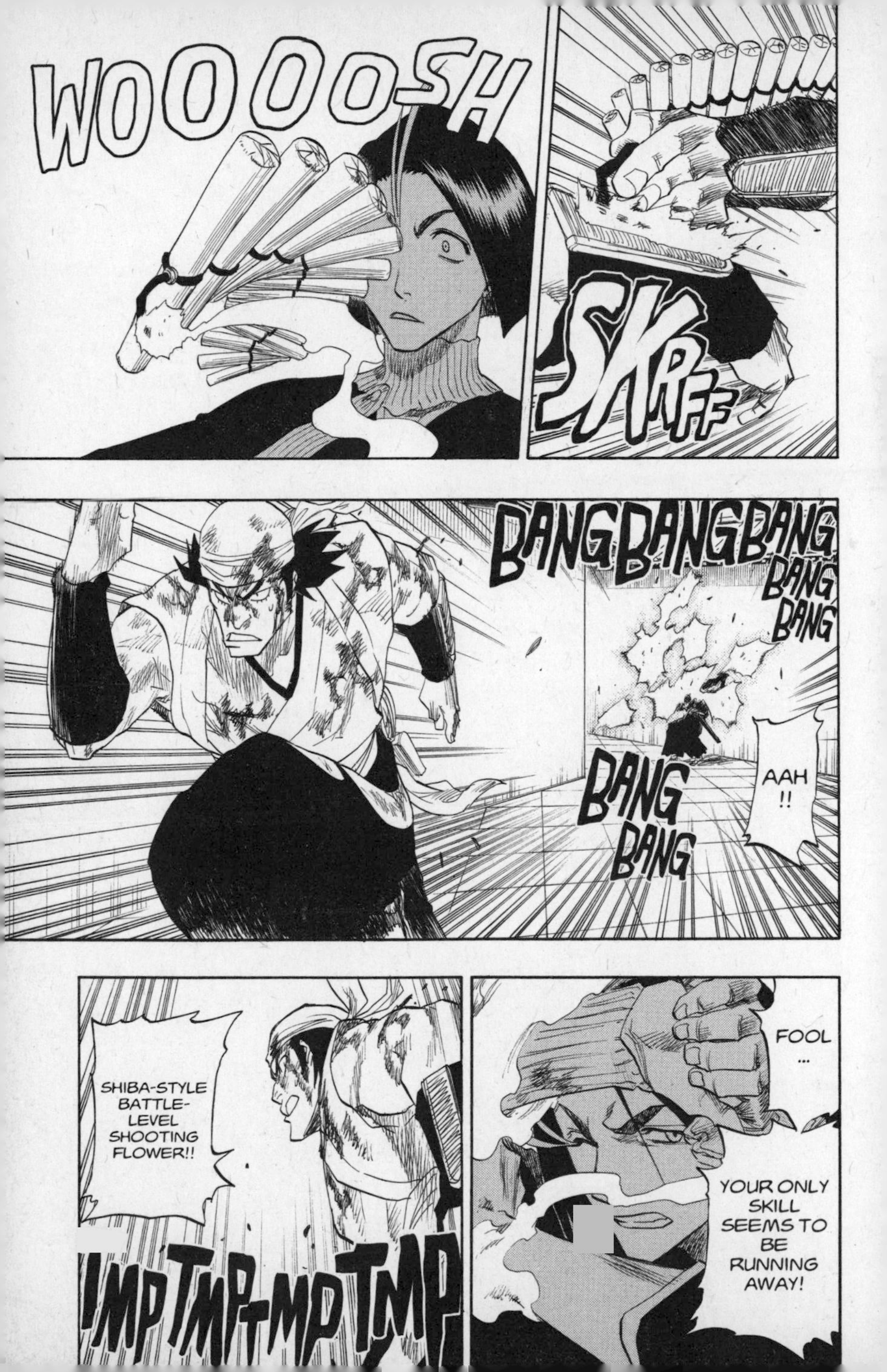
SKRFF
WOOOOSH
BANG BANG BANG BANG BANG
BANG BANG
AAH !!
FOOL ...
YOUR ONLY SKILL SEEMS TO BE RUNNING AWAY!
SHIBA-STYLE BATTLE-LEVEL SHOOTING FLOWER!!

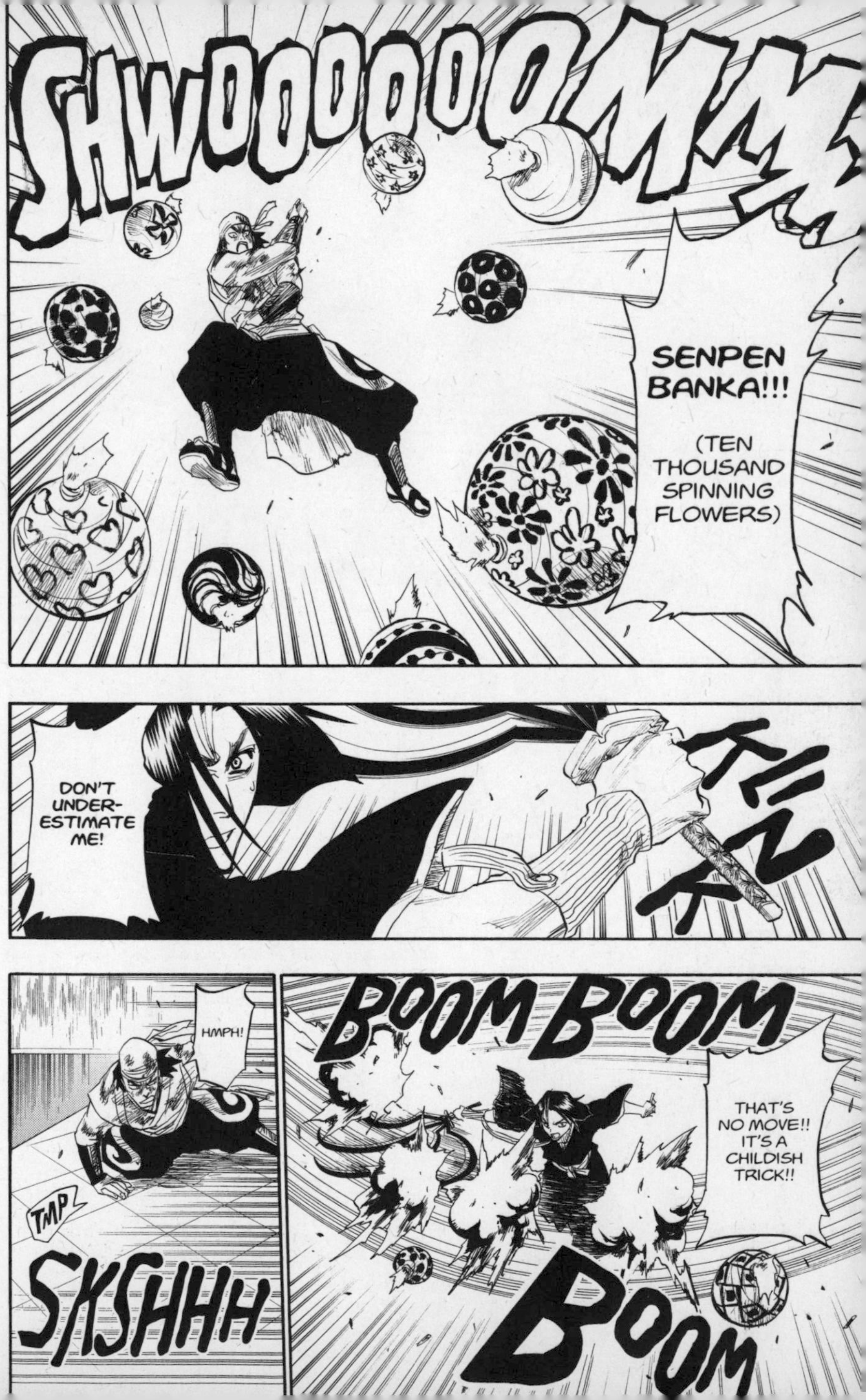
SHWOOOOOOMM
SENPEN BANKA!!!
(TEN THOUSAND SPINNING FLOWERS)
KLINK
DON'T UNDER-ESTIMATE ME!
BOOM BOOM
THAT'S NO MOVE!! IT'S A CHILDISH TRICK!!
BOOM
HMPH!
TMP
SKSHHH

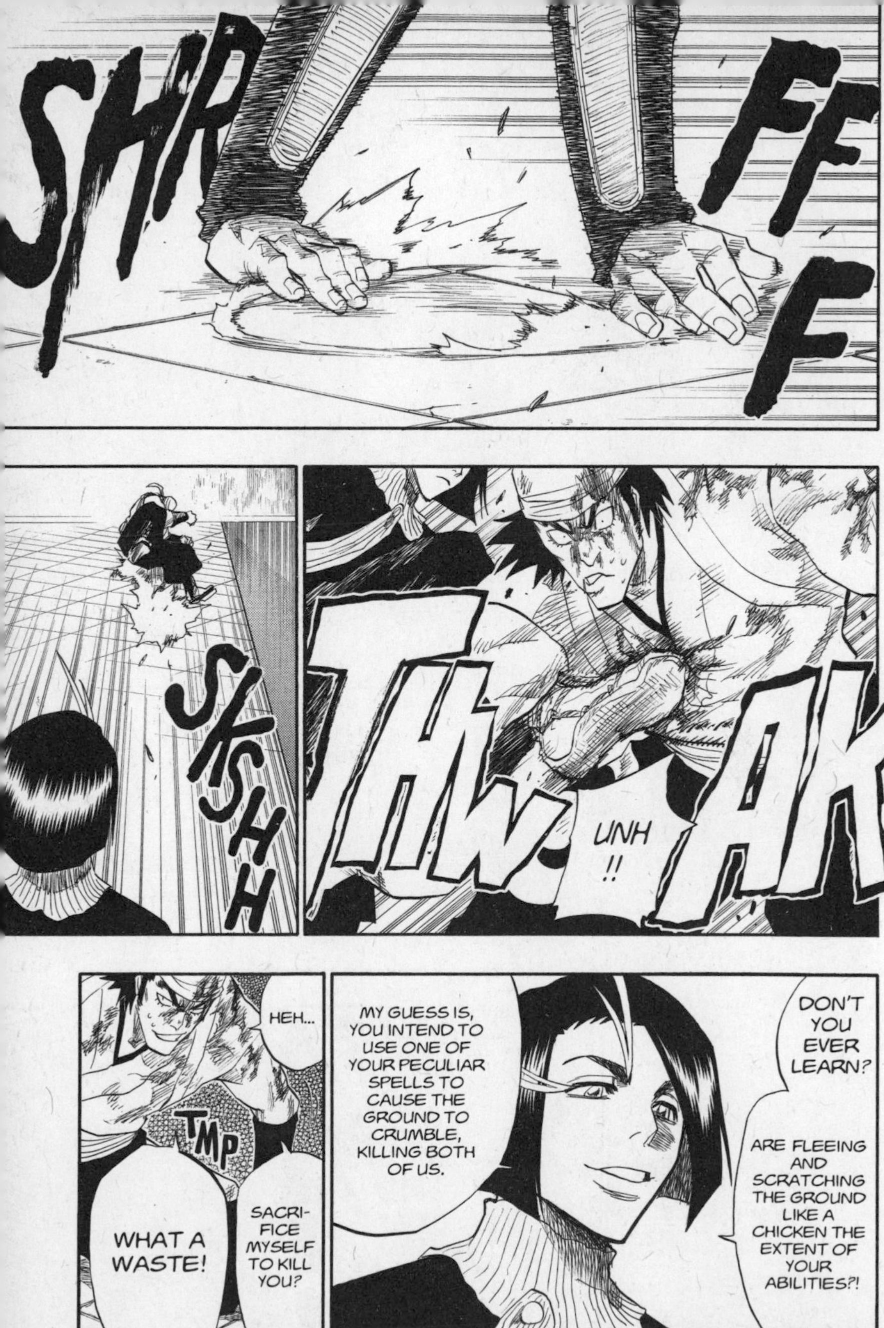
SHRFFF
THWAK
UNH !!
SKSHH
DON'T YOU EVER LEARN?
ARE FLEEING AND SCRATCHING THE GROUND LIKE A CHICKEN THE EXTENT OF YOUR ABILITIES?!
MY GUESS IS, YOU INTEND TO USE ONE OF YOUR PECULIAR SPELLS TO CAUSE THE GROUND TO CRUMBLE, KILLING BOTH OF US.
HEH...
TMP
SACRI-FICE MYSELF TO KILL YOU?
WHAT A WASTE!

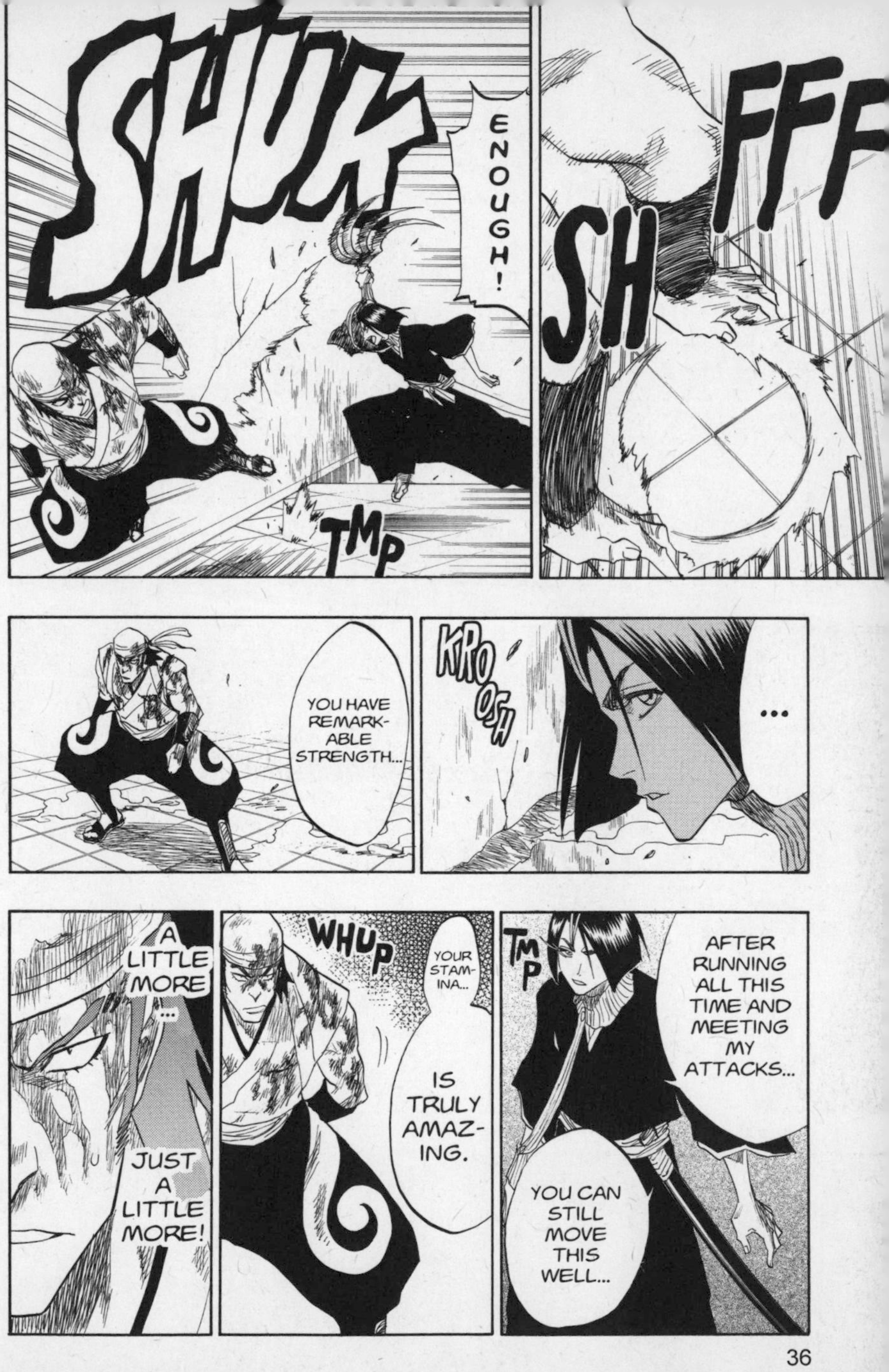
SHFFF
ENOUGH!
SHUK
TMP
KROOSH
...
YOU HAVE REMARKABLE STRENGTH...
AFTER RUNNING ALL THIS TIME AND MEETING MY ATTACKS...
TMP
YOU CAN STILL MOVE THIS WELL...
YOUR STAMINA...
WHUP
IS TRULY AMAZING.
A LITTLE MORE...
JUST A LITTLE MORE!

READ THIS WAY

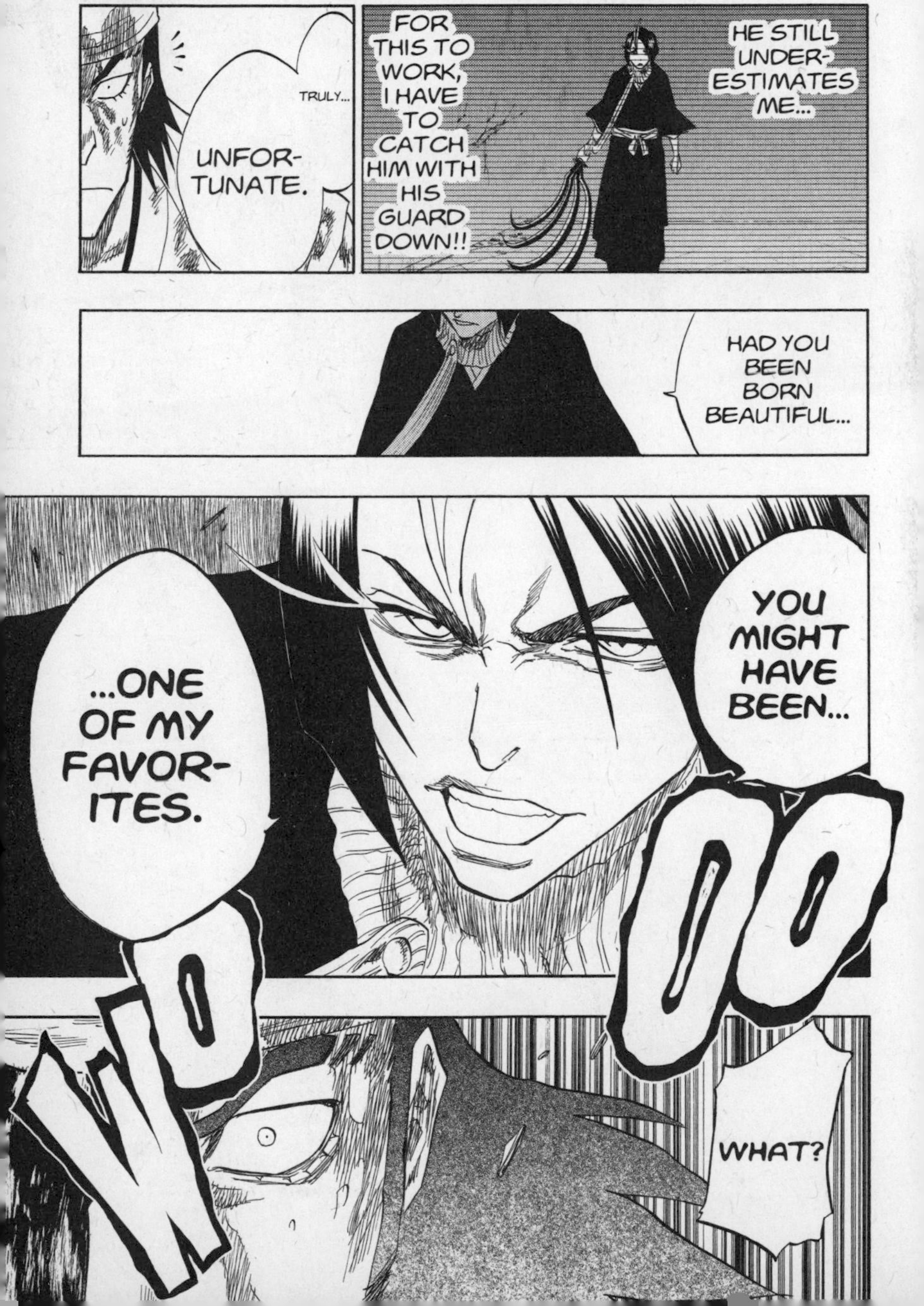
HE STILL UNDER-ESTIMATES ME...
FOR THIS TO WORK, I HAVE TO CATCH HIM WITH HIS GUARD DOWN!!
TRULY...
UNFOR-TUNATE.
HAD YOU BEEN BORN BEAUTIFUL...
YOU MIGHT HAVE BEEN...
...ONE OF MY FAVOR-ITES.
WHAT?

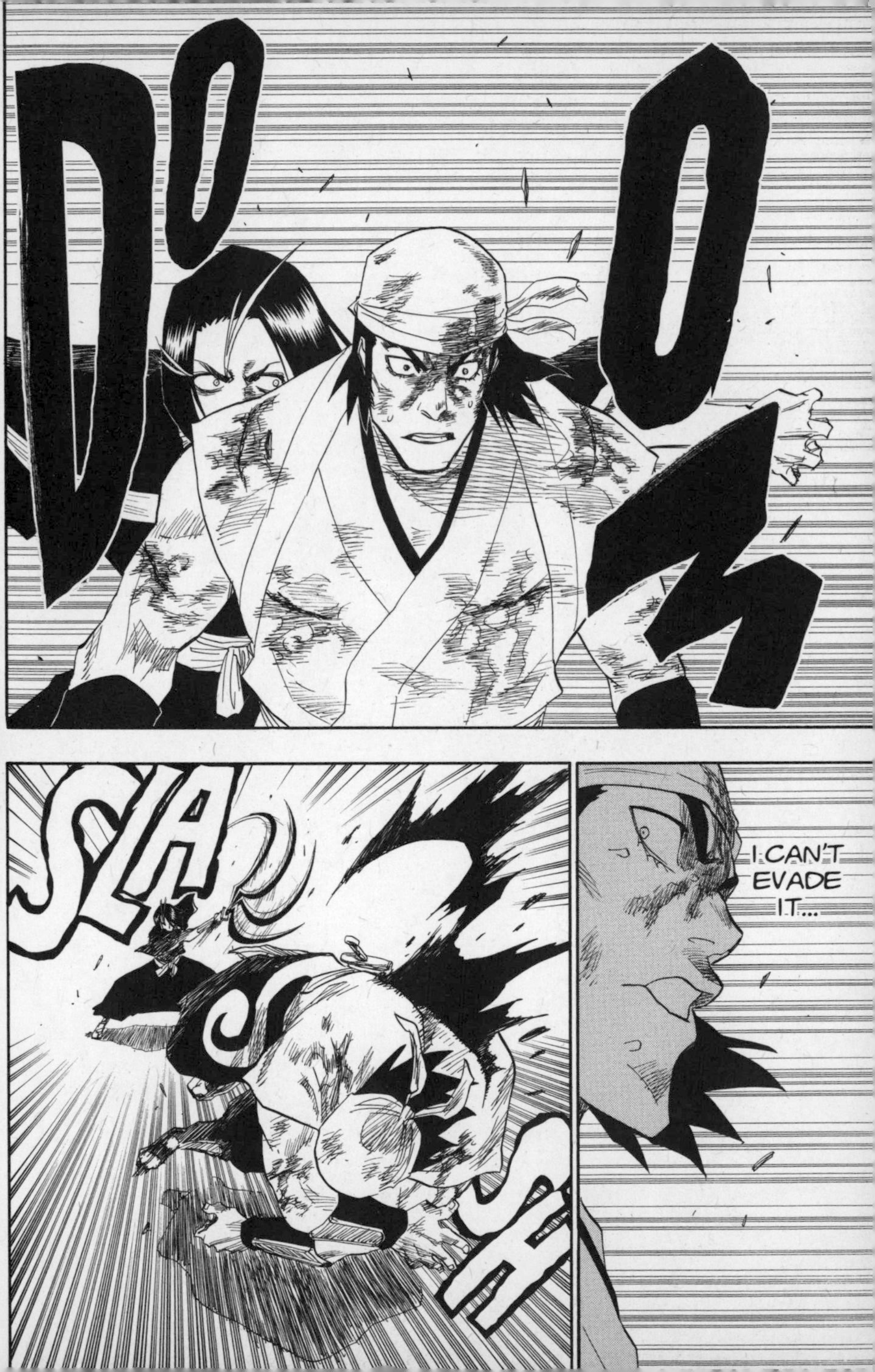
DOOM
I CAN'T EVADE IT...
SLASH

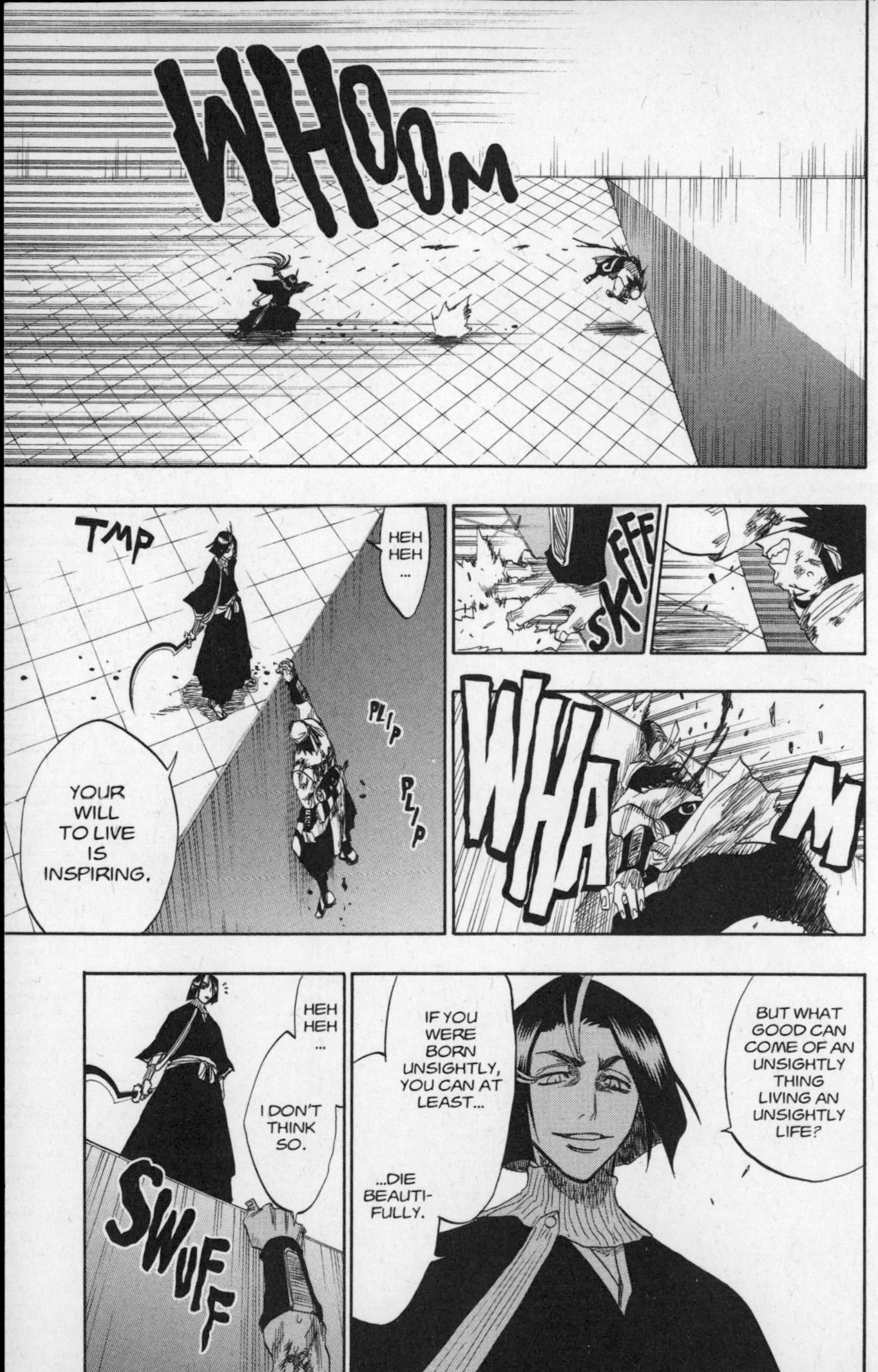
WHOOM
SKIFFF
WHA M
TMP
HEH HEH ...
PLIP PLIP
YOUR WILL TO LIVE IS INSPIRING.
BUT WHAT GOOD CAN COME OF AN UNSIGHTLY THING LIVING AN UNSIGHTLY LIFE?
IF YOU WERE BORN UNSIGHTLY, YOU CAN AT LEAST...
...DIE BEAUTI-FULLY.
HEH HEH ...
I DON'T THINK SO.
SWUFF

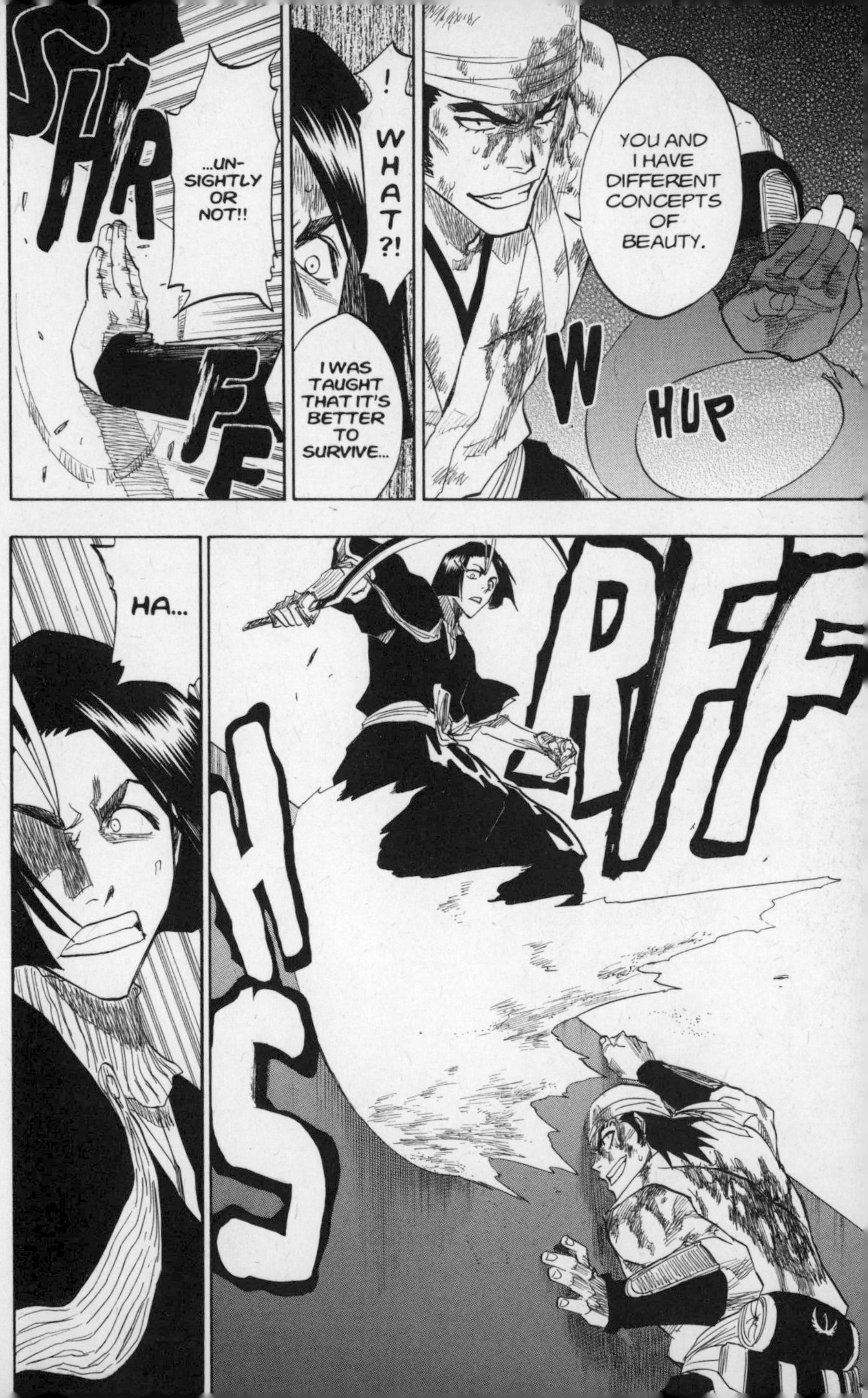
YOU AND I HAVE DIFFERENT CONCEPTS OF BEAUTY.
WHUP
!
WHAT?!
I WAS TAUGHT THAT IT'S BETTER TO SURVIVE...
...UN-SIGHTLY OR NOT!!
SHRFF
SHRFF
HA...

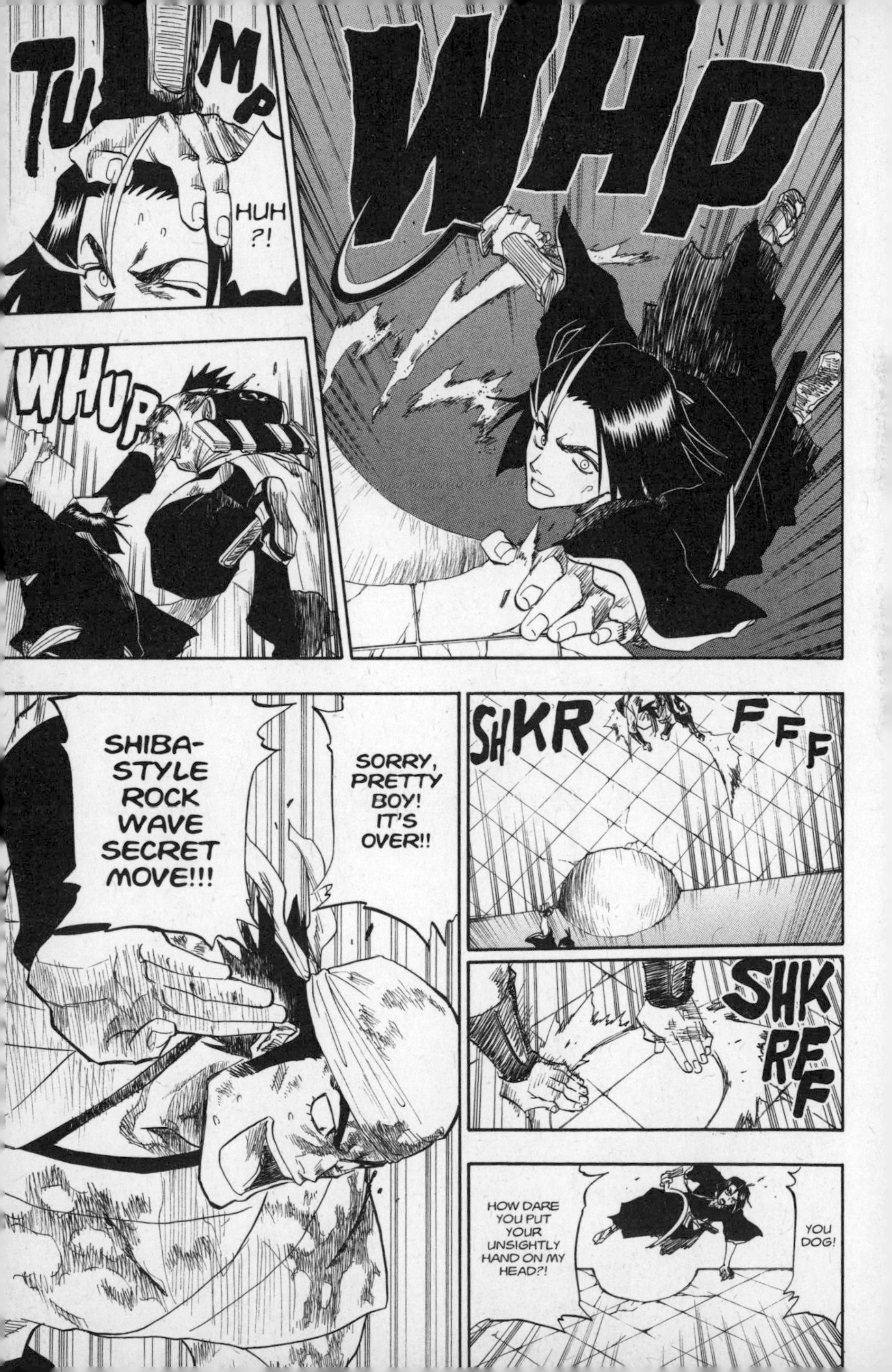
WAP
TUMP
HUH?!
WHUP
SHKR
FFF
SHK RFF
HOW DARE YOU PUT YOUR UNSIGHTLY HAND ON MY HEAD?!
YOU DOG!
SORRY, PRETTY BOY! IT'S OVER!!
SHIBA-STYLE ROCK WAVE SECRET MOVE!!!

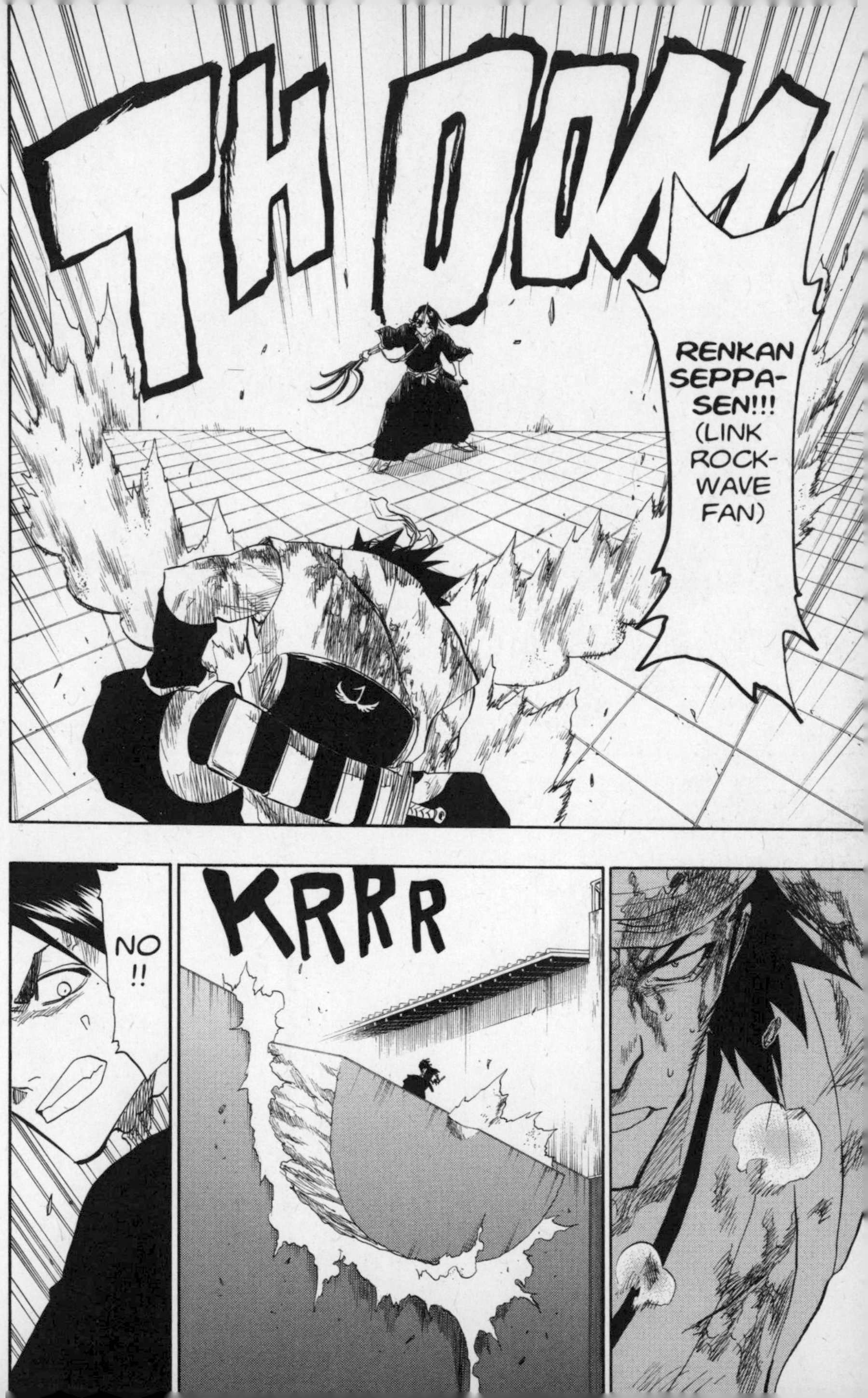
THOOM
RENKAN SEPPA-SEN!!! (LINK ROCK-WAVE FAN)
KRRR
NO !!

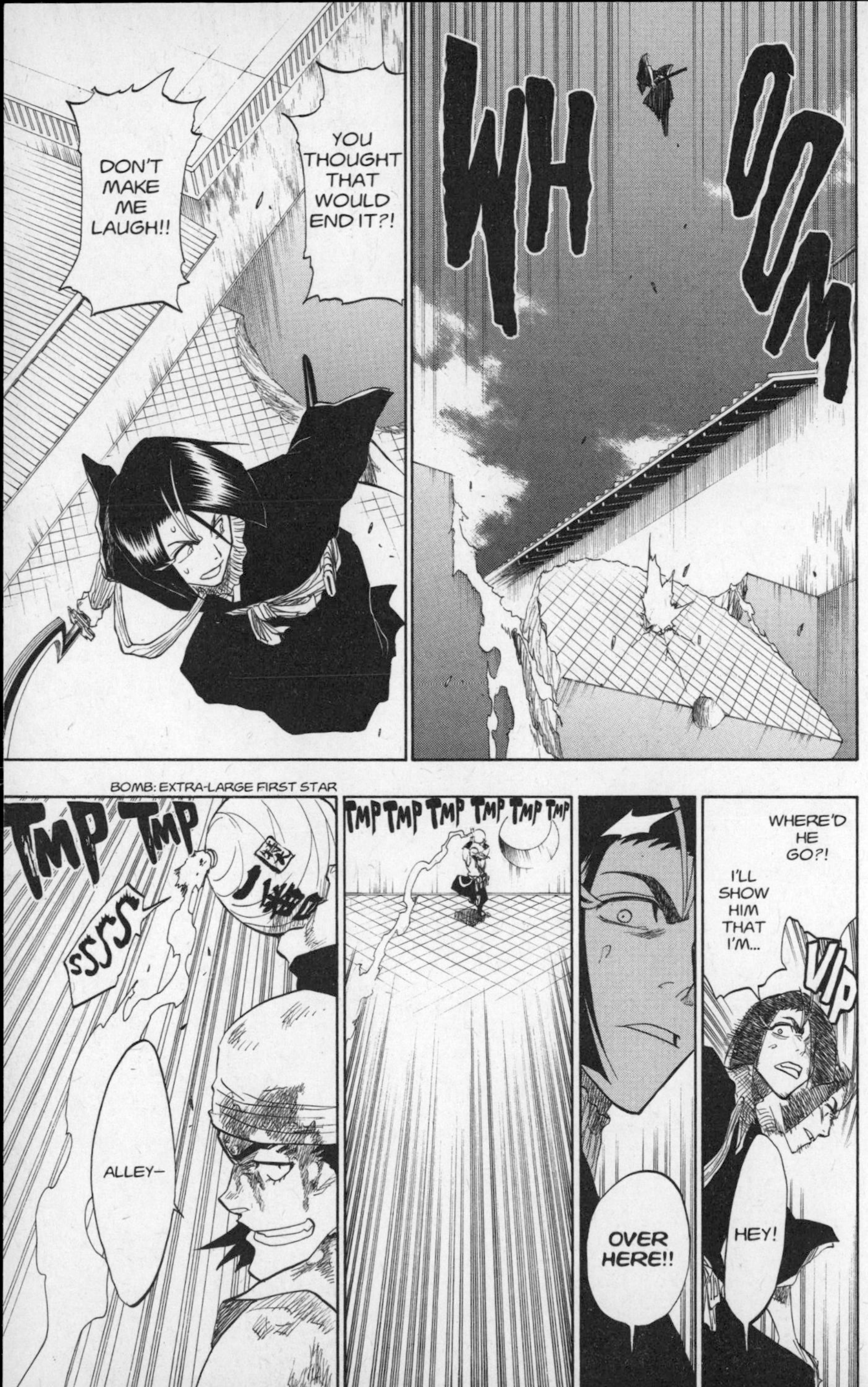
WH
OOOM
YOU THOUGHT THAT WOULD END IT?!
DON'T MAKE ME LAUGH!!
BOMB: EXTRA-LARGE FIRST STAR
WHERE'D HE GO?!
I'LL SHOW HIM THAT I'M...
VIP
HEY!
OVER HERE!!
TMP TMP TMP TMP TMP TMP
TMP TMP
SSSS
ALLEY—

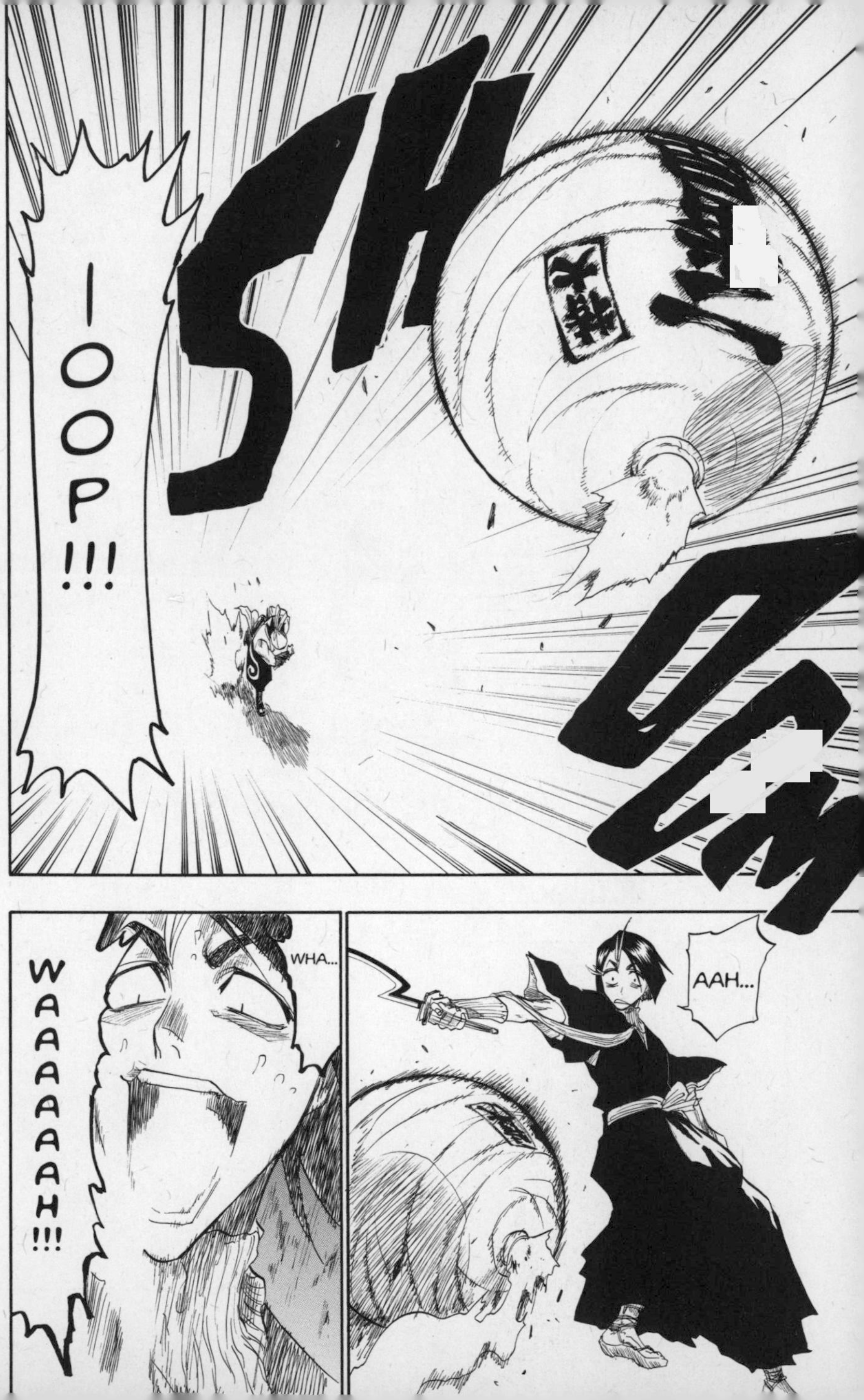
SH
OOM
IOOP!!!
AAH...
WHA...
WAAAAAAAAH!!!

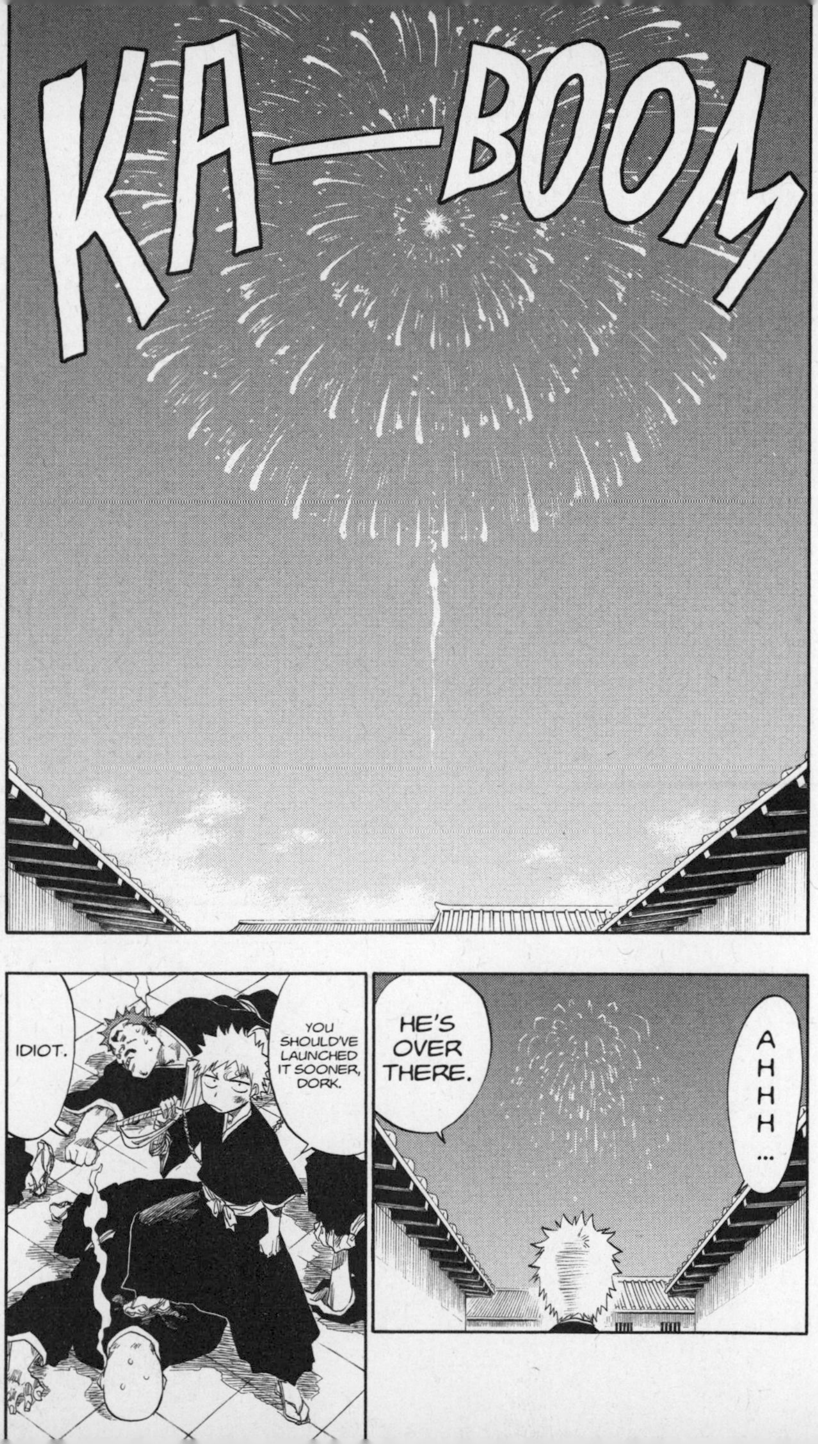
KA—BOOM
AHHH...
HE'S OVER THERE.
YOU SHOULD'VE LAUNCHED IT SOONER, DORK.
IDIOT.

AW...

YUMICHIKA
LOST.

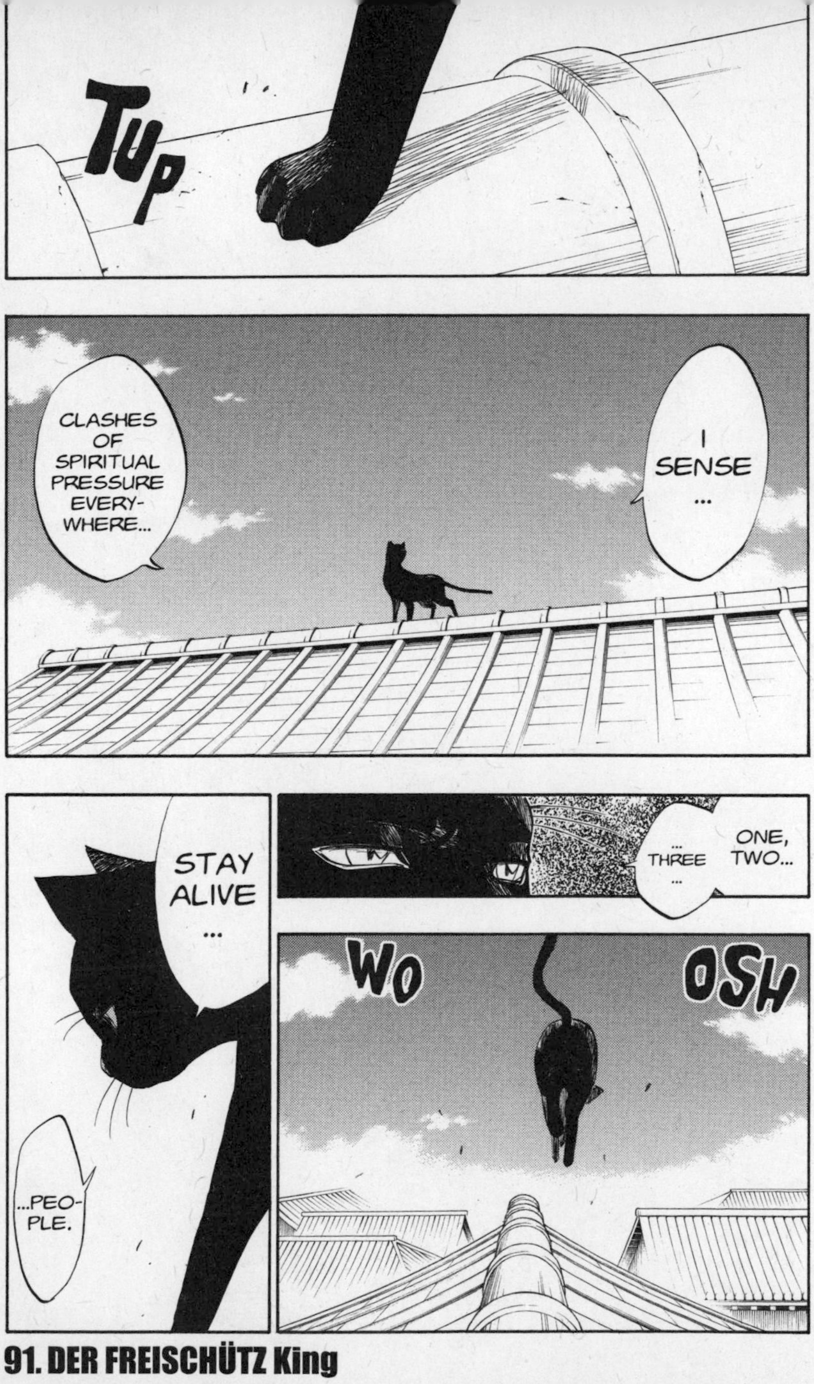
TUP
I SENSE ...
CLASHES OF SPIRITUAL PRESSURE EVERYWHERE...
ONE, TWO...
... THREE ...
WO OSH
STAY ALIVE ...
...PEO-PLE.

91. DER FREISCHÜTZ King

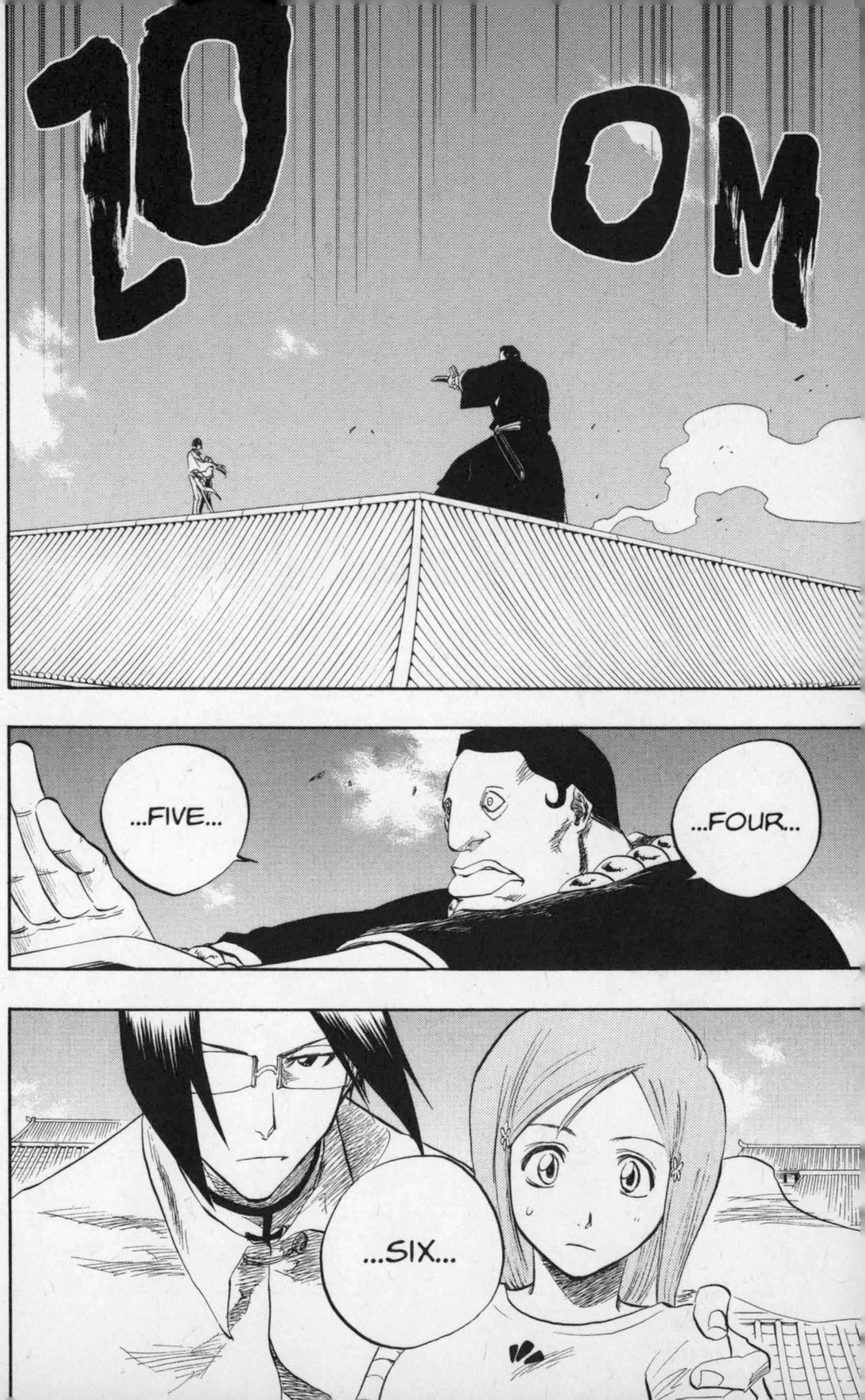
...FOUR...
...FIVE...
...SIX...

READ THIS WAY

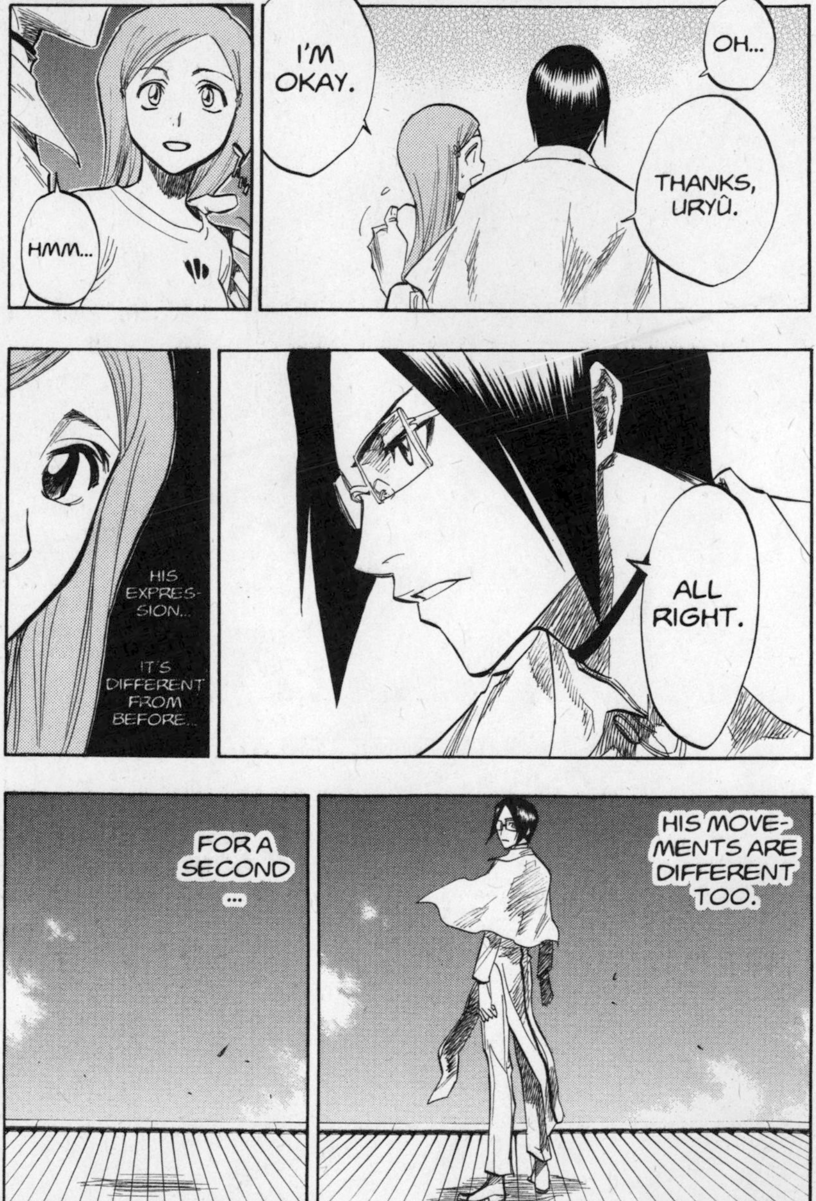
OH...
THANKS, URYÛ.
I'M OKAY.
HMM...
ALL RIGHT.
HIS EXPRES-SION...
IT'S DIFFERENT FROM BEFORE...
HIS MOVE-MENTS ARE DIFFERENT TOO.
FOR A SECOND ...

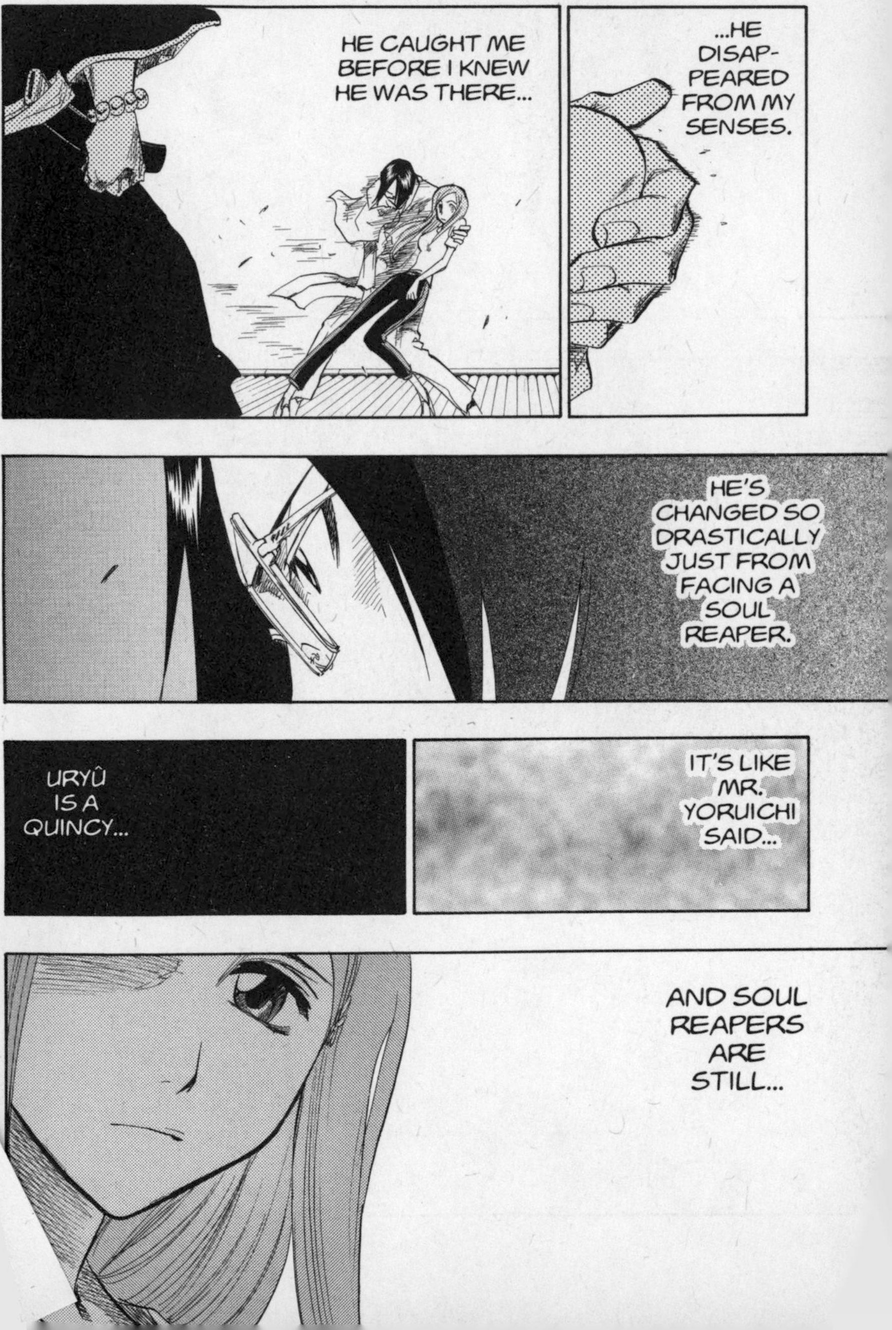
...HE DISAP-PEARED FROM MY SENSES.
HE CAUGHT ME BEFORE I KNEW HE WAS THERE...
HE'S CHANGED SO DRASTICALLY JUST FROM FACING A SOUL REAPER.
IT'S LIKE MR. YORUICHI SAID...
URYÛ IS A QUINCY...
AND SOUL REAPERS ARE STILL...

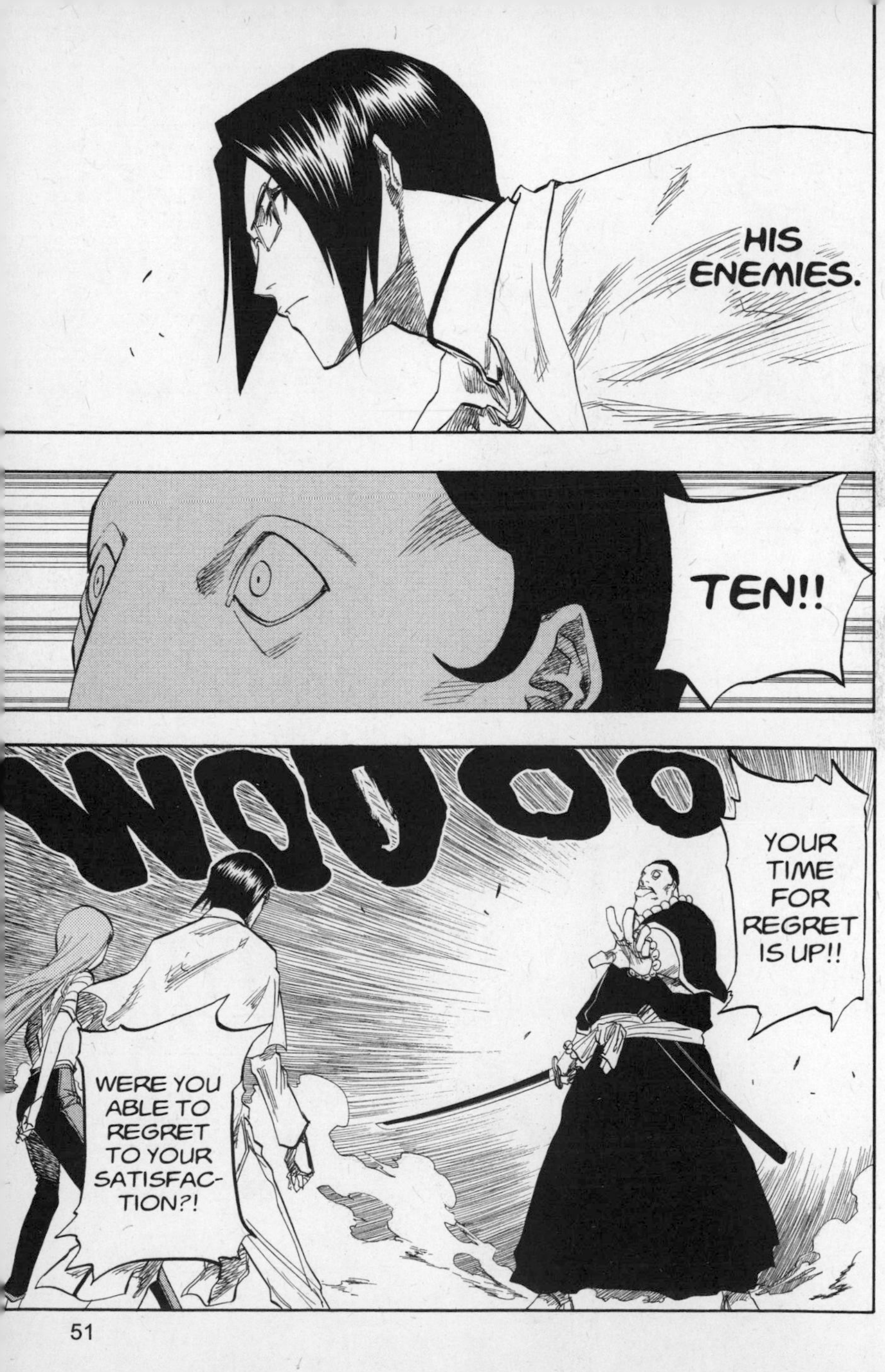
HIS ENEMIES.
TEN!!
YOUR TIME FOR REGRET IS UP!!
WERE YOU ABLE TO REGRET TO YOUR SATISFACTION?!

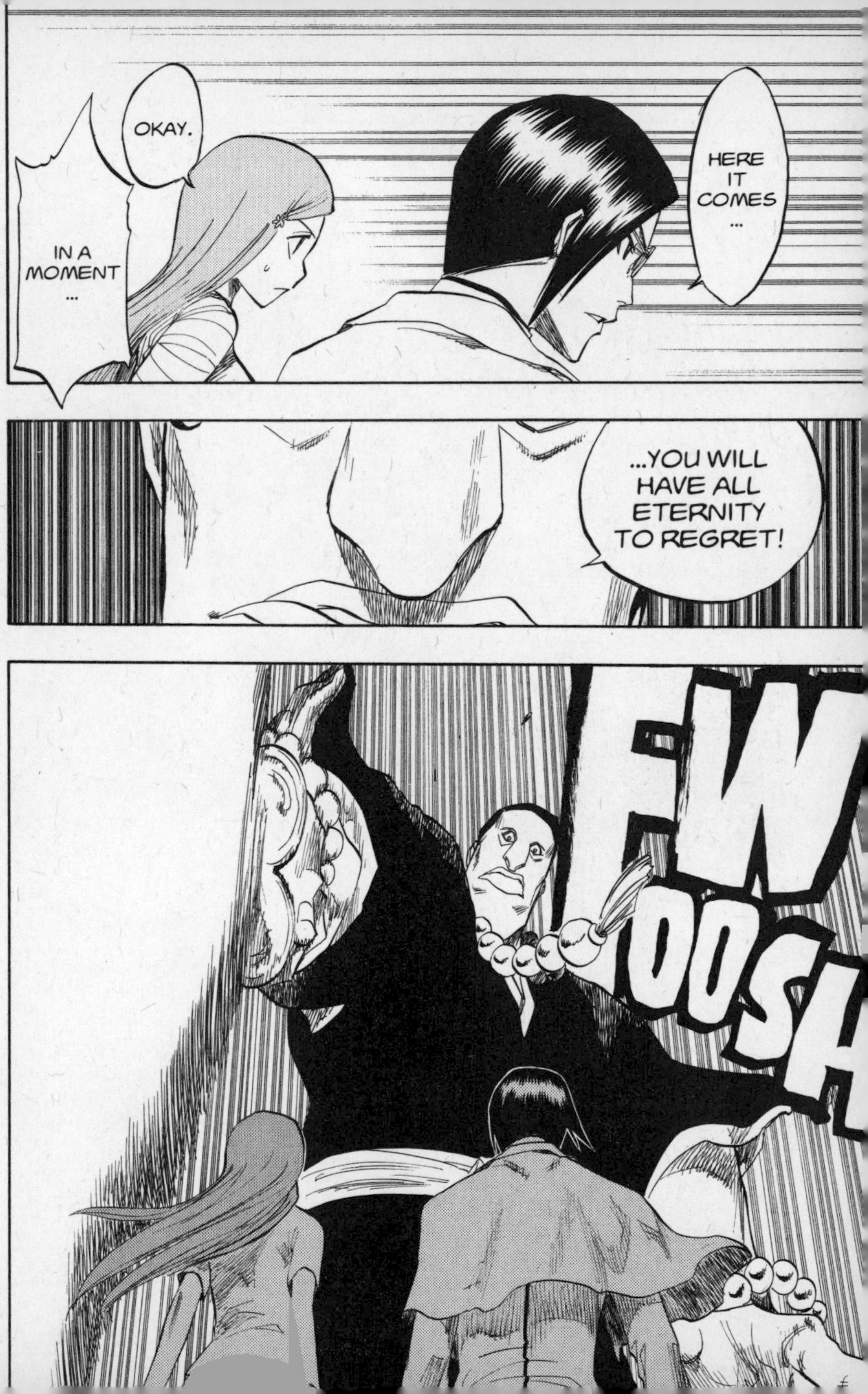
HERE IT COMES ...
OKAY.
IN A MOMENT ...
...YOU WILL HAVE ALL ETERNITY TO REGRET!
FWOOSH

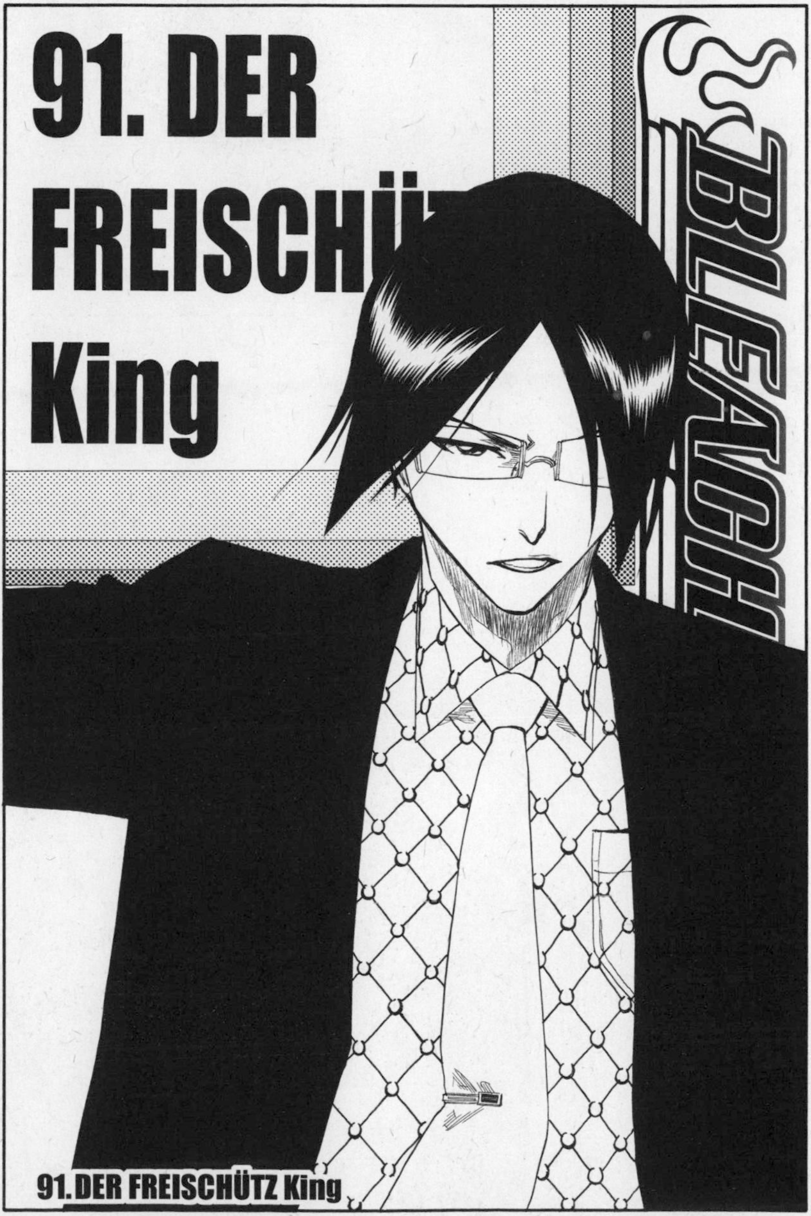
91. DER
FREISCHÜ
King
BLEACH
91. DER FREISCHÜTZ King

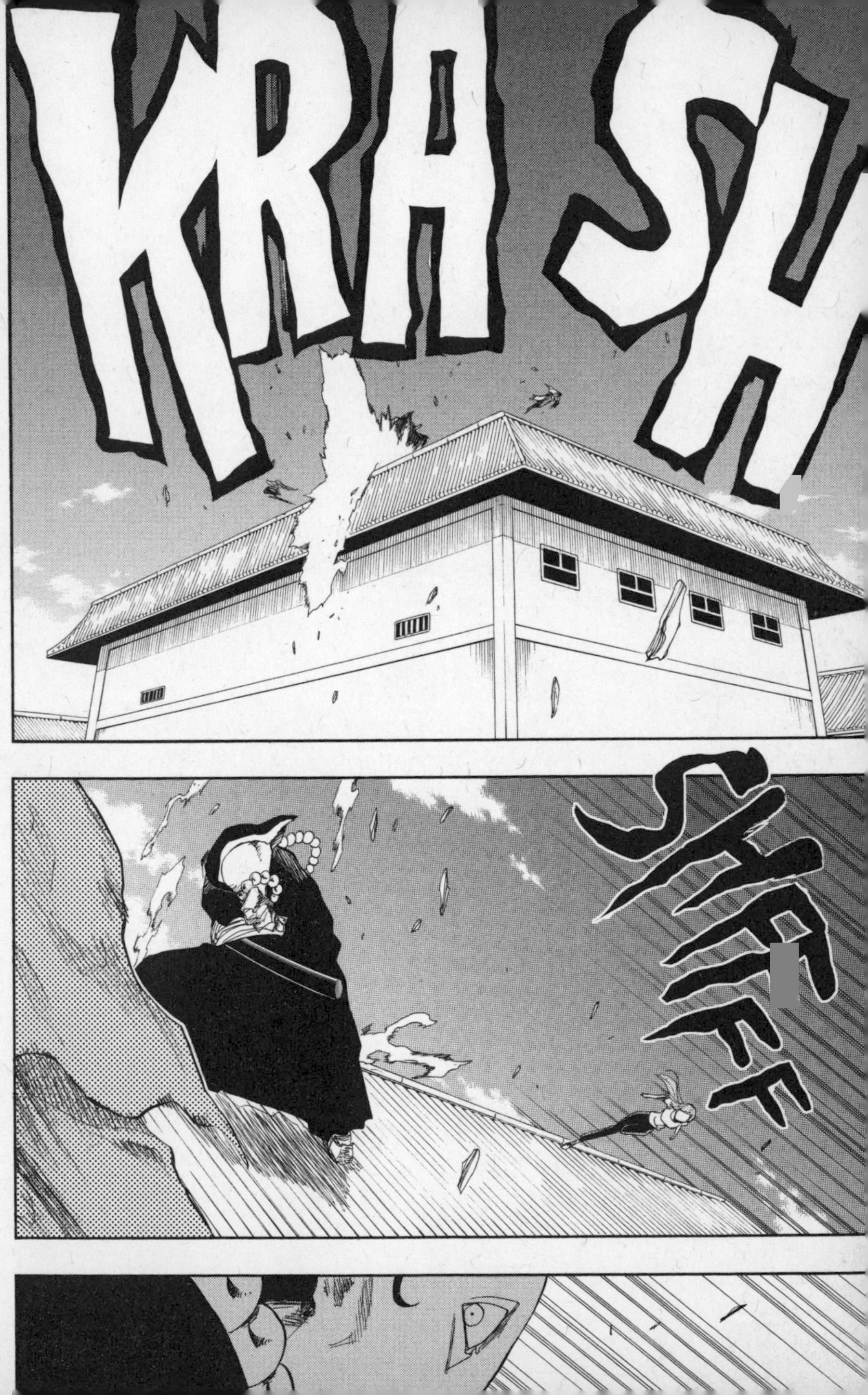

KRASH
SHFFF

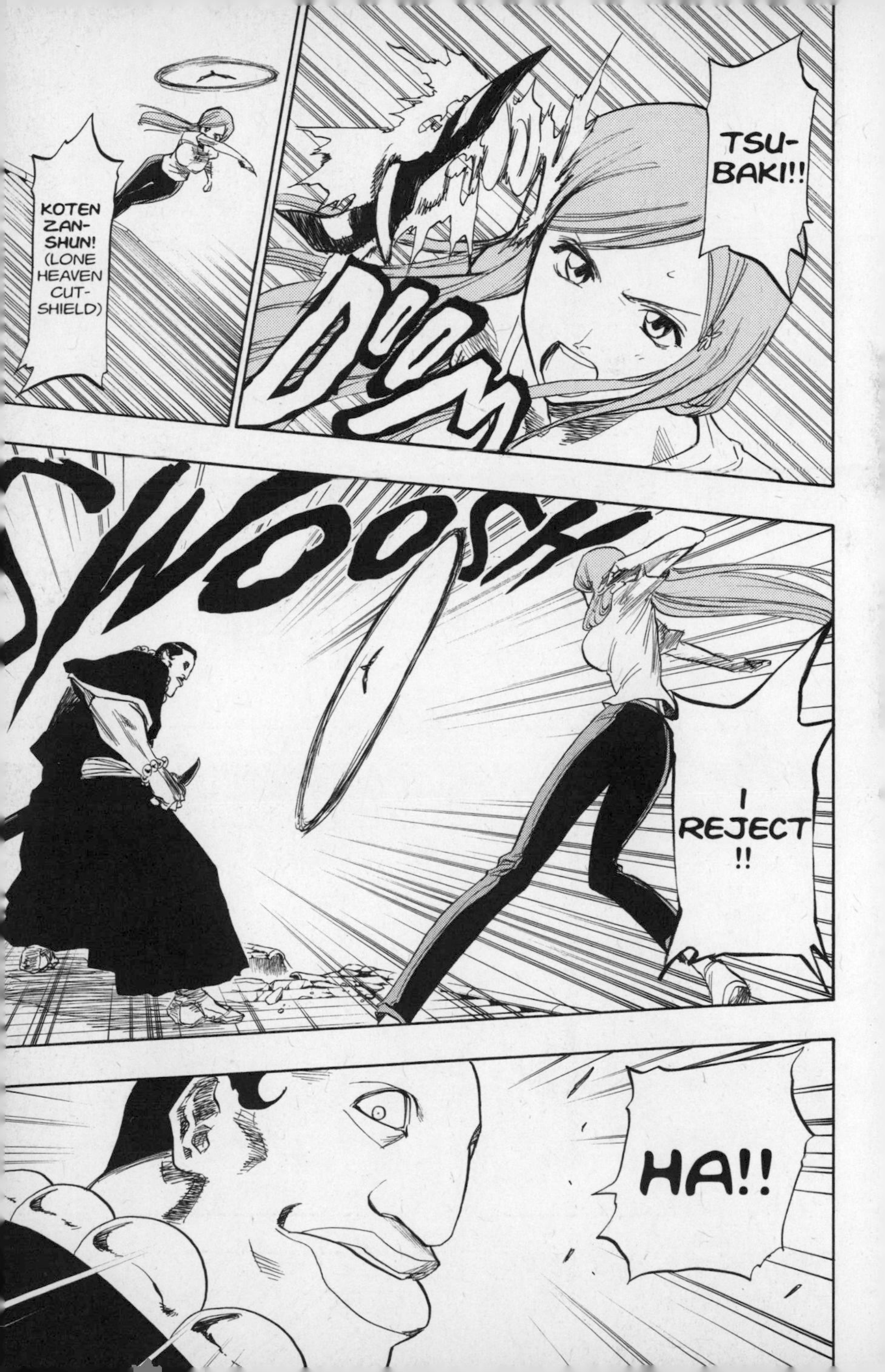
TSU-BAKI!!
DOOM
KOTEN ZAN-SHUN! (LONE HEAVEN CUT-SHIELD)
SWOOSH
I REJECT!!
HA!!

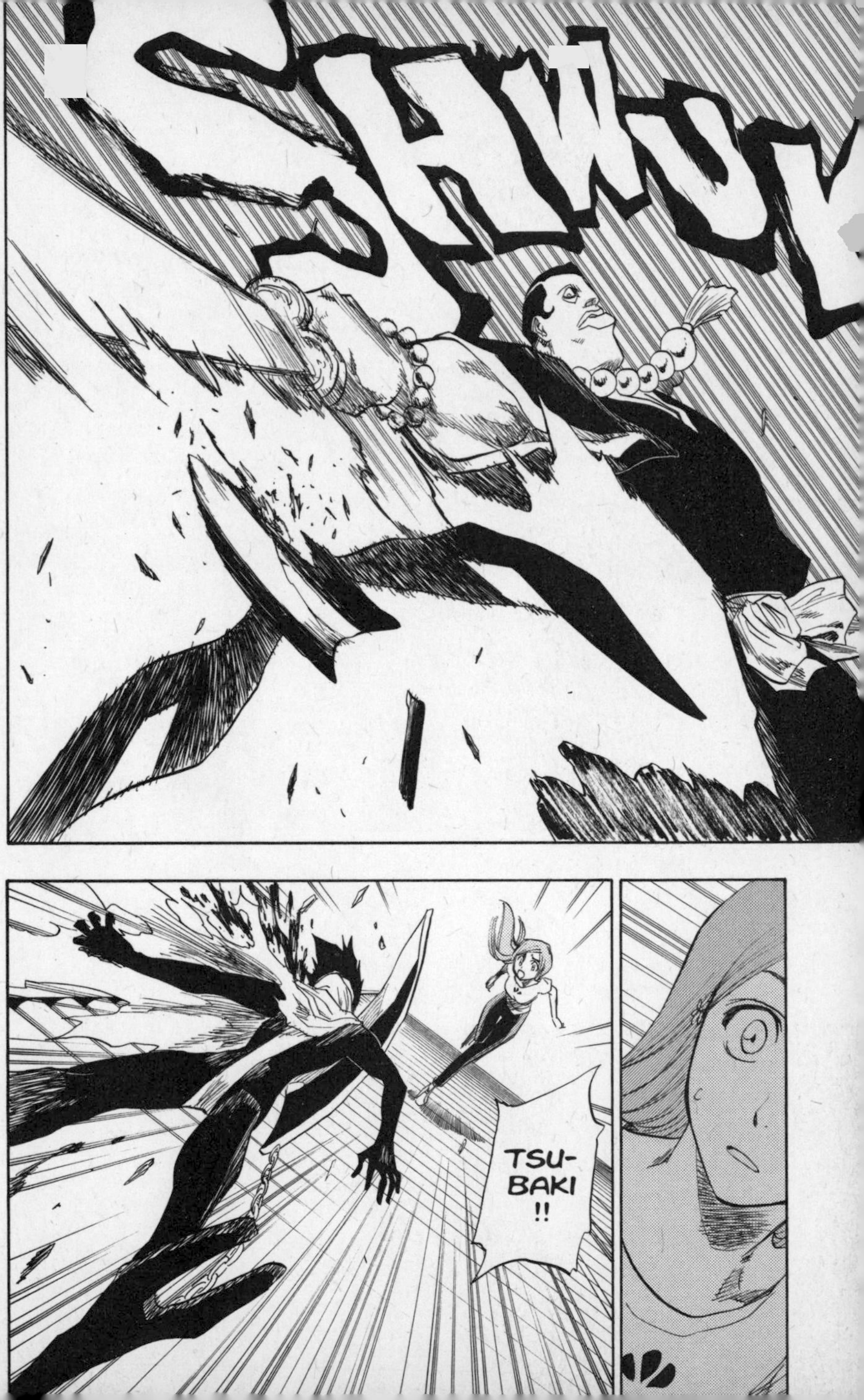
TSU-
BAKI
!!

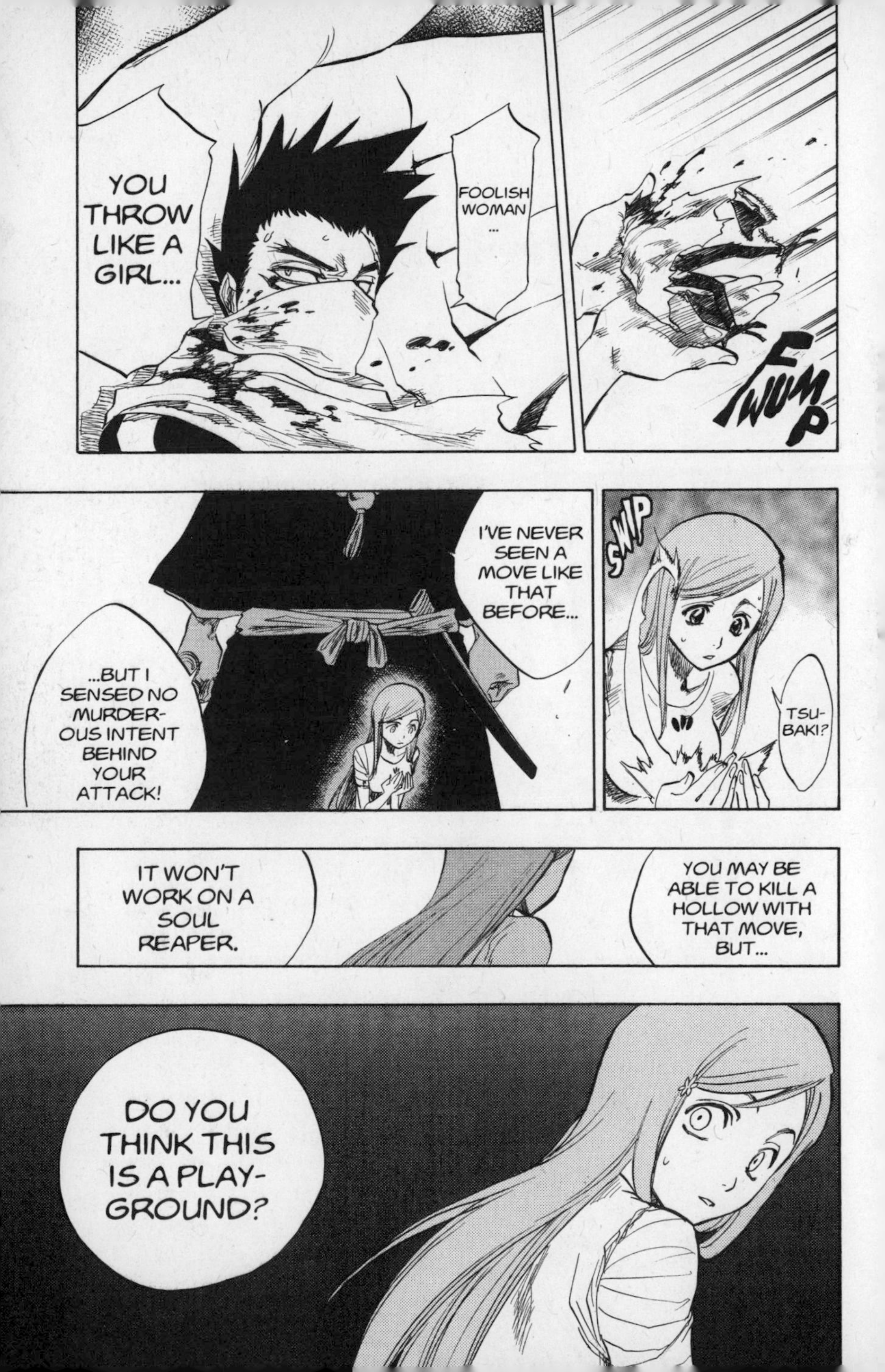
FWUMP
FOOLISH WOMAN ...
YOU THROW LIKE A GIRL...
SWIP
TSUBAKI?
I'VE NEVER SEEN A MOVE LIKE THAT BEFORE...
...BUT I SENSED NO MURDEROUS INTENT BEHIND YOUR ATTACK!
YOU MAY BE ABLE TO KILL A HOLLOW WITH THAT MOVE, BUT...
IT WON'T WORK ON A SOUL REAPER.
DO YOU THINK THIS IS A PLAYGROUND?

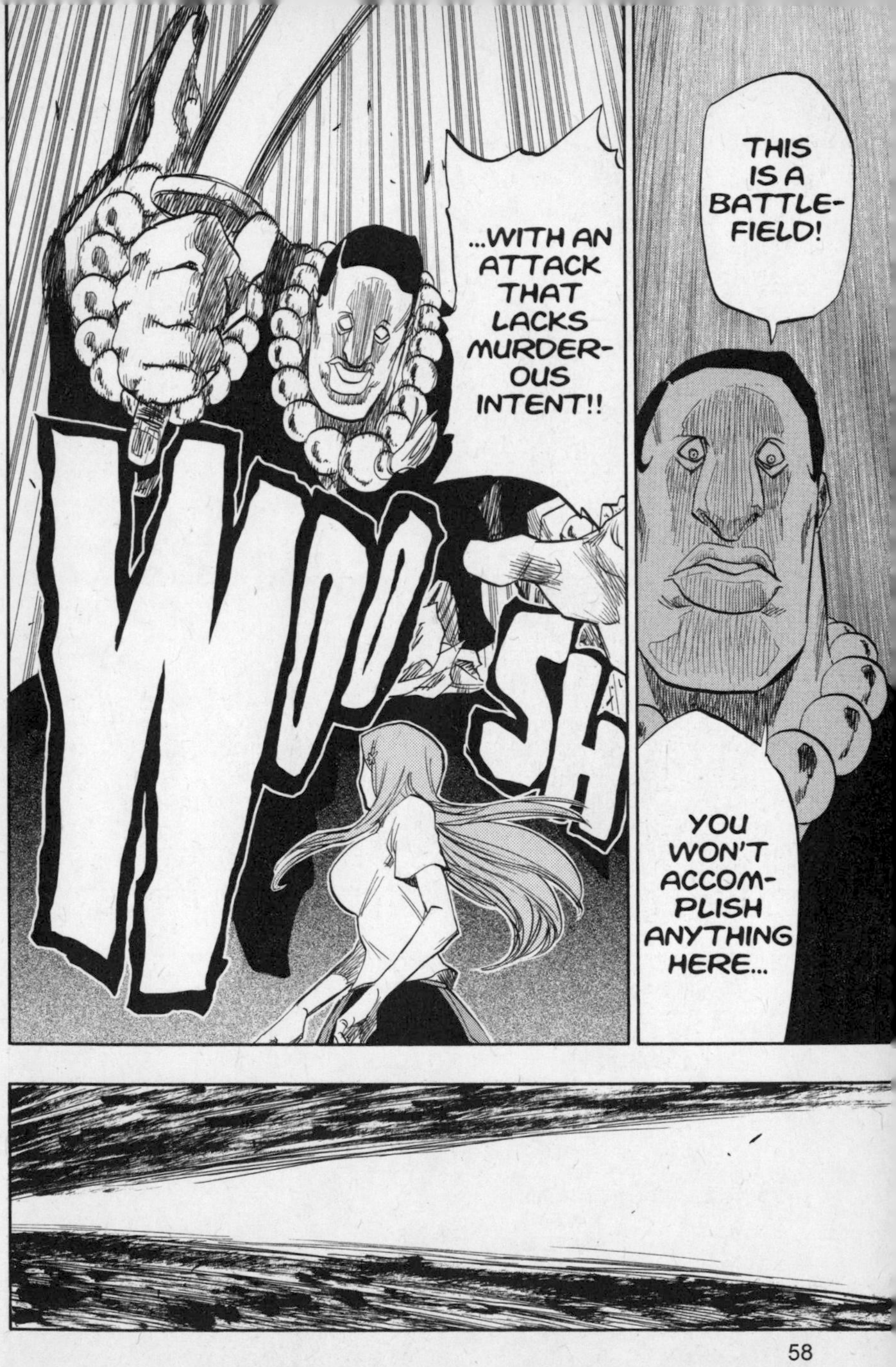
THIS IS A BATTLE-FIELD!
YOU WON'T ACCOM-PLISH ANYTHING HERE...
...WITH AN ATTACK THAT LACKS MURDER-OUS INTENT!!
WOOSH

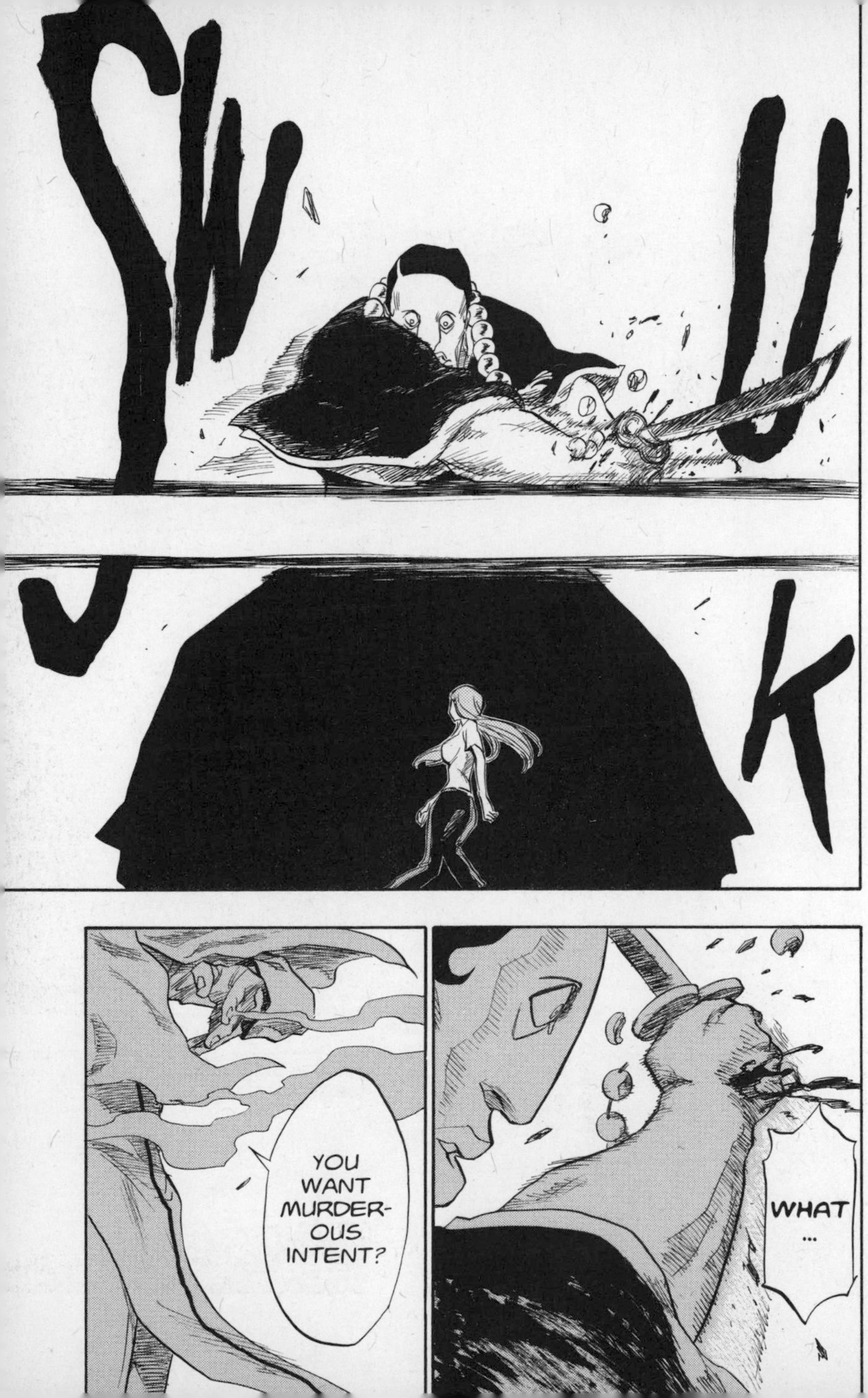
SWUK
WHAT ...
YOU WANT MURDER-OUS INTENT?

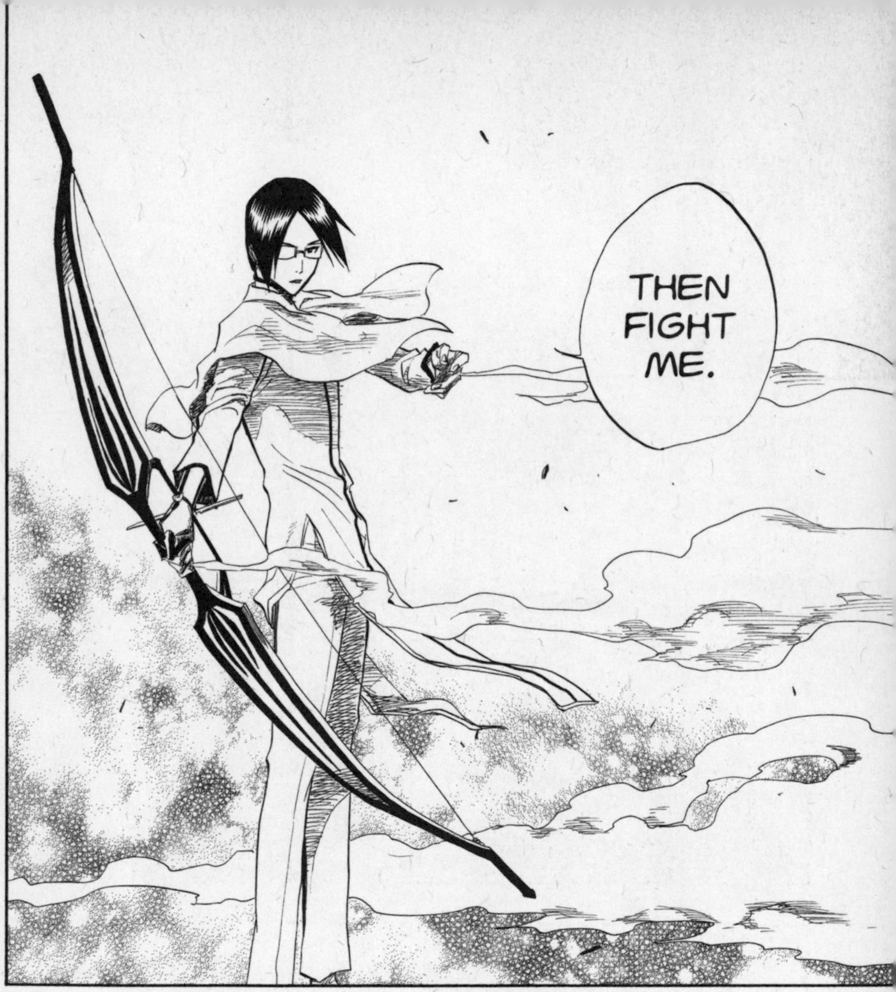
THEN FIGHT ME.

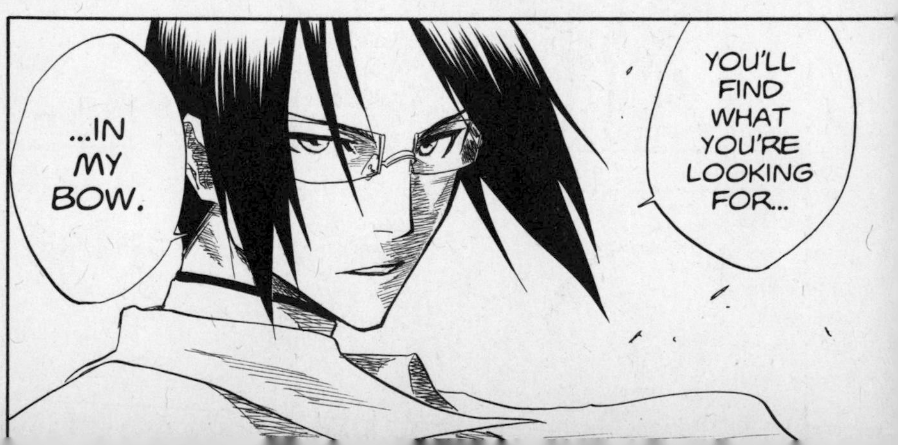
YOU'LL FIND WHAT YOU'RE LOOKING FOR...
...IN MY BOW.

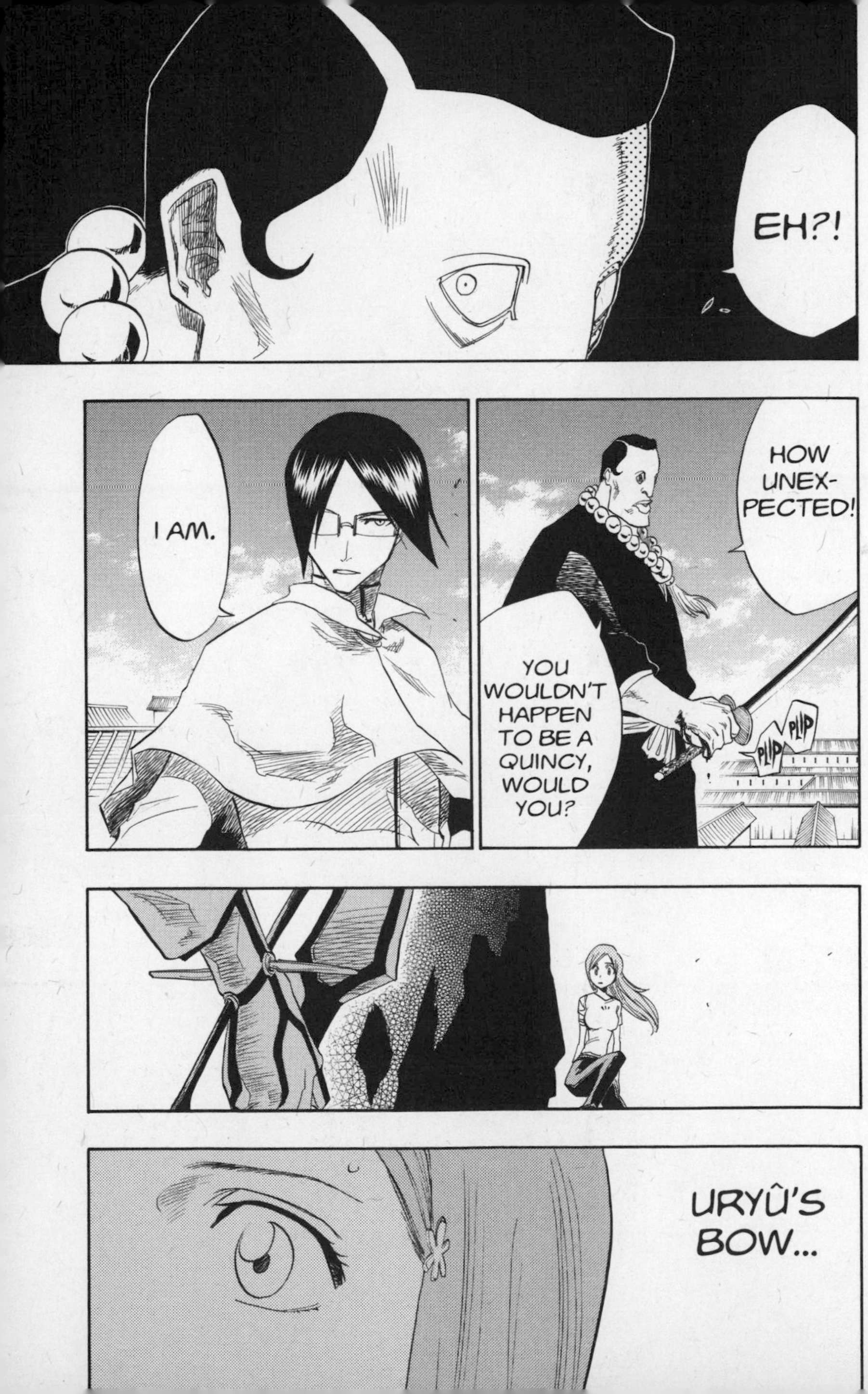
EH?!
HOW UNEX-PECTED!
YOU WOULDN'T HAPPEN TO BE A QUINCY, WOULD YOU?
PLIP
PLIP
I AM.
URYÛ'S BOW...

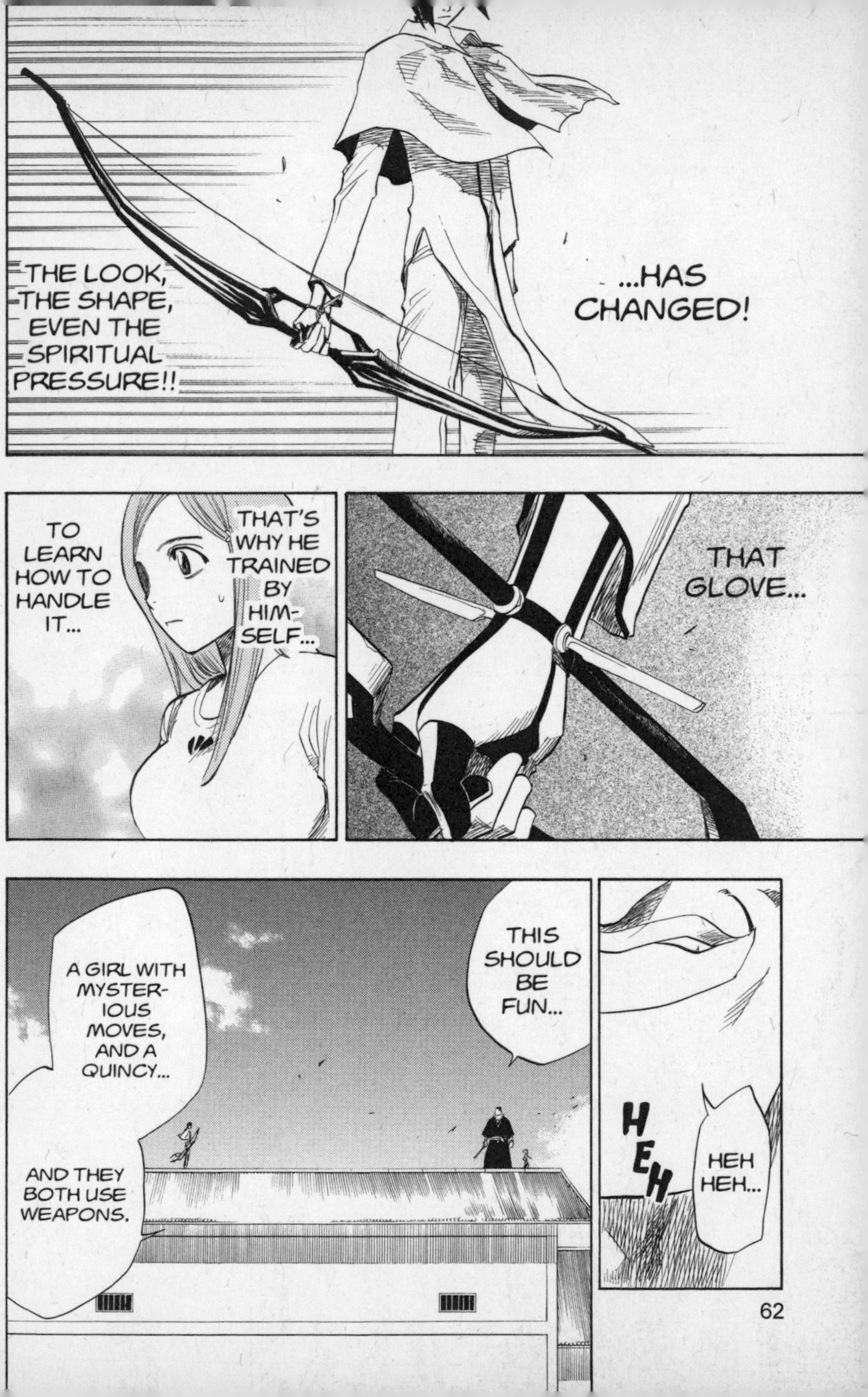
THE LOOK, THE SHAPE, EVEN THE SPIRITUAL PRESSURE!!
...HAS CHANGED!
THAT GLOVE...
THAT'S WHY HE TRAINED BY HIM-SELF...
TO LEARN HOW TO HANDLE IT...
HEH
HEH HEH...
THIS SHOULD BE FUN...
A GIRL WITH MYSTER-IOUS MOVES, AND A QUINCY...
AND THEY BOTH USE WEAPONS.

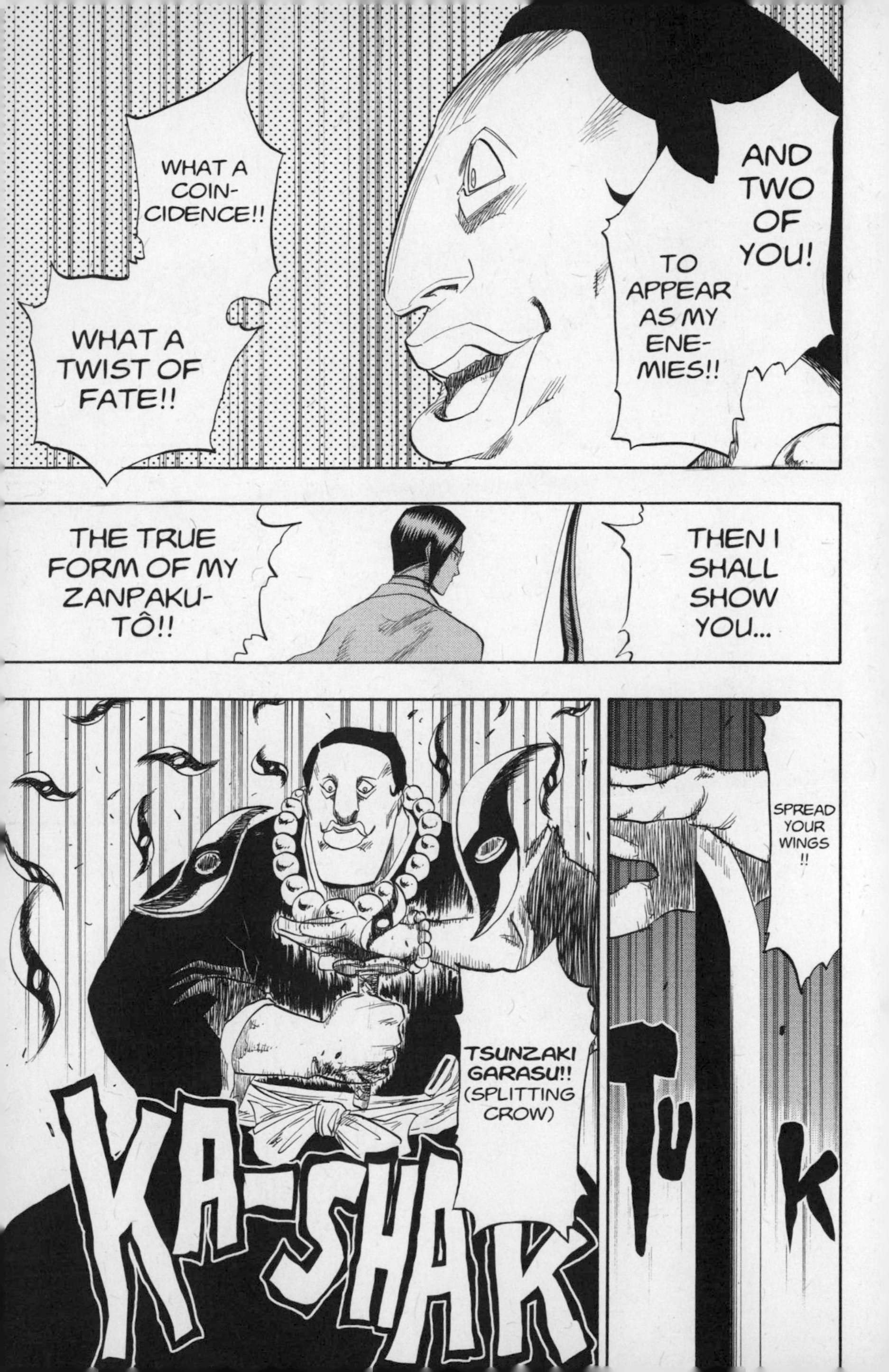
AND TWO OF YOU!
TO APPEAR AS MY ENE-MIES!!
WHAT A COIN-CIDENCE!!
WHAT A TWIST OF FATE!!
THEN I SHALL SHOW YOU...
THE TRUE FORM OF MY ZANPAKU-TÔ!!
SPREAD YOUR WINGS !!
TUK
TSUNZAKI GARASU!! (SPLITTING CROW)
KA-SHAK

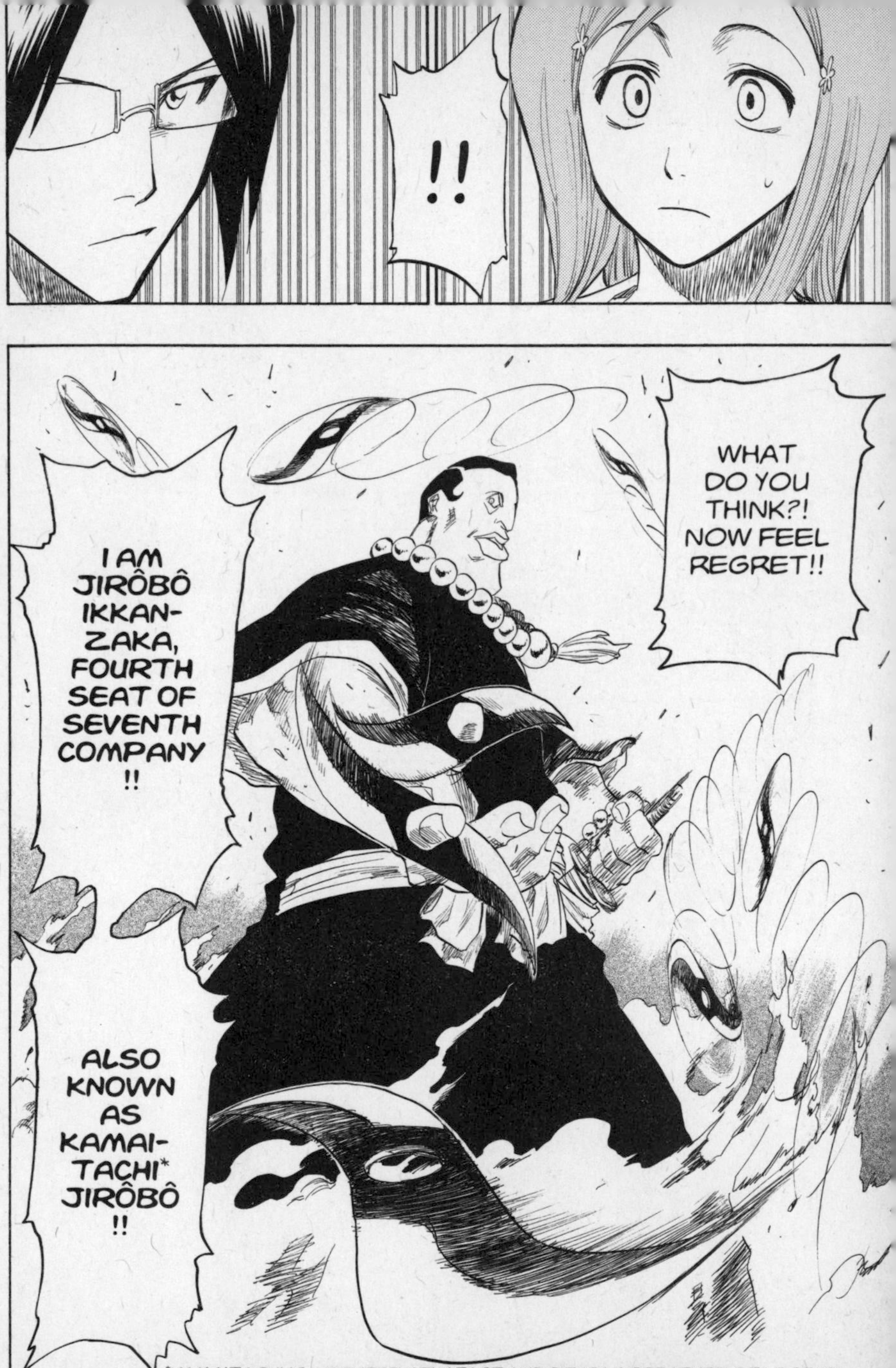
!!
WHAT DO YOU THINK?! NOW FEEL REGRET!!
I AM JIRÔBÔ IKKAN-ZAKA, FOURTH SEAT OF SEVENTH COMPANY !!
ALSO KNOWN AS KAMAI-TACHI* JIRÔBÔ !!

*KAMAITACHI IS AN EXTREMELY FAST AND DEADLY CREATURE OF LEGEND. THE WORD LITERALLY MEANS "SICKLE WEASEL."

READ THIS WAY

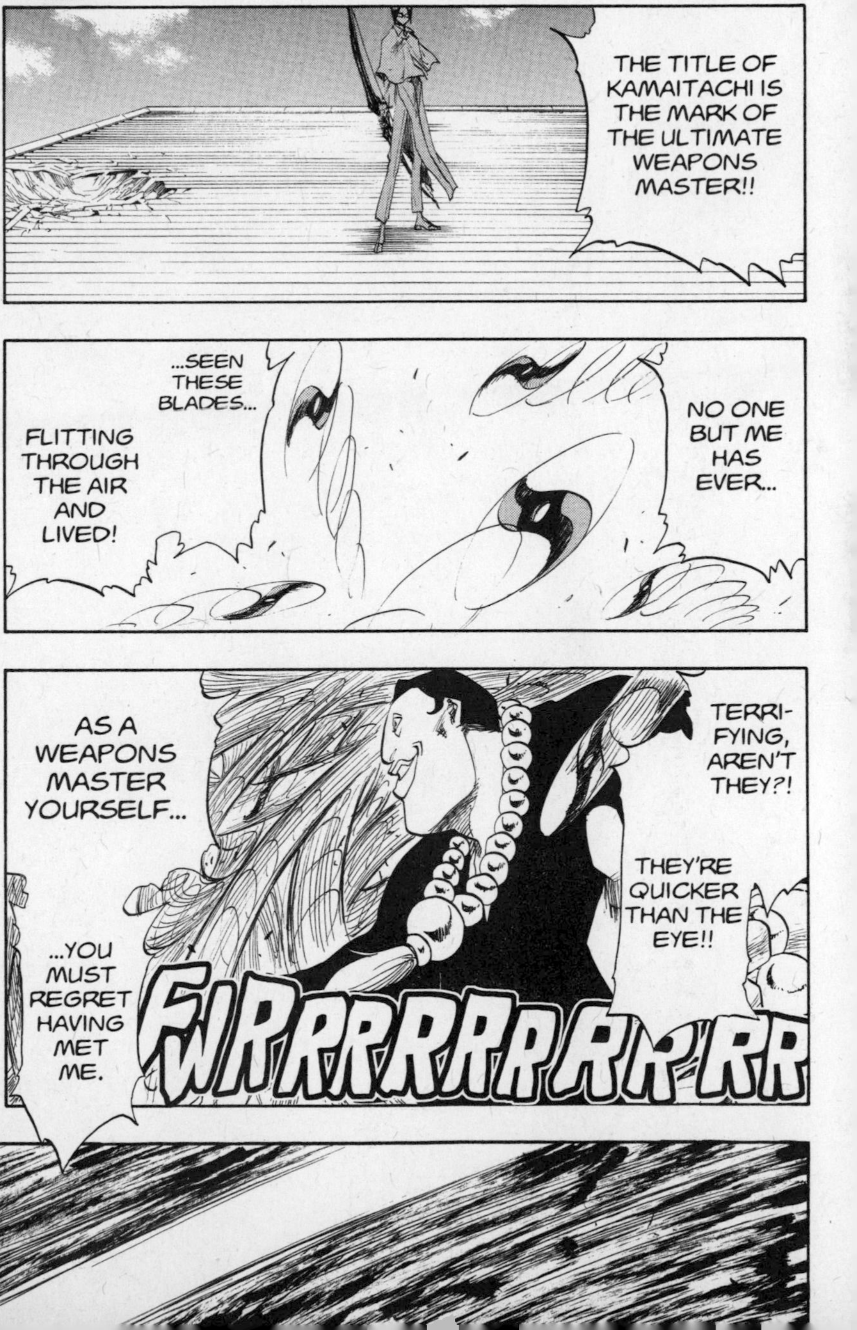
THE TITLE OF KAMAITACHI IS THE MARK OF THE ULTIMATE WEAPONS MASTER!!
NO ONE BUT ME HAS EVER...
...SEEN THESE BLADES...
FLITTING THROUGH THE AIR AND LIVED!
TERRI-FYING, AREN'T THEY?!
THEY'RE QUICKER THAN THE EYE!!
AS A WEAPONS MASTER YOURSELF...
...YOU MUST REGRET HAVING MET ME.
FWRRRRRRRRR

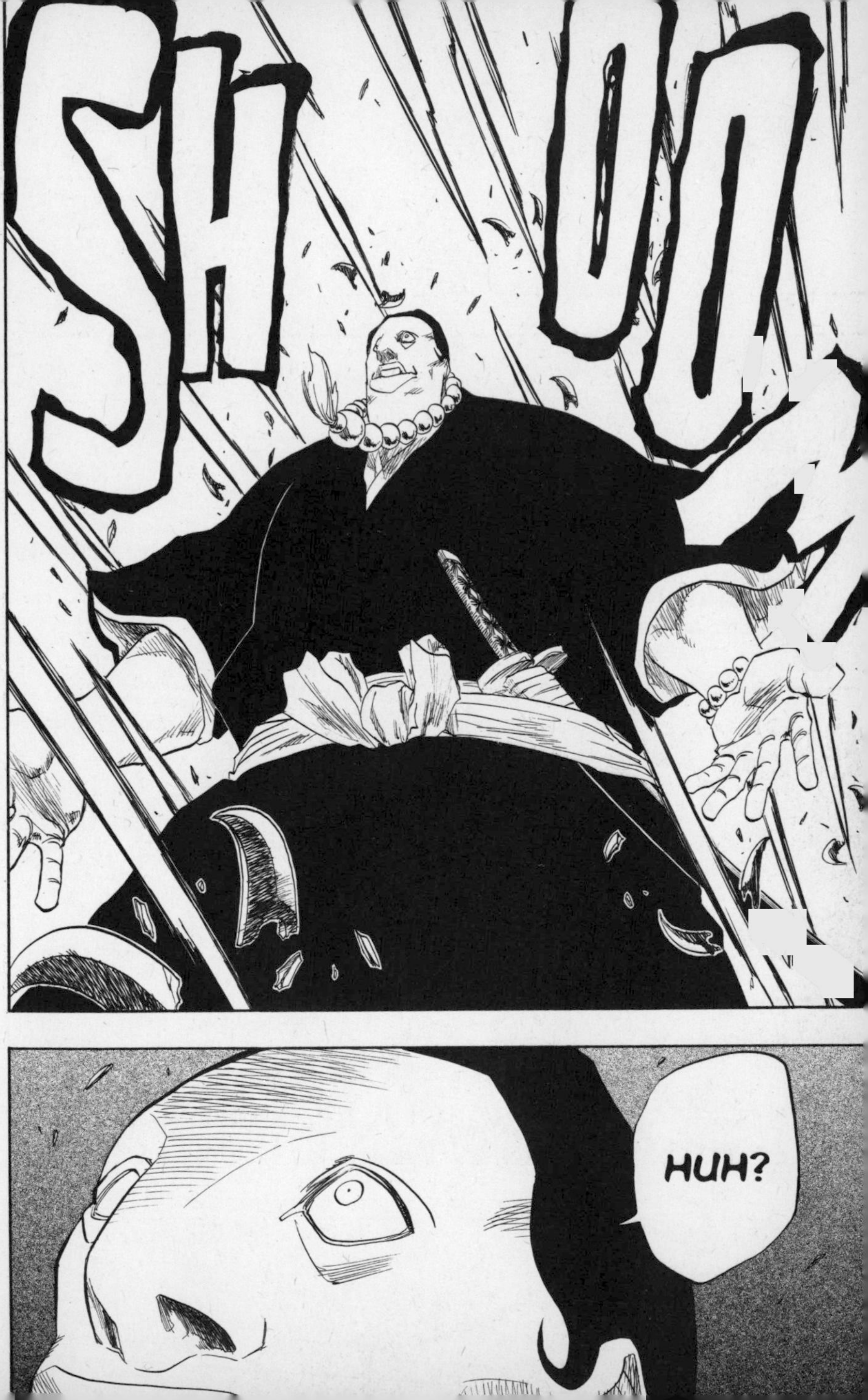
HUH?

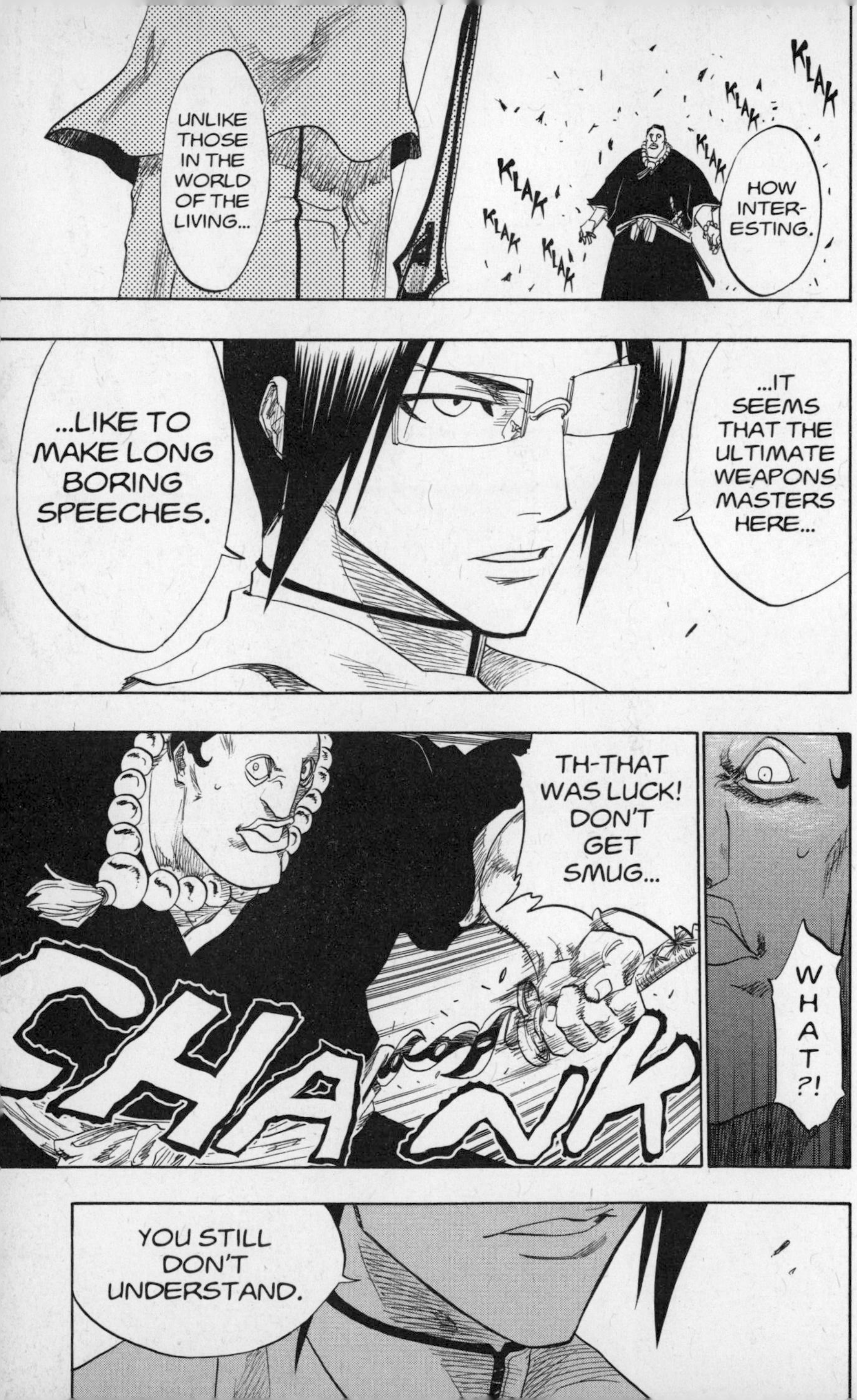
KLAK
KLAK
KLAK
KLAK
KLAK
KLAK
HOW INTERESTING.
UNLIKE THOSE IN THE WORLD OF THE LIVING...
...IT SEEMS THAT THE ULTIMATE WEAPONS MASTERS HERE...
...LIKE TO MAKE LONG BORING SPEECHES.
WHAT?!
TH-THAT WAS LUCK! DON'T GET SMUG...
CHANK
YOU STILL DON'T UNDERSTAND.

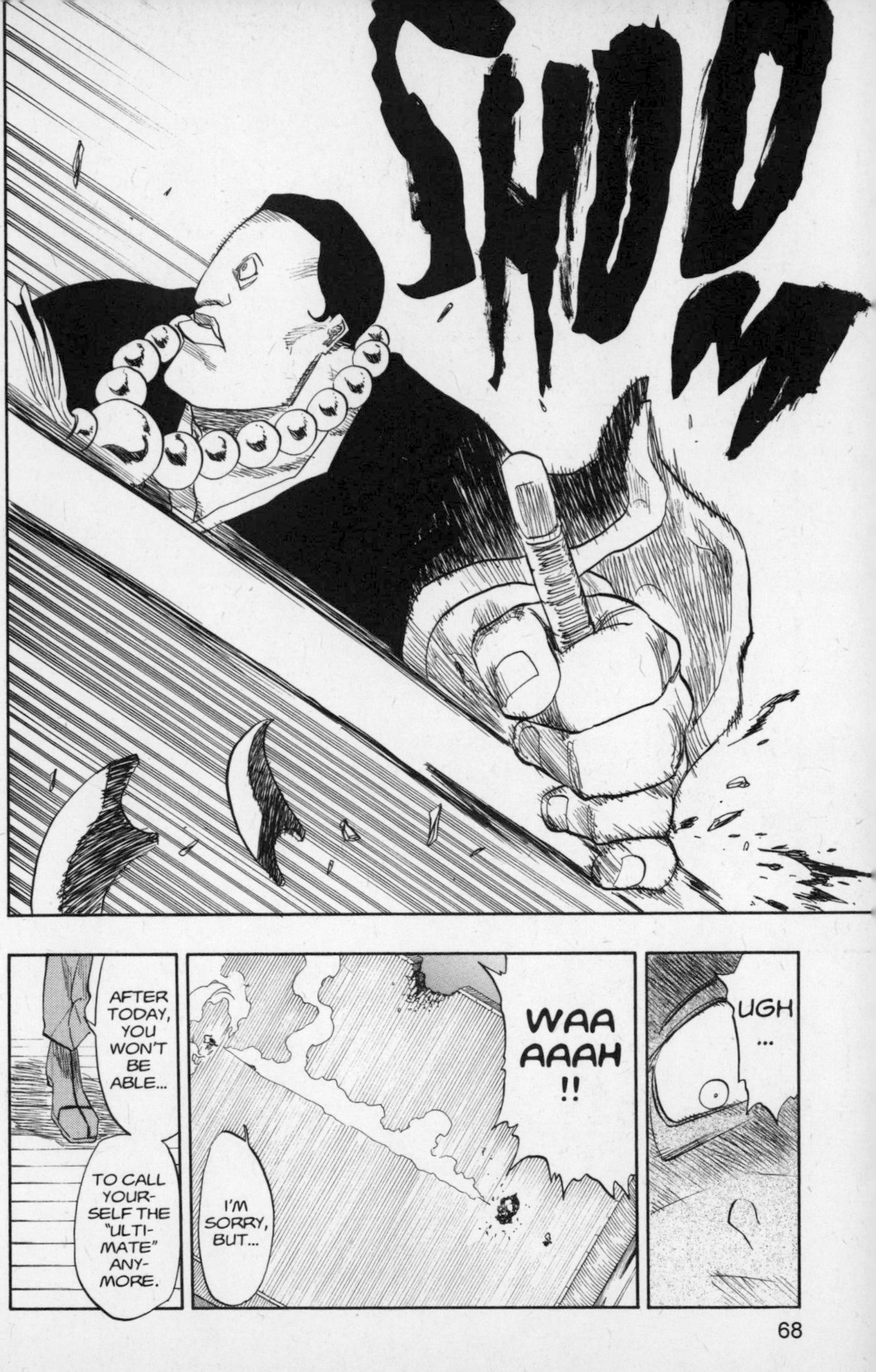
SHOOM
UGH ...
WAA AAAH !!
I'M SORRY, BUT...
AFTER TODAY, YOU WON'T BE ABLE...
TO CALL YOURSELF THE "ULTIMATE" ANYMORE.

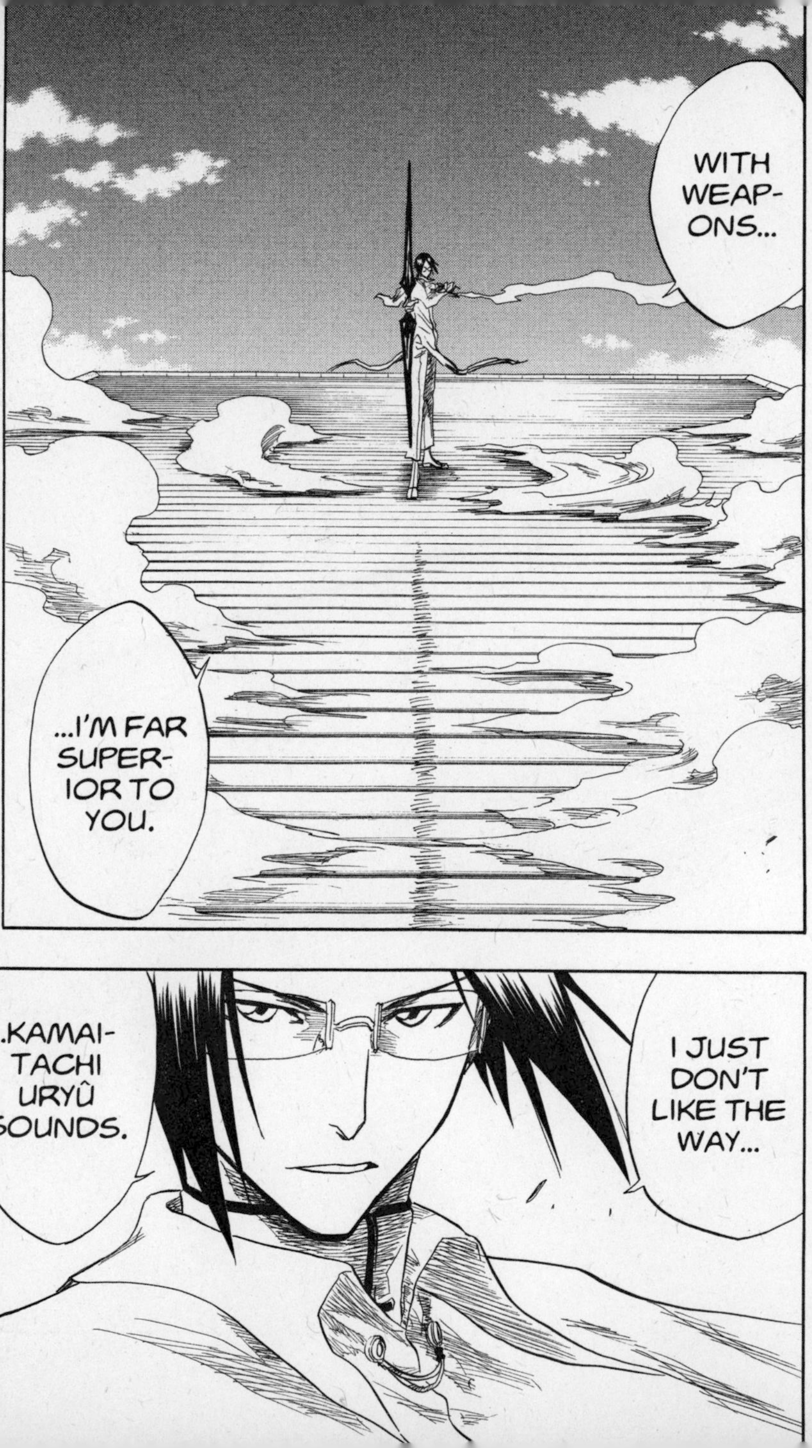
WITH WEAPONS...
...I'M FAR SUPERIOR TO YOU.
I JUST DON'T LIKE THE WAY...
...KAMAITACHI URYÛ SOUNDS.

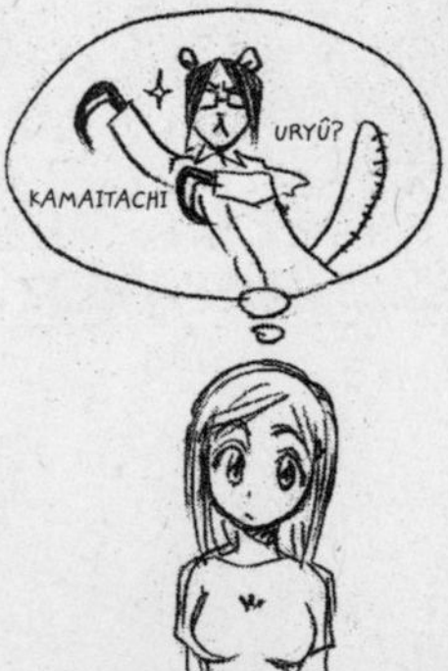
URYÛ?
KAMAITACHI

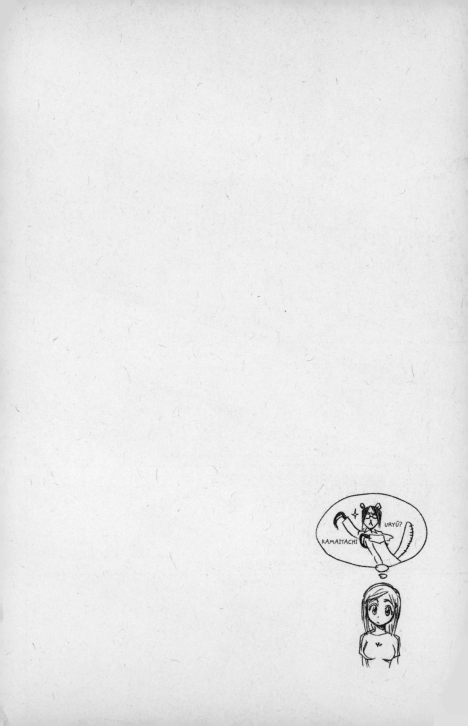

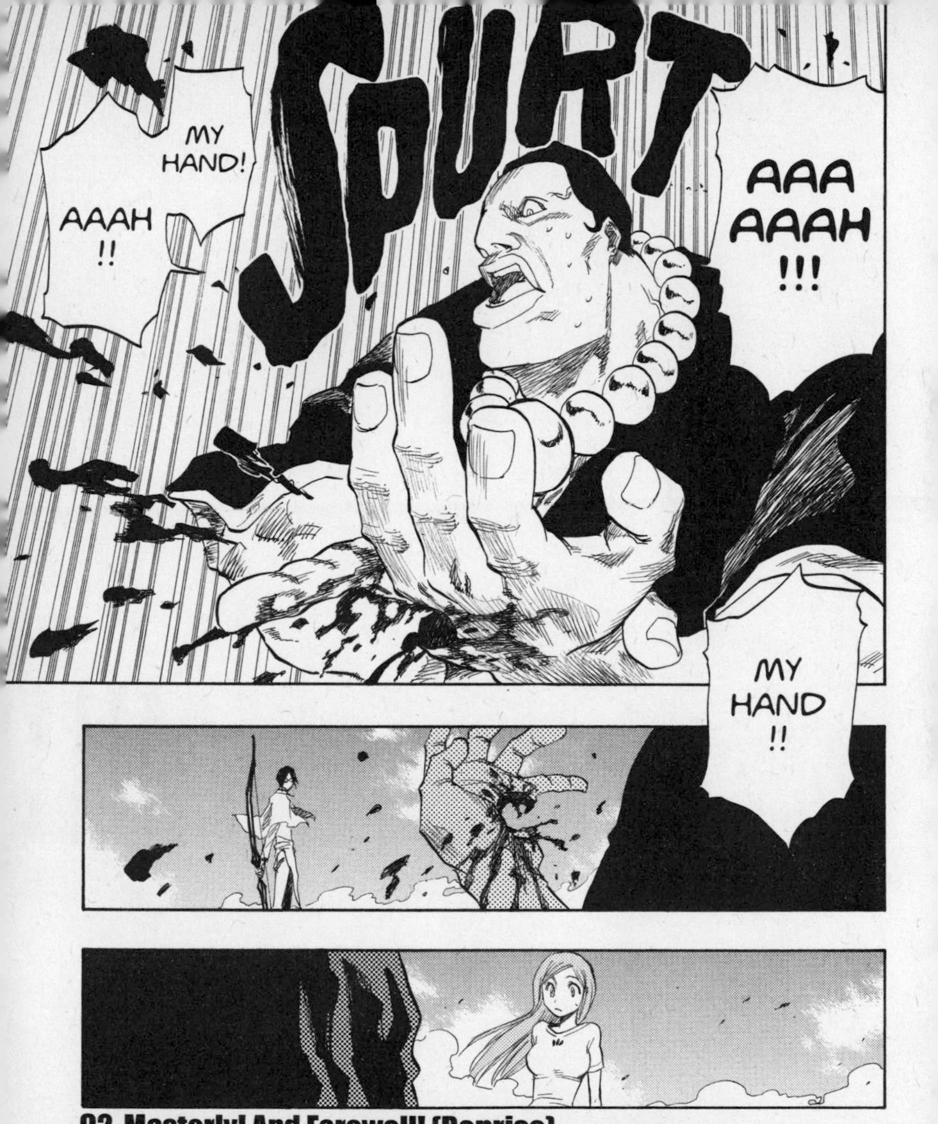
AAA AAAH !!!
SPURT
MY HAND!
AAAH !!
MY HAND !!

92. Masterly! And Farewell! (Reprise)

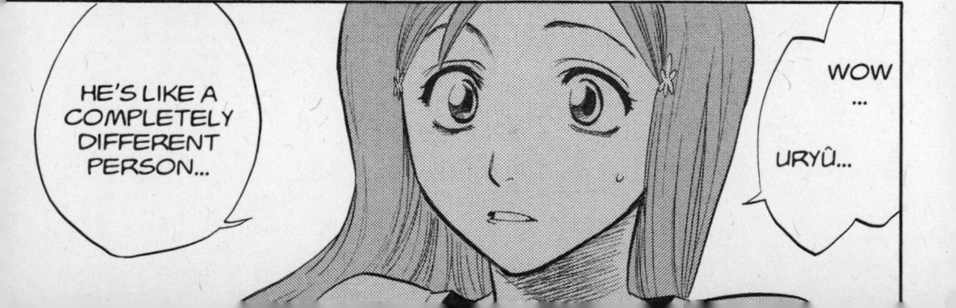
WOW ... URYÛ...
HE'S LIKE A COMPLETELY DIFFERENT PERSON...

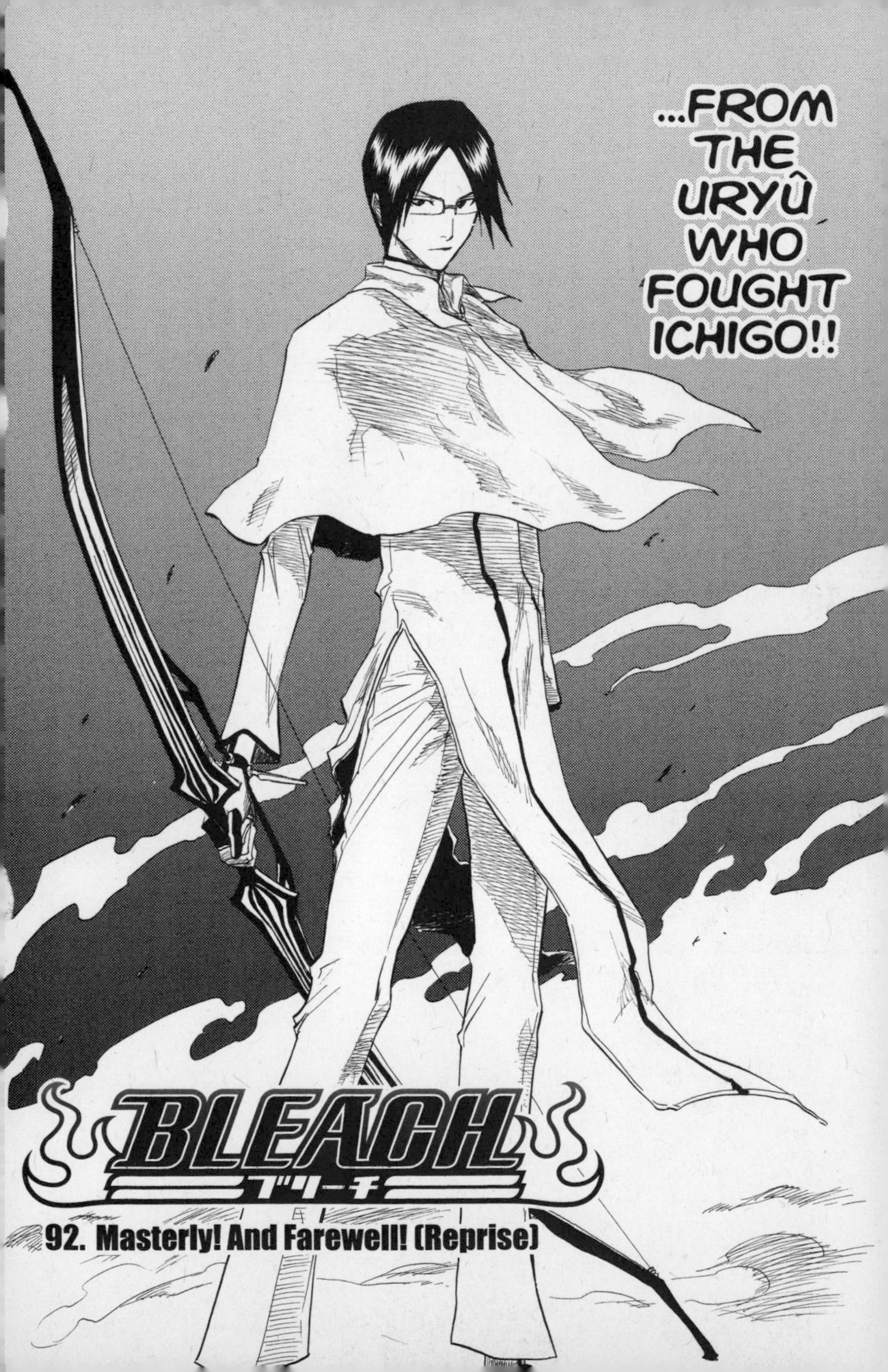
...FROM THE URYÛ WHO FOUGHT ICHIGO!!
BLEACH
ブリーチ
92. Masterly! And Farewell! (Reprise)

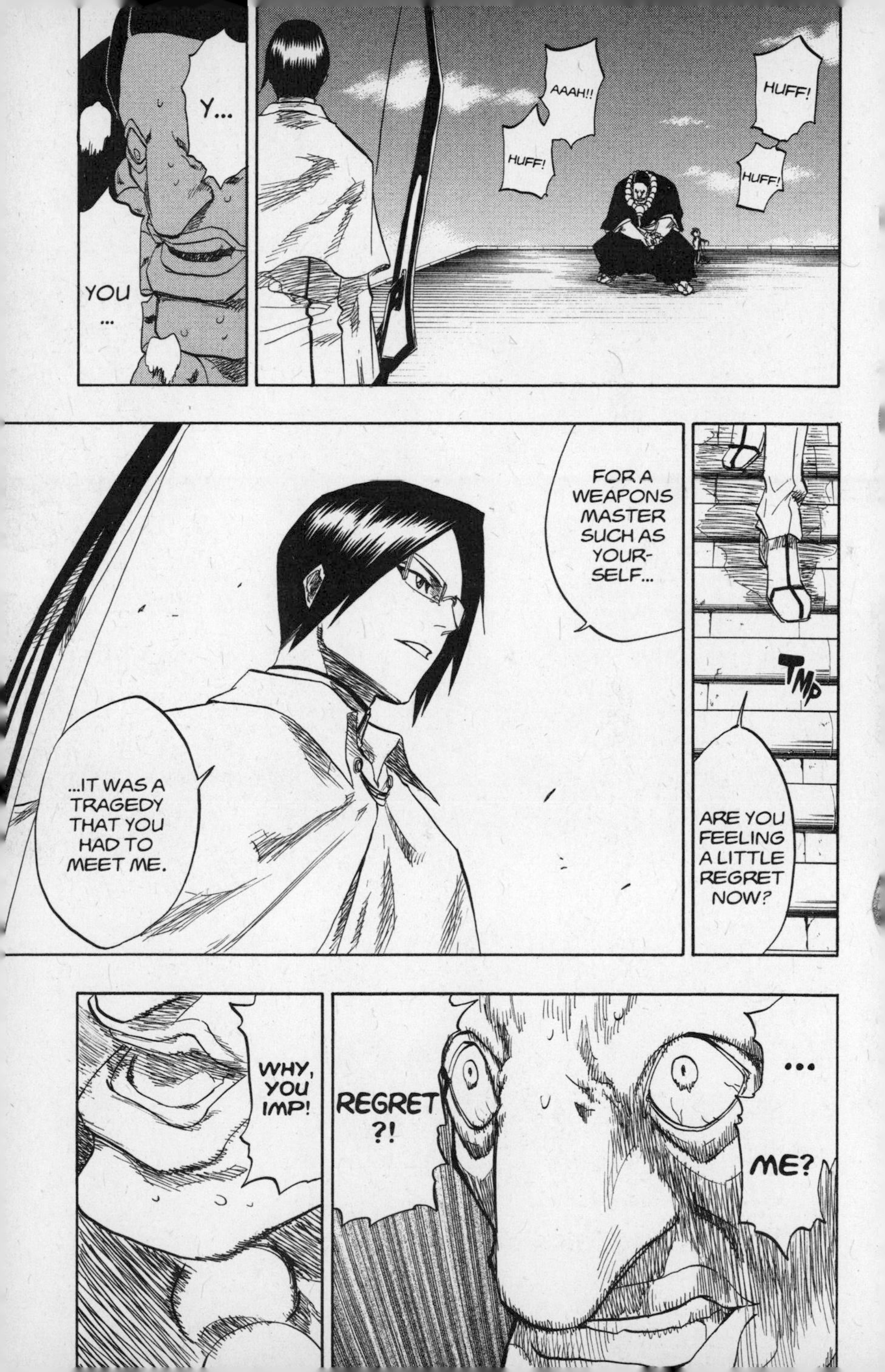
HUFF!
HUFF!
AAAH!!
HUFF!
Y...
YOU ...
TMP
ARE YOU FEELING A LITTLE REGRET NOW?
FOR A WEAPONS MASTER SUCH AS YOURSELF...
...IT WAS A TRAGEDY THAT YOU HAD TO MEET ME.
...
ME?
REGRET ?!
WHY, YOU IMP!

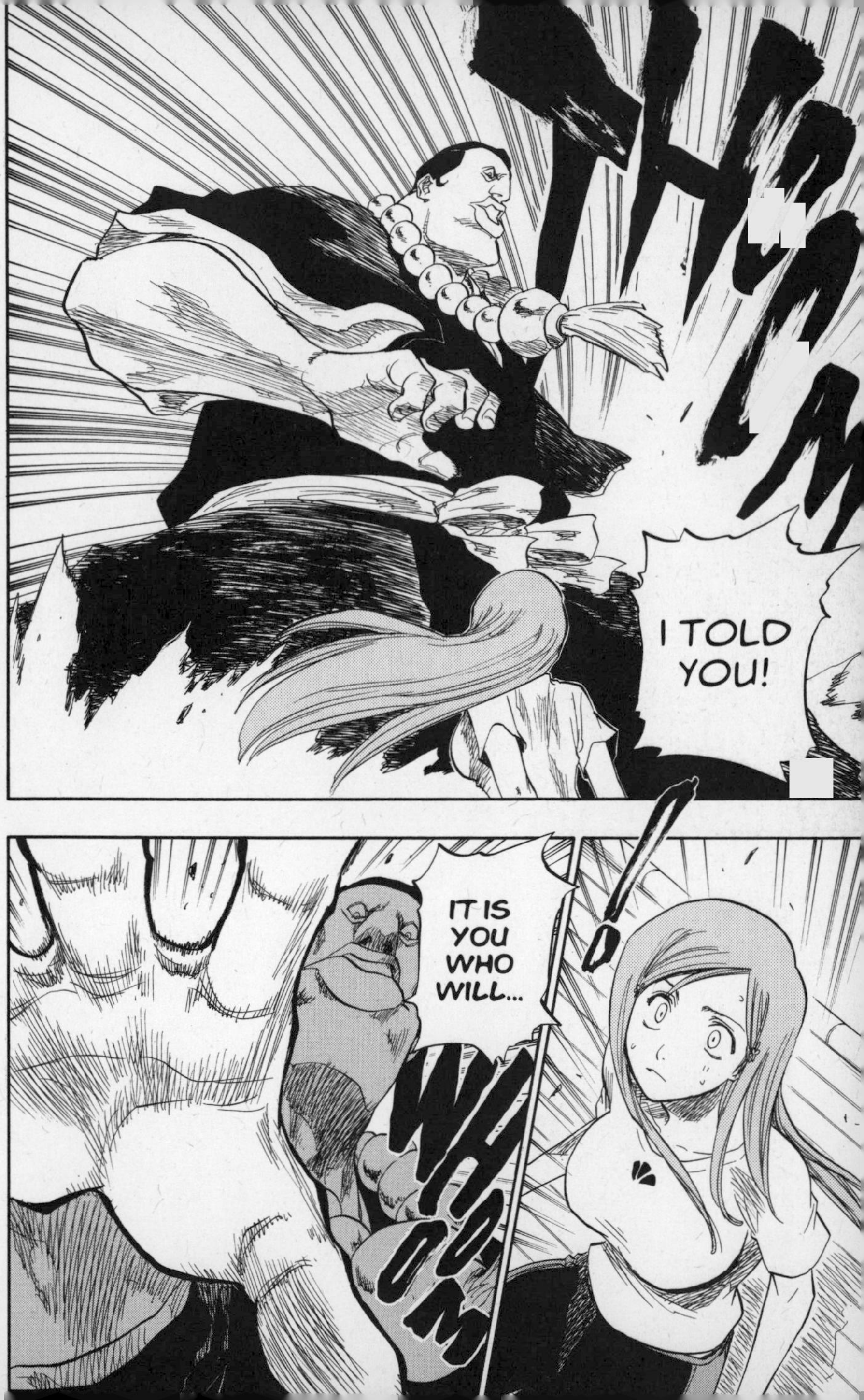
I TOLD YOU!
IT IS YOU WHO WILL...
WHOOM

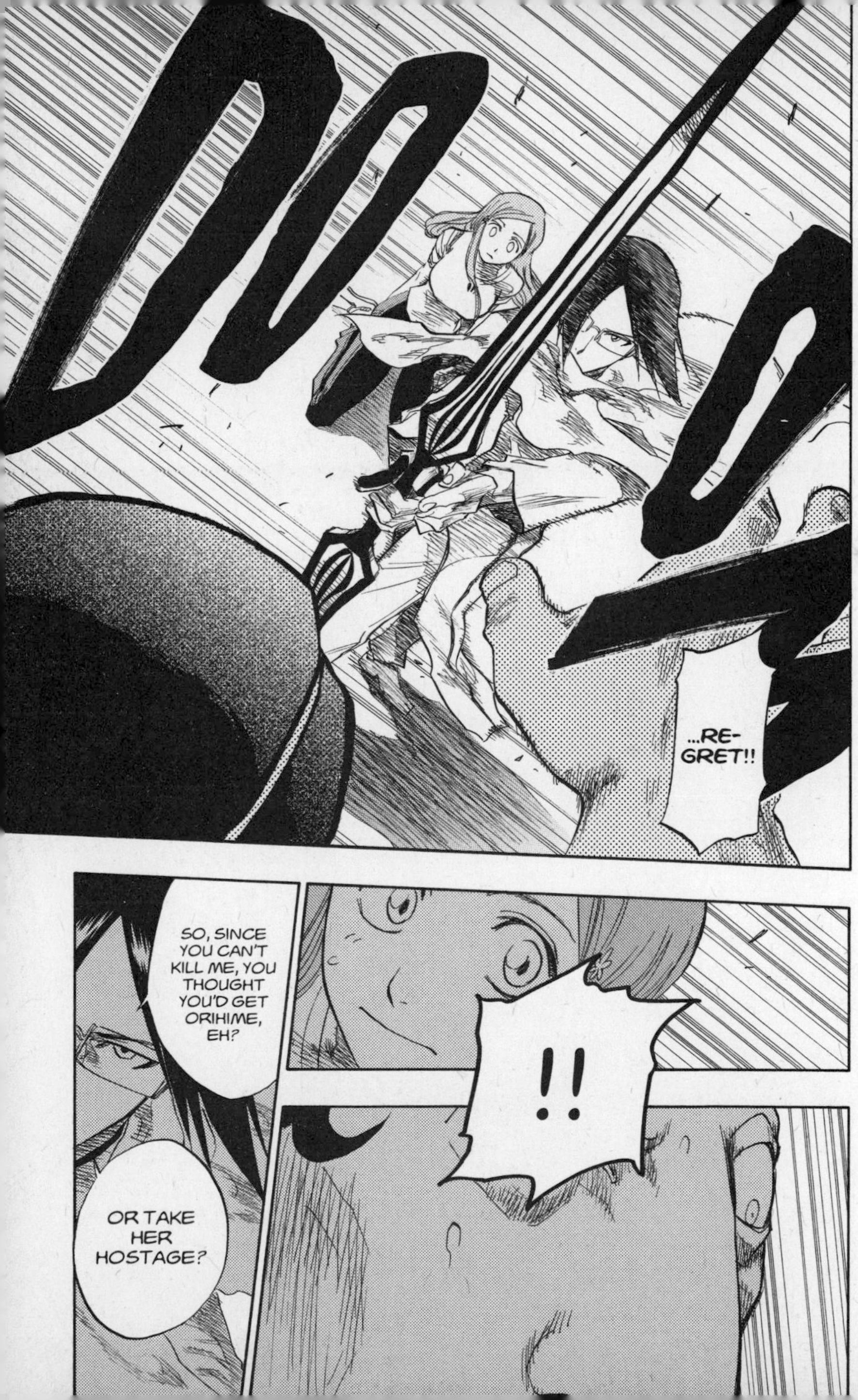
...RE-
GRET!!
SO, SINCE YOU CAN'T KILL ME, YOU THOUGHT YOU'D GET ORIHIME, EH?
!!
OR TAKE HER HOSTAGE?

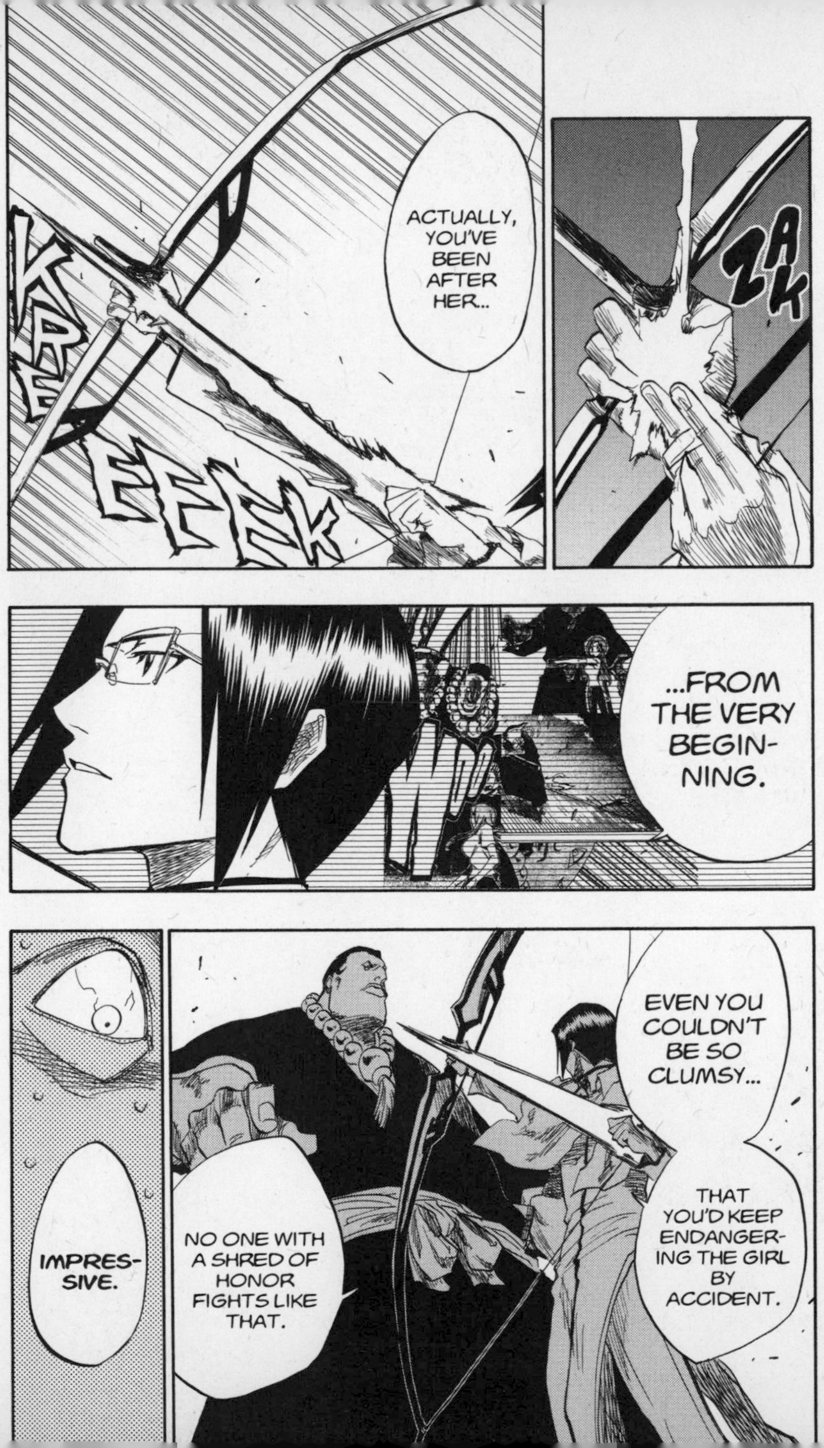
ZAK
ACTUALLY, YOU'VE BEEN AFTER HER...
KREEEK
...FROM THE VERY BEGIN-NING.
EVEN YOU COULDN'T BE SO CLUMSY...
THAT YOU'D KEEP ENDANGER-ING THE GIRL BY ACCIDENT.
NO ONE WITH A SHRED OF HONOR FIGHTS LIKE THAT.
IMPRES-SIVE.

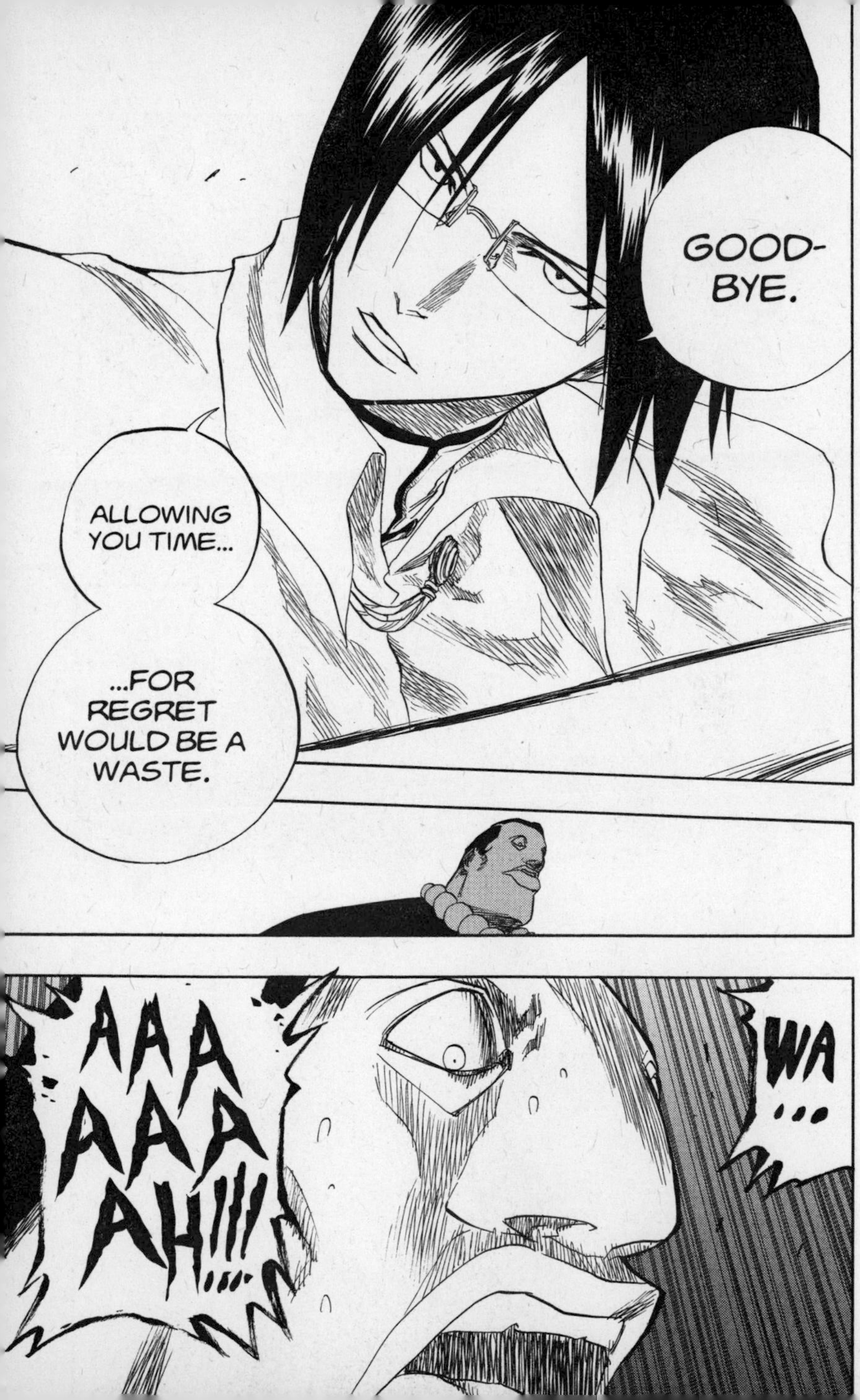
GOOD-BYE.
ALLOWING YOU TIME...
...FOR REGRET WOULD BE A WASTE.
WA...
AAAAAAAH!!!

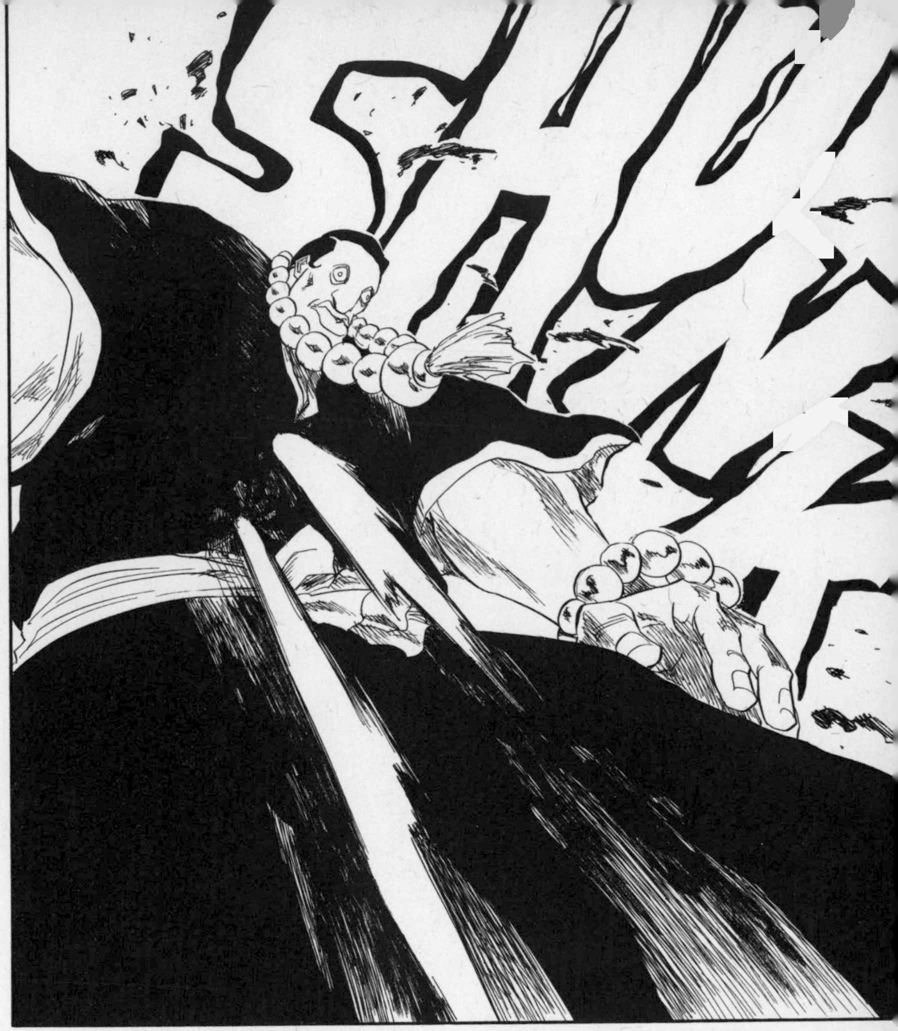

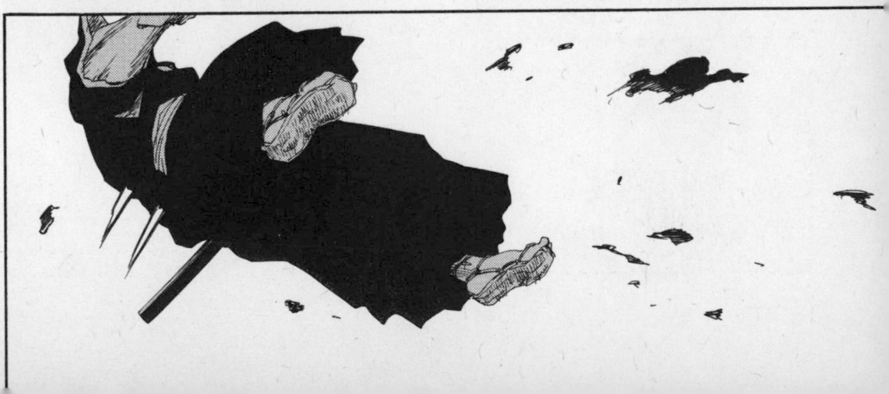

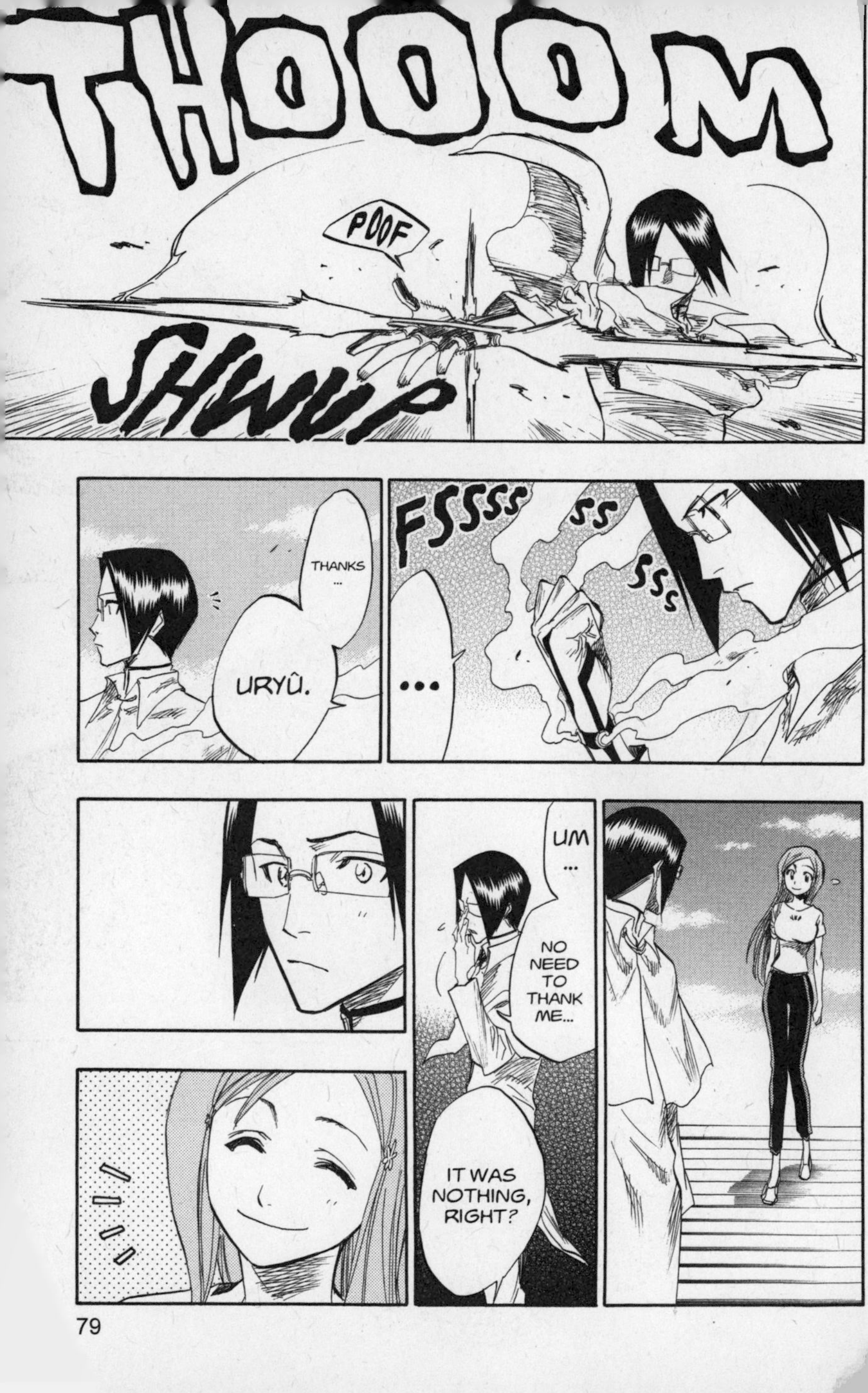
THOOOM
POOF
SHWUP
FSSSS
SS
SSS
...
THANKS...
URYÛ.
UM...
NO NEED TO THANK ME...
IT WAS NOTHING, RIGHT?

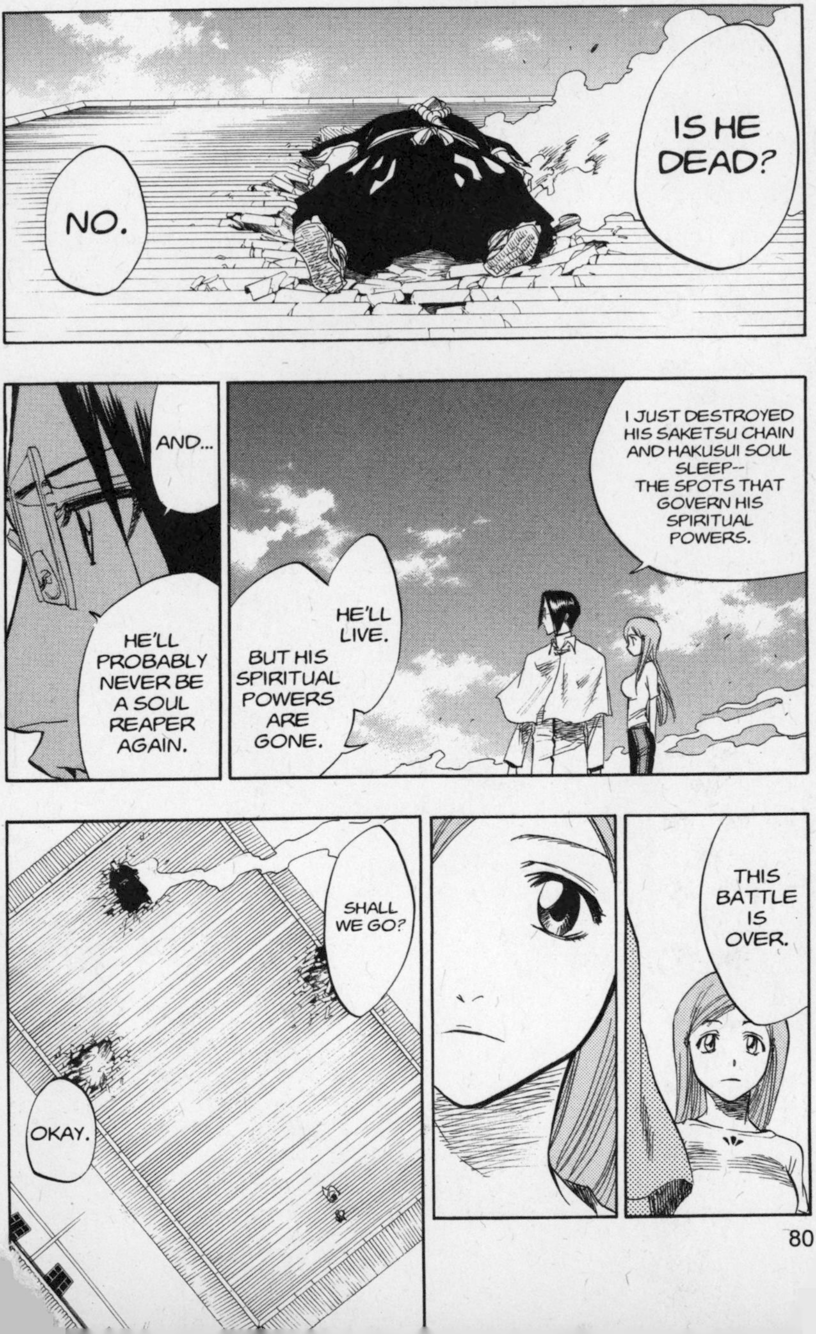
IS HE DEAD?
NO.
I JUST DESTROYED HIS SAKETSU CHAIN AND HAKUSUI SOUL SLEEP-- THE SPOTS THAT GOVERN HIS SPIRITUAL POWERS.
HE'LL LIVE.
BUT HIS SPIRITUAL POWERS ARE GONE.
AND...
HE'LL PROBABLY NEVER BE A SOUL REAPER AGAIN.
THIS BATTLE IS OVER.
SHALL WE GO?
OKAY.

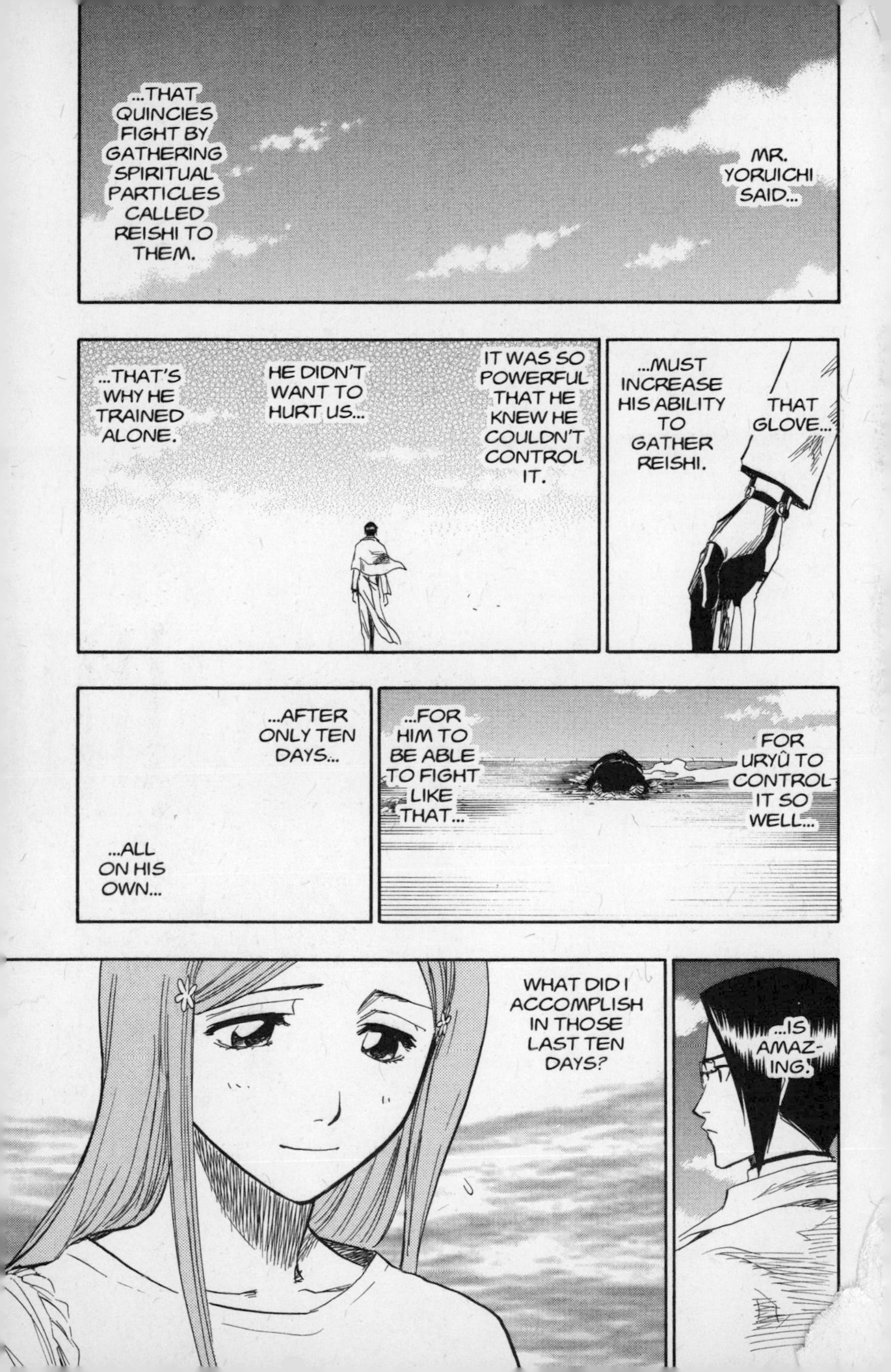
MR. YORUICHI SAID...
...THAT QUINCIES FIGHT BY GATHERING SPIRITUAL PARTICLES CALLED REISHI TO THEM.
THAT GLOVE...
...MUST INCREASE HIS ABILITY TO GATHER REISHI.
IT WAS SO POWERFUL THAT HE KNEW HE COULDN'T CONTROL IT.
HE DIDN'T WANT TO HURT US...
...THAT'S WHY HE TRAINED ALONE.
FOR URYÛ TO CONTROL IT SO WELL...
...FOR HIM TO BE ABLE TO FIGHT LIKE THAT...
...AFTER ONLY TEN DAYS...
...ALL ON HIS OWN...
...IS AMAZING.
WHAT DID I ACCOMPLISH IN THOSE LAST TEN DAYS?

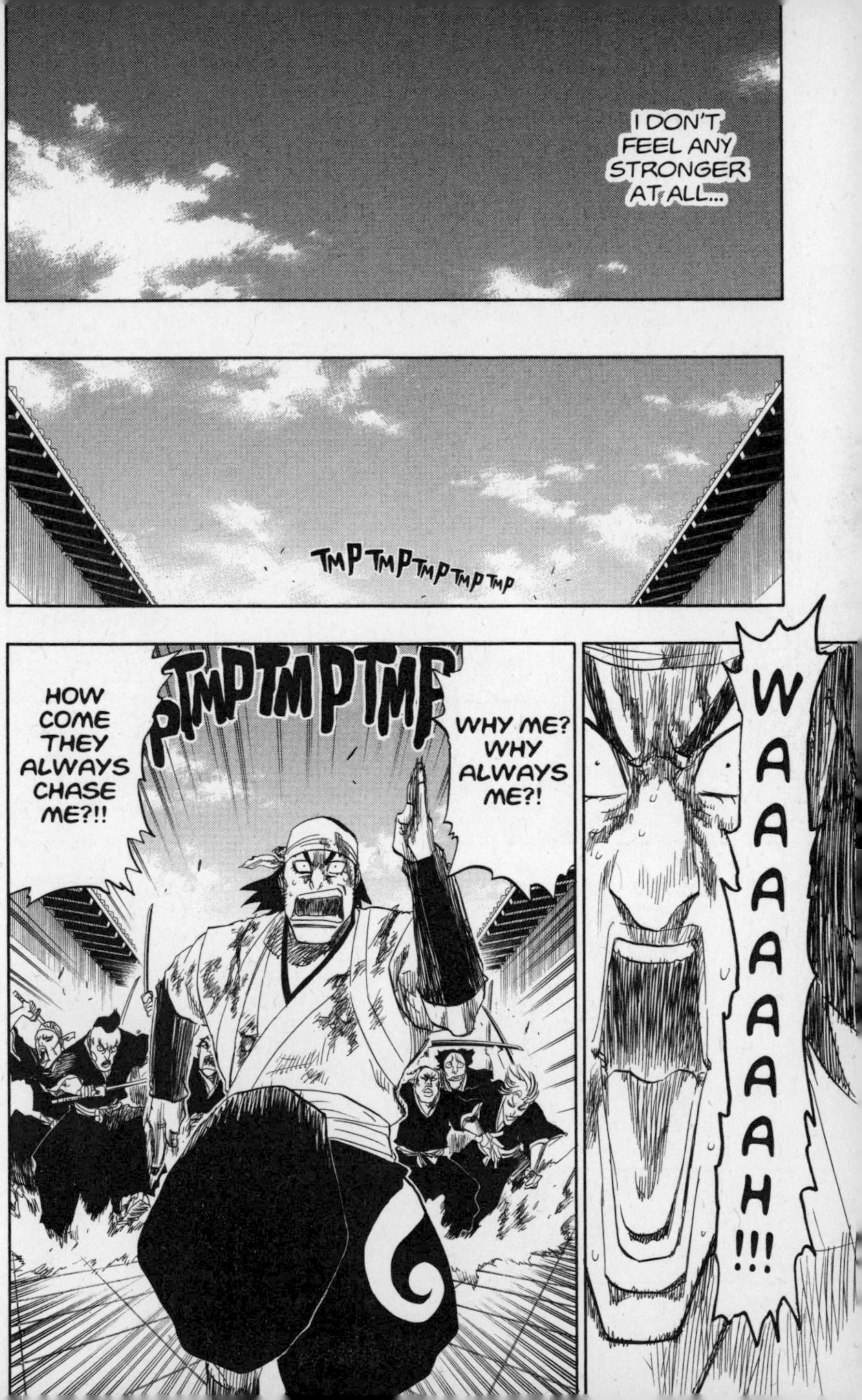
I DON'T FEEL ANY STRONGER AT ALL...
TMP TMP TMP TMP TMP
WAAAAAAAH!!!
PTMPTMPTMP
WHY ME? WHY ALWAYS ME?!
HOW COME THEY ALWAYS CHASE ME?!!

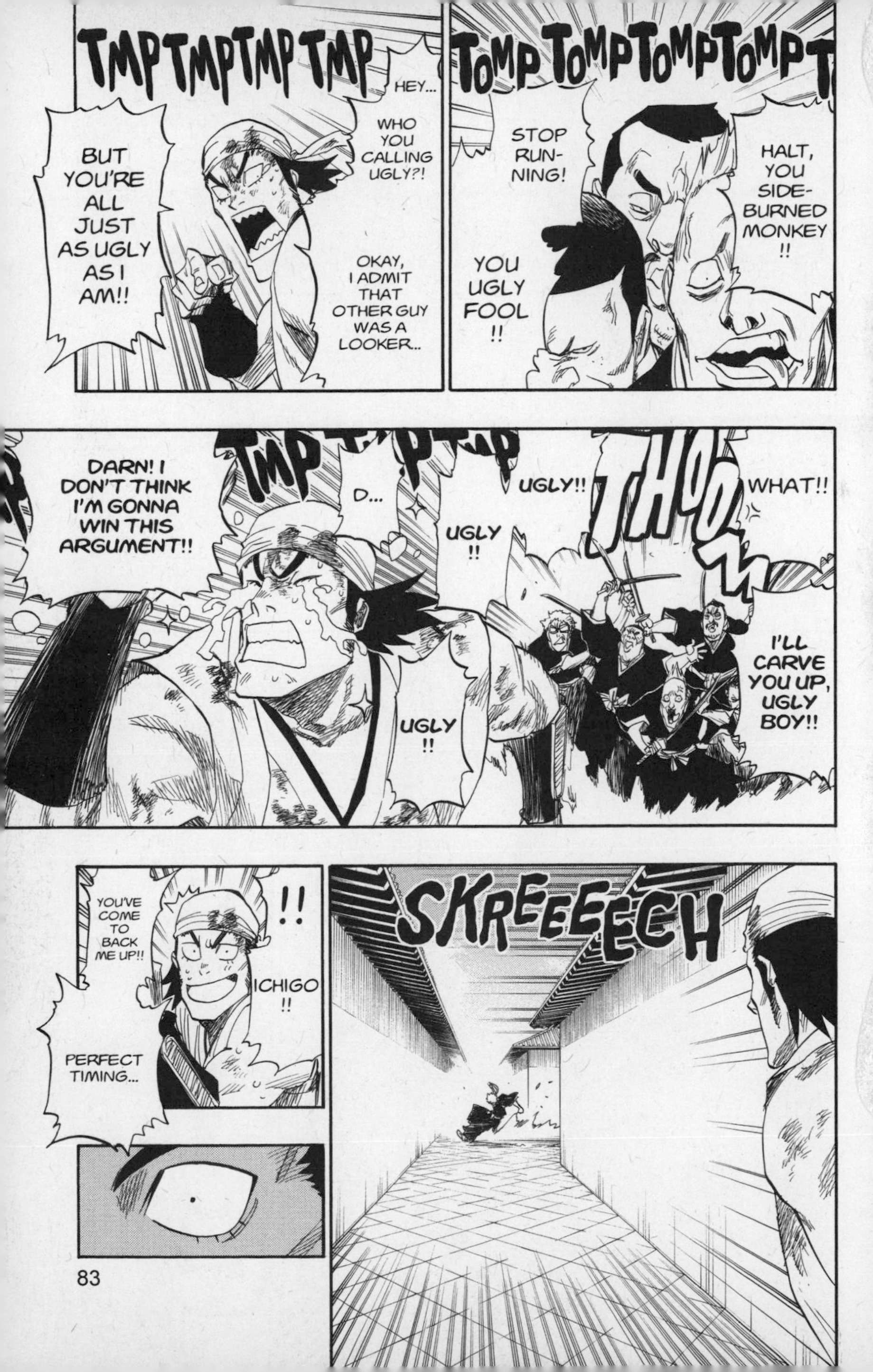
TOMP TOMP TOMP TOMP
HALT, YOU SIDE-BURNED MONKEY!!
STOP RUN-NING!
YOU UGLY FOOL!!
TMP TMP TMP TMP
HEY...
WHO YOU CALLING UGLY?!
OKAY, I ADMIT THAT OTHER GUY WAS A LOOKER...
BUT YOU'RE ALL JUST AS UGLY AS I AM!!
THOOM
WHAT!!
I'LL CARVE YOU UP, UGLY BOY!!
UGLY!!
UGLY!!
UGLY!!
D...
TMP
DARN! I DON'T THINK I'M GONNA WIN THIS ARGUMENT!!
SKREEEECH
!!
YOU'VE COME TO BACK ME UP!!
ICHIGO!!
PERFECT TIMING...

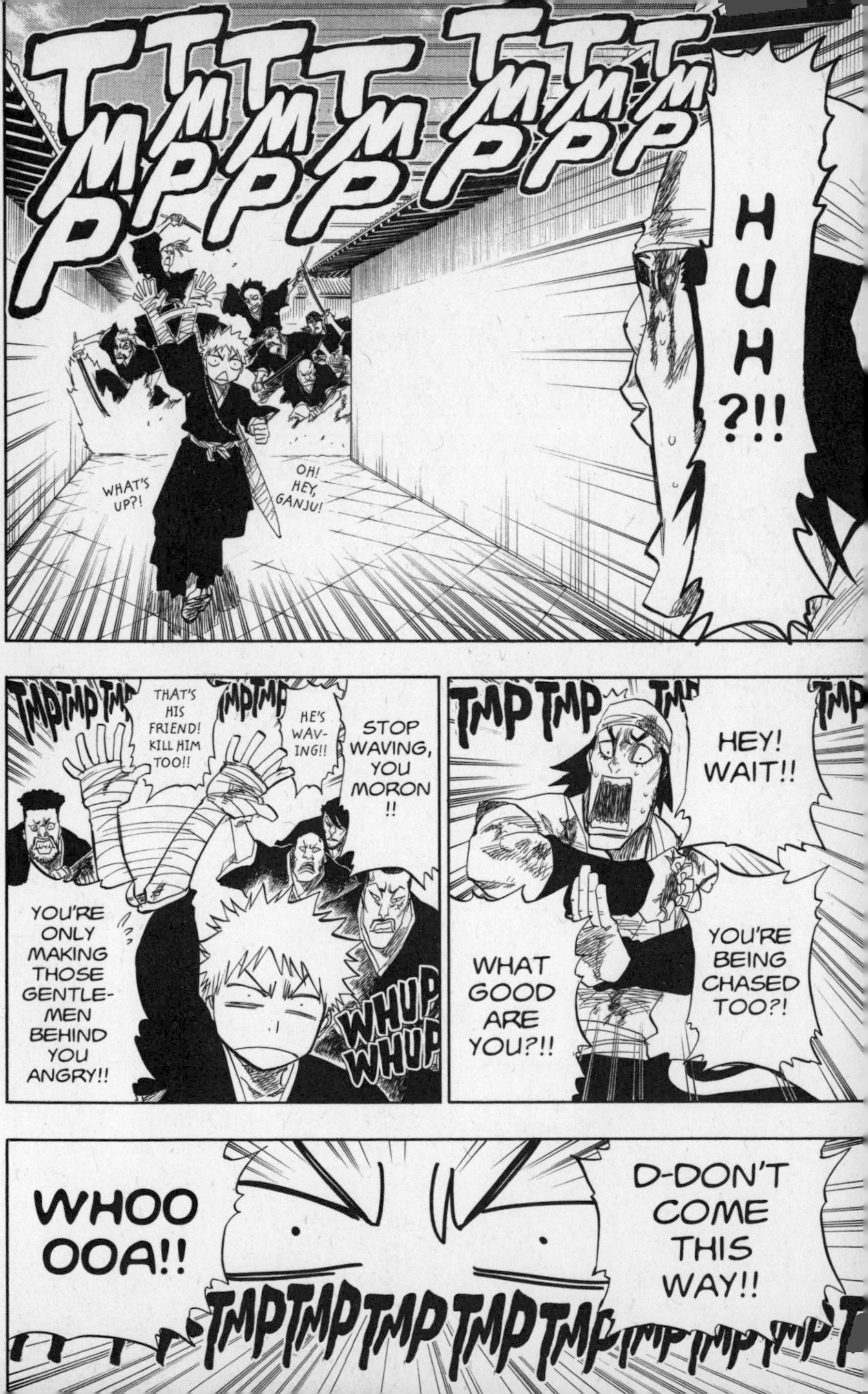
HUH?!!
TMMP TMMP TMMP TMMP TMMP TMMP TMMP TMMP
OH! HEY, GANJU!
WHAT'S UP?!
TMP TMP TMP
HEY! WAIT!!
YOU'RE BEING CHASED TOO?!
WHAT GOOD ARE YOU?!!
STOP WAVING, YOU MORON!!
HE'S WAVING!!
TMPTMP
THAT'S HIS FRIEND! KILL HIM TOO!!
TMPTMPTMP
YOU'RE ONLY MAKING THOSE GENTLEMEN BEHIND YOU ANGRY!!
WHUP WHUP
D-DON'T COME THIS WAY!!
WHOO OOA!!
TMPTMP TMP TMP TMP TMP TMP TMP

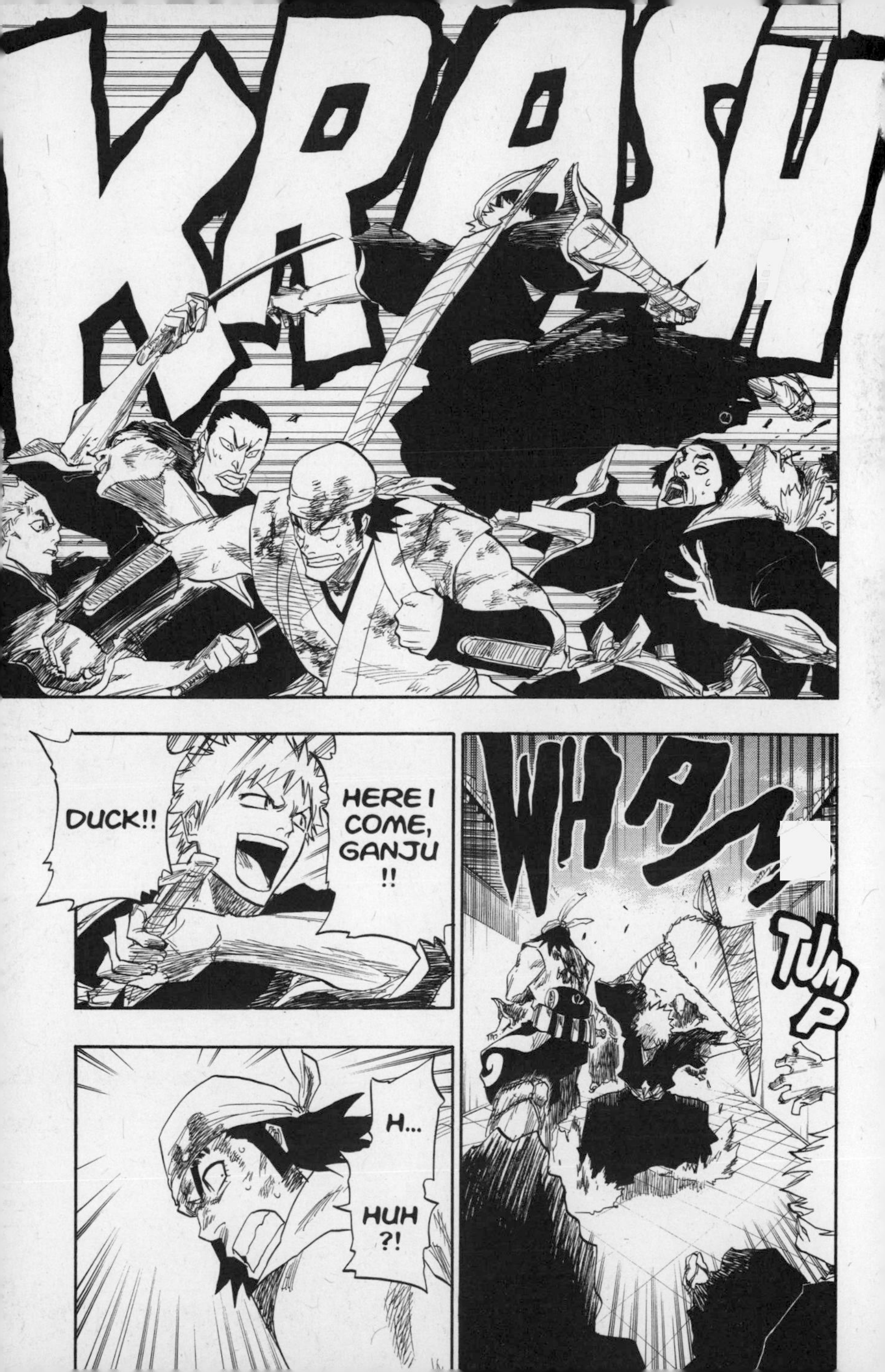
KRASH
WHAM
TUMP
HERE I COME, GANJU!!
DUCK!!
H...
HUH?!

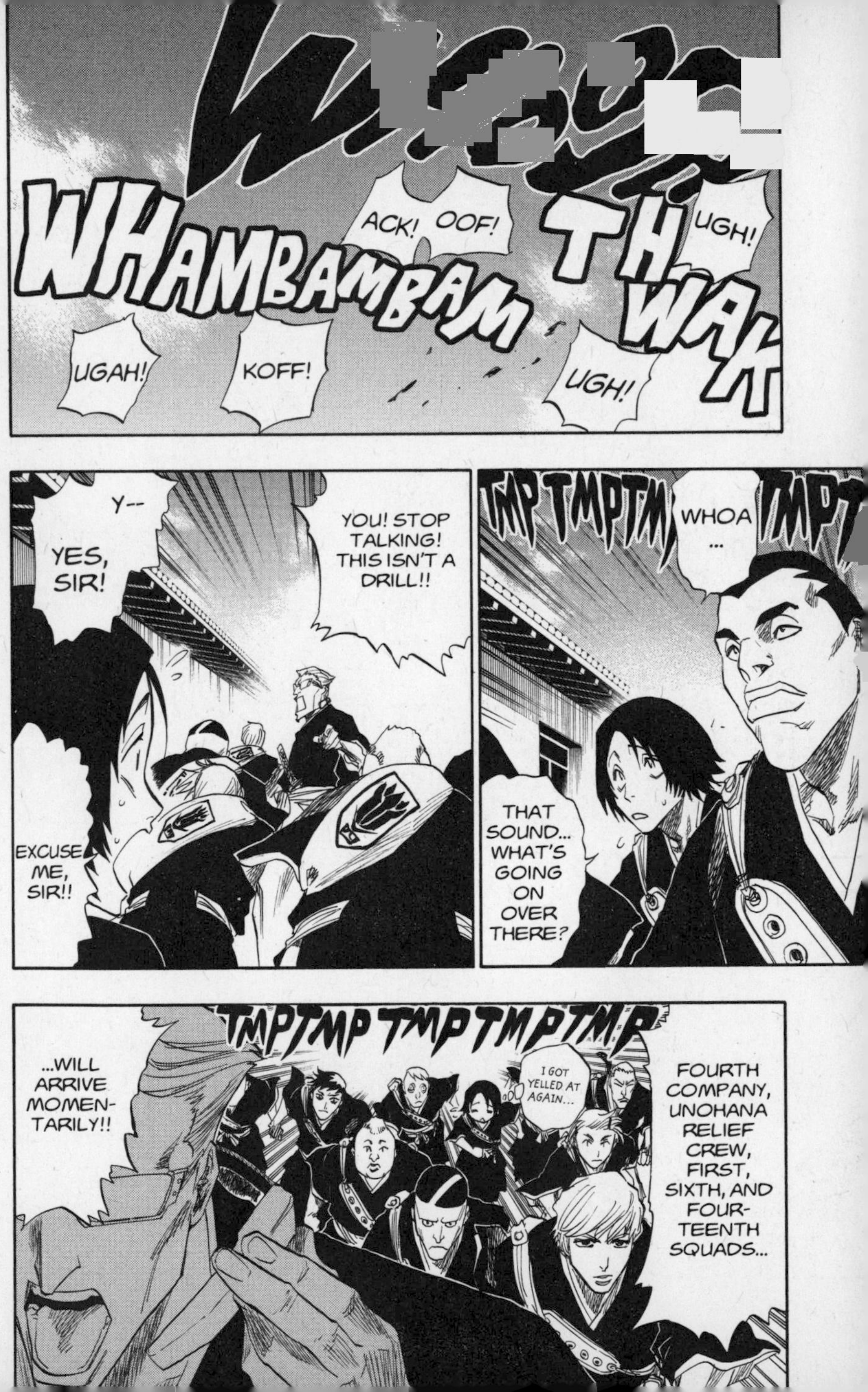
UGH!
THWAK
ACK! OOF!
WHAMBAMBAM
UGH!
KOFF!
UGAH!
TMP TMPTMP
WHOA ...
THAT SOUND... WHAT'S GOING ON OVER THERE?
YOU! STOP TALKING! THIS ISN'T A DRILL!!
Y--
YES, SIR!
EXCUSE ME, SIR!!
TMPTMP TMP TMP TMP
FOURTH COMPANY, UNOHANA RELIEF CREW, FIRST, SIXTH, AND FOURTEENTH SQUADS...
I GOT YELLED AT AGAIN...
...WILL ARRIVE MOMENTARILY!!

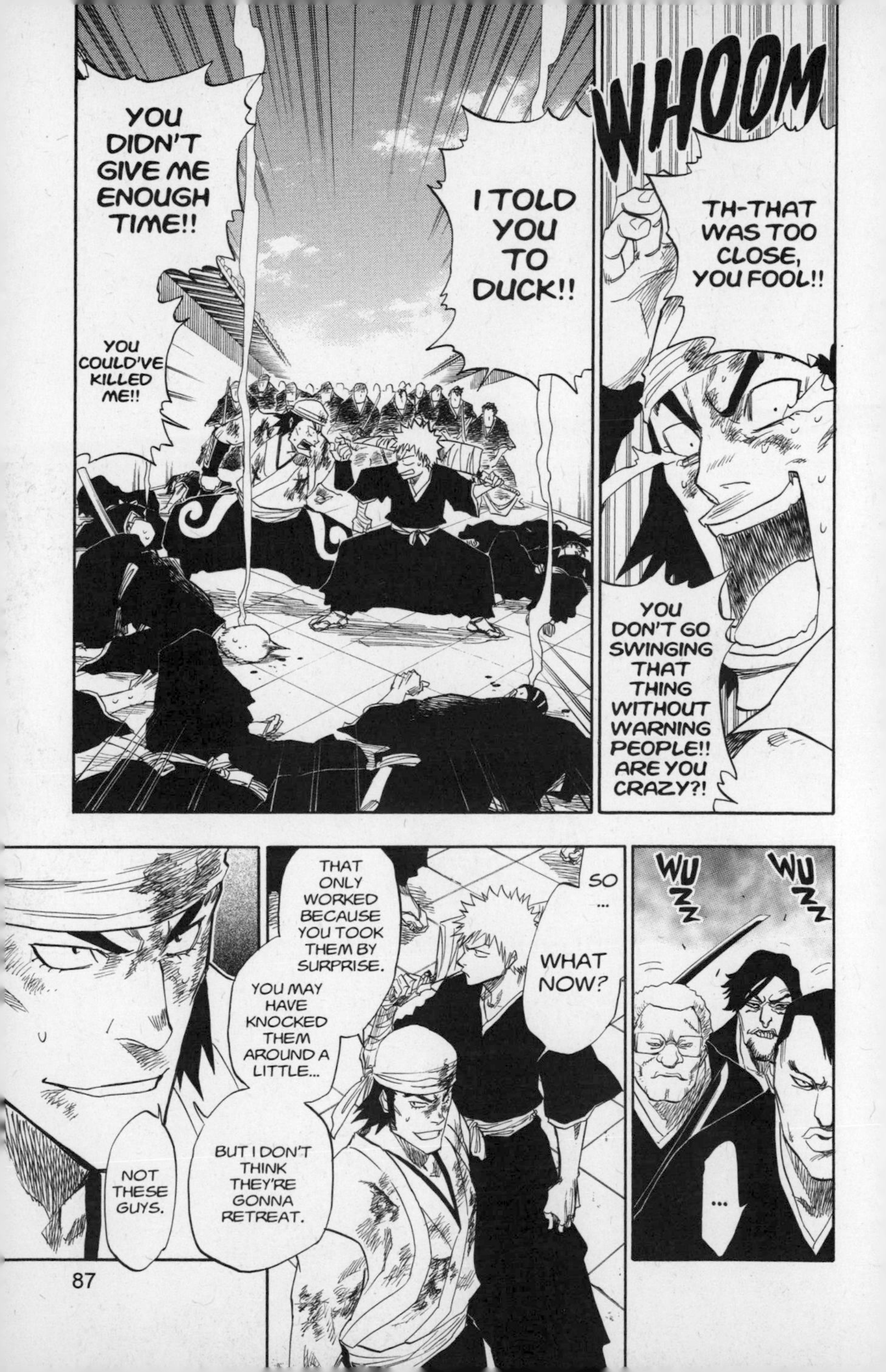
WHOOM
TH-THAT WAS TOO CLOSE, YOU FOOL!!
YOU DON'T GO SWINGING THAT THING WITHOUT WARNING PEOPLE!! ARE YOU CRAZY?!
I TOLD YOU TO DUCK!!
YOU DIDN'T GIVE ME ENOUGH TIME!!
YOU COULD'VE KILLED ME!!
WUZZ
WUZZ
...
SO ... WHAT NOW?
THAT ONLY WORKED BECAUSE YOU TOOK THEM BY SURPRISE.
YOU MAY HAVE KNOCKED THEM AROUND A LITTLE...
BUT I DON'T THINK THEY'RE GONNA RETREAT.
NOT THESE GUYS.

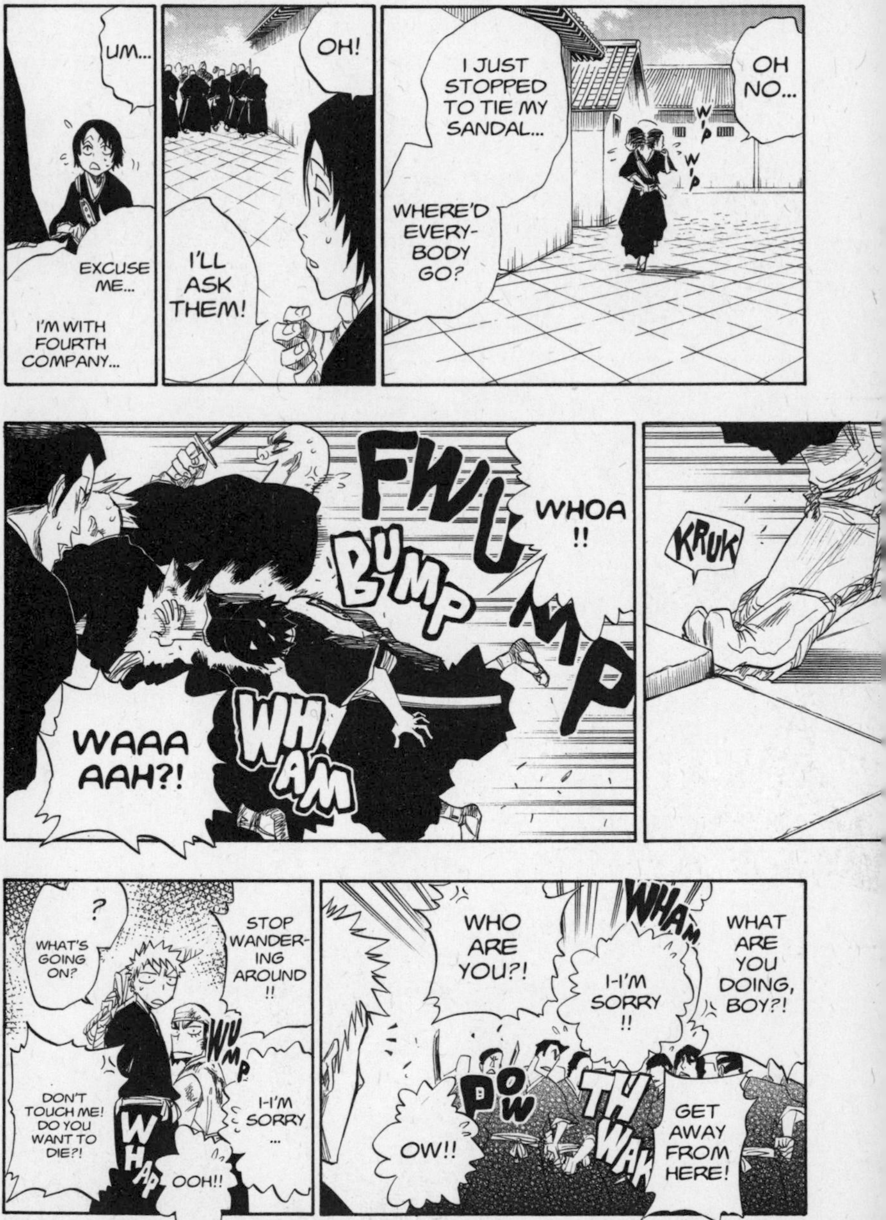
OH NO...
WIP WIP
I JUST STOPPED TO TIE MY SANDAL...
WHERE'D EVERY-BODY GO?
OH!
I'LL ASK THEM!
UM...
EXCUSE ME...
I'M WITH FOURTH COMPANY...
KRUK
WHOA!!
FWUMP
BUMP
WHAM
WAAAAAH?!
WHAT ARE YOU DOING, BOY?!
WHAM
I-I'M SORRY!!
WHO ARE YOU?!
GET AWAY FROM HERE!
THWAK
POW
OW!!
STOP WANDER-ING AROUND!!
?
WHAT'S GOING ON?
WUMP
I-I'M SORRY...
DON'T TOUCH ME! DO YOU WANT TO DIE?!
WHAP
OOH!!

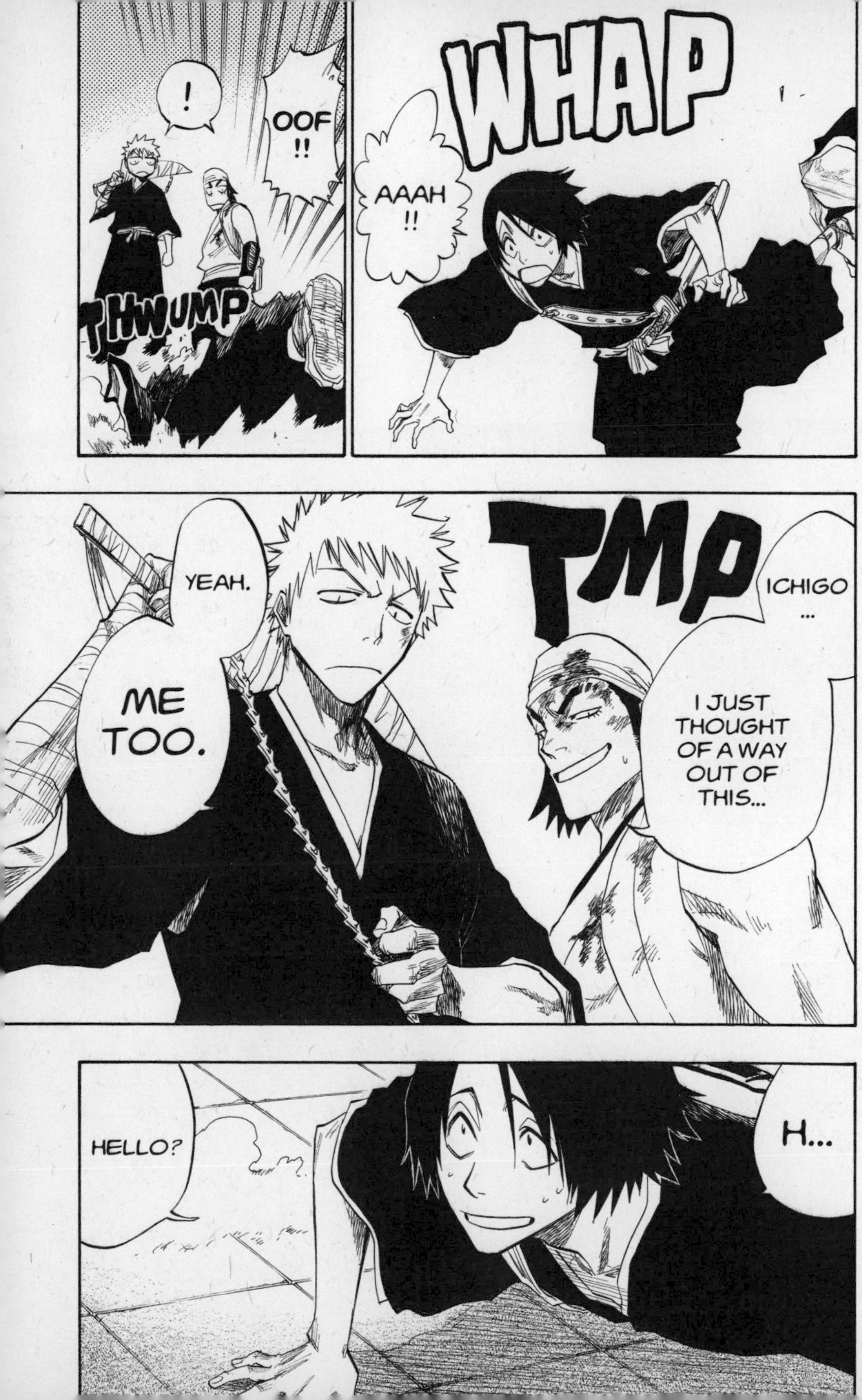
WHAP
AAAH !!
OOF !!
!
THWUMP
TMP
ICHIGO ...
I JUST THOUGHT OF A WAY OUT OF THIS...
YEAH.
ME TOO.
H...
HELLO?

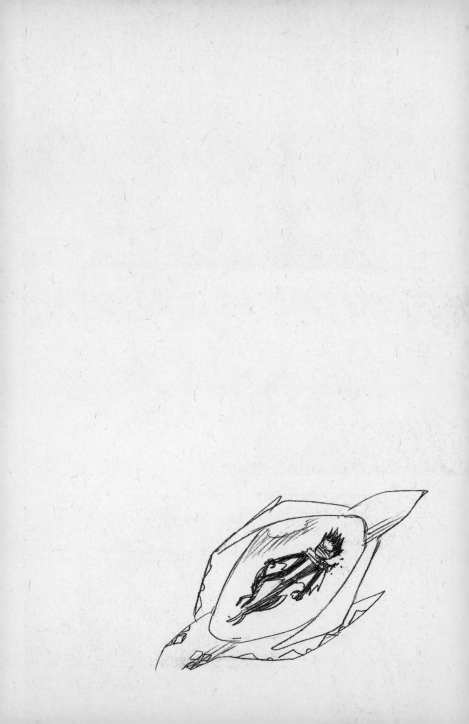

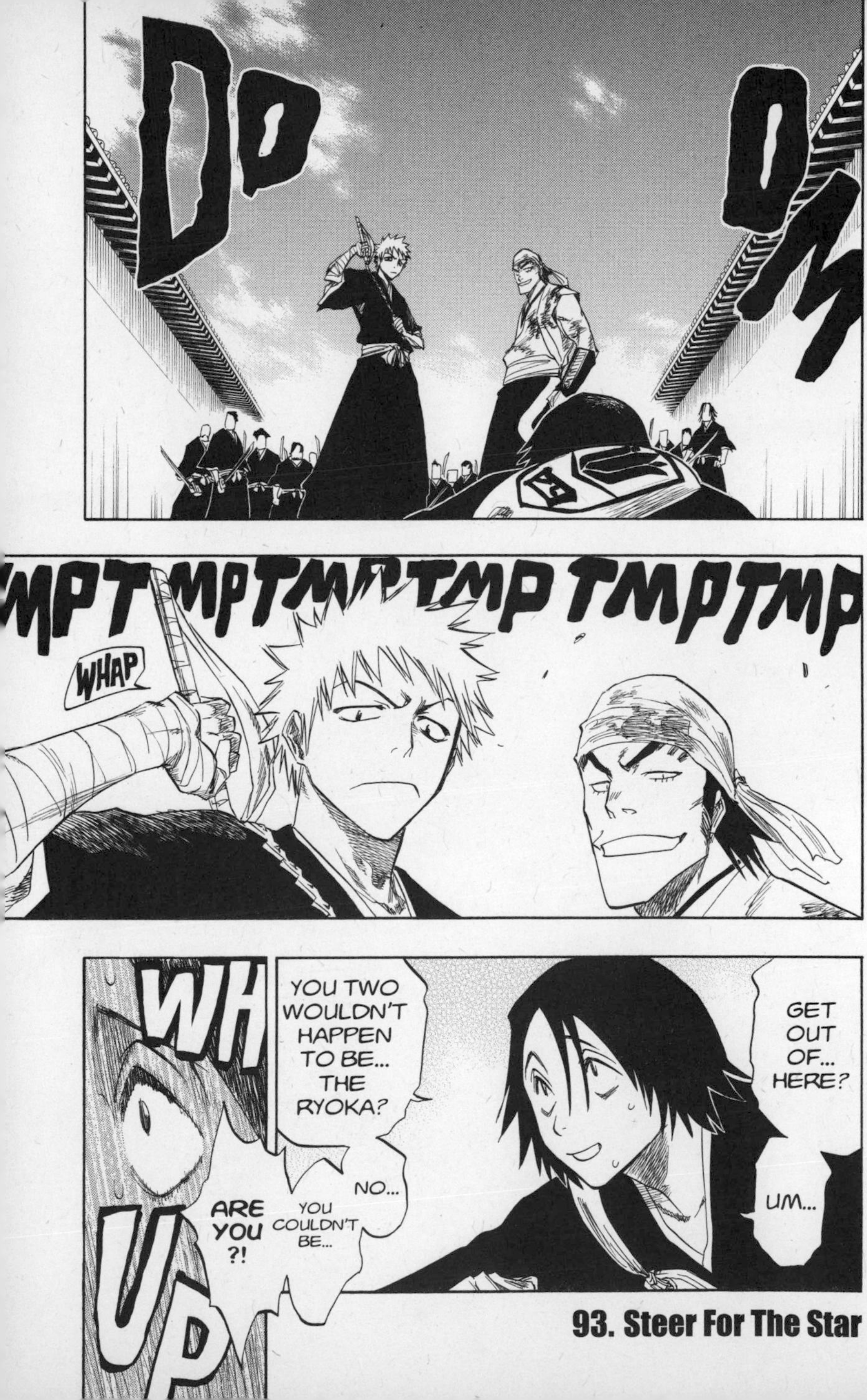
DOOM
TMP TMP TMP TMP TMP TMP
WHAP
GET OUT OF... HERE?
UM...
YOU TWO WOULDN'T HAPPEN TO BE... THE RYOKA?
NO... YOU COULDN'T BE...
ARE YOU ?!
WHUP

93. Steer For The Star

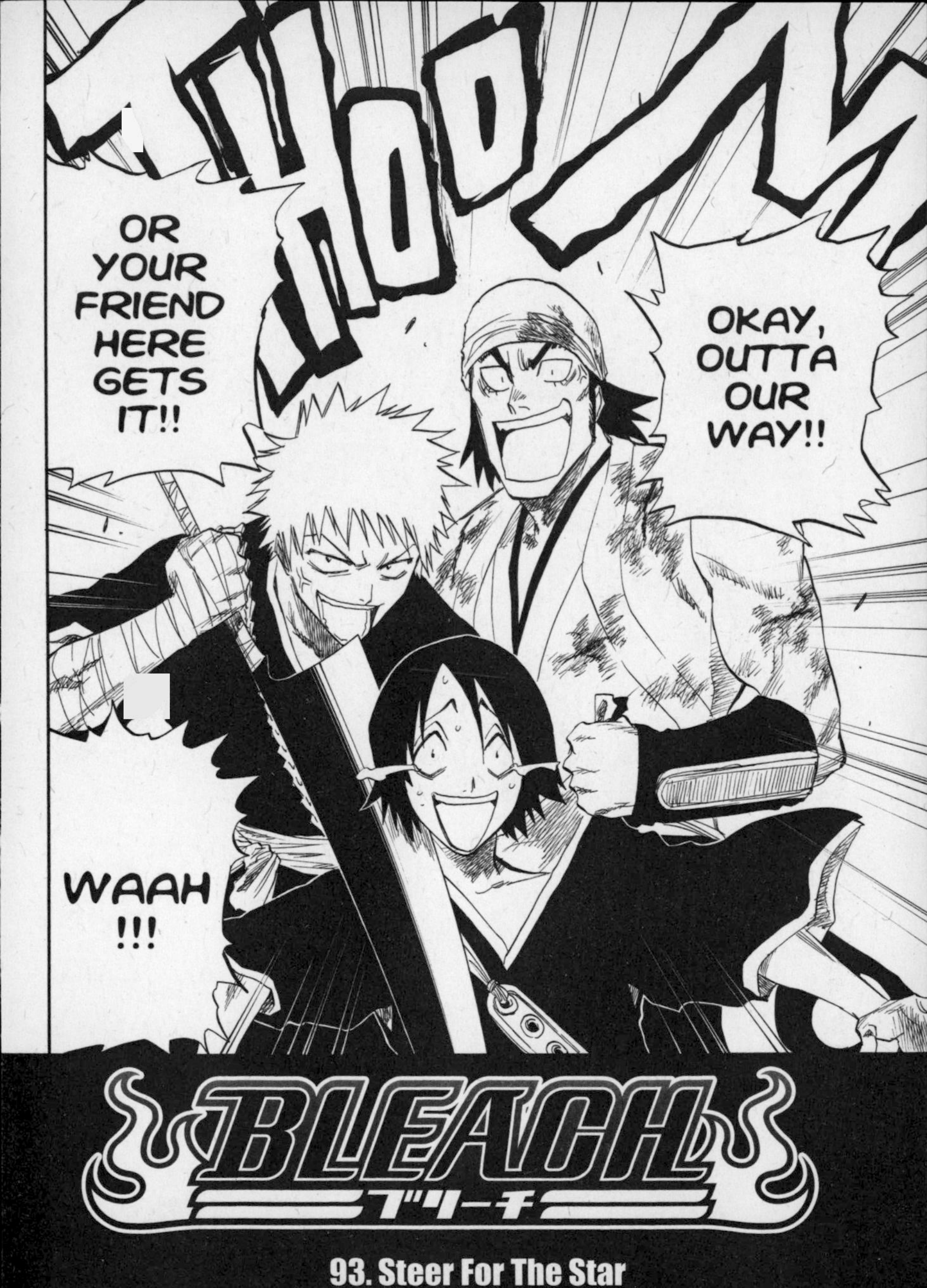
OKAY, OUTTA OUR WAY!!
OR YOUR FRIEND HERE GETS IT!!
WAAH!!!

BLEACH
ブリーチ

93. Steer For The Star

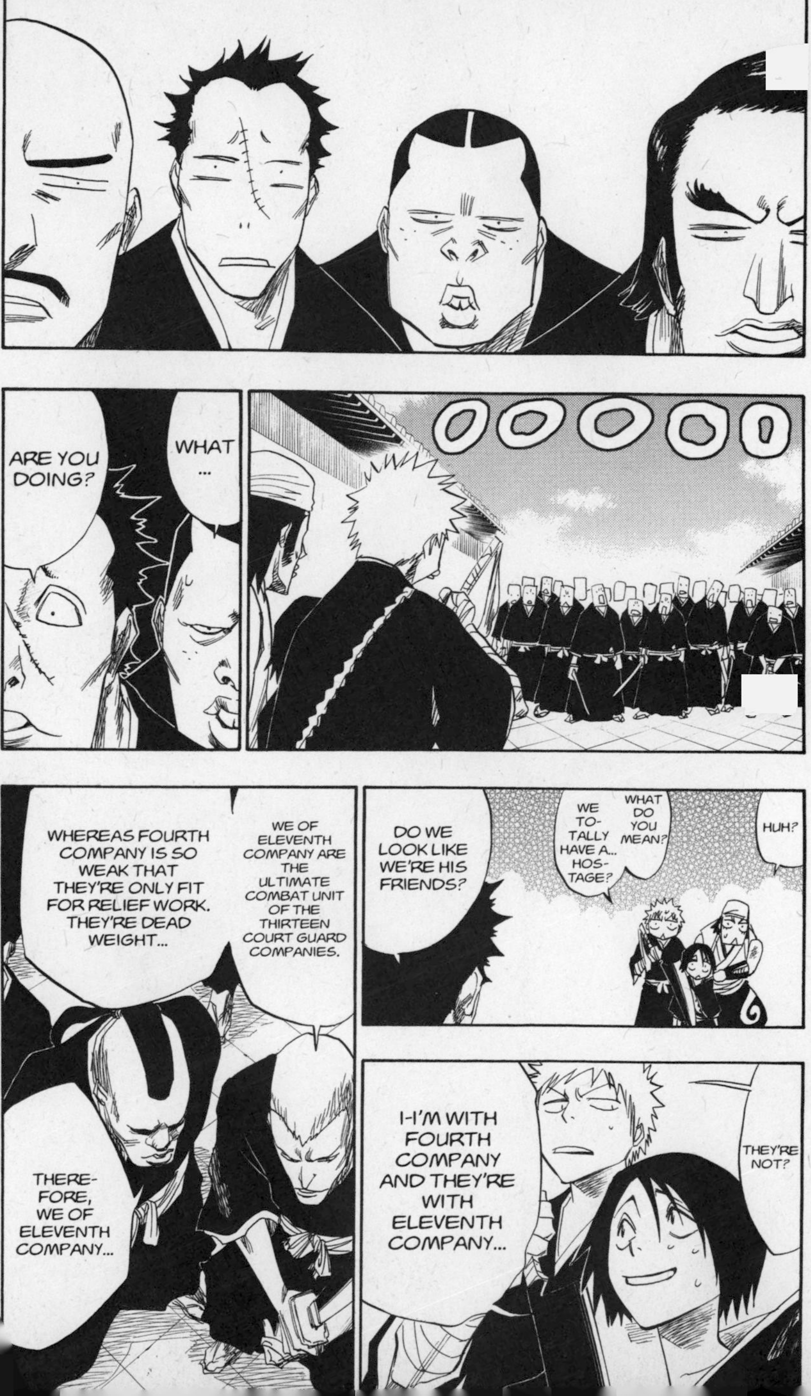

WHAT ...
ARE YOU DOING?
HUH?
WHAT DO YOU MEAN?
WE TOTALLY HAVE A... HOSTAGE?
DO WE LOOK LIKE WE'RE HIS FRIENDS?
THEY'RE NOT?
I-I'M WITH FOURTH COMPANY AND THEY'RE WITH ELEVENTH COMPANY...
WE OF ELEVENTH COMPANY ARE THE ULTIMATE COMBAT UNIT OF THE THIRTEEN COURT GUARD COMPANIES.
WHEREAS FOURTH COMPANY IS SO WEAK THAT THEY'RE ONLY FIT FOR RELIEF WORK. THEY'RE DEAD WEIGHT...
THEREFORE, WE OF ELEVENTH COMPANY...

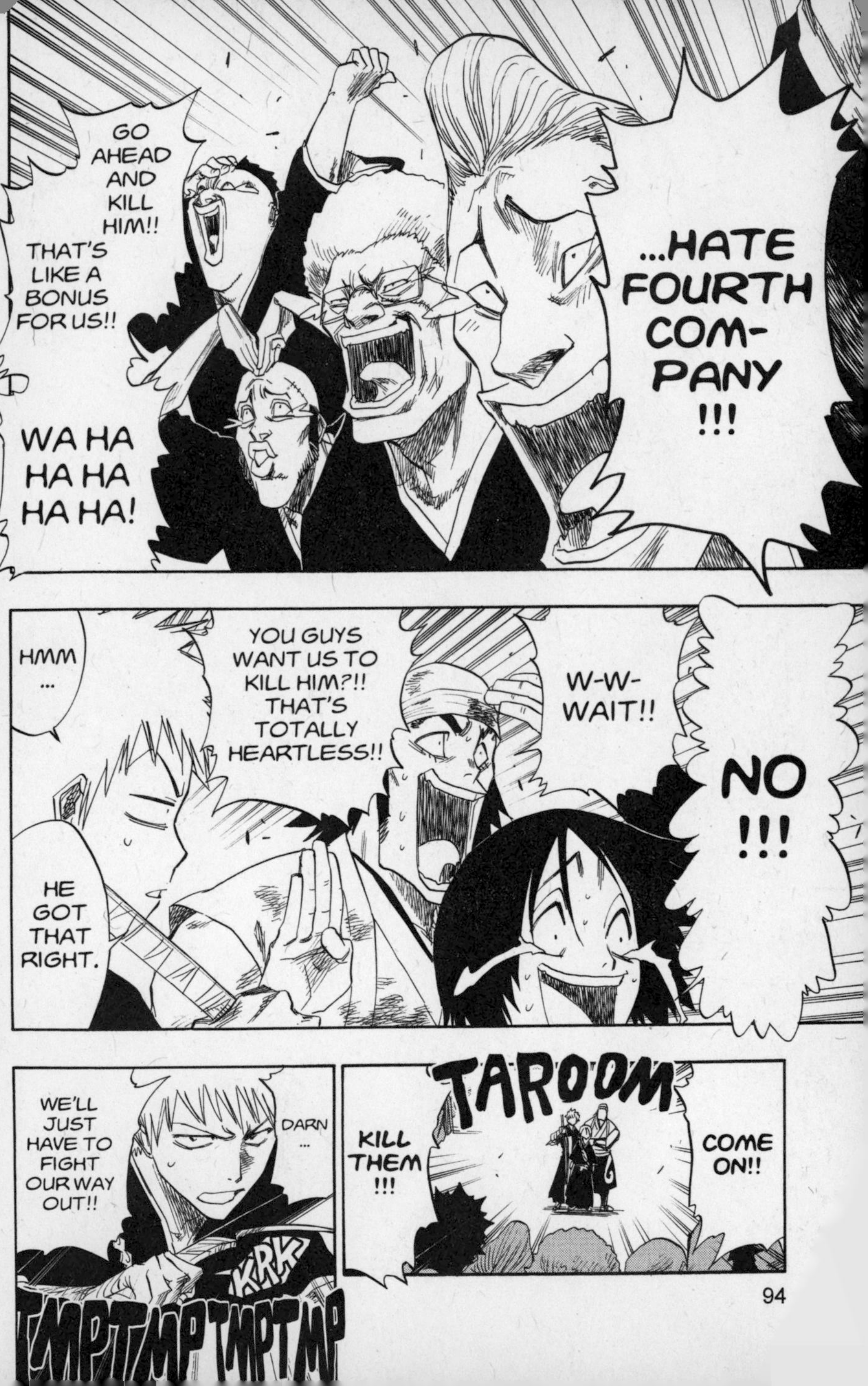
...HATE FOURTH COMPANY!!!
GO AHEAD AND KILL HIM!! THAT'S LIKE A BONUS FOR US!!
WA HA HA HA HA HA!
NO!!!
W-W-WAIT!!
YOU GUYS WANT US TO KILL HIM?!! THAT'S TOTALLY HEARTLESS!!
HMM...
HE GOT THAT RIGHT.
TAROOM
COME ON!!
KILL THEM!!!
DARN...
WE'LL JUST HAVE TO FIGHT OUR WAY OUT!!
KRK
TMPTMP TMPTMP

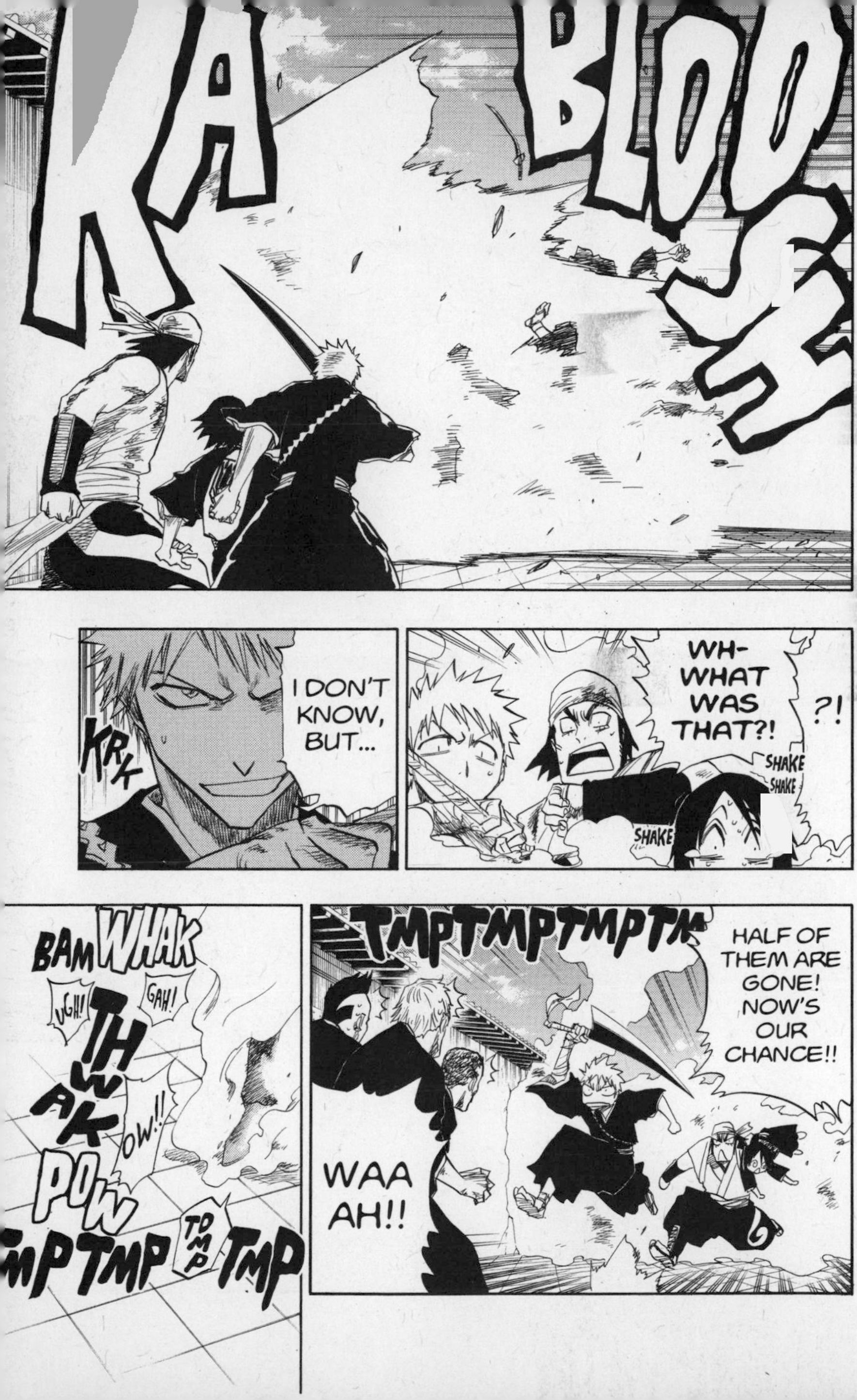
KA BLOOSH
WH- WHAT WAS THAT?!
?!
SHAKE SHAKE
SHAKE
KRK
I DON'T KNOW, BUT...
TMPTMPTMPTM
HALF OF THEM ARE GONE! NOW'S OUR CHANCE!!
WAA AH!!
BAM WHAK
UGH!
GAH!
THWAK
OW!!
POW
TMPTMP
TOMP
TMP

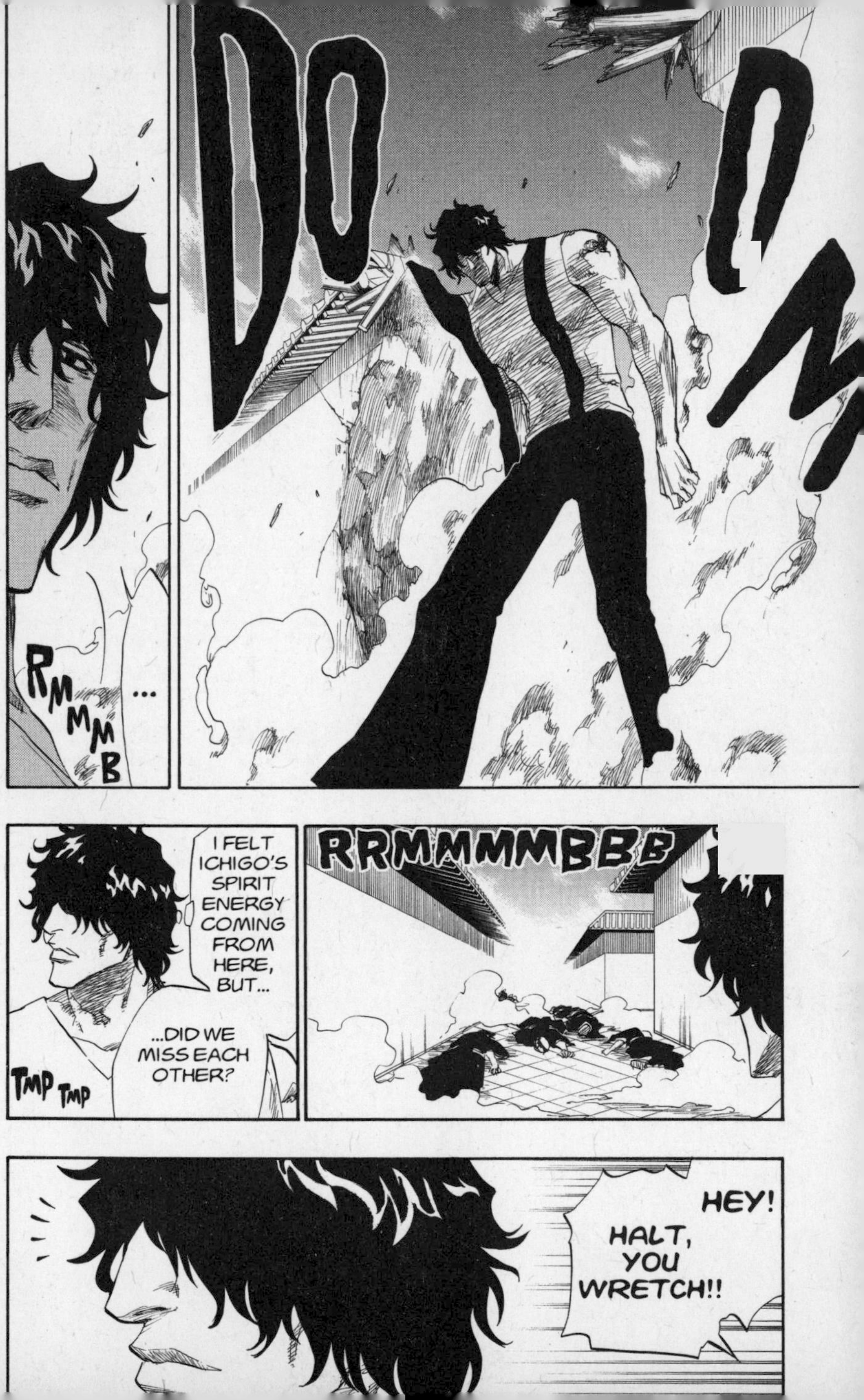
DOOM
RMMMB
...
RRMMMMMBBB
I FELT ICHIGO'S SPIRIT ENERGY COMING FROM HERE, BUT...
...DID WE MISS EACH OTHER?
TMP TMP
HEY!
HALT, YOU WRETCH!!

READ THIS WAY

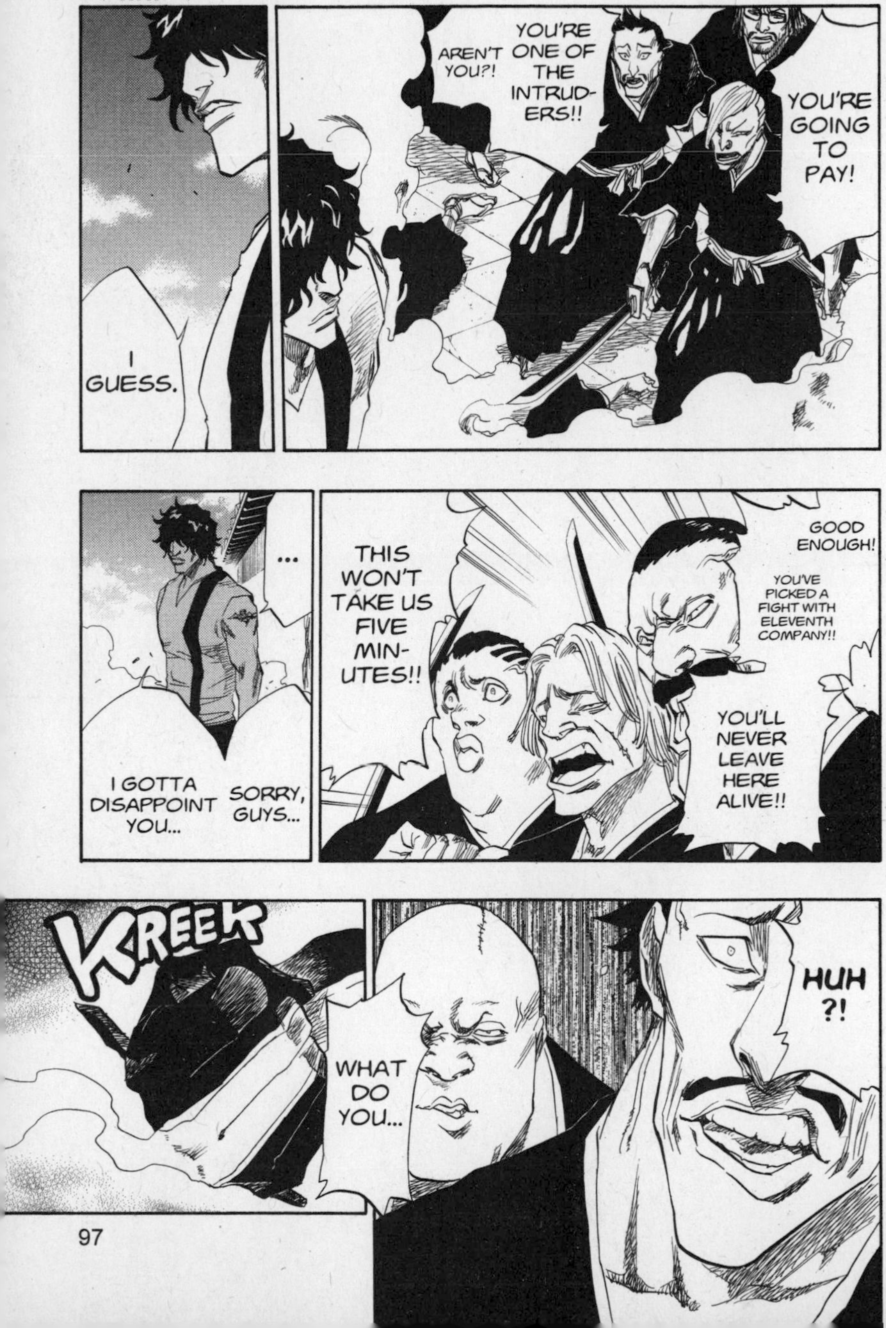
YOU'RE ONE OF THE INTRUDERS!!
AREN'T YOU?!
YOU'RE GOING TO PAY!
I GUESS.
GOOD ENOUGH!
YOU'VE PICKED A FIGHT WITH ELEVENTH COMPANY!!
THIS WON'T TAKE US FIVE MIN-UTES!!
YOU'LL NEVER LEAVE HERE ALIVE!!
...
SORRY, GUYS...
I GOTTA DISAPPOINT YOU...
HUH ?!
WHAT DO YOU...
KREEK

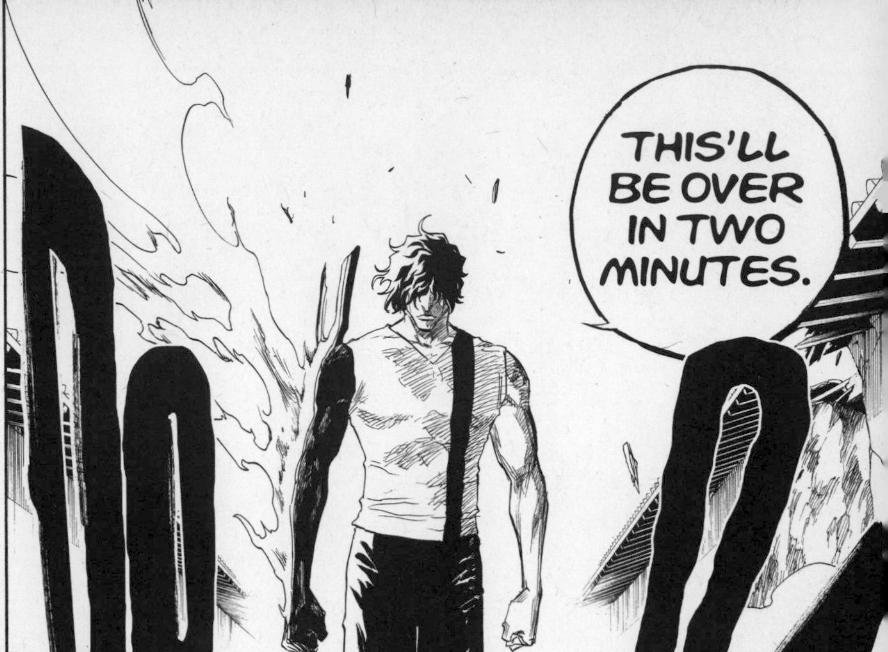
THIS'LL BE OVER IN TWO MINUTES.
DOOM
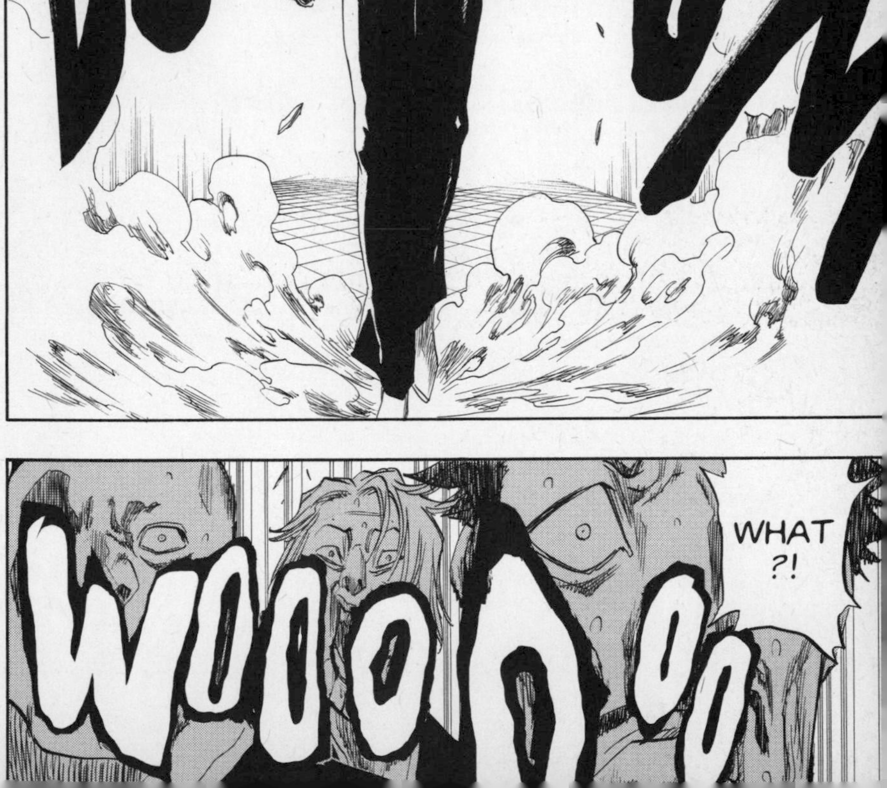
WHAT ?!

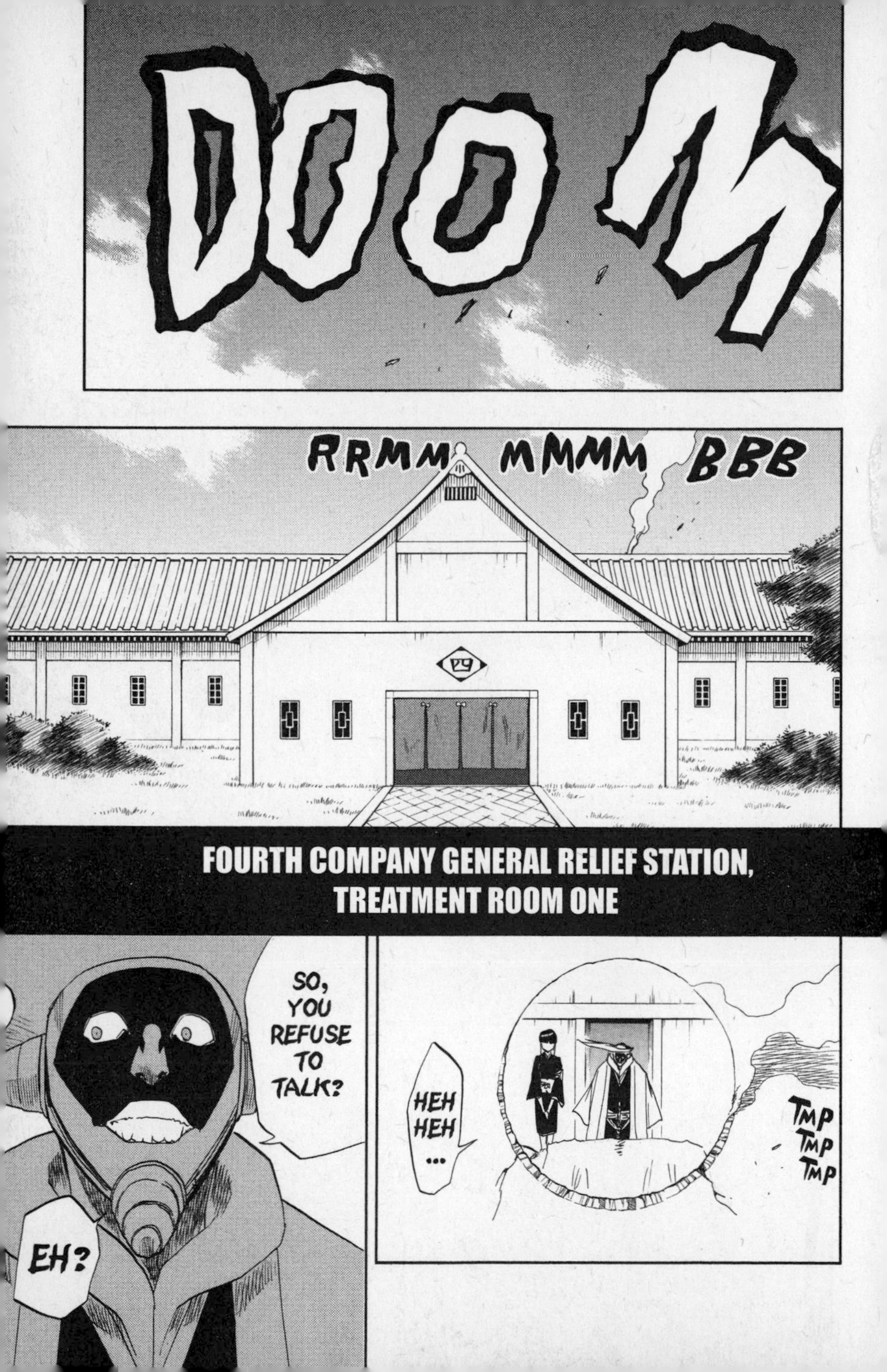
DOOM
RRMM MMMM BBB
FOURTH COMPANY GENERAL RELIEF STATION, TREATMENT ROOM ONE
HEH HEH ...
TMP TMP TMP
SO, YOU REFUSE TO TALK?
EH?

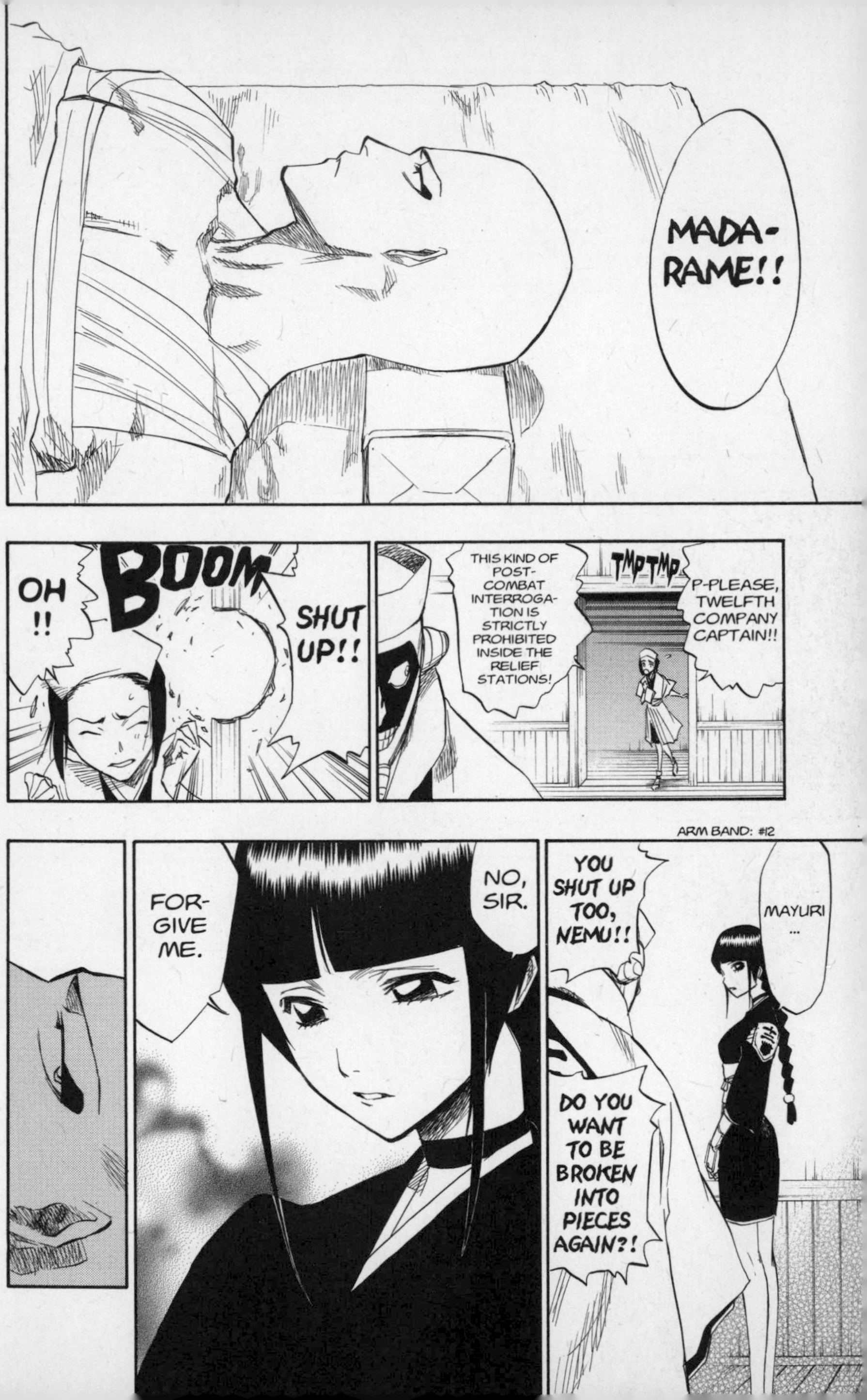
MADA-
RAME!!
TMPTMP
P-PLEASE, TWELFTH COMPANY CAPTAIN!!
THIS KIND OF POST-COMBAT INTERROGATION IS STRICTLY PROHIBITED INSIDE THE RELIEF STATIONS!
SHUT UP!!
BOOM
OH !!
ARM BAND: #12
MAYURI ...
YOU SHUT UP TOO, NEMU!!
DO YOU WANT TO BE BROKEN INTO PIECES AGAIN?!
NO, SIR.
FOR-
GIVE
ME.

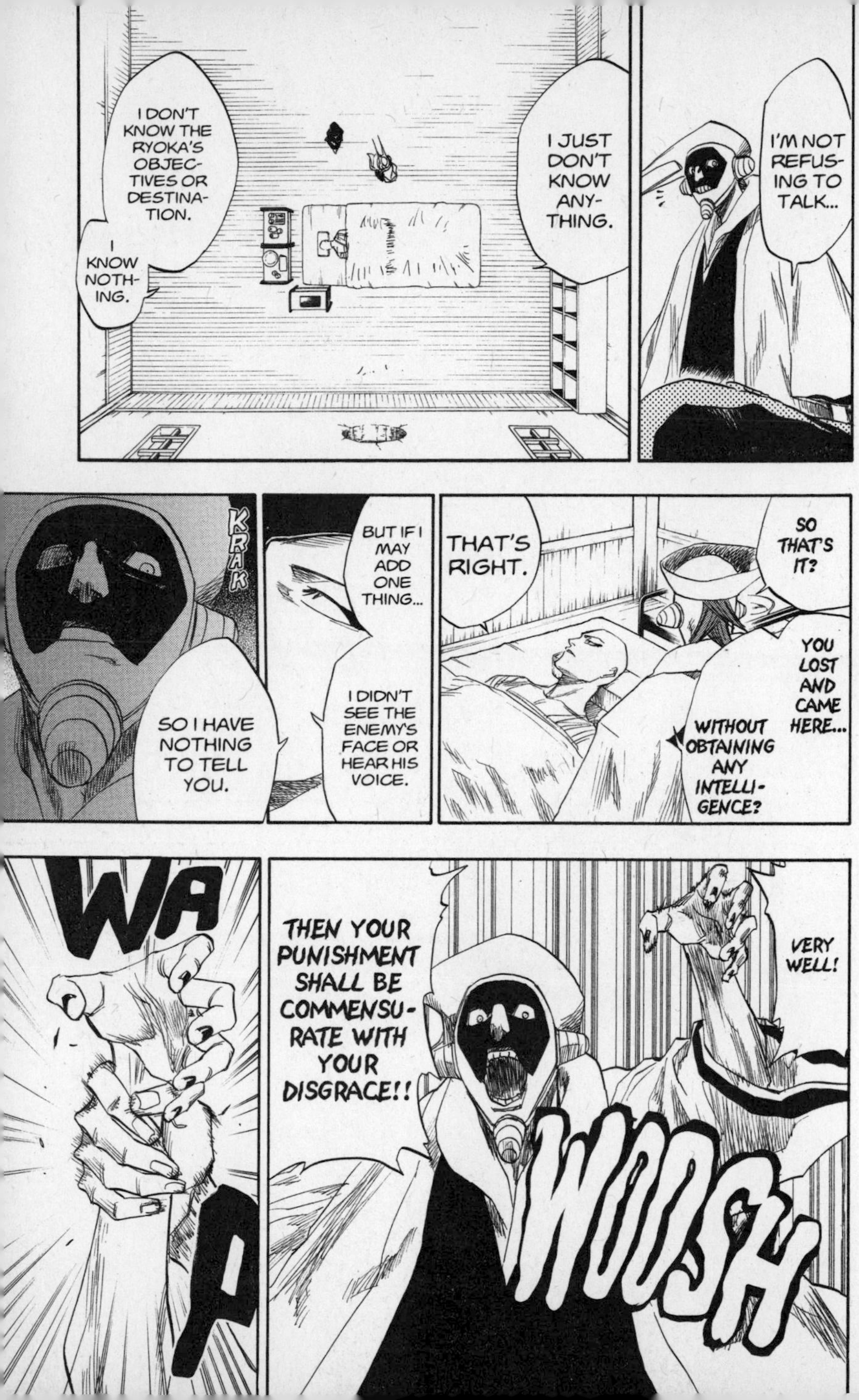
I'M NOT REFUSING TO TALK...
I JUST DON'T KNOW ANYTHING.
I DON'T KNOW THE RYOKA'S OBJECTIVES OR DESTINATION.
I KNOW NOTHING.
SO THAT'S IT?
YOU LOST AND CAME HERE...
WITHOUT OBTAINING ANY INTELLIGENCE?
THAT'S RIGHT.
BUT IF I MAY ADD ONE THING...
I DIDN'T SEE THE ENEMY'S FACE OR HEAR HIS VOICE.
KRAK
SO I HAVE NOTHING TO TELL YOU.
VERY WELL!
THEN YOUR PUNISHMENT SHALL BE COMMENSURATE WITH YOUR DISGRACE!!
WOOSH
WAP

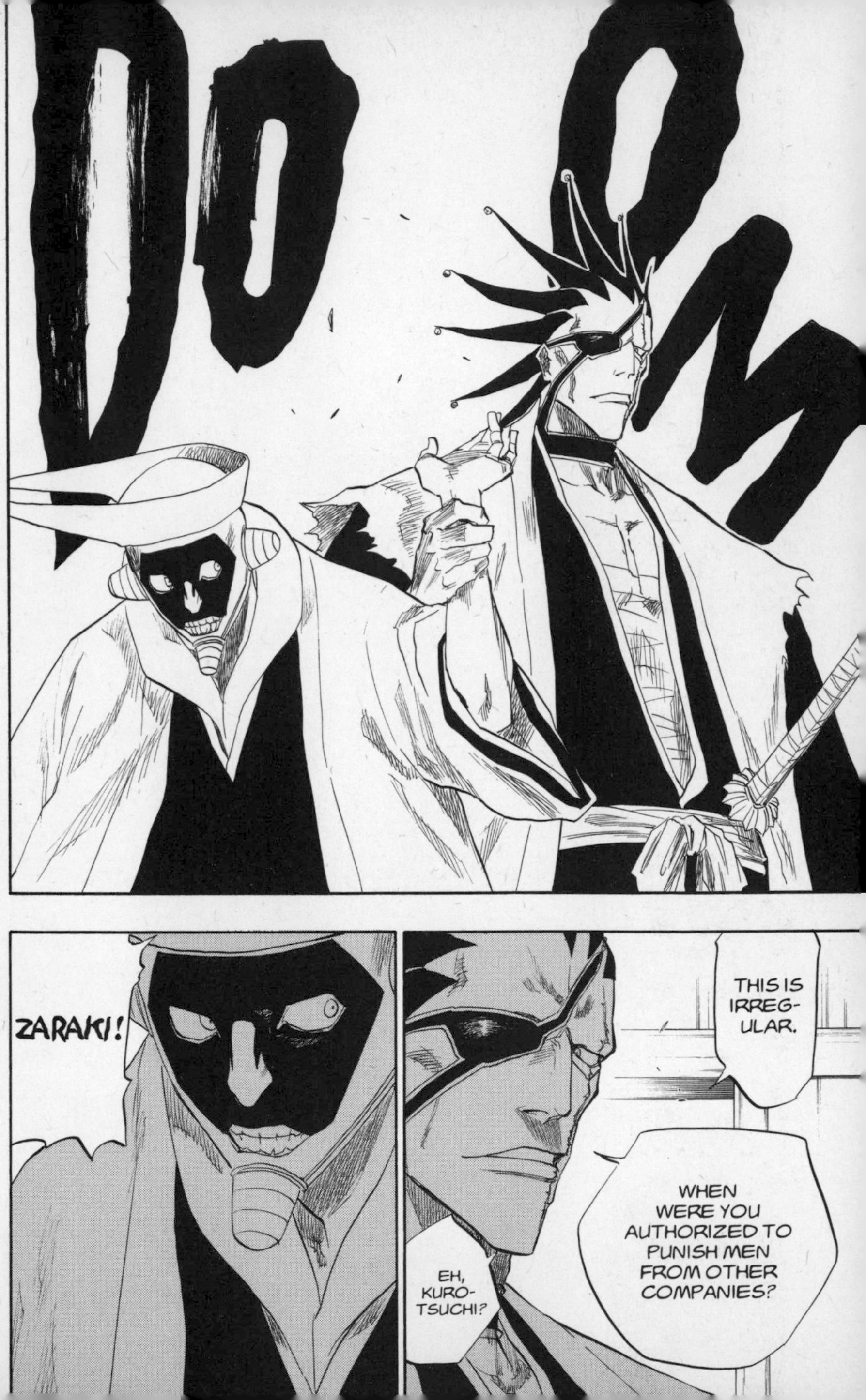
DOOM
THIS IS IRREG-ULAR.
WHEN WERE YOU AUTHORIZED TO PUNISH MEN FROM OTHER COMPANIES?
EH, KURO-TSUCHI?
ZARAKI!

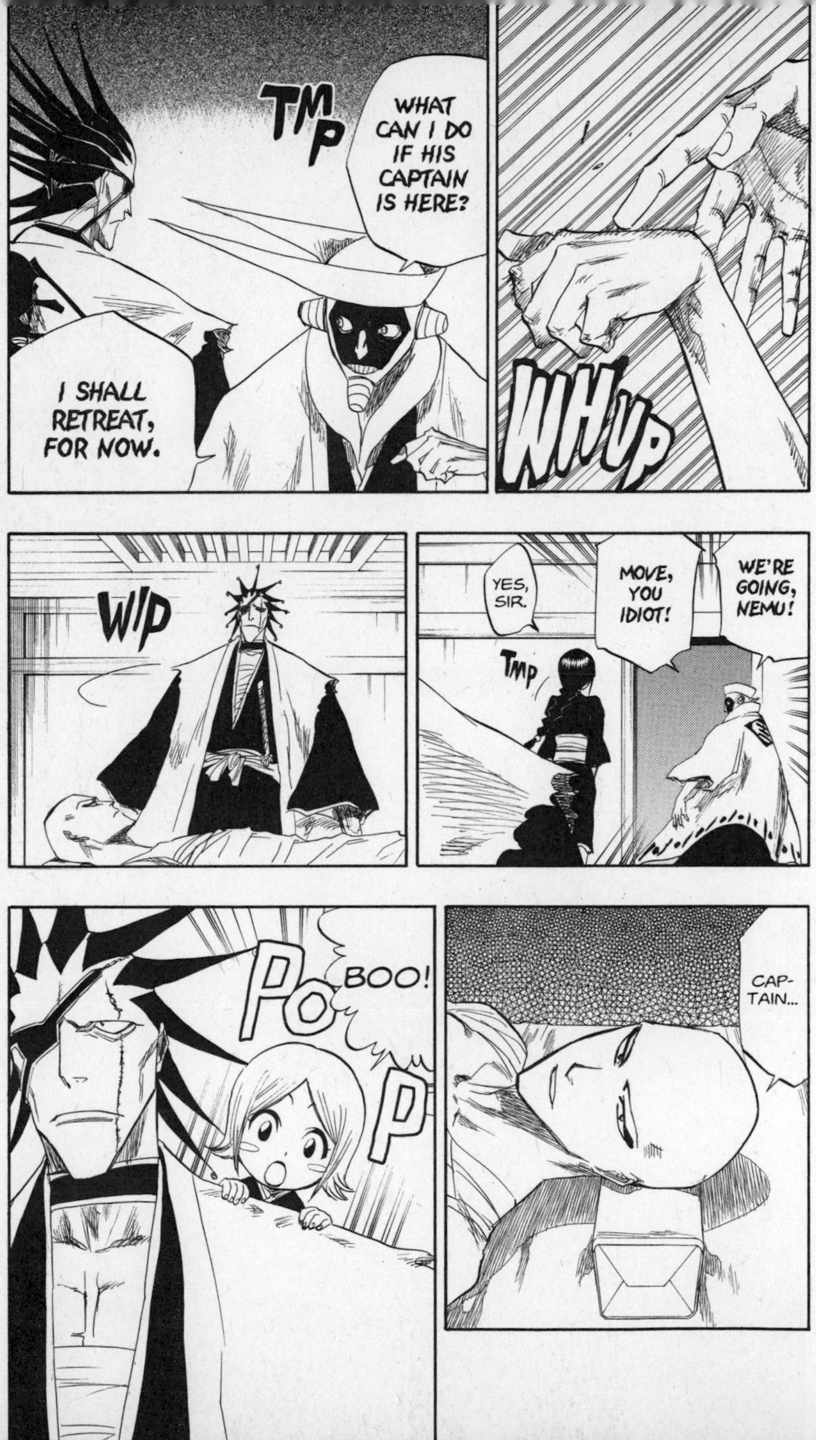
WHUP
TMP
WHAT CAN I DO IF HIS CAPTAIN IS HERE?
I SHALL RETREAT, FOR NOW.
WE'RE GOING, NEMU!
MOVE, YOU IDIOT!
YES, SIR.
TMP
WIP
CAP-TAIN...
POP
BOO!

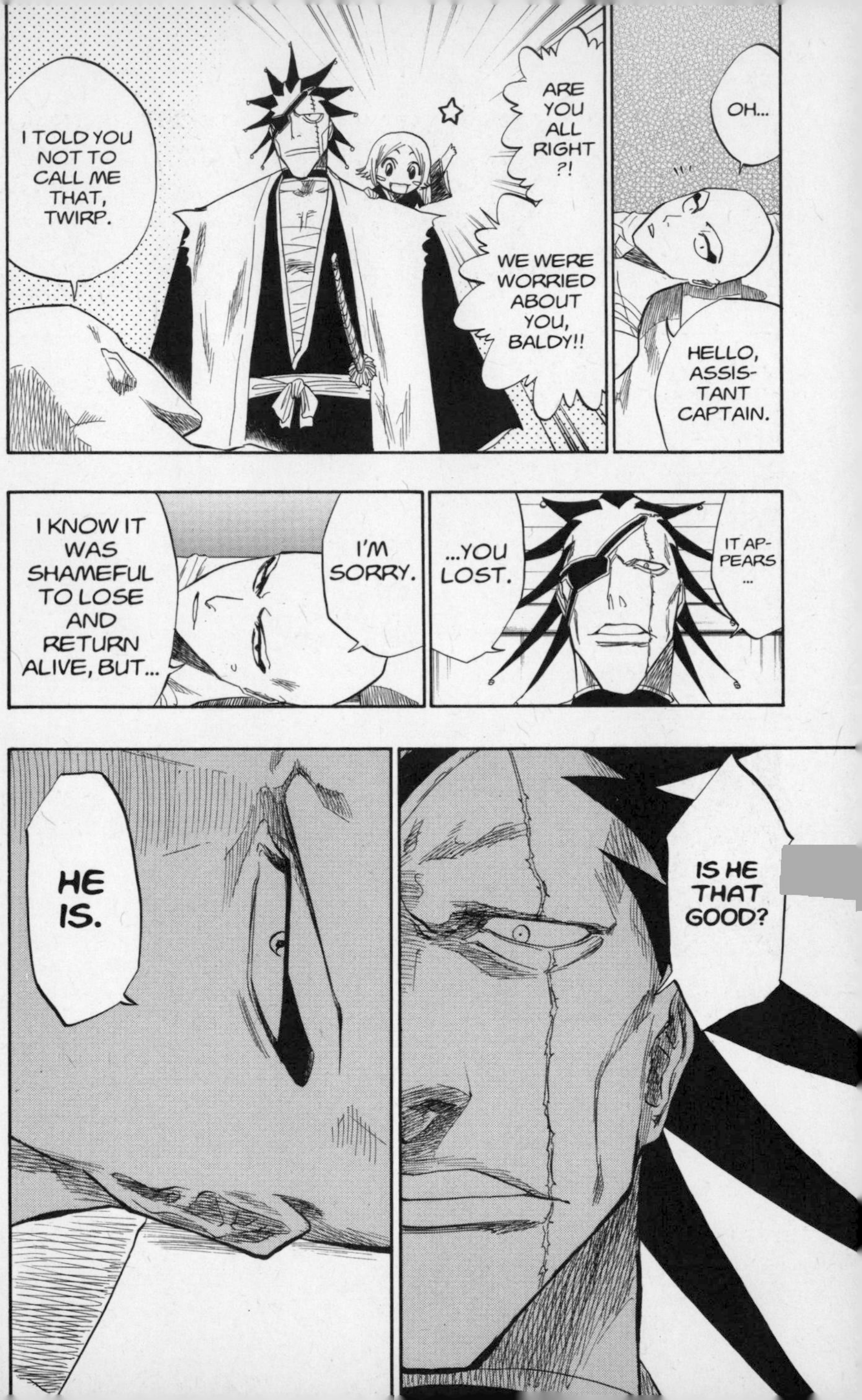
OH...
HELLO, ASSISTANT CAPTAIN.
ARE YOU ALL RIGHT ?!
WE WERE WORRIED ABOUT YOU, BALDY!!
I TOLD YOU NOT TO CALL ME THAT, TWIRP.
IT APPEARS ...
...YOU LOST.
I'M SORRY.
I KNOW IT WAS SHAMEFUL TO LOSE AND RETURN ALIVE, BUT...
IS HE THAT GOOD?
HE IS.

READ THIS WAY

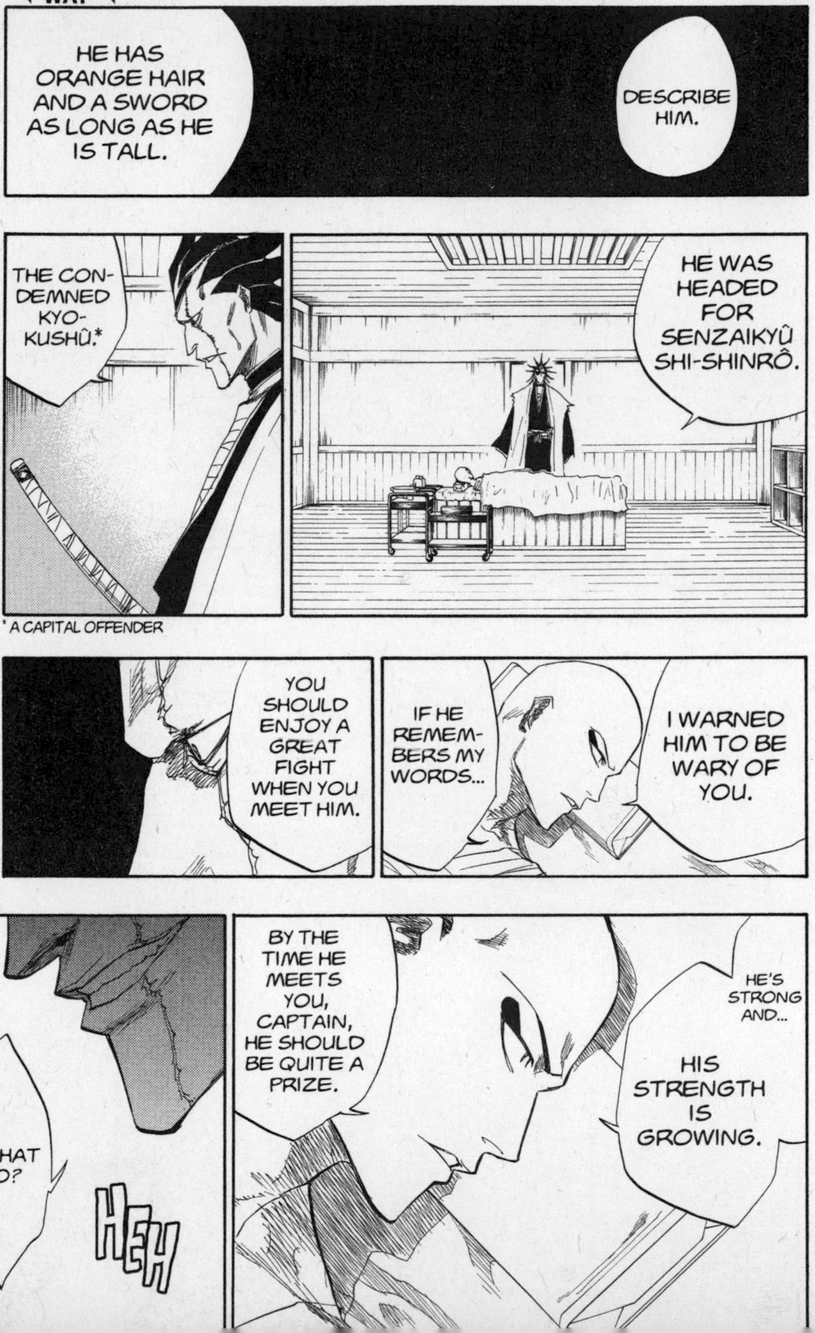
DESCRIBE HIM.
HE HAS ORANGE HAIR AND A SWORD AS LONG AS HE IS TALL.
HE WAS HEADED FOR SENZAIKYÛ SHI-SHINRÔ.
THE CONDEMNED KYOKUSHÛ.*
I WARNED HIM TO BE WARY OF YOU.
IF HE REMEMBERS MY WORDS...
YOU SHOULD ENJOY A GREAT FIGHT WHEN YOU MEET HIM.
HE'S STRONG AND...
HIS STRENGTH IS GROWING.
BY THE TIME HE MEETS YOU, CAPTAIN, HE SHOULD BE QUITE A PRIZE.
IS THAT SO?
HEH

* A CAPITAL OFFENDER

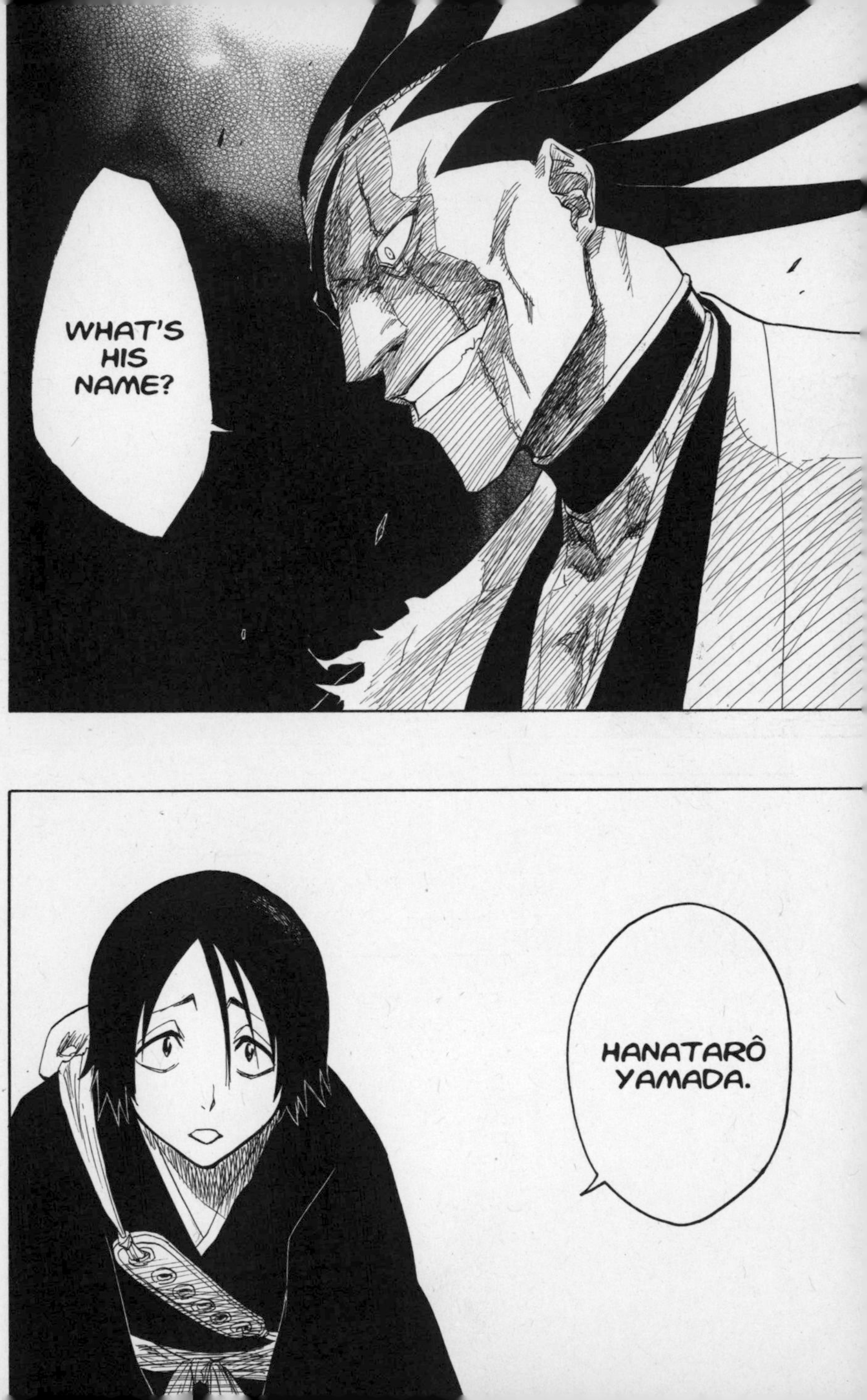
WHAT'S HIS NAME?
HANATARÔ YAMADA.

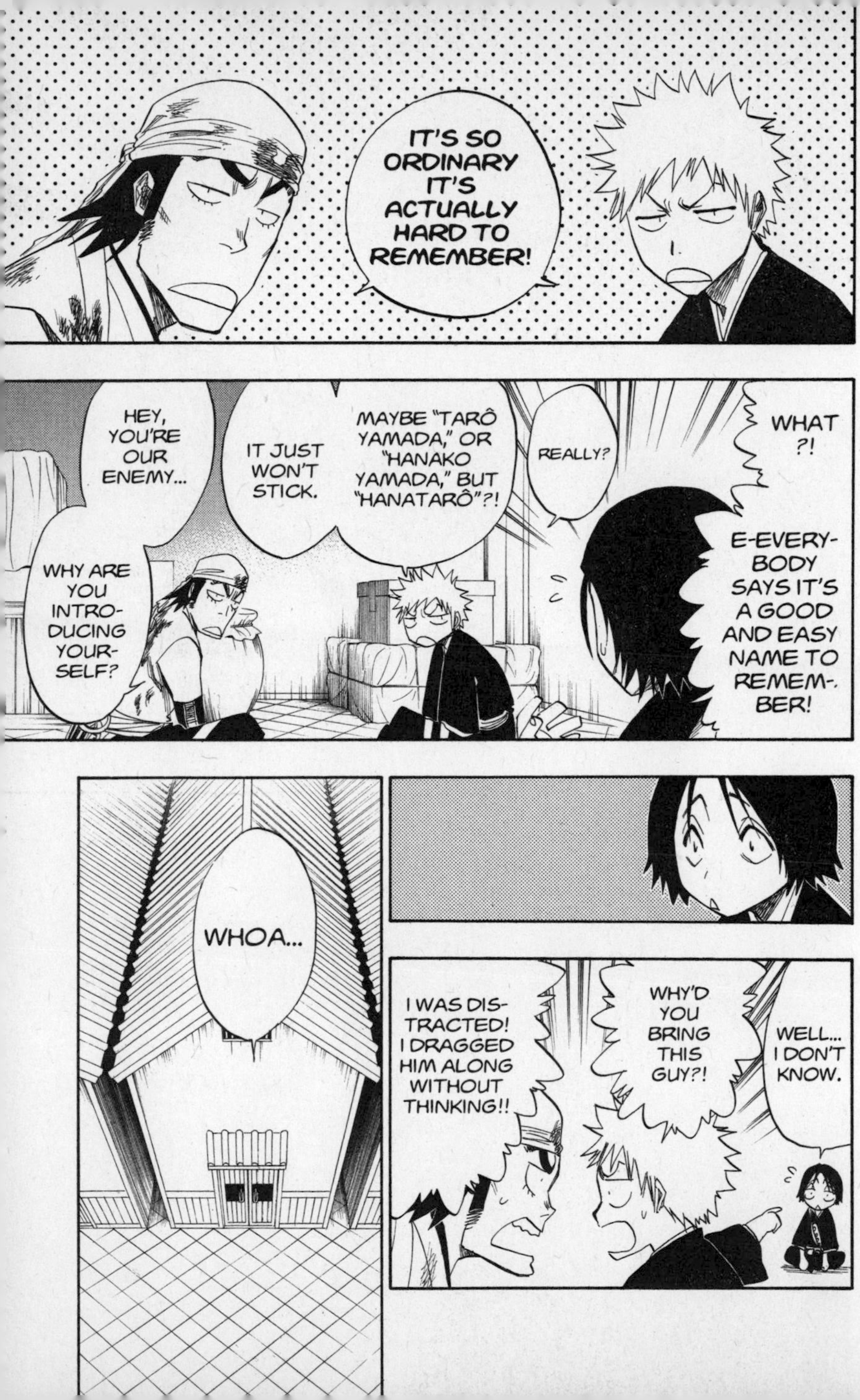
IT'S SO ORDINARY IT'S ACTUALLY HARD TO REMEMBER!
WHAT?!
E-EVERYBODY SAYS IT'S A GOOD AND EASY NAME TO REMEMBER!
REALLY?
MAYBE "TARÔ YAMADA," OR "HANAKO YAMADA," BUT "HANATARÔ"?!
IT JUST WON'T STICK.
HEY, YOU'RE OUR ENEMY...
WHY ARE YOU INTRODUCING YOURSELF?
WELL... I DON'T KNOW.
WHY'D YOU BRING THIS GUY?!
I WAS DISTRACTED! I DRAGGED HIM ALONG WITHOUT THINKING!!
WHOA...

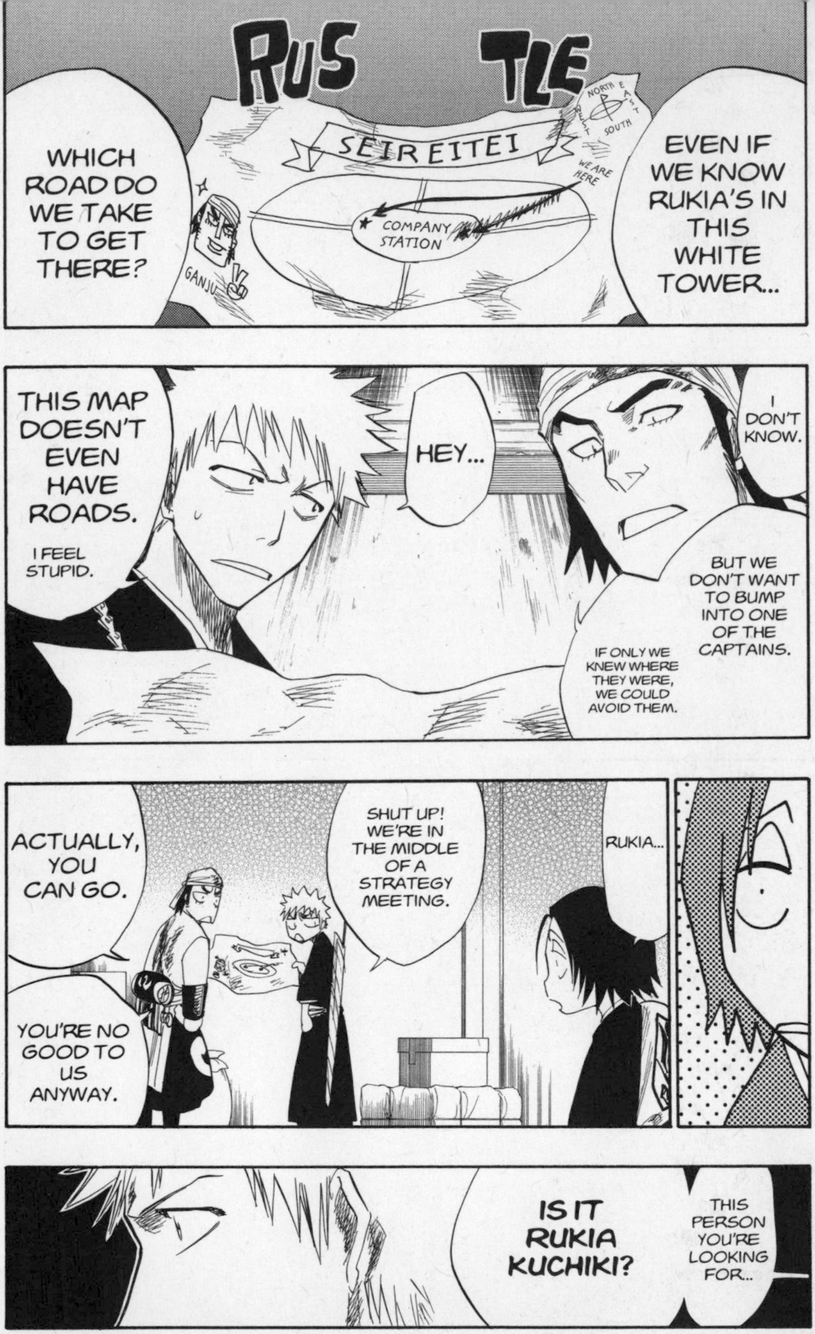
RUSTLE
EVEN IF WE KNOW RUKIA'S IN THIS WHITE TOWER...
NORTH EAST SOUTH WEST
SEIREITEI
WE ARE HERE
COMPANY STATION
GANJU
WHICH ROAD DO WE TAKE TO GET THERE?
I DON'T KNOW.
BUT WE DON'T WANT TO BUMP INTO ONE OF THE CAPTAINS.
IF ONLY WE KNEW WHERE THEY WERE, WE COULD AVOID THEM.
HEY...
THIS MAP DOESN'T EVEN HAVE ROADS.
I FEEL STUPID.
RUKIA...
SHUT UP! WE'RE IN THE MIDDLE OF A STRATEGY MEETING.
ACTUALLY, YOU CAN GO.
YOU'RE NO GOOD TO US ANYWAY.
THIS PERSON YOU'RE LOOKING FOR..
IS IT RUKIA KUCHIKI?

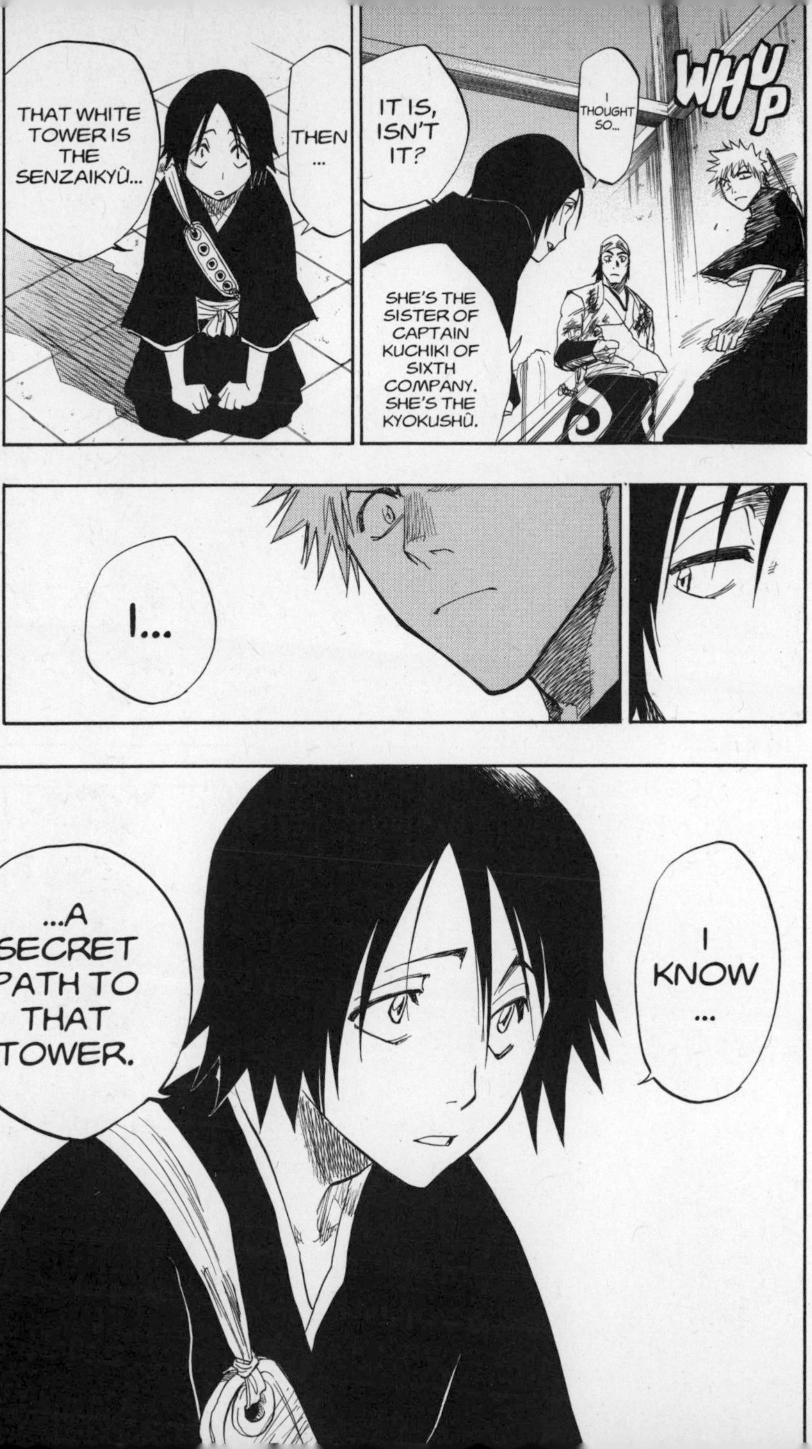
WHUP
I THOUGHT SO...
IT IS, ISN'T IT?
SHE'S THE SISTER OF CAPTAIN KUCHIKI OF SIXTH COMPANY. SHE'S THE KYOKUSHÛ.
THEN...
THAT WHITE TOWER IS THE SENZAIKYÛ...
I...
I KNOW...
...A SECRET PATH TO THAT TOWER.

BACK

NURSE

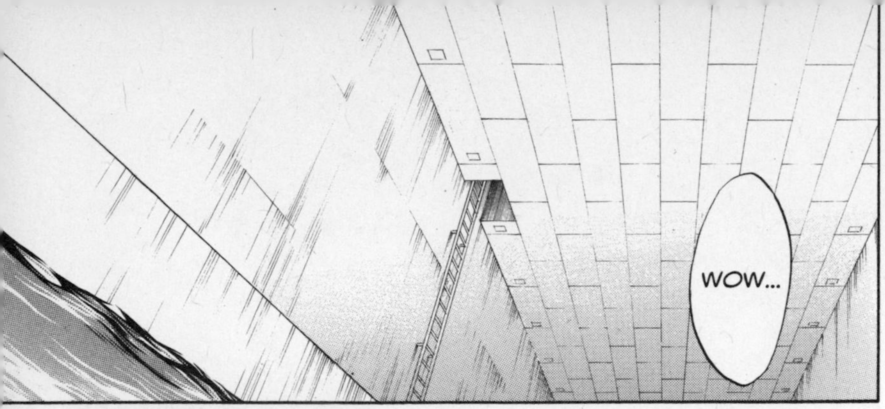
WOW...

94. A Jail Called Remorse

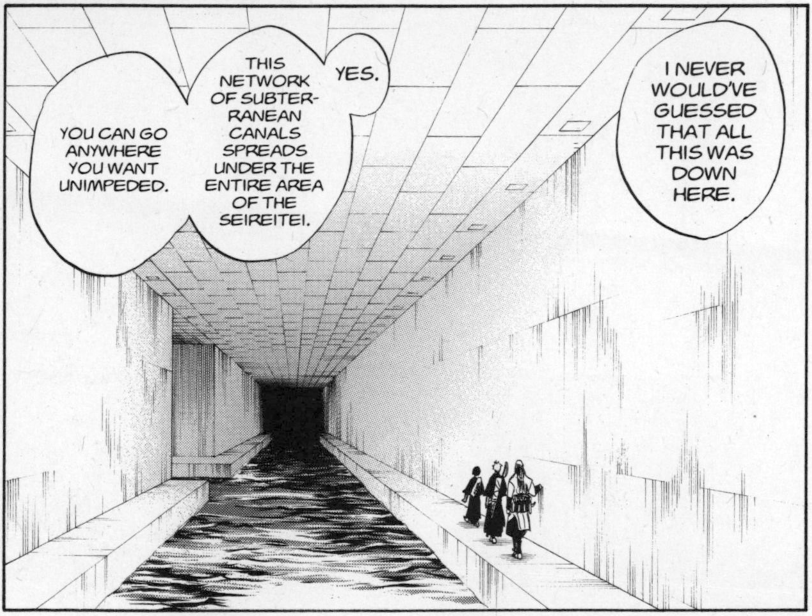
I NEVER WOULD'VE GUESSED THAT ALL THIS WAS DOWN HERE.
YES.
THIS NETWORK OF SUBTER-RANEAN CANALS SPREADS UNDER THE ENTIRE AREA OF THE SEIREITEI.
YOU CAN GO ANYWHERE YOU WANT UNIMPEDED.

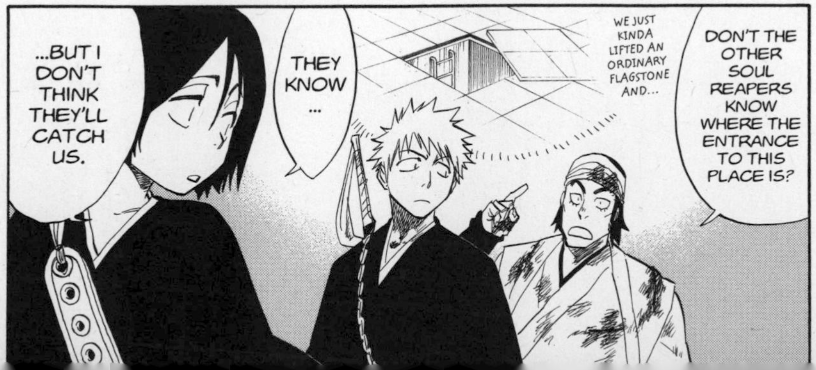
DON'T THE OTHER SOUL REAPERS KNOW WHERE THE ENTRANCE TO THIS PLACE IS?
WE JUST KINDA LIFTED AN ORDINARY FLAGSTONE AND...
THEY KNOW ...
...BUT I DON'T THINK THEY'LL CATCH US.

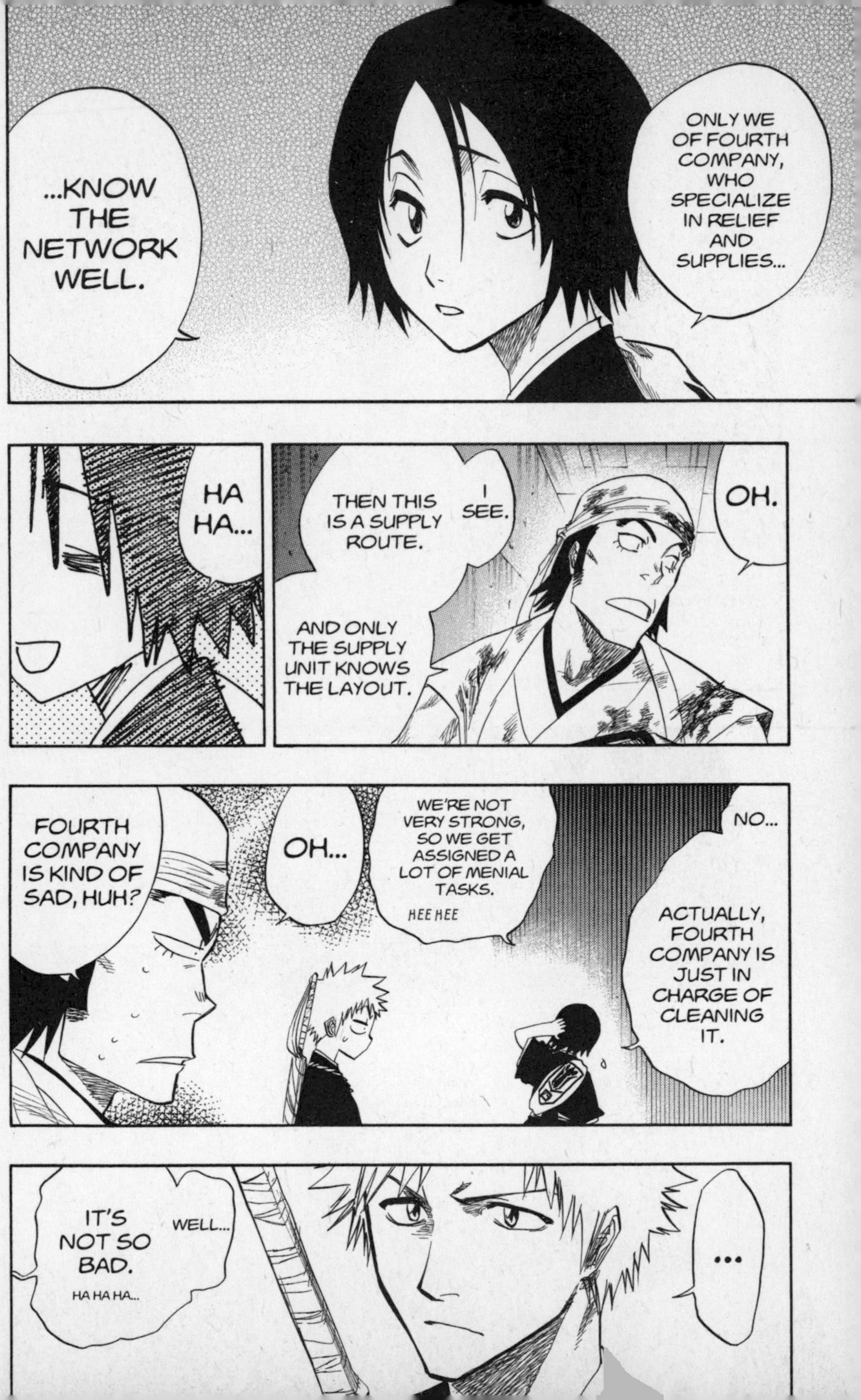
ONLY WE OF FOURTH COMPANY, WHO SPECIALIZE IN RELIEF AND SUPPLIES...
...KNOW THE NETWORK WELL.
OH.
I SEE.
THEN THIS IS A SUPPLY ROUTE.
AND ONLY THE SUPPLY UNIT KNOWS THE LAYOUT.
HA HA...
NO...
ACTUALLY, FOURTH COMPANY IS JUST IN CHARGE OF CLEANING IT.
WE'RE NOT VERY STRONG, SO WE GET ASSIGNED A LOT OF MENIAL TASKS.
HEE HEE
OH...
FOURTH COMPANY IS KIND OF SAD, HUH?
...
WELL...
IT'S NOT SO BAD.
HA HA HA...

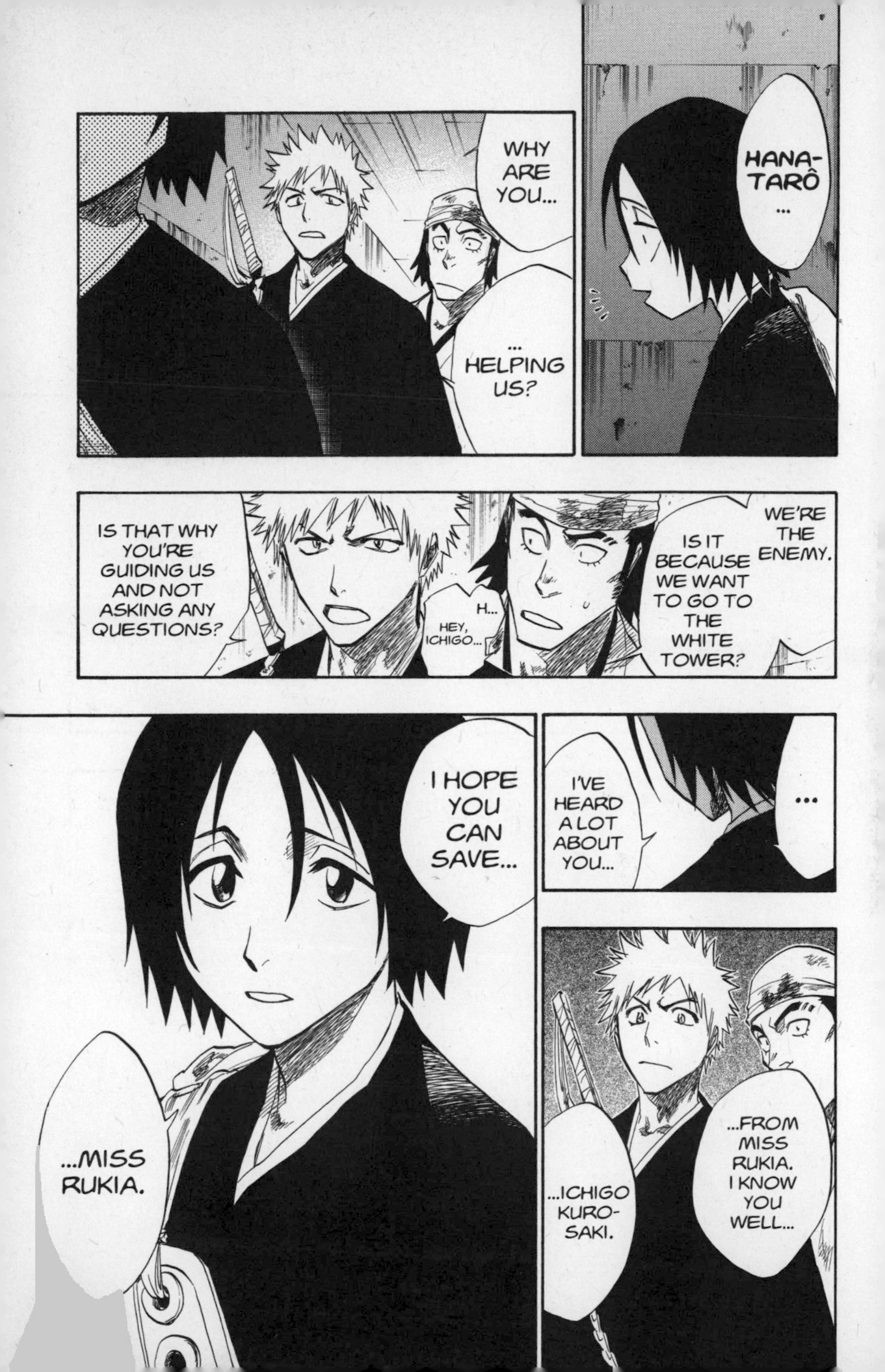
HANA-TARÔ ...
WHY ARE YOU...
... HELPING US?
WE'RE THE ENEMY.
IS IT BECAUSE WE WANT TO GO TO THE WHITE TOWER?
H... HEY, ICHIGO...
IS THAT WHY YOU'RE GUIDING US AND NOT ASKING ANY QUESTIONS?
...
I'VE HEARD A LOT ABOUT YOU...
...FROM MISS RUKIA. I KNOW YOU WELL...
...ICHIGO KURO-SAKI.
I HOPE YOU CAN SAVE...
...MISS RUKIA.

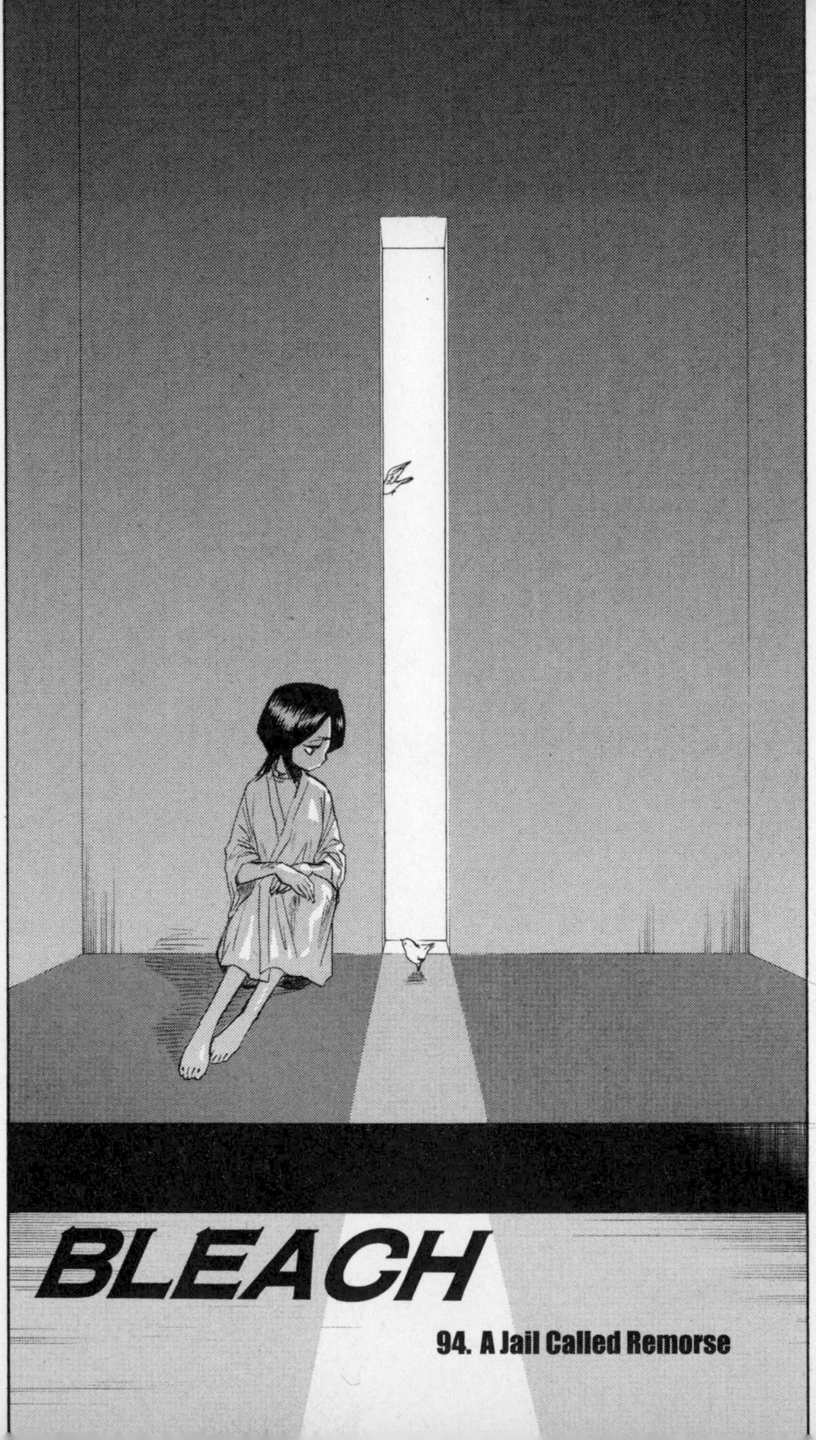
BLEACH
94. A Jail Called Remorse

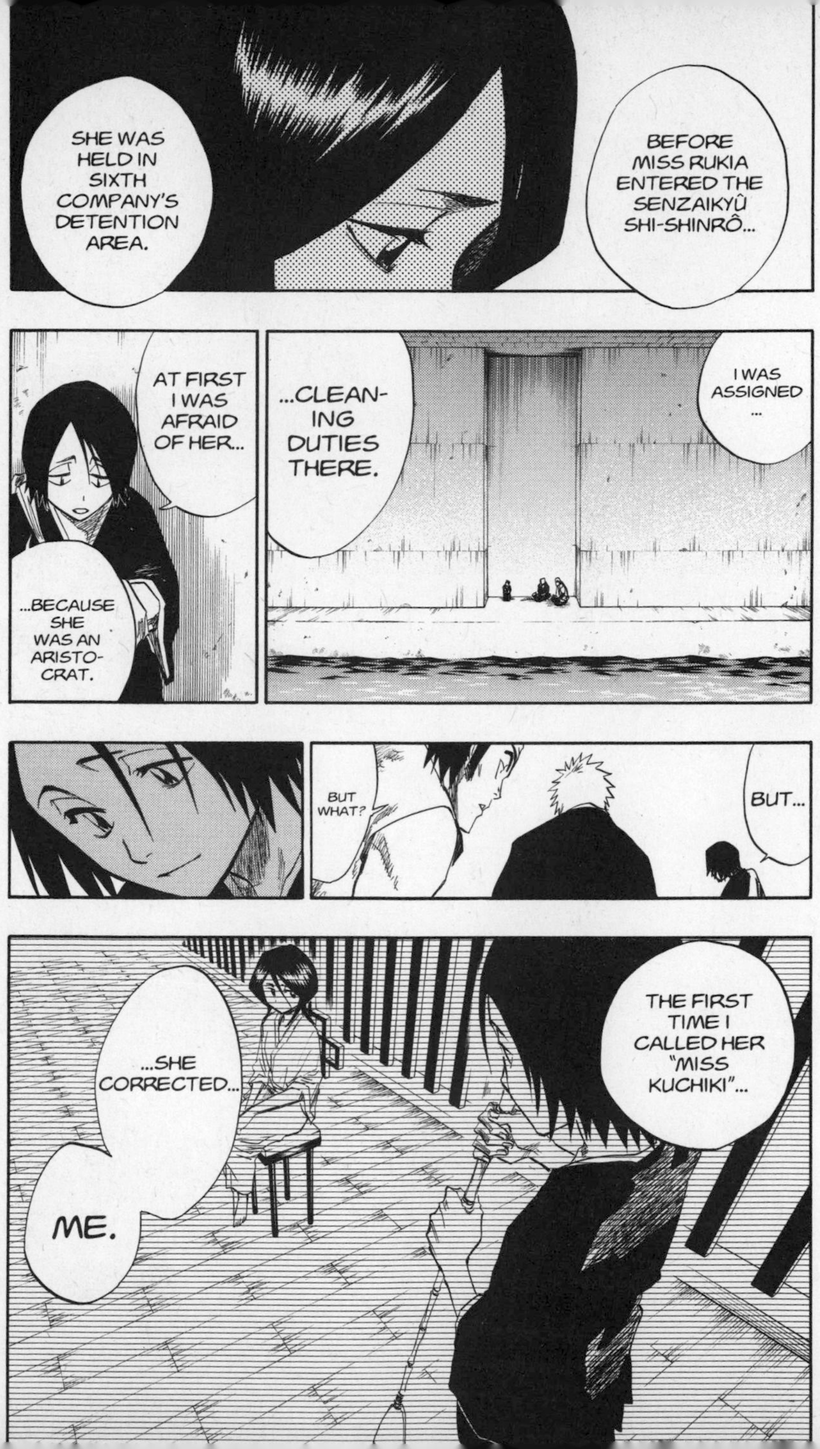
BEFORE MISS RUKIA ENTERED THE SENZAIKYÛ SHI-SHINRÔ...
SHE WAS HELD IN SIXTH COMPANY'S DETENTION AREA.
I WAS ASSIGNED ...
...CLEAN-ING DUTIES THERE.
AT FIRST I WAS AFRAID OF HER...
...BECAUSE SHE WAS AN ARISTO-CRAT.
BUT...
BUT WHAT?
THE FIRST TIME I CALLED HER "MISS KUCHIKI"...
...SHE CORRECTED...
ME.

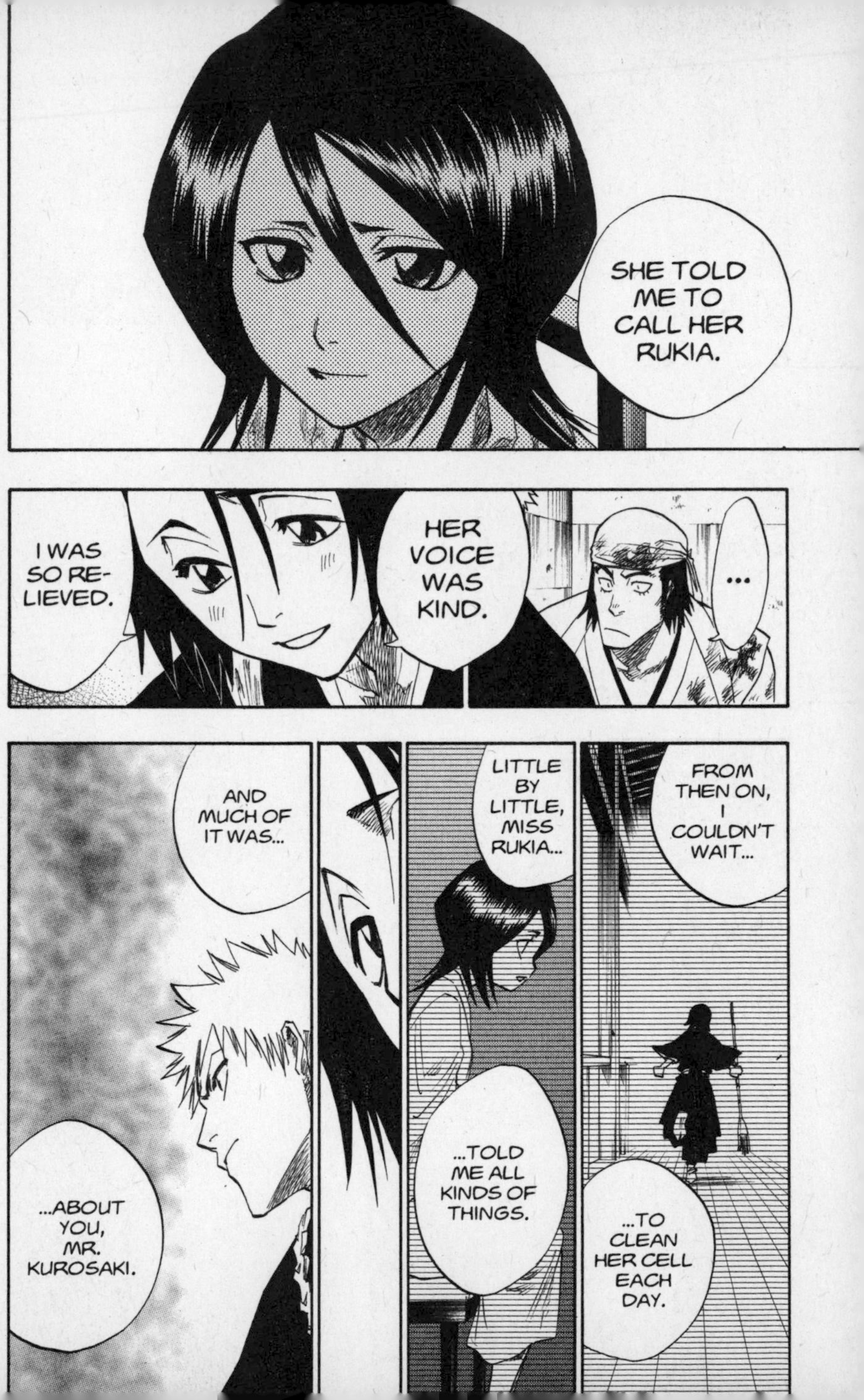
SHE TOLD ME TO CALL HER RUKIA.
...
HER VOICE WAS KIND.
I WAS SO RE-LIEVED.
FROM THEN ON, I COULDN'T WAIT...
...TO CLEAN HER CELL EACH DAY.
LITTLE BY LITTLE, MISS RUKIA...
...TOLD ME ALL KINDS OF THINGS.
AND MUCH OF IT WAS...
...ABOUT YOU, MR. KUROSAKI.

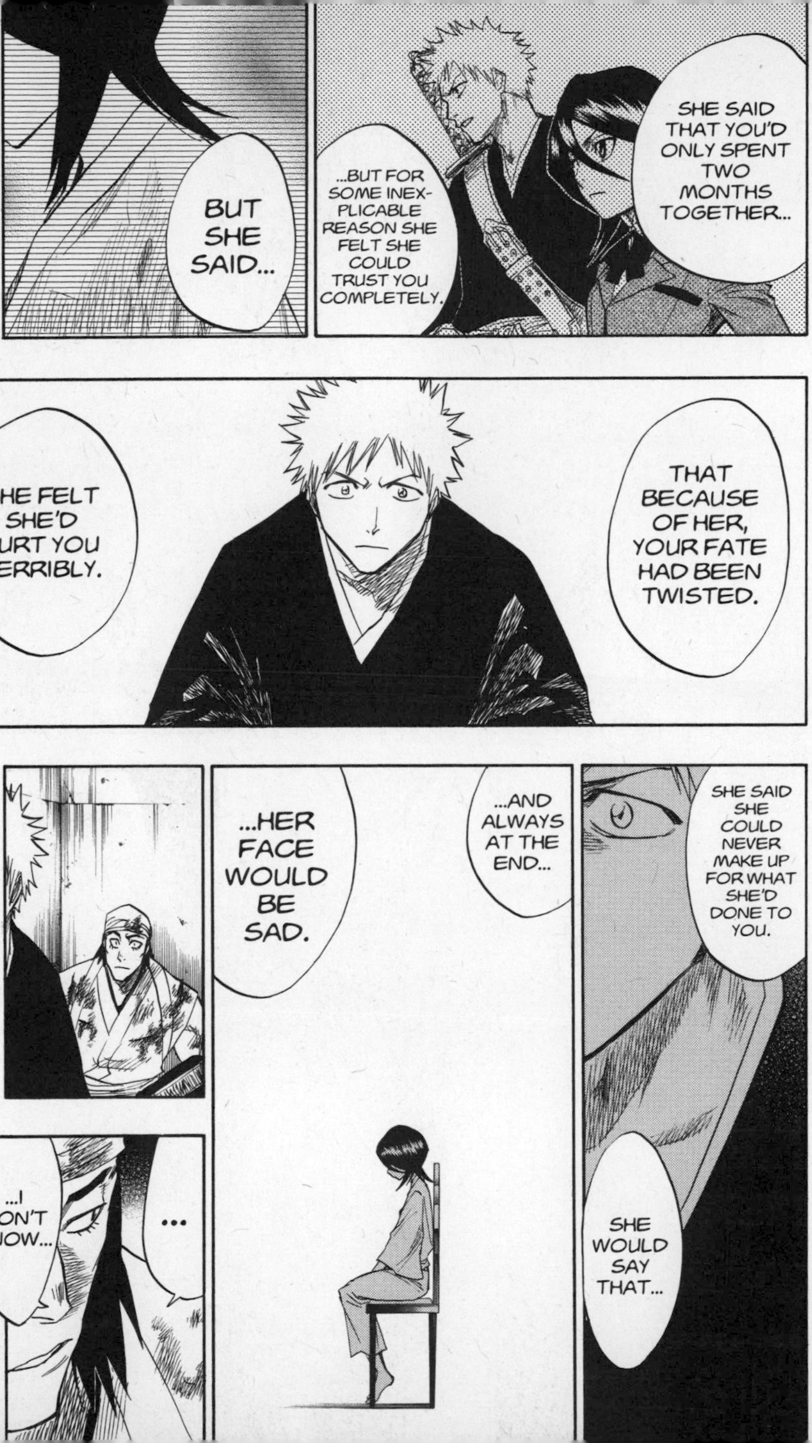
SHE SAID THAT YOU'D ONLY SPENT TWO MONTHS TOGETHER...
...BUT FOR SOME INEXPLICABLE REASON SHE FELT SHE COULD TRUST YOU COMPLETELY.
BUT SHE SAID...
THAT BECAUSE OF HER, YOUR FATE HAD BEEN TWISTED.
SHE FELT SHE'D HURT YOU TERRIBLY.
SHE SAID SHE COULD NEVER MAKE UP FOR WHAT SHE'D DONE TO YOU.
SHE WOULD SAY THAT...
...AND ALWAYS AT THE END...
...HER FACE WOULD BE SAD.
...
...I DON'T KNOW...

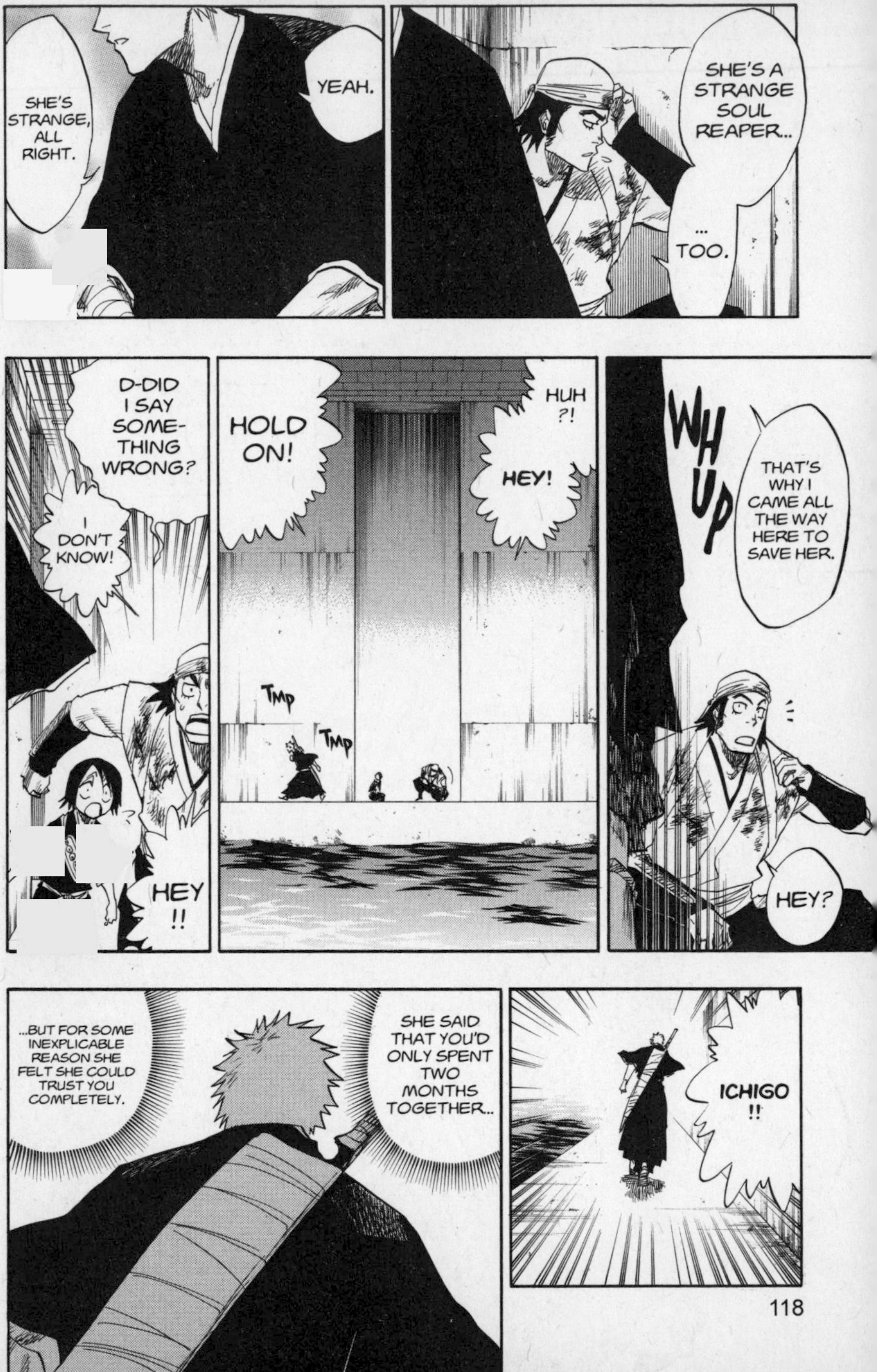
SHE'S A STRANGE SOUL REAPER...
... TOO.
YEAH.
SHE'S STRANGE, ALL RIGHT.
WHUP
THAT'S WHY I CAME ALL THE WAY HERE TO SAVE HER.
HEY?
HUH ?!
HEY!
HOLD ON!
TMP
TMP
D-DID I SAY SOME-THING WRONG?
I DON'T KNOW!
HEY !!
ICHIGO !!
SHE SAID THAT YOU'D ONLY SPENT TWO MONTHS TOGETHER..
...BUT FOR SOME INEXPLICABLE REASON SHE FELT SHE COULD TRUST YOU COMPLETELY.

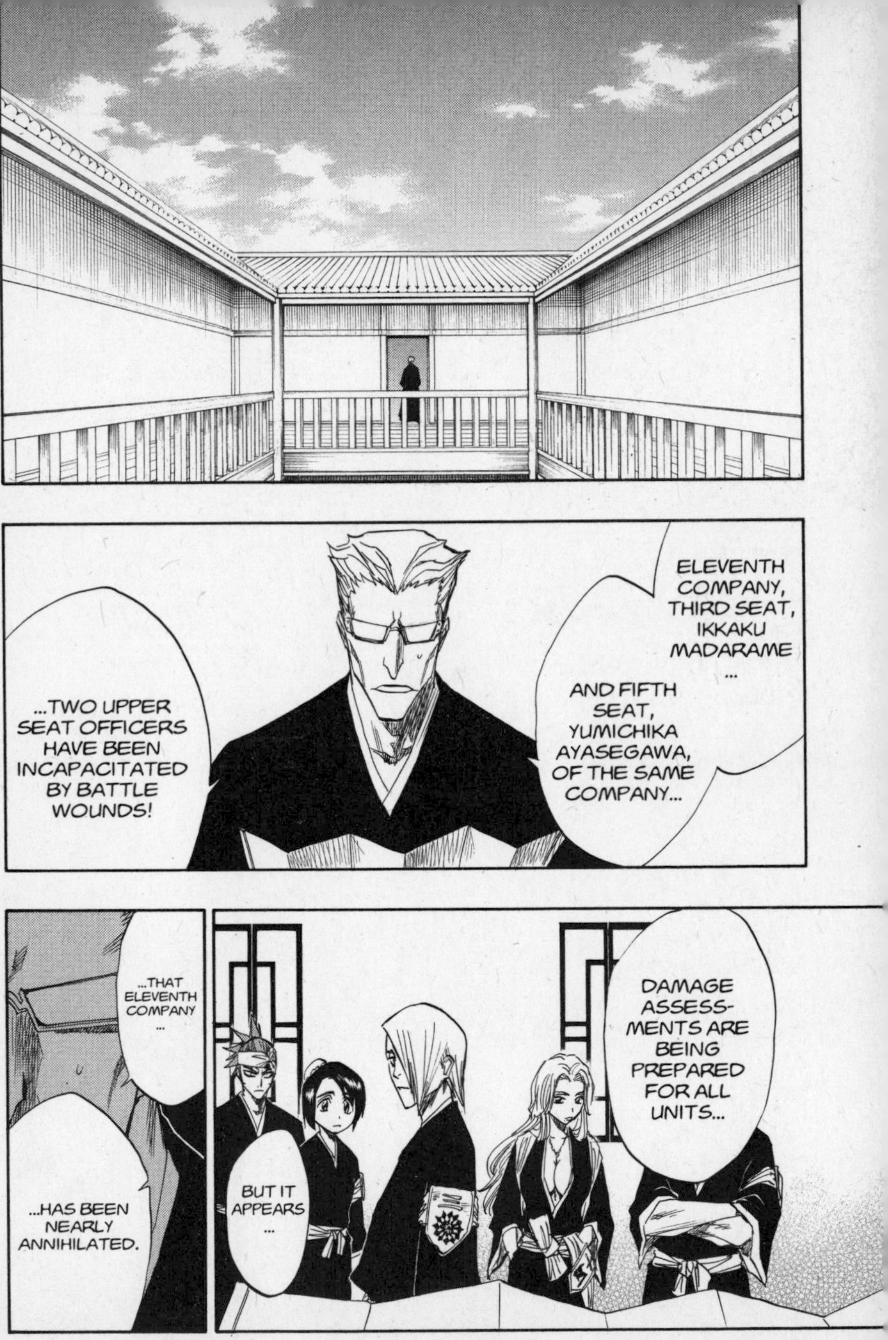
ELEVENTH COMPANY, THIRD SEAT, IKKAKU MADARAME ...
AND FIFTH SEAT, YUMICHIKA AYASEGAWA, OF THE SAME COMPANY...
...TWO UPPER SEAT OFFICERS HAVE BEEN INCAPACITATED BY BATTLE WOUNDS!
DAMAGE ASSESS-MENTS ARE BEING PREPARED FOR ALL UNITS...
BUT IT APPEARS ...
...THAT ELEVENTH COMPANY ...
...HAS BEEN NEARLY ANNIHILATED.

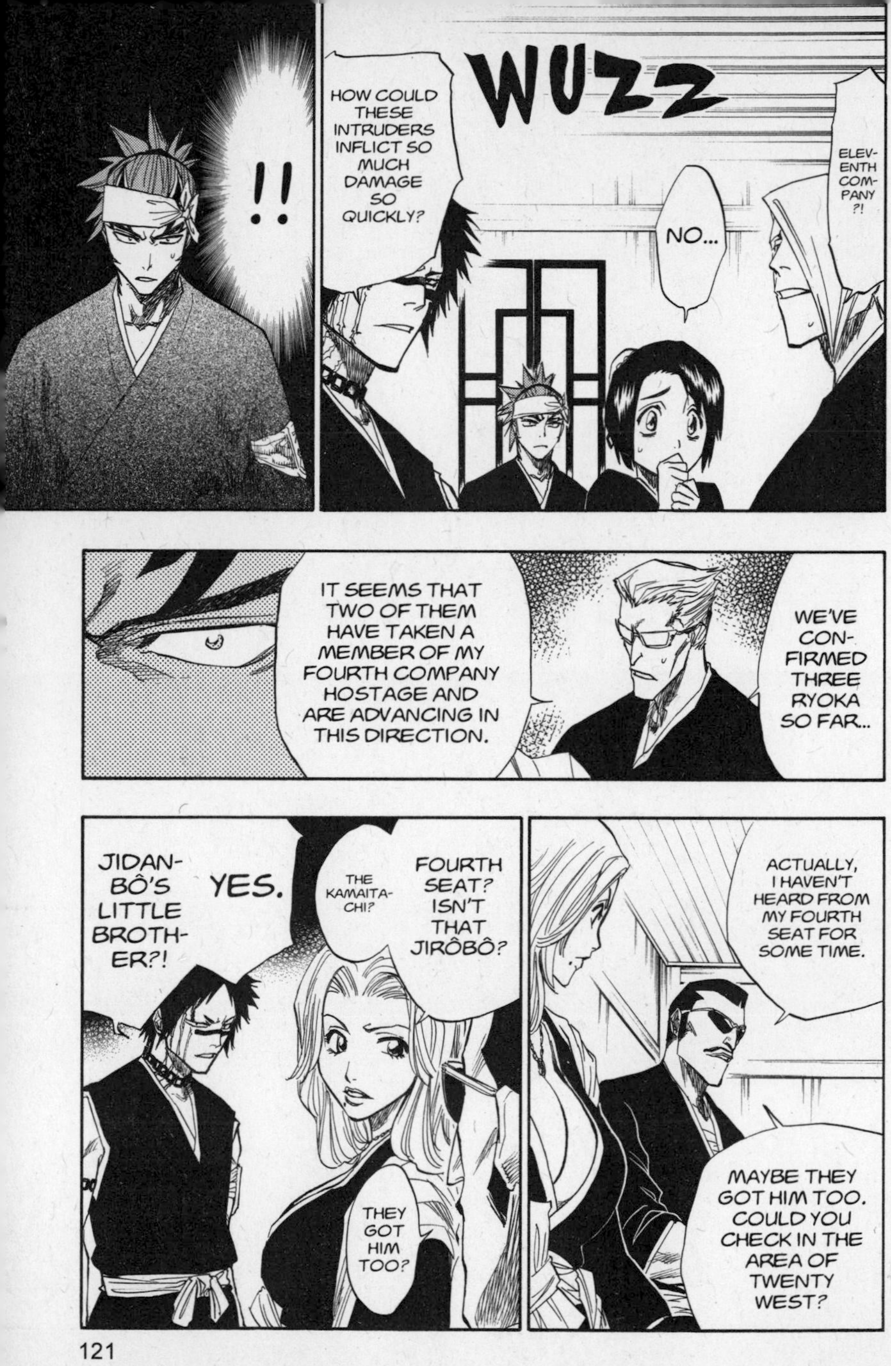
ELEVENTH COMPANY?!
WUZZ
NO...
HOW COULD THESE INTRUDERS INFLICT SO MUCH DAMAGE SO QUICKLY?
!!
WE'VE CONFIRMED THREE RYOKA SO FAR...
IT SEEMS THAT TWO OF THEM HAVE TAKEN A MEMBER OF MY FOURTH COMPANY HOSTAGE AND ARE ADVANCING IN THIS DIRECTION.
ACTUALLY, I HAVEN'T HEARD FROM MY FOURTH SEAT FOR SOME TIME.
MAYBE THEY GOT HIM TOO. COULD YOU CHECK IN THE AREA OF TWENTY WEST?
FOURTH SEAT? ISN'T THAT JIRÔBÔ?
THE KAMAITACHI?
YES.
JIDANBÔ'S LITTLE BROTHER?!
THEY GOT HIM TOO?

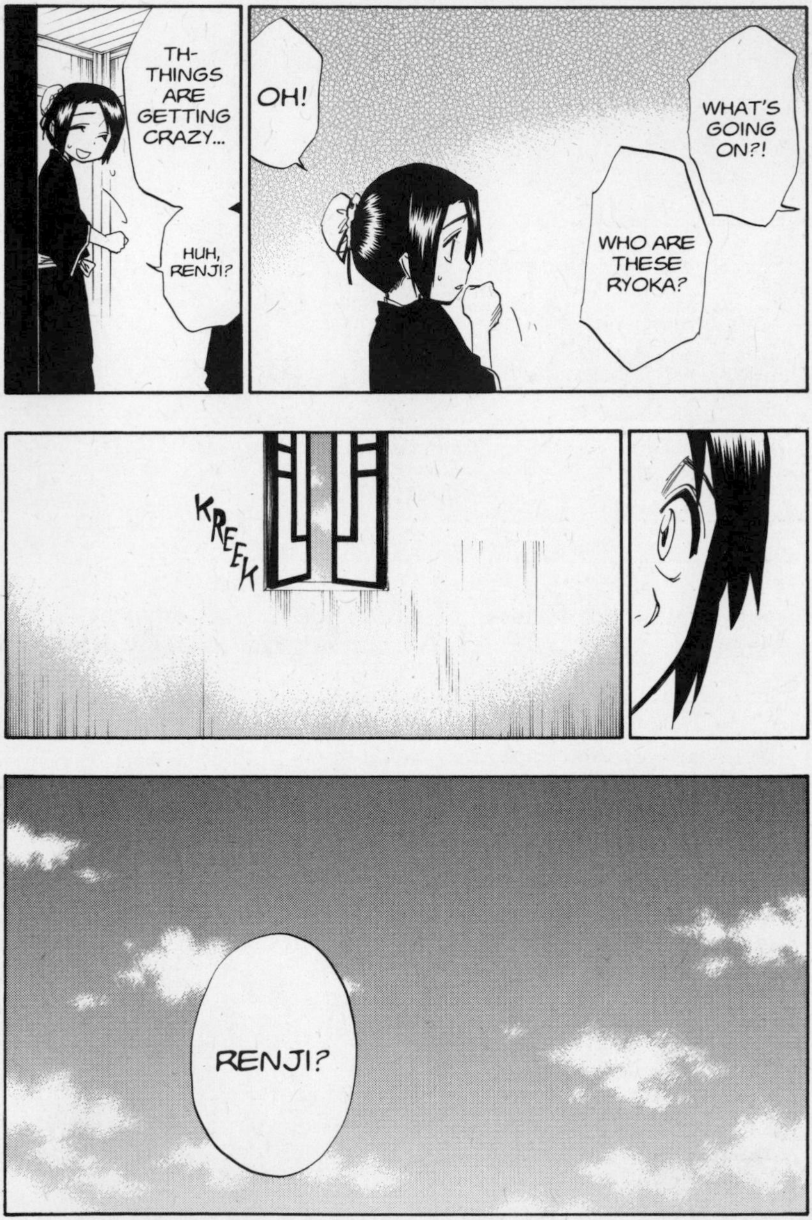
WHAT'S GOING ON?!
WHO ARE THESE RYOKA?
OH!
TH-THINGS ARE GETTING CRAZY...
HUH, RENJI?
KREEEK
RENJI?

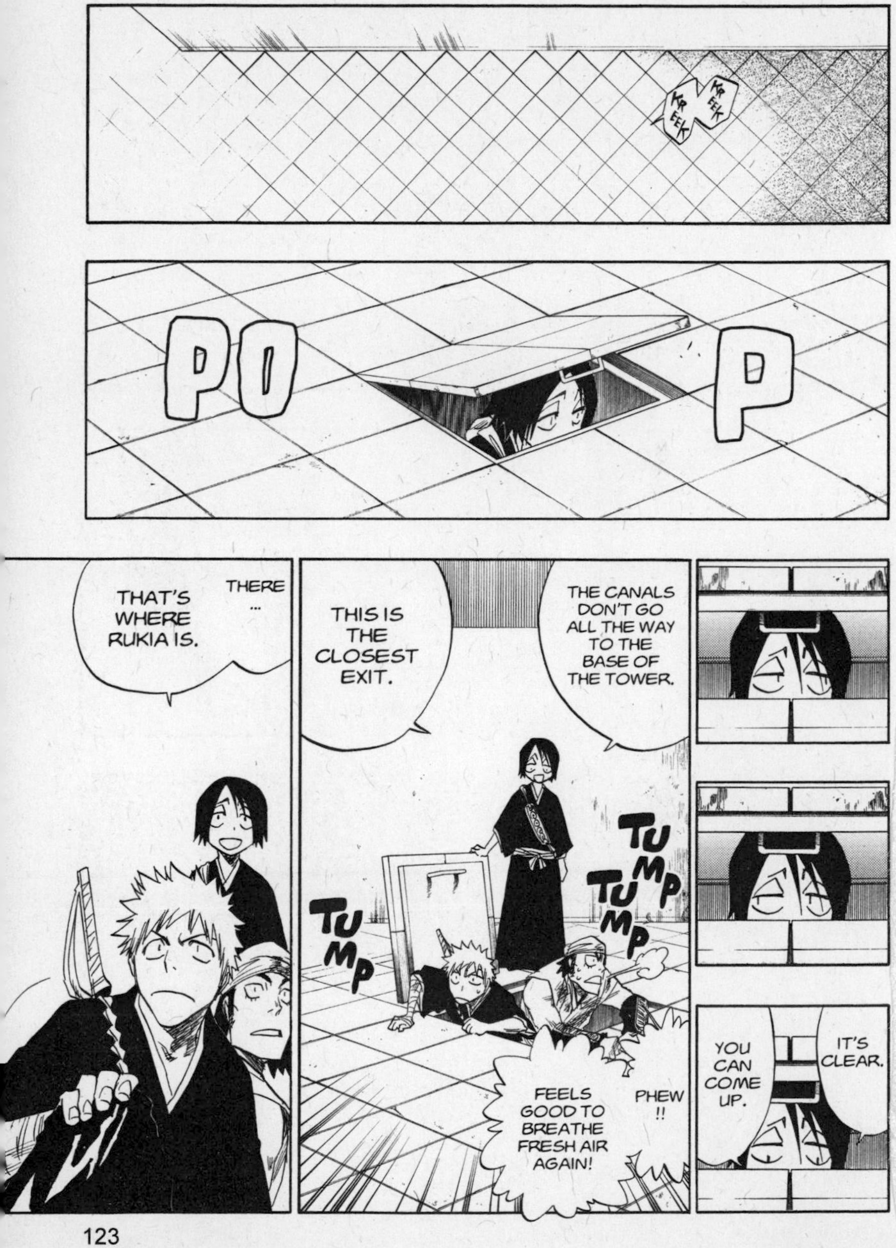
KREEK KREEK
POP
IT'S CLEAR.
YOU CAN COME UP.
THE CANALS DON'T GO ALL THE WAY TO THE BASE OF THE TOWER.
THIS IS THE CLOSEST EXIT.
TUMP TUMP
TUMP
PHEW!!
FEELS GOOD TO BREATHE FRESH AIR AGAIN!
THERE...
THAT'S WHERE RUKIA IS.

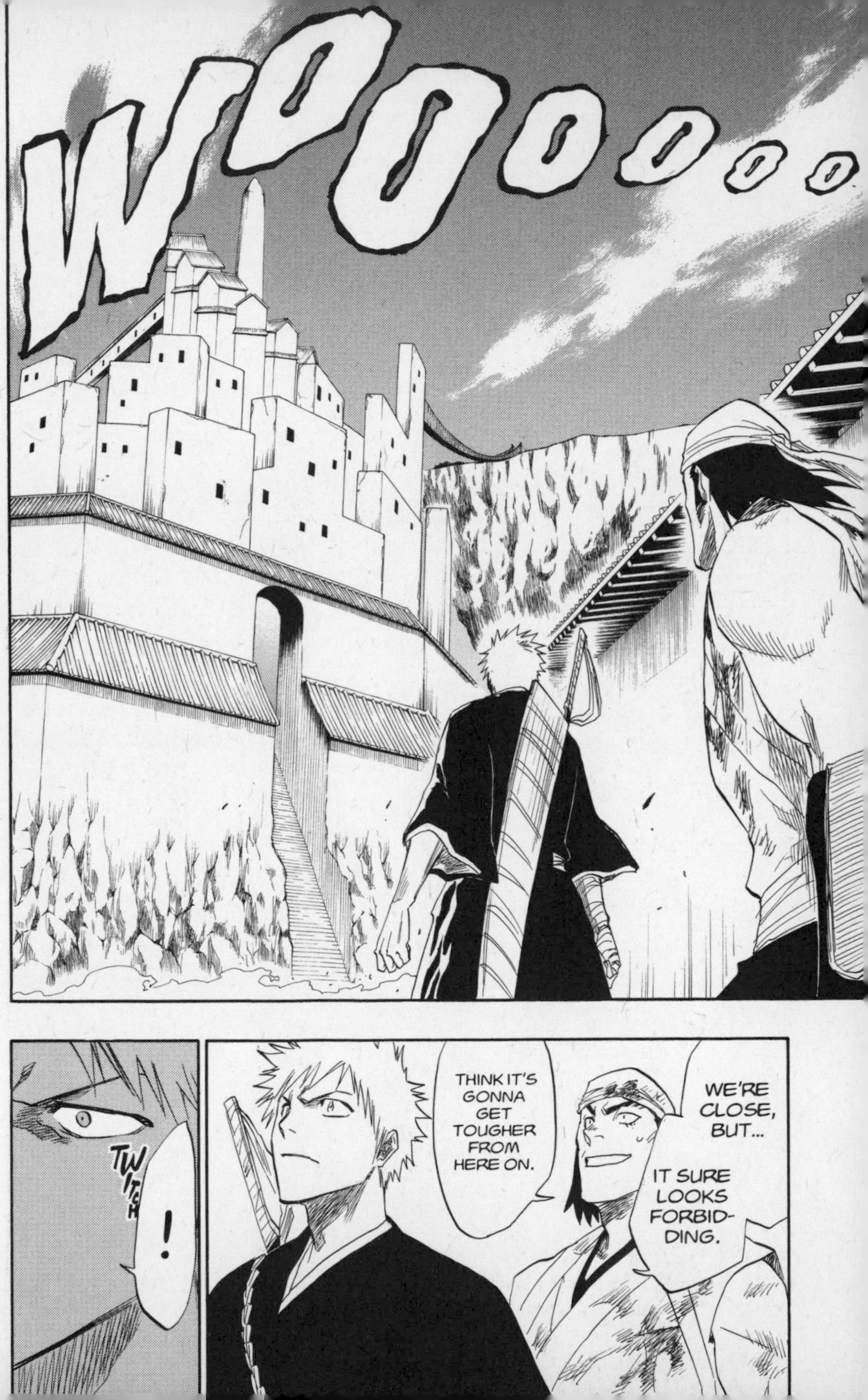
WOOOOOO...
WE'RE CLOSE, BUT...
IT SURE LOOKS FORBID-DING.
THINK IT'S GONNA GET TOUGHER FROM HERE ON.
TWITCH
!

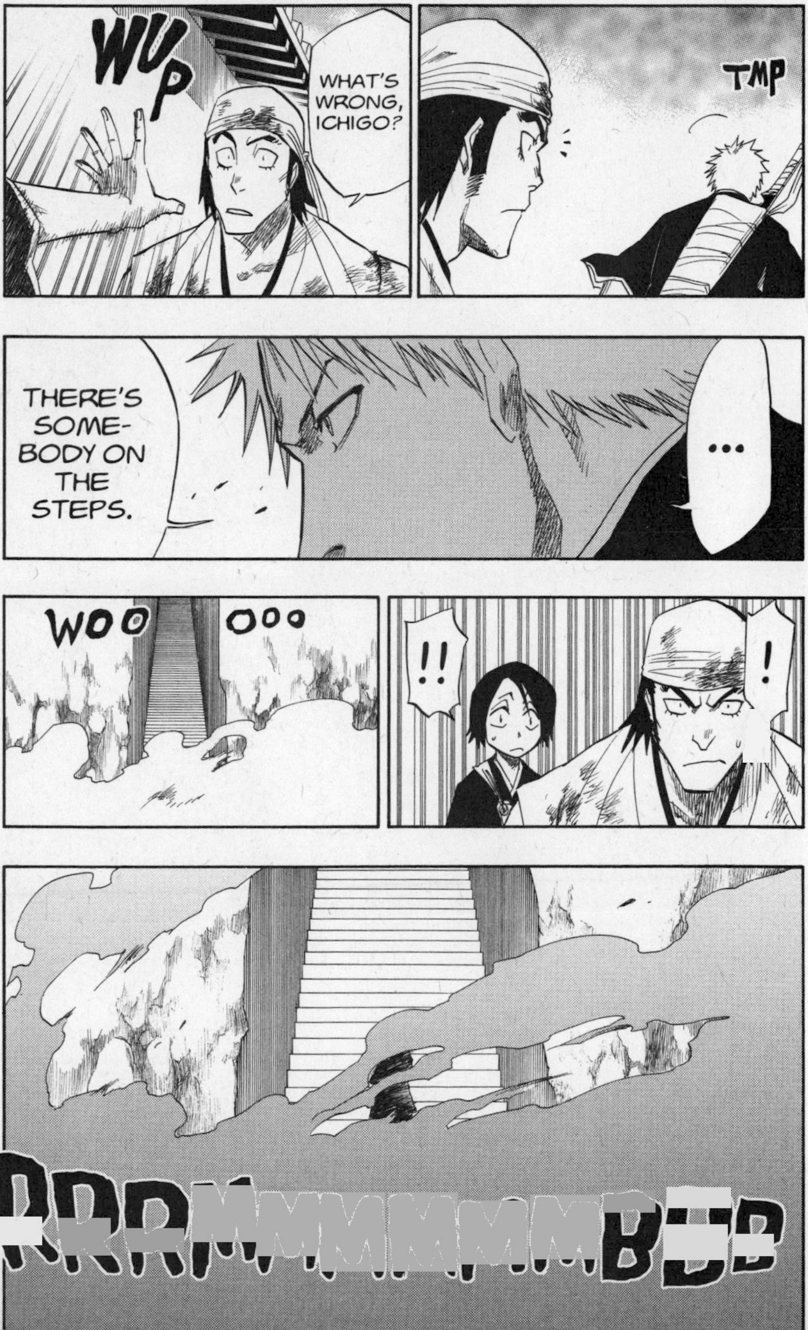
TMP
WUP
WHAT'S WRONG, ICHIGO?
...
THERE'S SOME-BODY ON THE STEPS.
!
!!
WOO OOO
RRRMMMMMMMMBBB

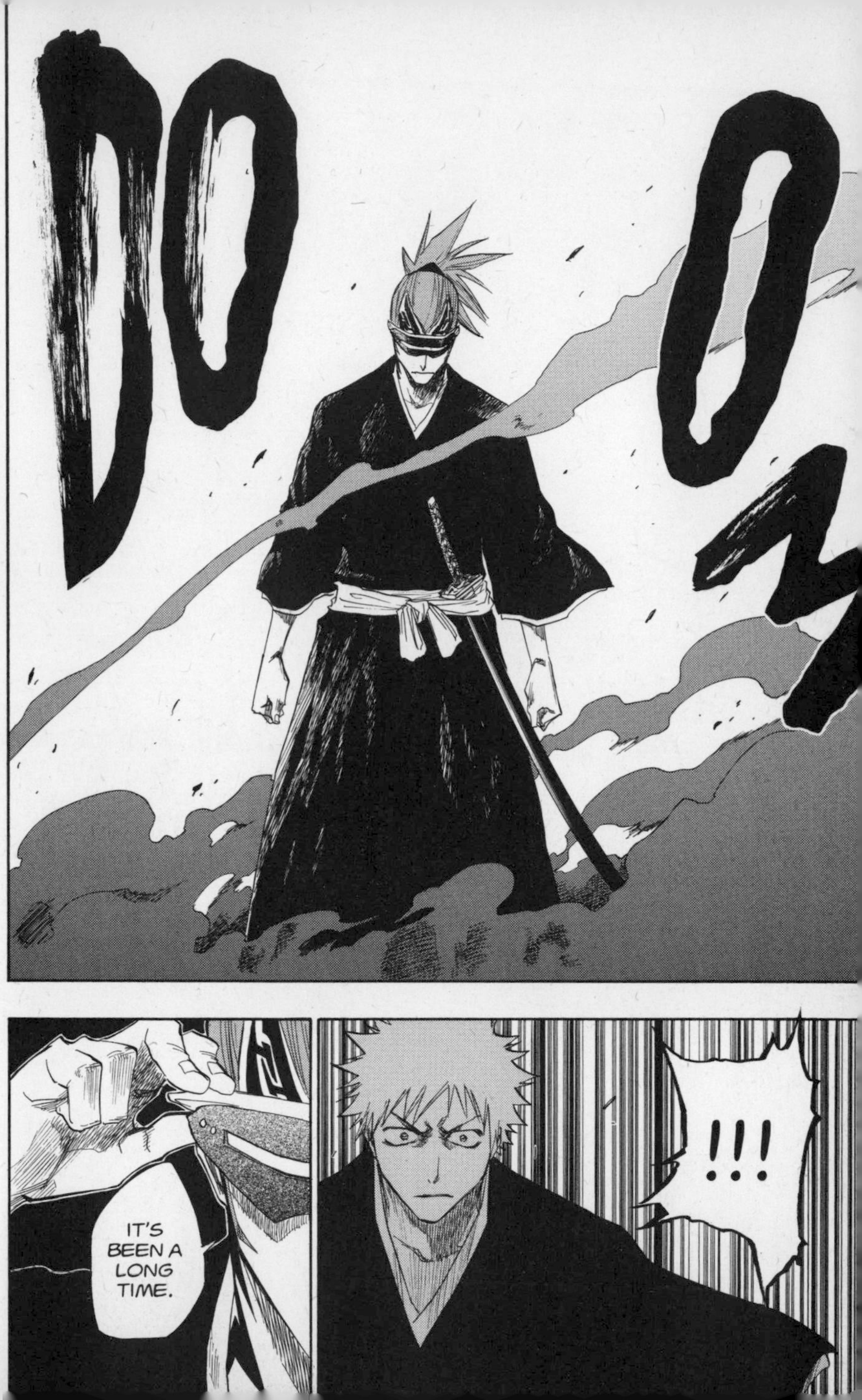
DOOM
!!!
IT'S BEEN A LONG TIME.

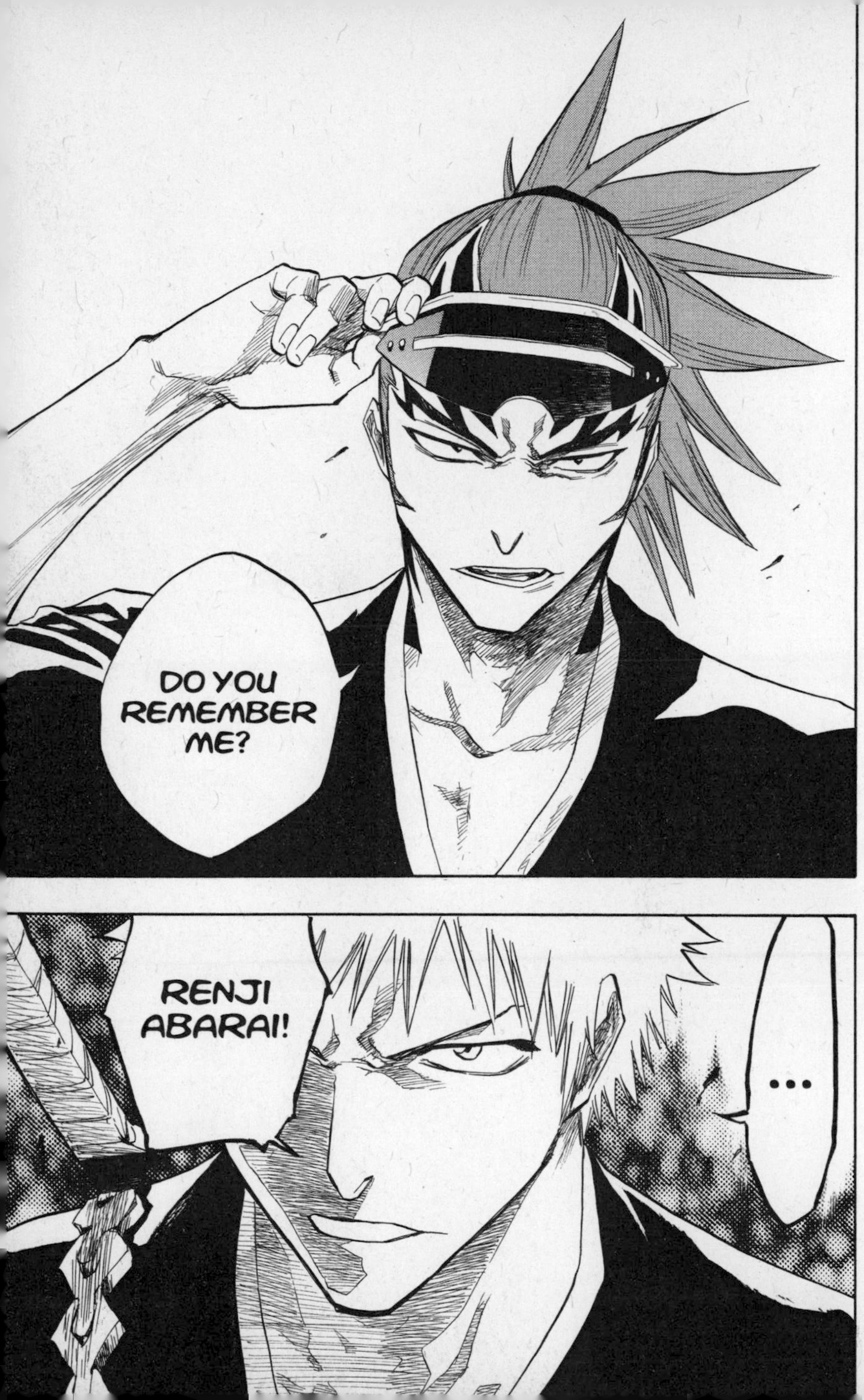
DO YOU REMEMBER ME?
...
RENJI ABARAI!

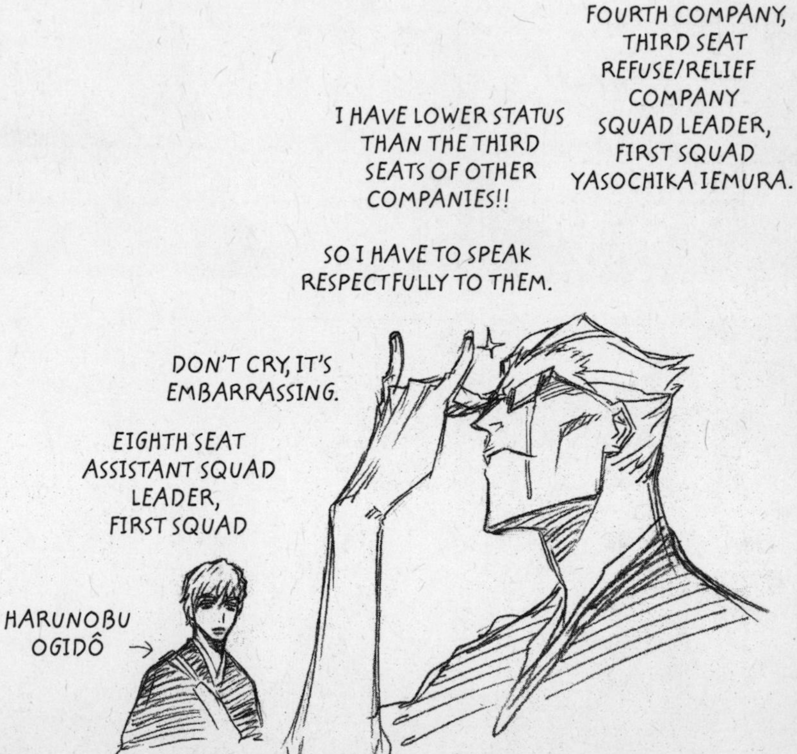
FOURTH COMPANY, THIRD SEAT REFUSE/RELIEF COMPANY SQUAD LEADER, FIRST SQUAD YASOCHIKA IEMURA.
I HAVE LOWER STATUS THAN THE THIRD SEATS OF OTHER COMPANIES!!
SO I HAVE TO SPEAK RESPECTFULLY TO THEM.
DON'T CRY, IT'S EMBARRASSING.
EIGHTH SEAT ASSISTANT SQUAD LEADER, FIRST SQUAD
HARUNOBU OGIDÔ

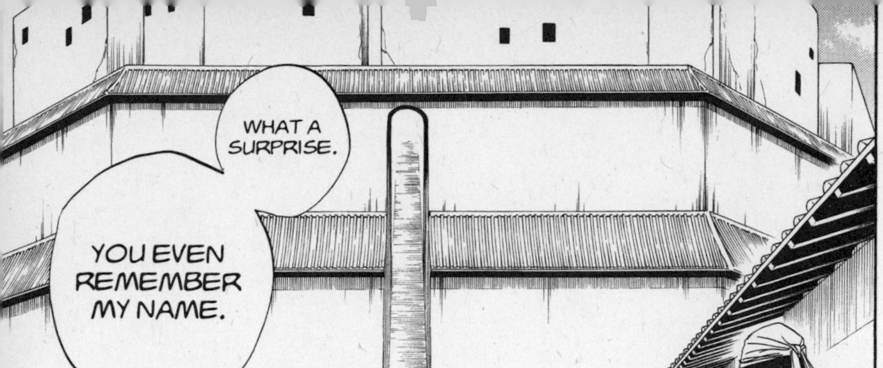
WHAT A SURPRISE.
YOU EVEN REMEMBER MY NAME.

95. CRUSH

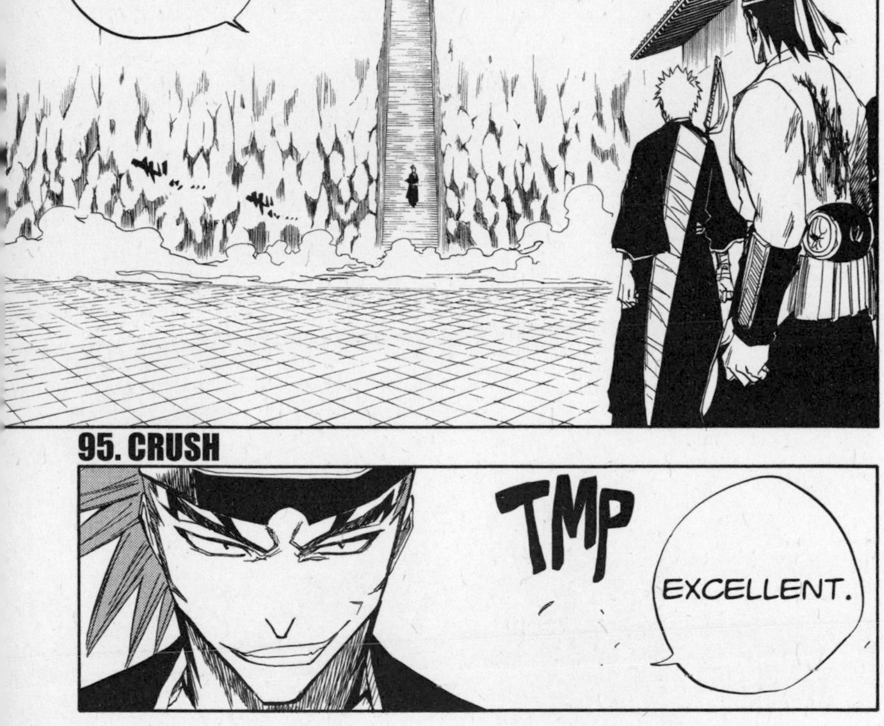
TMP
EXCELLENT.

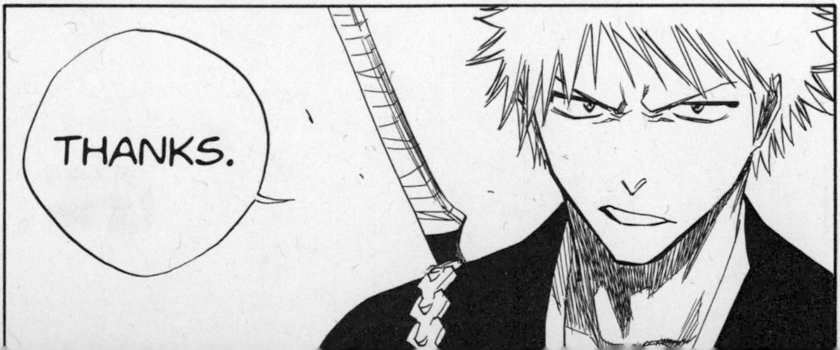
THANKS.

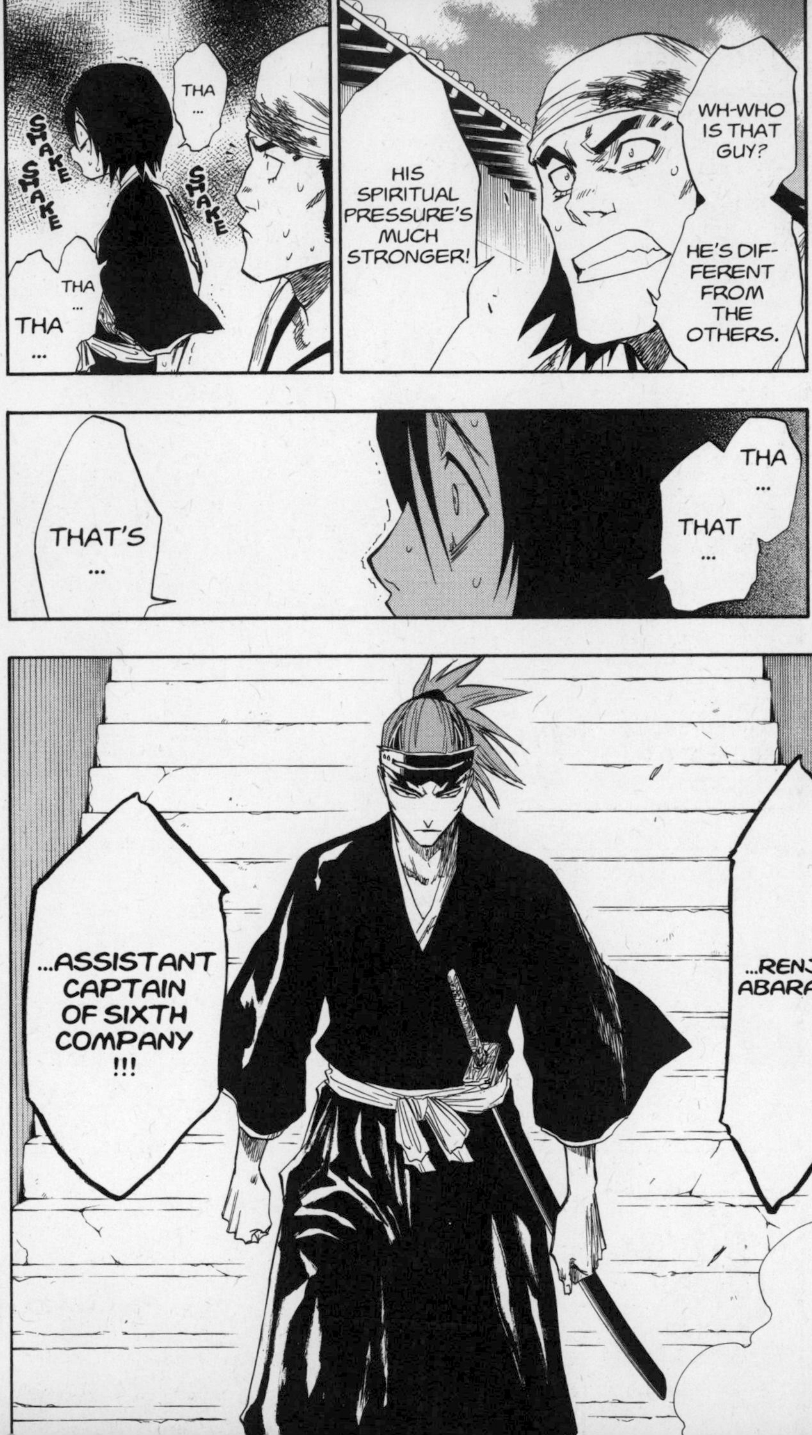
WH-WHO IS THAT GUY?
HE'S DIF-FERENT FROM THE OTHERS.
HIS SPIRITUAL PRESSURE'S MUCH STRONGER!
THA ...
SHAKE SHAKE
SHAKE
THA ...
THA ...
THA ... THAT ...
THAT'S ...
...RENJI ABARAI...
...ASSISTANT CAPTAIN OF SIXTH COMPANY !!!

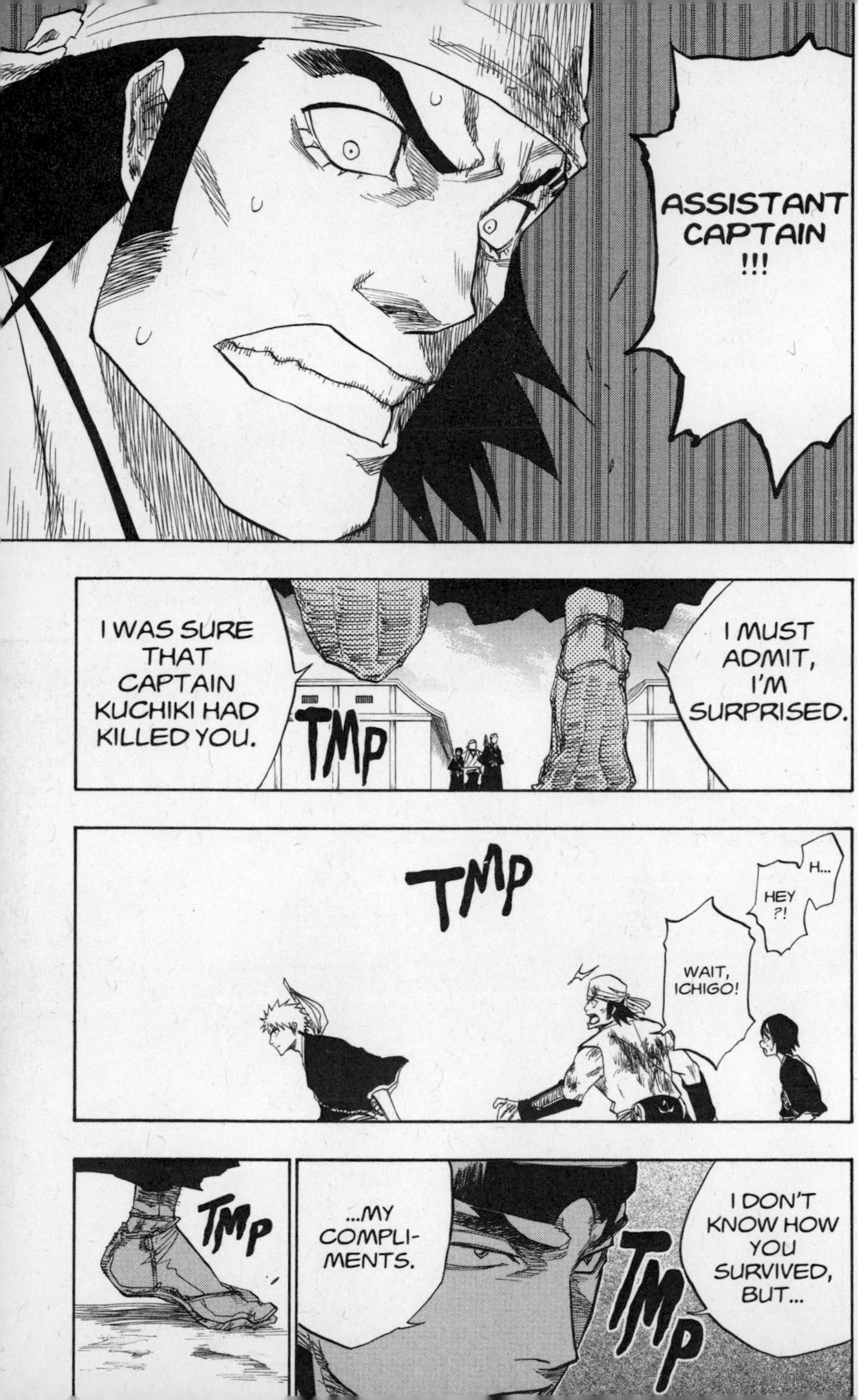
ASSISTANT CAPTAIN !!!
I MUST ADMIT, I'M SURPRISED.
I WAS SURE THAT CAPTAIN KUCHIKI HAD KILLED YOU.
TMP
TMP
H... HEY ?!
WAIT, ICHIGO!
I DON'T KNOW HOW YOU SURVIVED, BUT...
TMP
...MY COMPLI-MENTS.
TMP

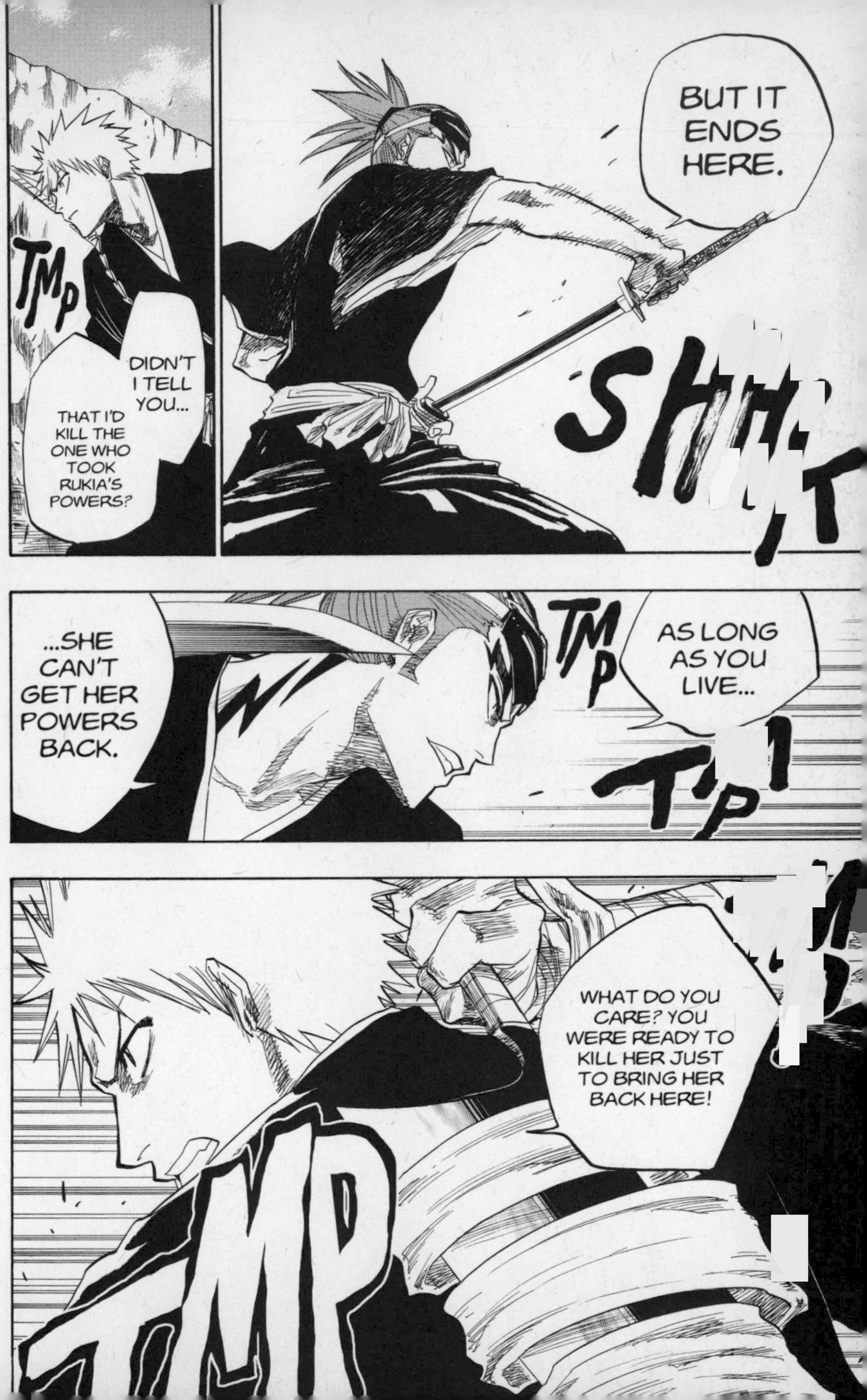
BUT IT ENDS HERE.
TMP
DIDN'T I TELL YOU...
THAT I'D KILL THE ONE WHO TOOK RUKIA'S POWERS?
AS LONG AS YOU LIVE...
TMP
...SHE CAN'T GET HER POWERS BACK.
WHAT DO YOU CARE? YOU WERE READY TO KILL HER JUST TO BRING HER BACK HERE!
TMP

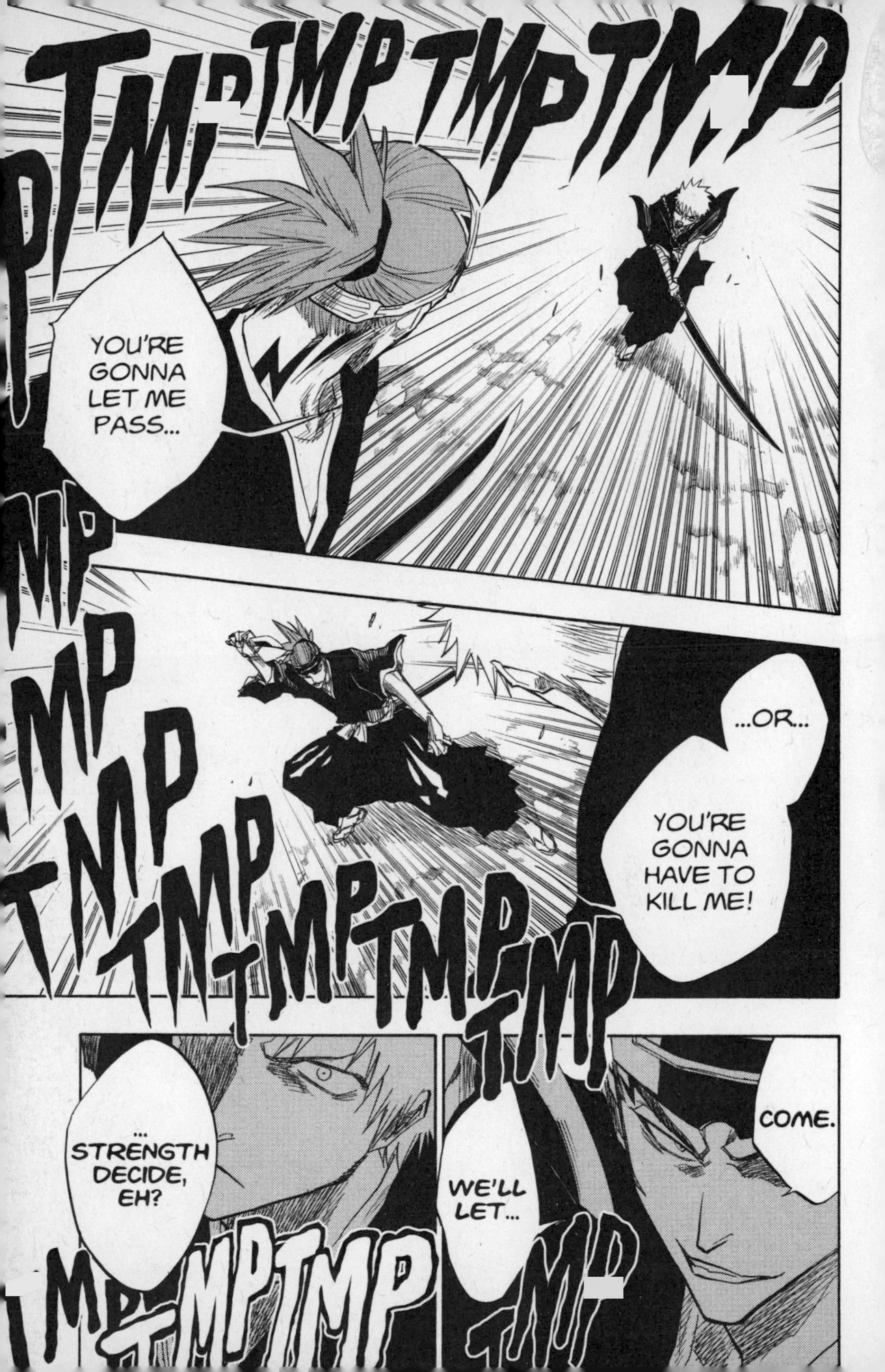
TMP TMP TMP TMP
YOU'RE GONNA LET ME PASS...
...OR...
YOU'RE GONNA HAVE TO KILL ME!
COME.
WE'LL LET...
... STRENGTH DECIDE, EH?

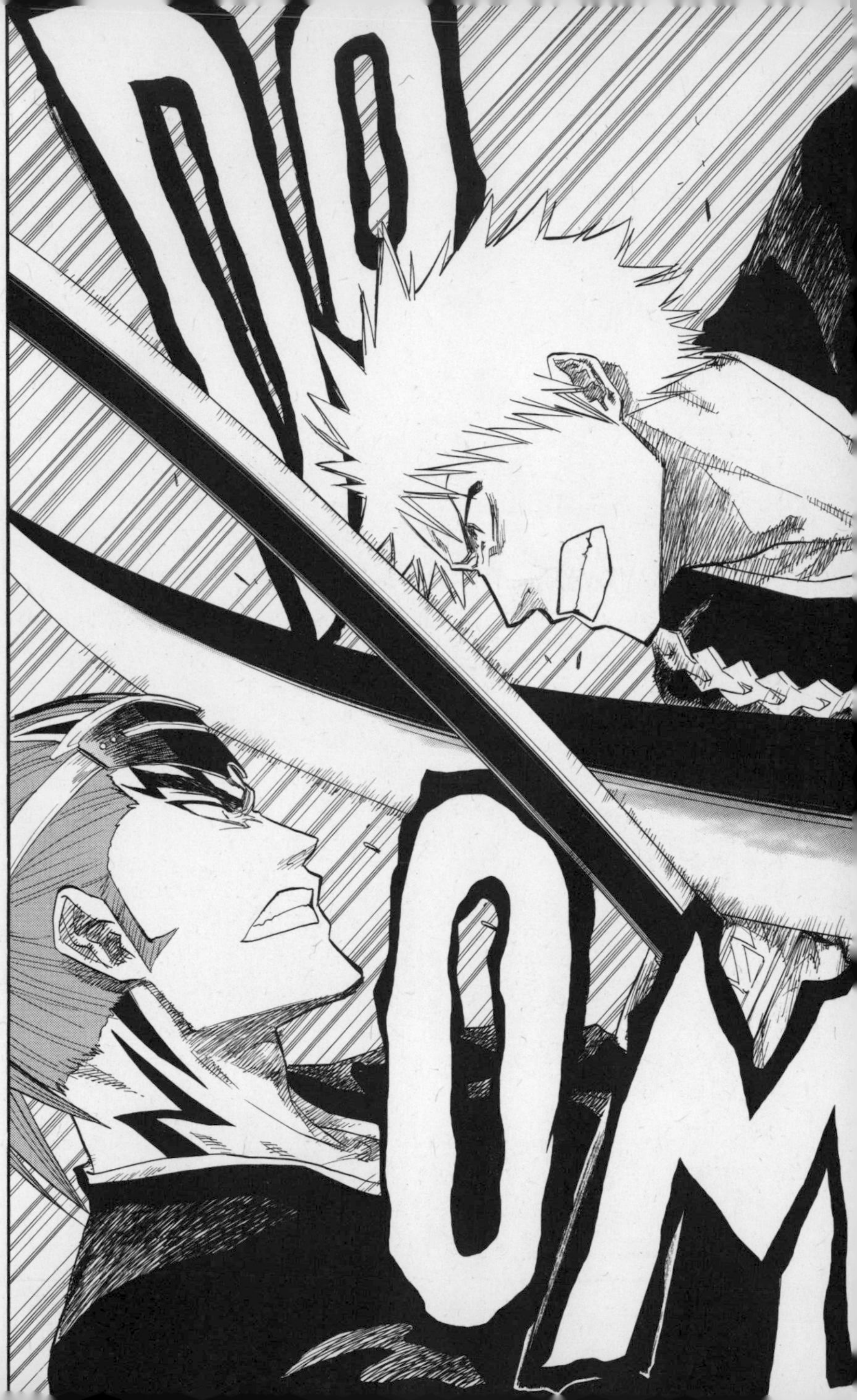
DOO
OM

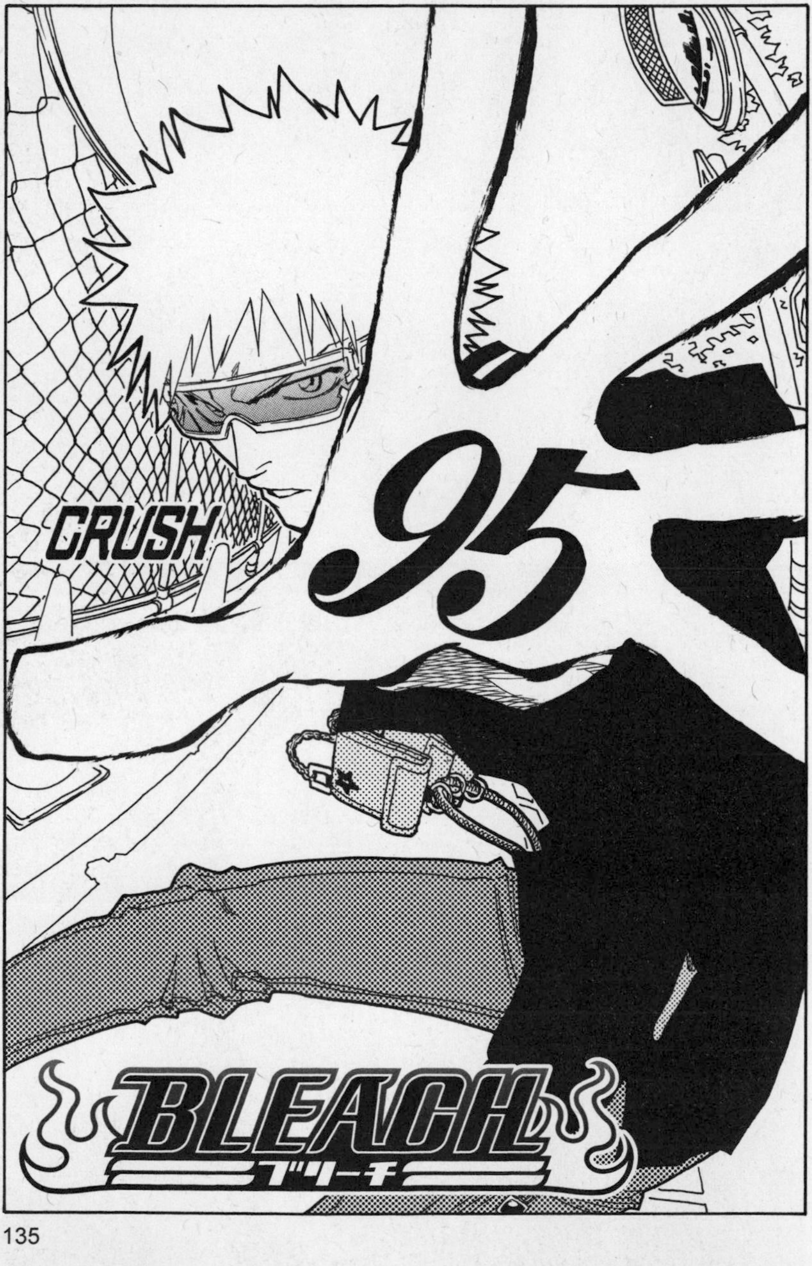
95
CRUSH
BLEACH
ブリーチ

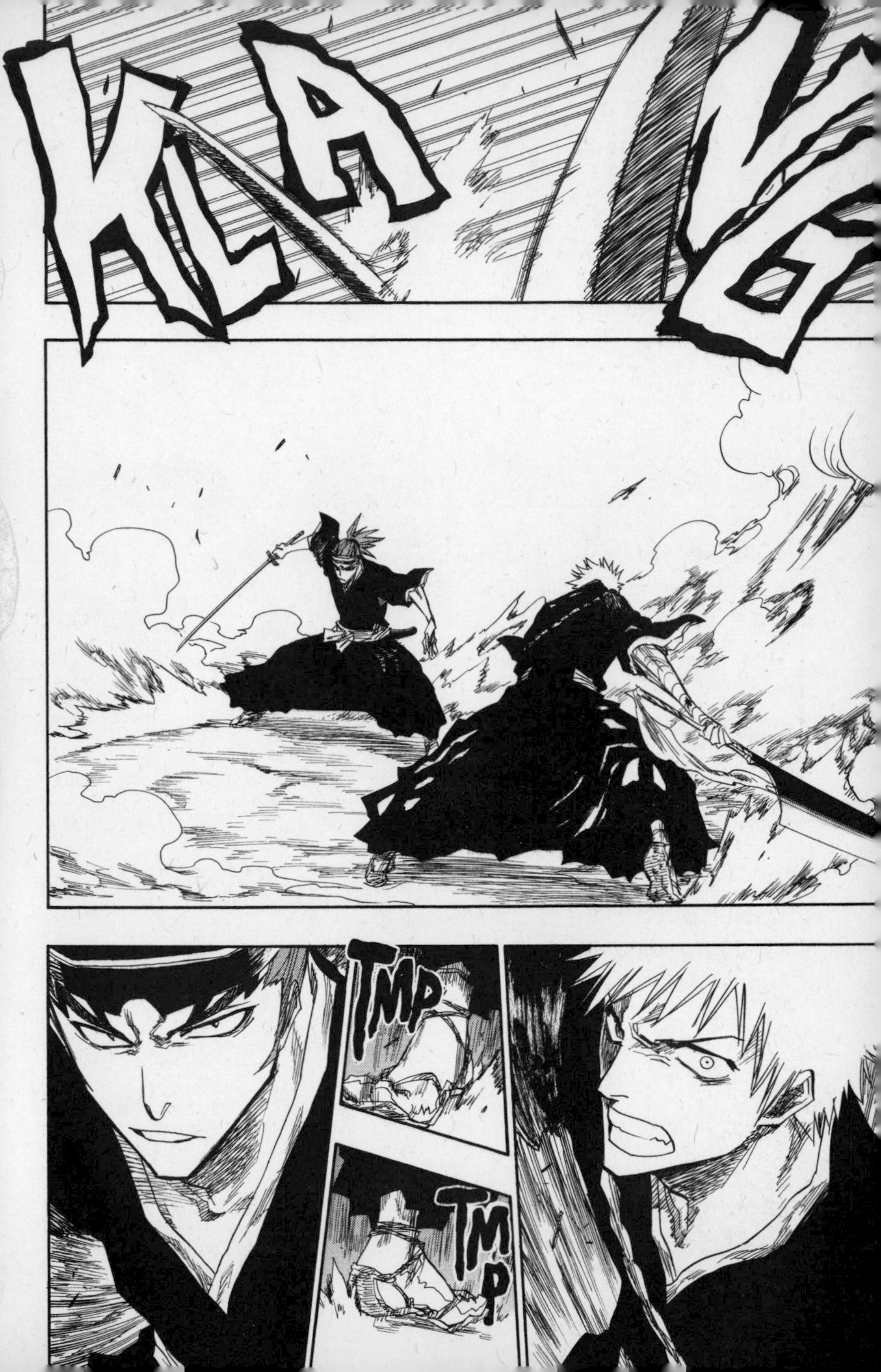
KLANG
TMP
TMP

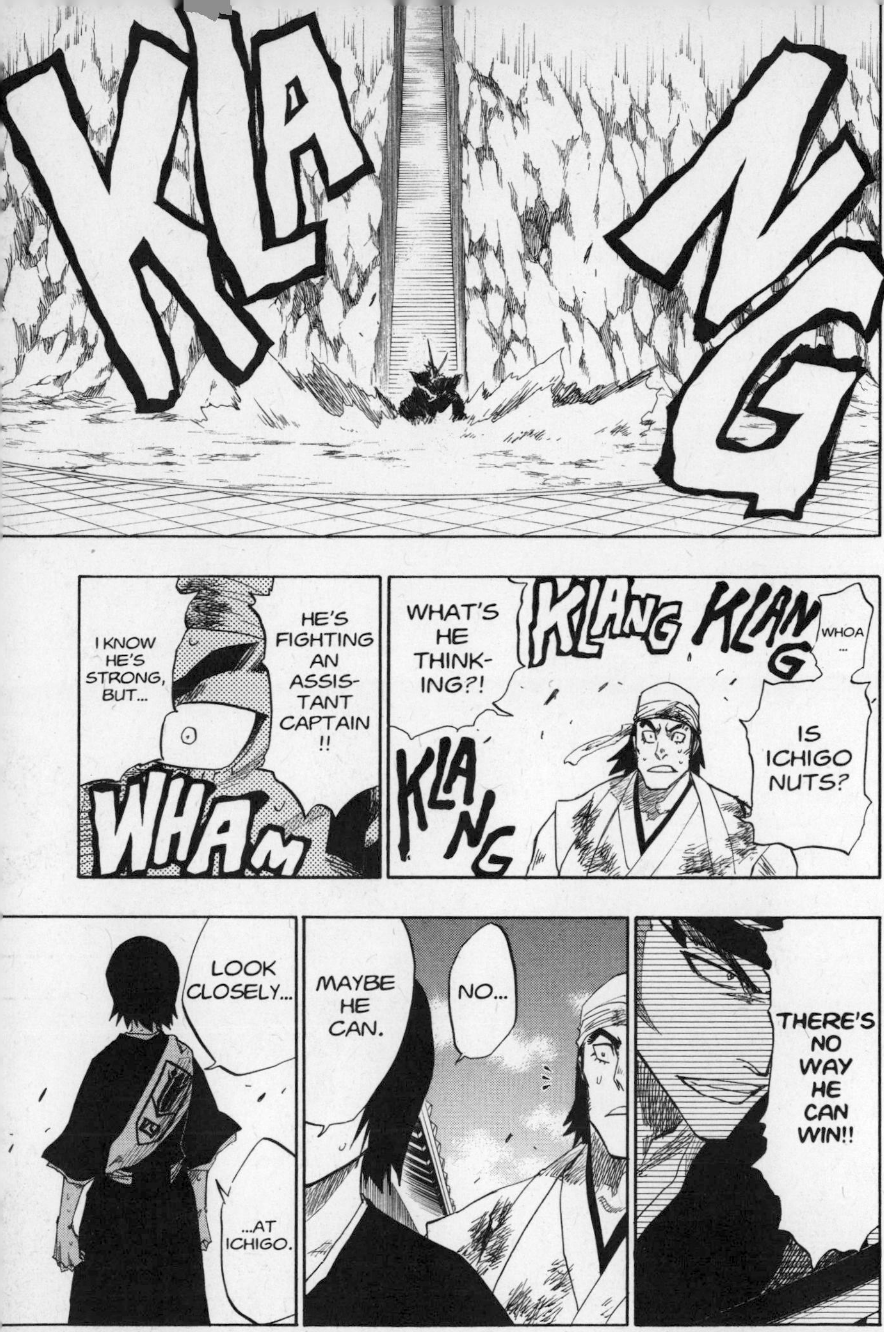
KLANG
WHOA...
KLANG KLANG
WHAT'S HE THINKING?!
IS ICHIGO NUTS?
KLANG
HE'S FIGHTING AN ASSISTANT CAPTAIN!!
I KNOW HE'S STRONG, BUT...
WHAM
THERE'S NO WAY HE CAN WIN!!
NO...
MAYBE HE CAN.
LOOK CLOSELY...
...AT ICHIGO.

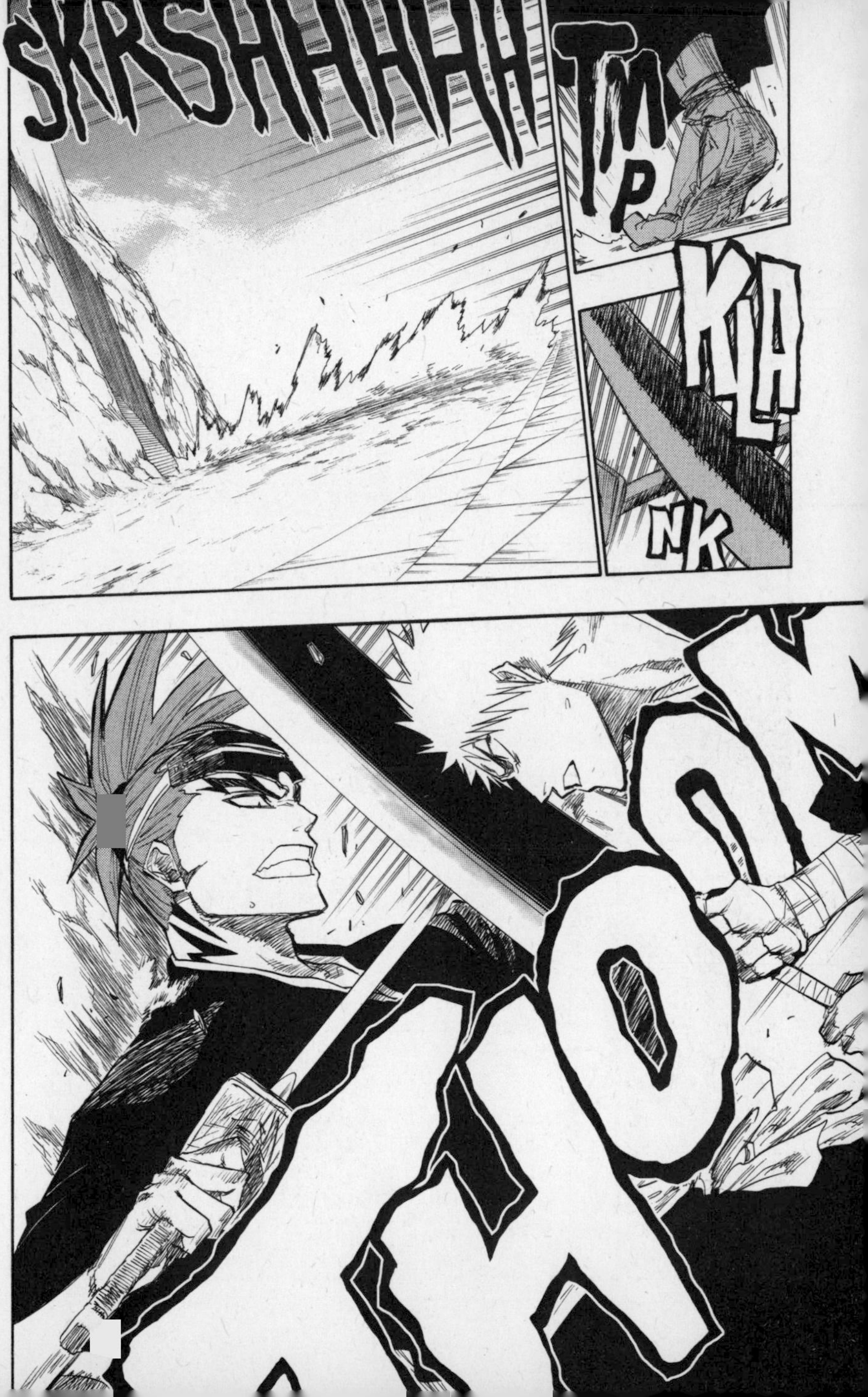
TMP
KLANK
SKRSHHHHH

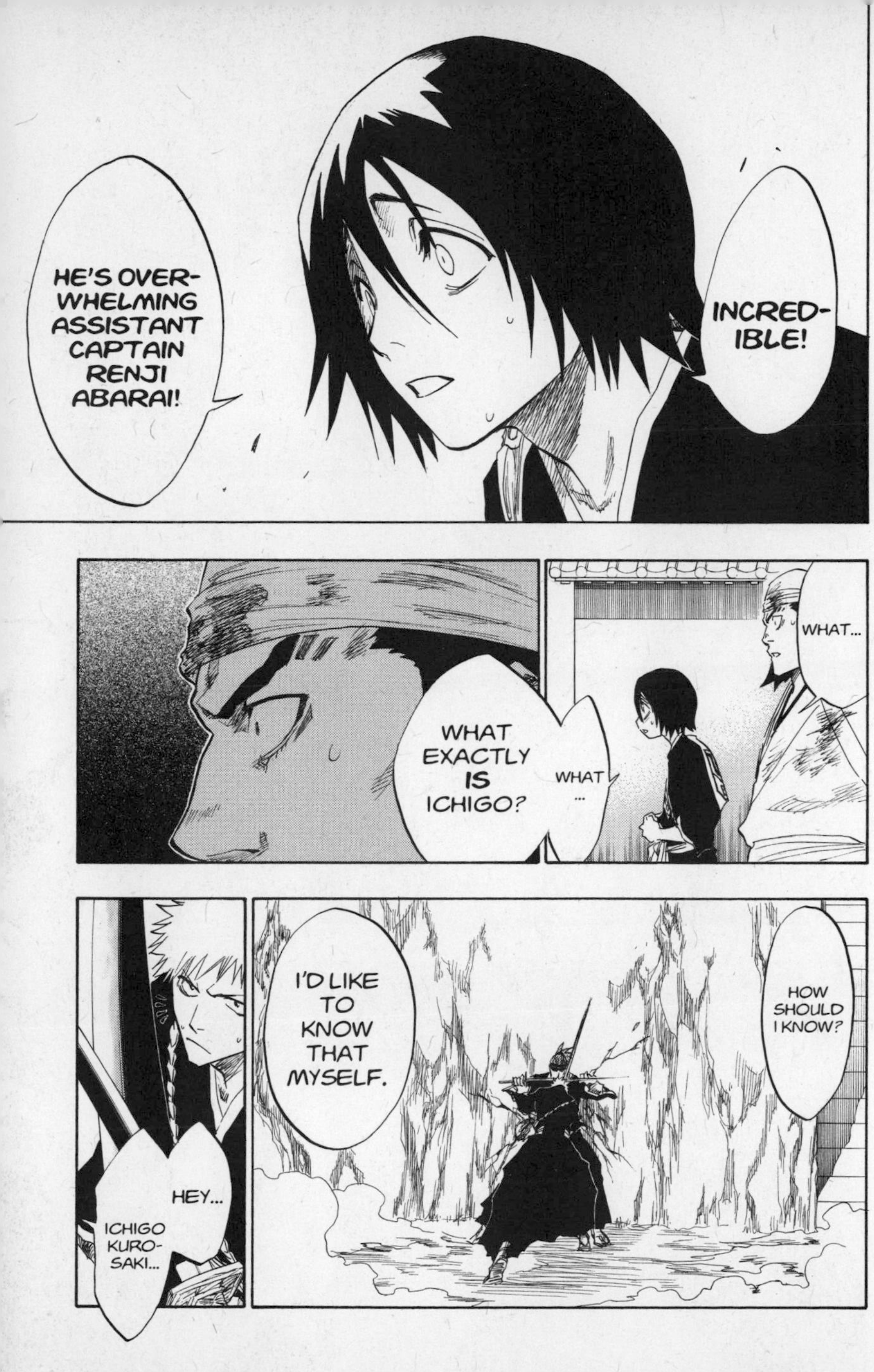
INCRED-IBLE!
HE'S OVER-WHELMING ASSISTANT CAPTAIN RENJI ABARAI!
WHAT...
WHAT ...
WHAT EXACTLY IS ICHIGO?
HOW SHOULD I KNOW?
I'D LIKE TO KNOW THAT MYSELF.
HEY...
ICHIGO KURO-SAKI...

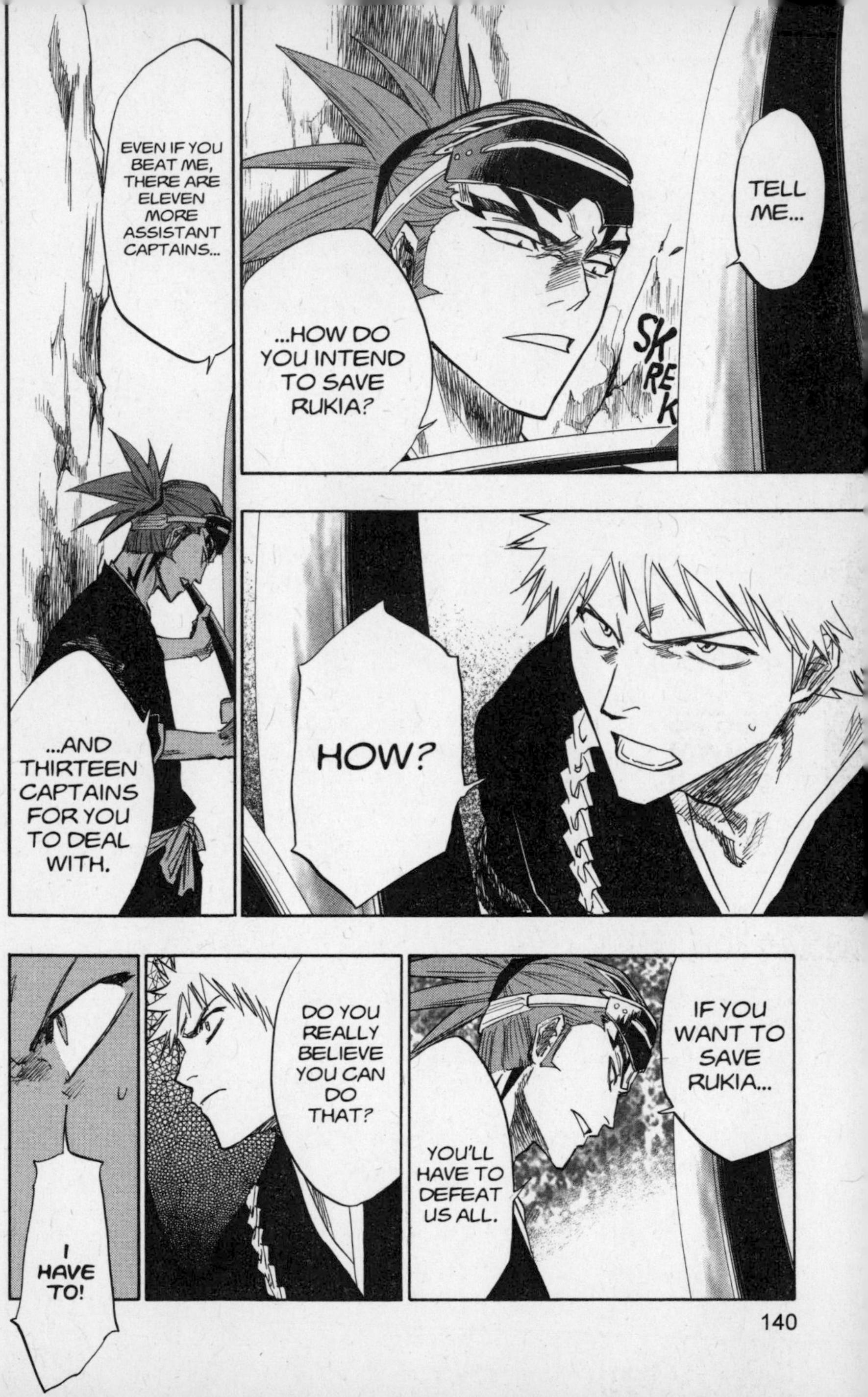
TELL ME...
SKREK
...HOW DO YOU INTEND TO SAVE RUKIA?
HOW?
EVEN IF YOU BEAT ME, THERE ARE ELEVEN MORE ASSISTANT CAPTAINS...
...AND THIRTEEN CAPTAINS FOR YOU TO DEAL WITH.
IF YOU WANT TO SAVE RUKIA...
YOU'LL HAVE TO DEFEAT US ALL.
DO YOU REALLY BELIEVE YOU CAN DO THAT?
I HAVE TO!

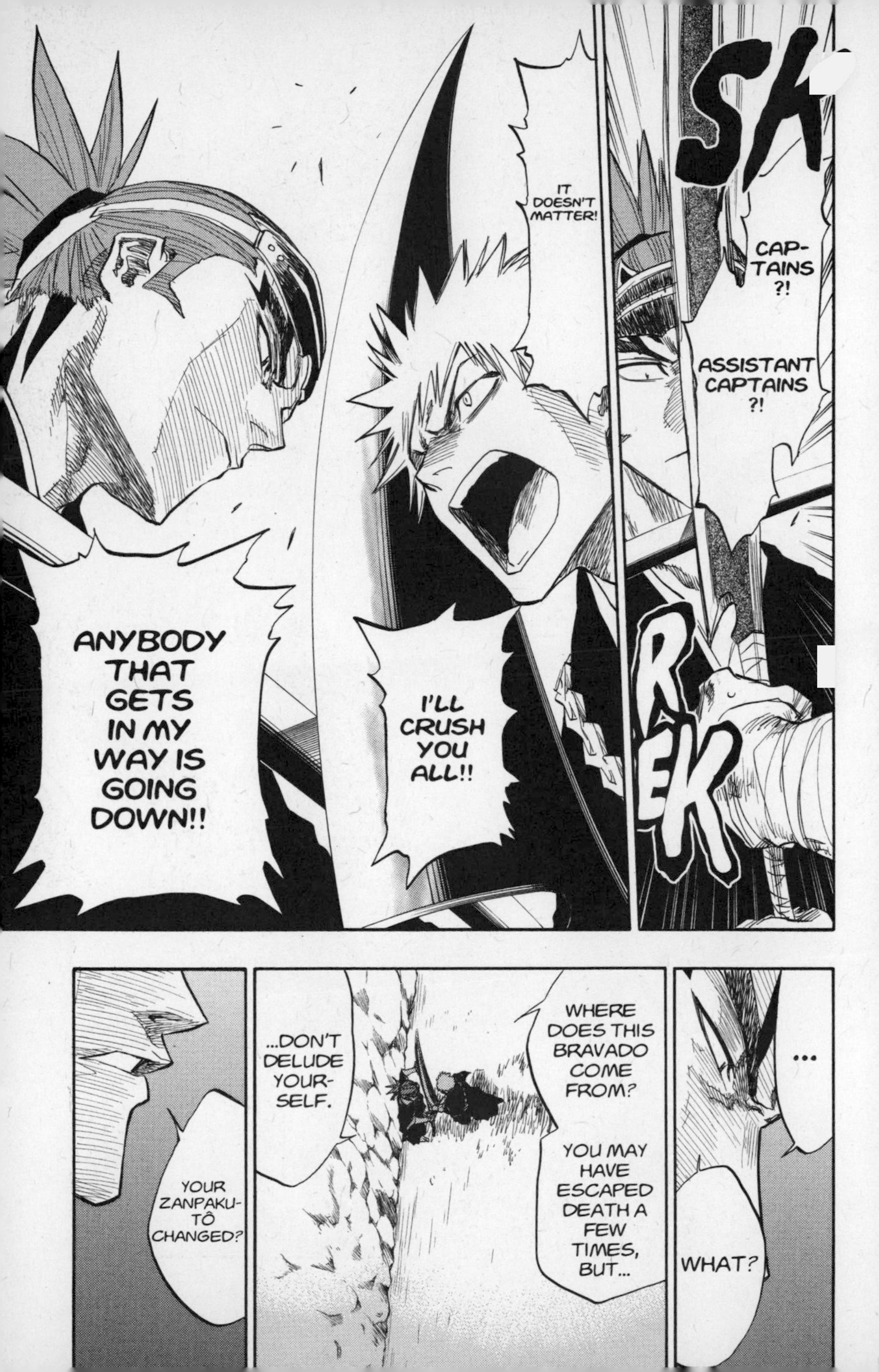
SKREK
CAPTAINS?!
ASSISTANT CAPTAINS?!
IT DOESN'T MATTER!
I'LL CRUSH YOU ALL!!
ANYBODY THAT GETS IN MY WAY IS GOING DOWN!!
...
WHAT?
WHERE DOES THIS BRAVADO COME FROM?
YOU MAY HAVE ESCAPED DEATH A FEW TIMES, BUT...
...DON'T DELUDE YOURSELF.
YOUR ZANPAKUTÔ CHANGED?

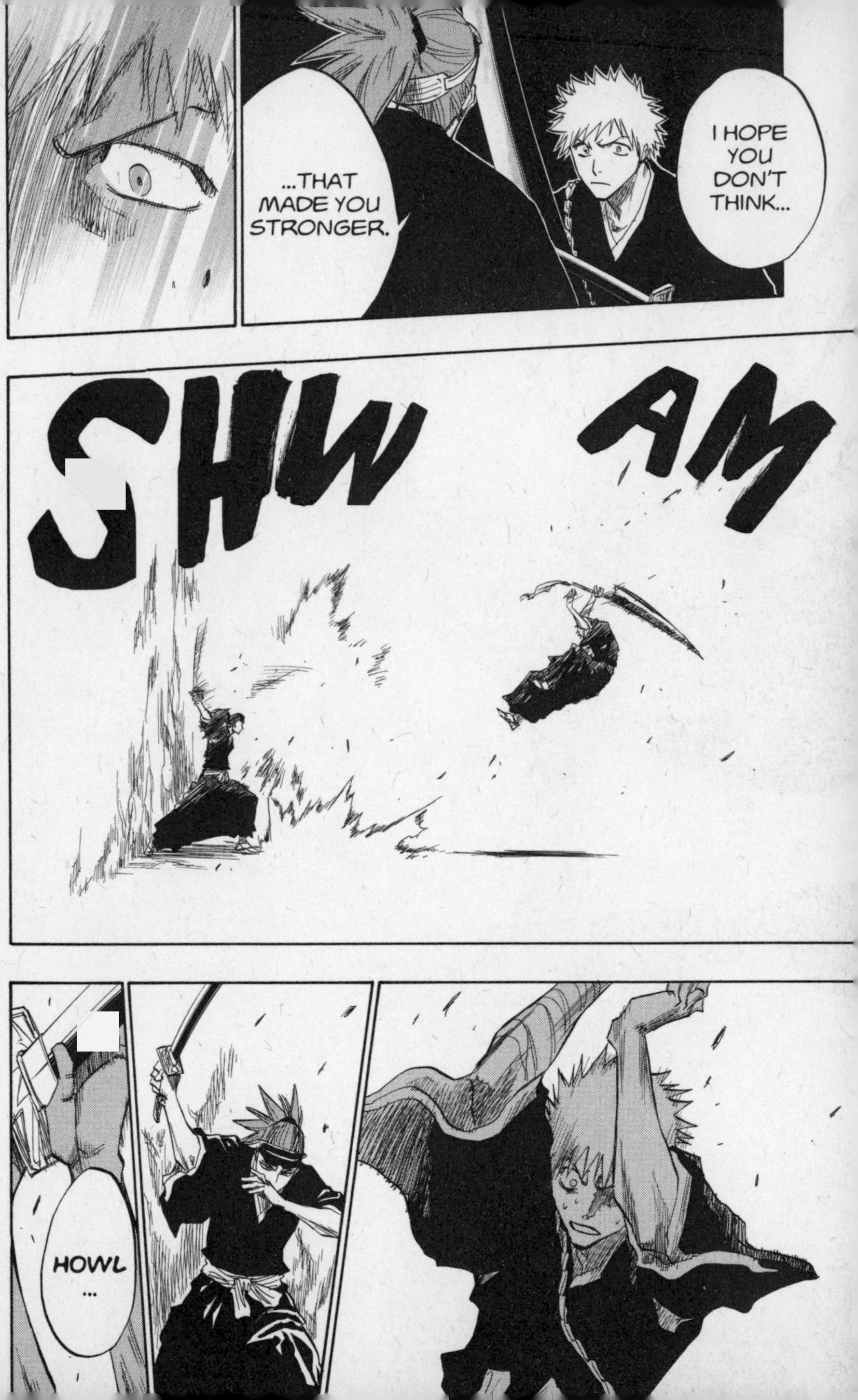
I HOPE YOU DON'T THINK...
...THAT MADE YOU STRONGER.
SHW AM
HOWL ...

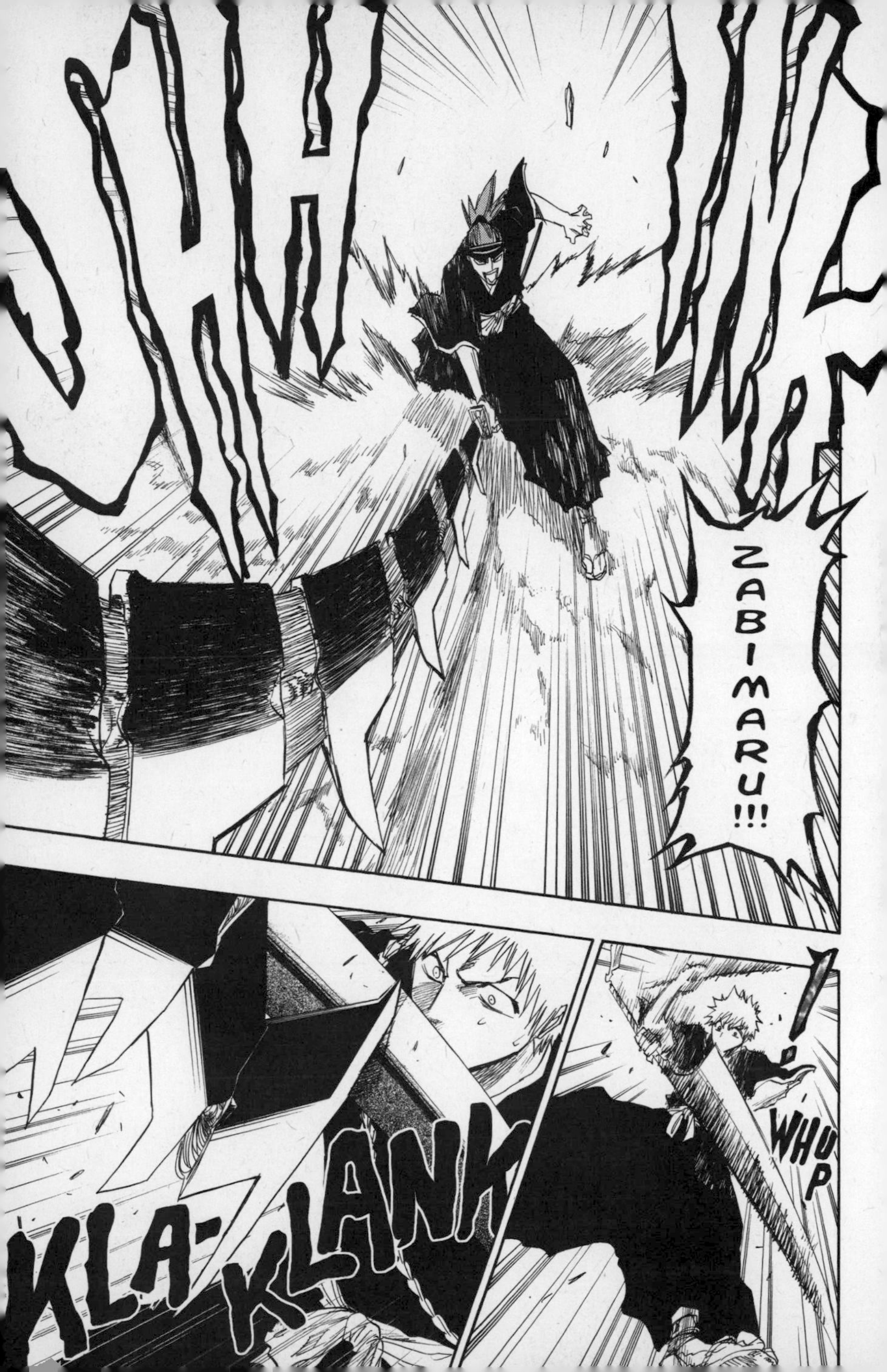
ZABIMARU!!!
!
WHUP
KLA-KLANK

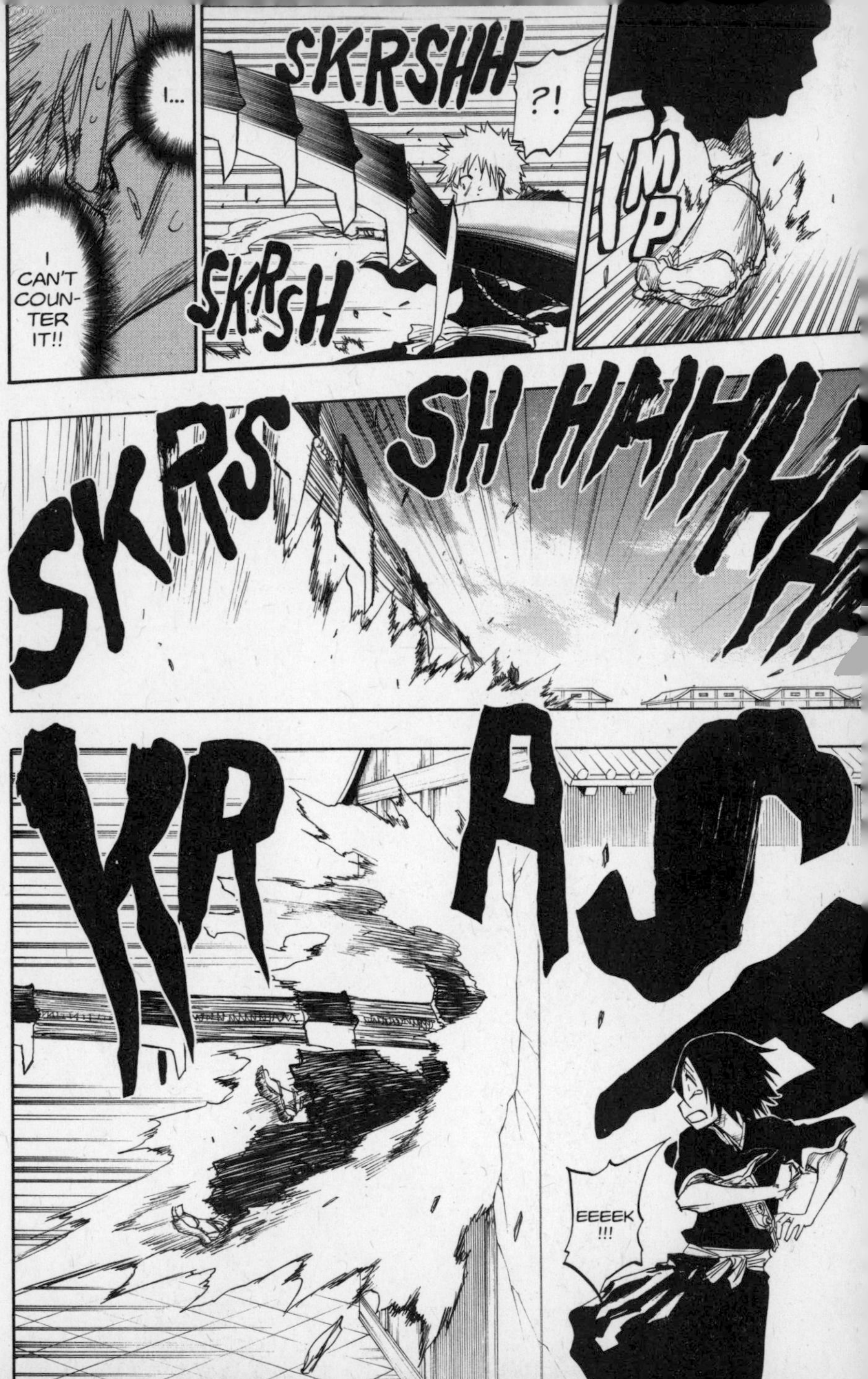
TMP
SKRSHH
?!
SKRSH
I...
I CAN'T COUNTER IT!!
SKRS SH HHHHH
KRASH
EEEEK !!!

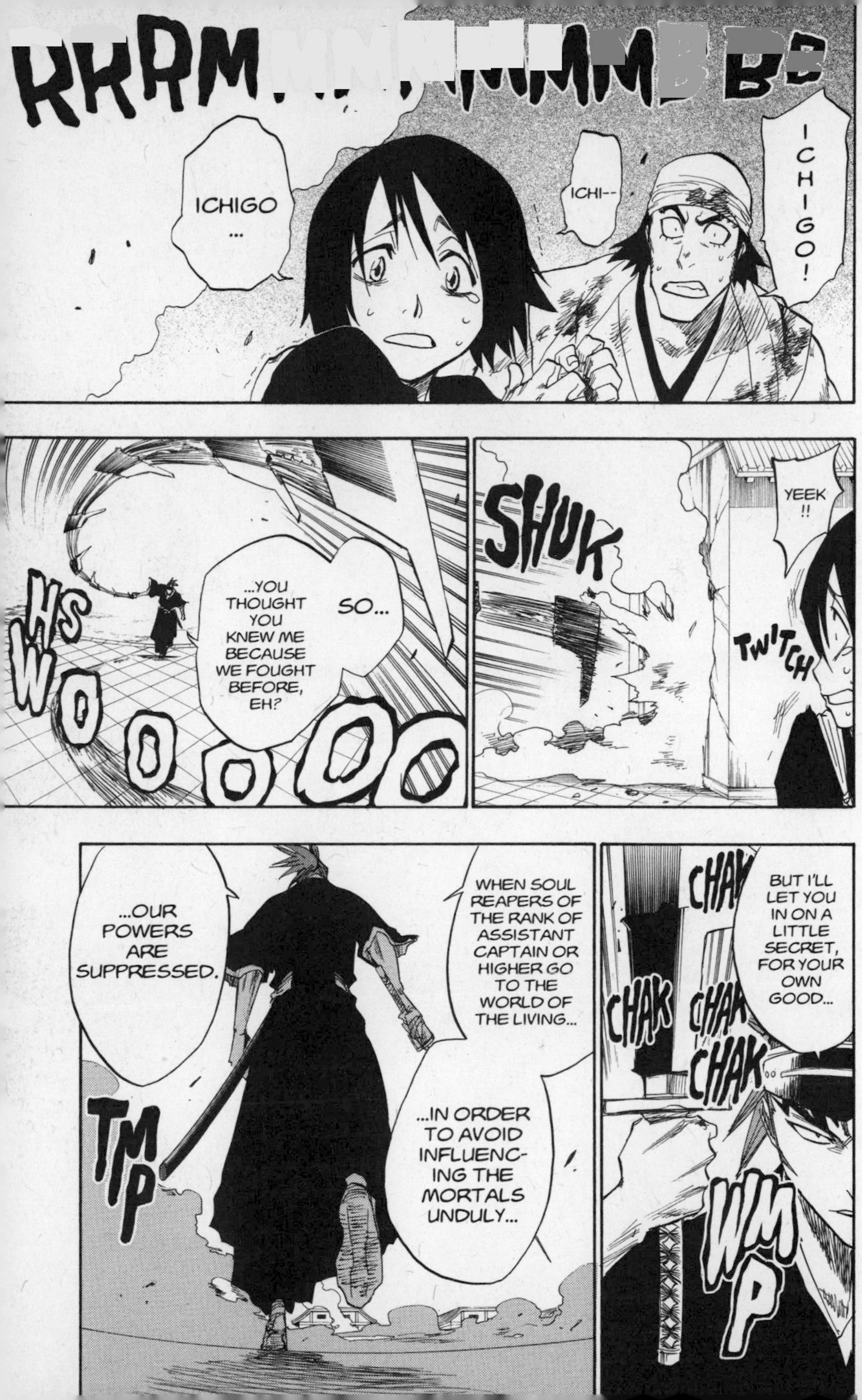
RRRM
ICHIGO!
ICHI--
ICHIGO ...
YEEK !!
TWITCH
SHUK
SO...
...YOU THOUGHT YOU KNEW ME BECAUSE WE FOUGHT BEFORE, EH?
HSWOOOOOO
BUT I'LL LET YOU IN ON A LITTLE SECRET, FOR YOUR OWN GOOD...
CHAK
CHAK
CHAK
CHAK
WMP
WHEN SOUL REAPERS OF THE RANK OF ASSISTANT CAPTAIN OR HIGHER GO TO THE WORLD OF THE LIVING...
...IN ORDER TO AVOID INFLUENCING THE MORTALS UNDULY...
...OUR POWERS ARE SUPPRESSED.
TMP

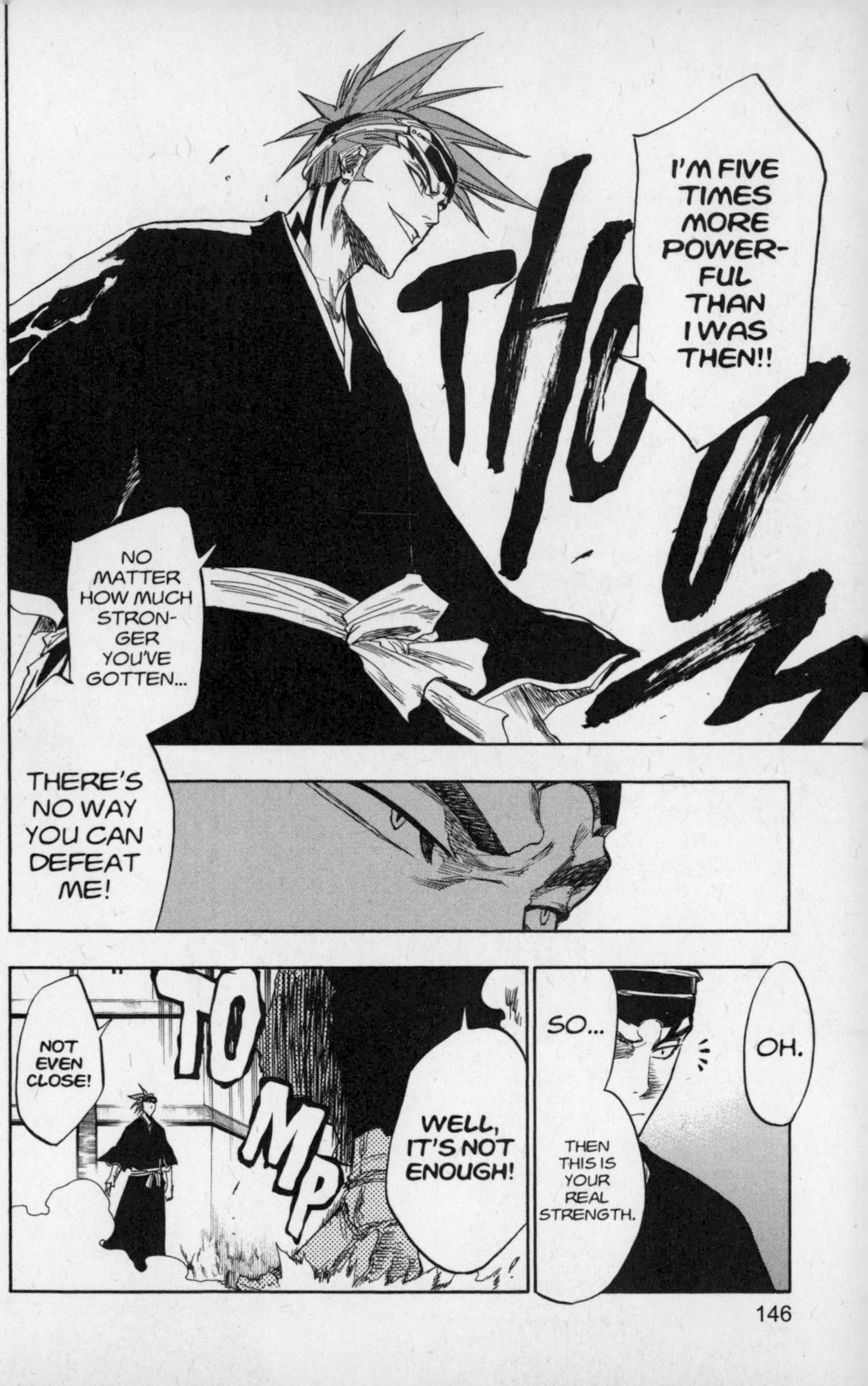
I'M FIVE TIMES MORE POWERFUL THAN I WAS THEN!!
THOOM
NO MATTER HOW MUCH STRONGER YOU'VE GOTTEN...
THERE'S NO WAY YOU CAN DEFEAT ME!
OH.
SO...
THEN THIS IS YOUR REAL STRENGTH.
WELL, IT'S NOT ENOUGH!
TOMP
NOT EVEN CLOSE!

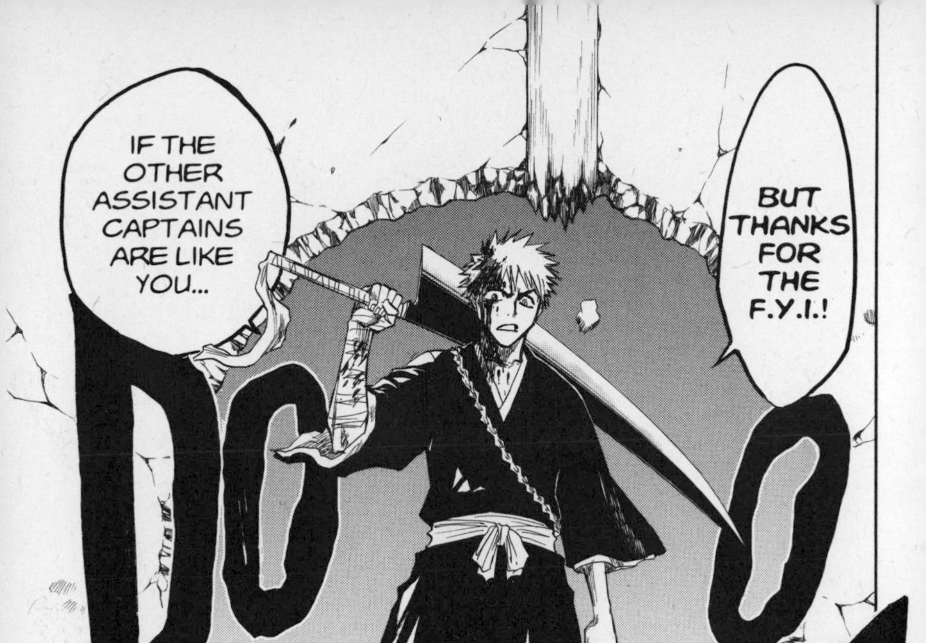
BUT THANKS FOR THE F.Y.I.!
IF THE OTHER ASSISTANT CAPTAINS ARE LIKE YOU...
DOOM
I JUST MAY HAVE A CHANCE!

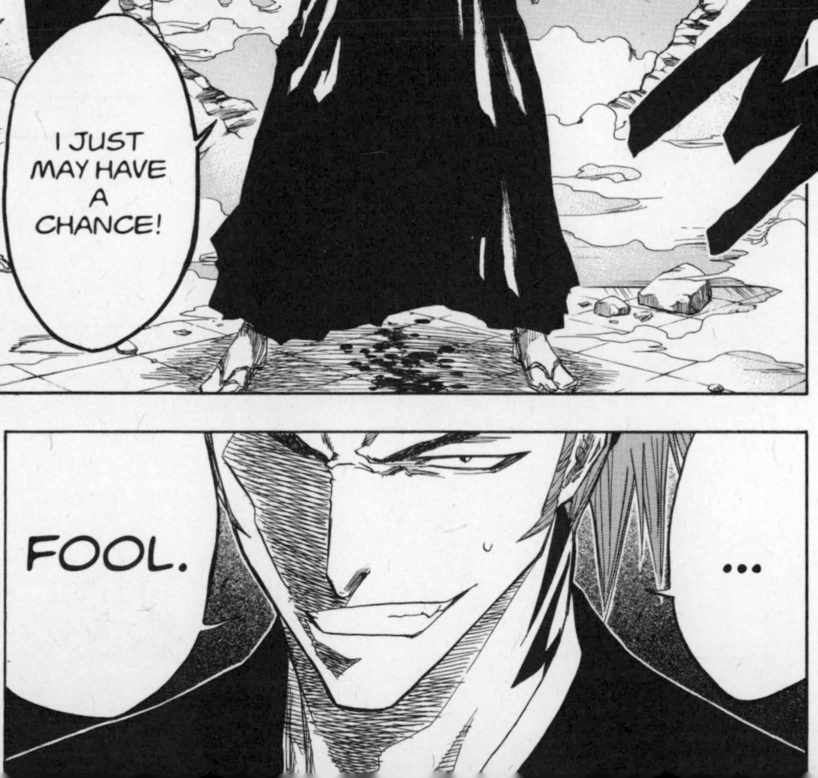
...
FOOL.

BRAND NEW.
LOOKS LIKE IT'S HARD
TO SEE THROUGH.

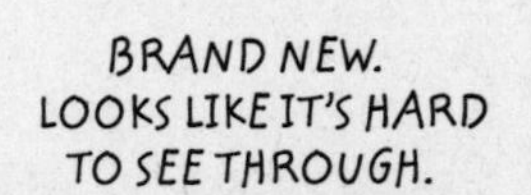

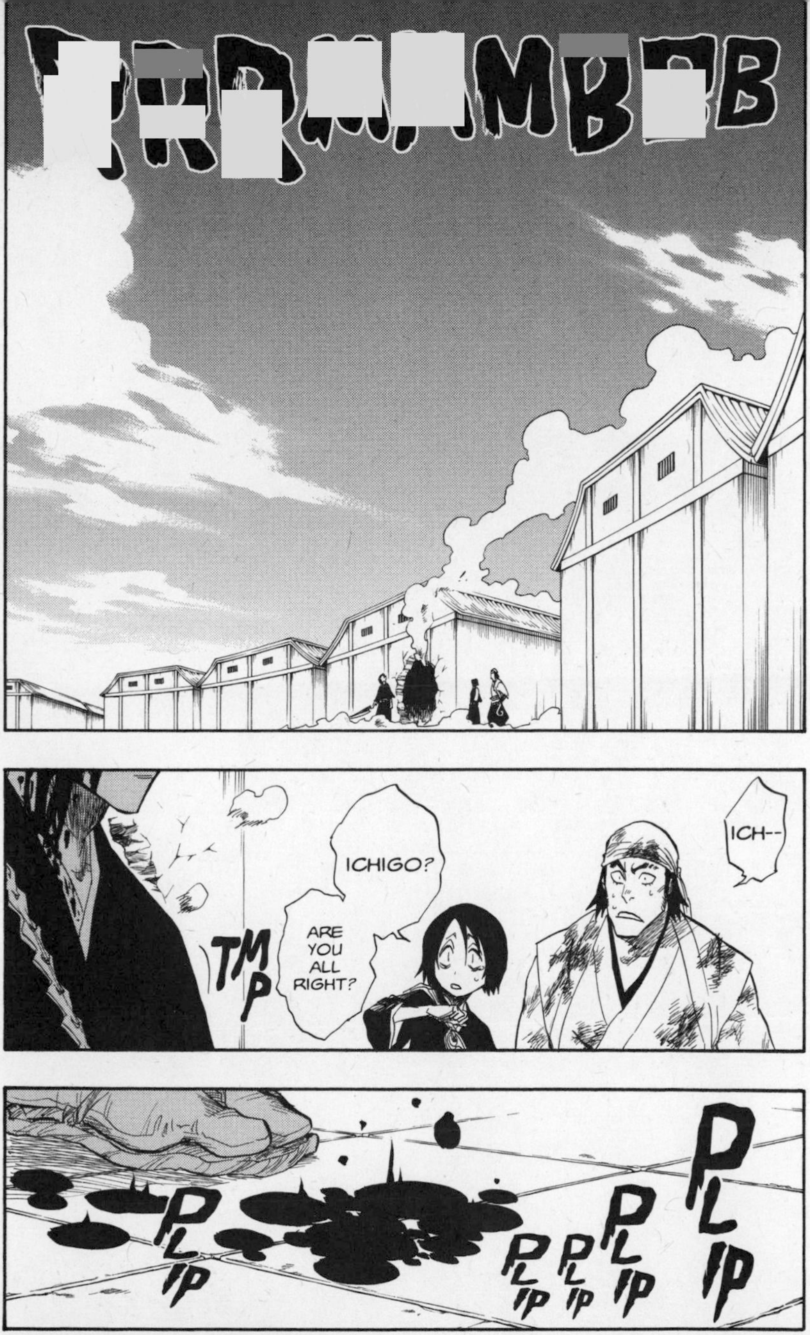
ICH--
ICHIGO?
ARE YOU ALL RIGHT?
TMP
PLIP
PLIP
PLIP
PLIP
PLIP

96. BLOODRED CONFLICT

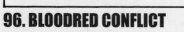

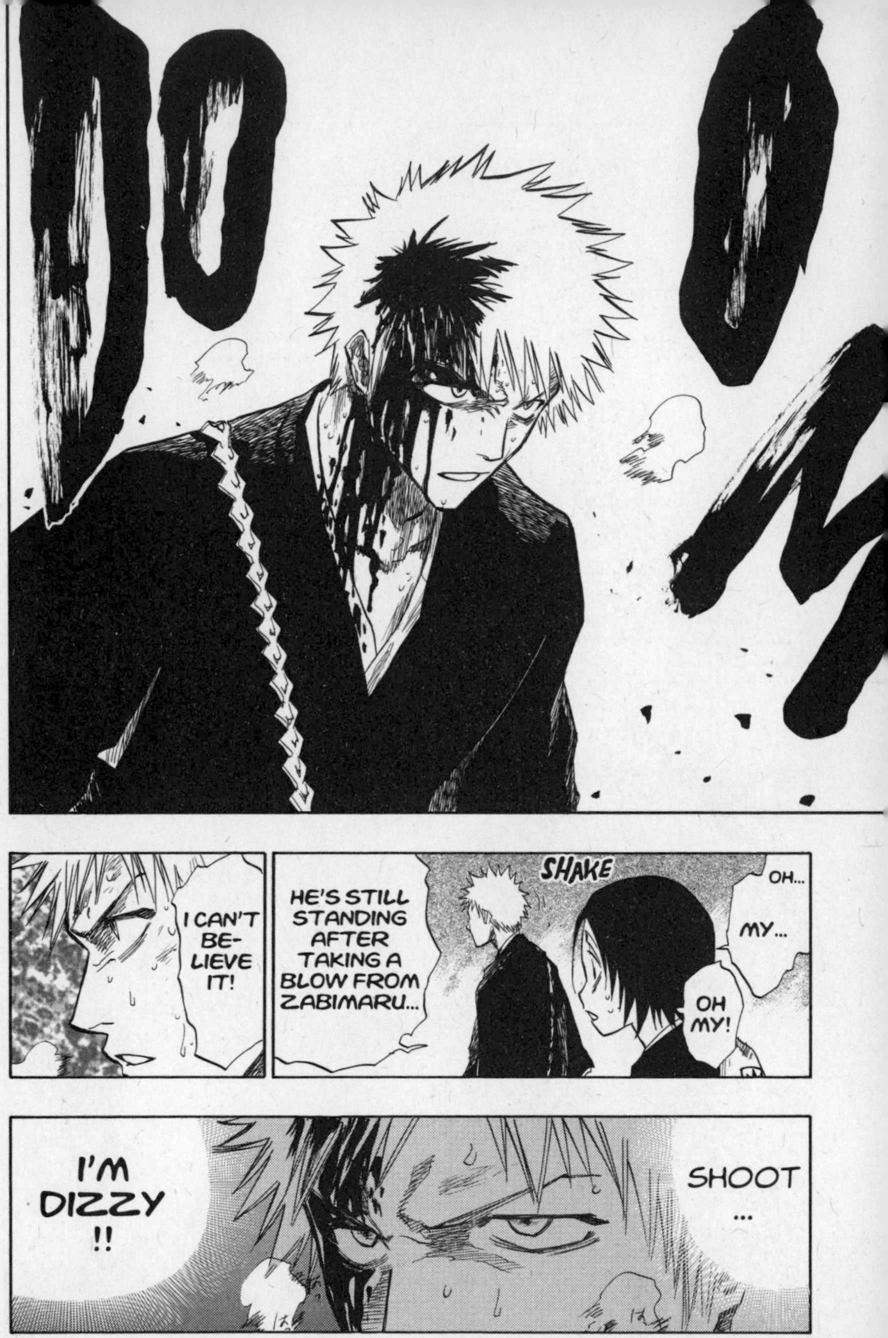
DOOM
OH... MY...
SHAKE
HE'S STILL STANDING AFTER TAKING A BLOW FROM ZABIMARU...
OH MY!
I CAN'T BE-LIEVE IT!
SHOOT ...
I'M DIZZY !!

READ THIS WAY

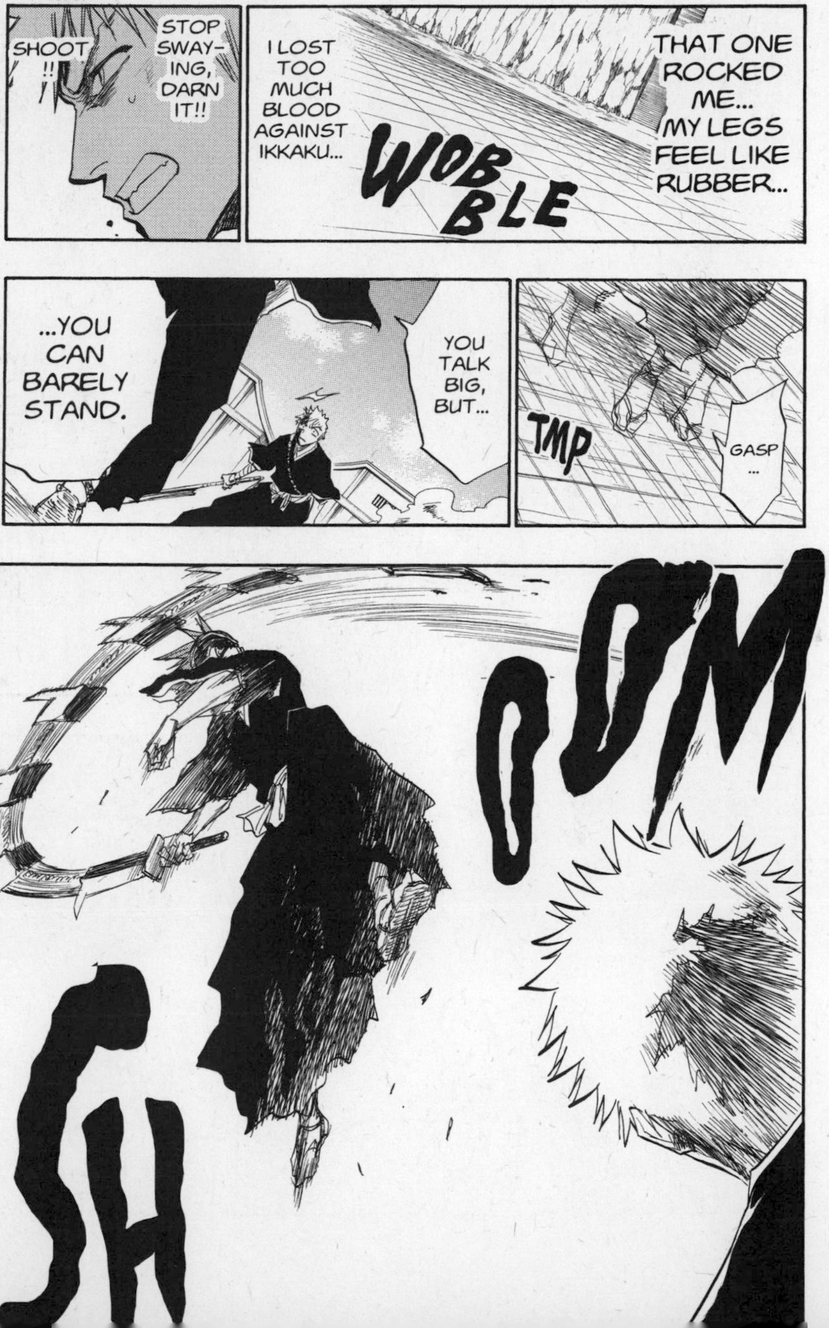
THAT ONE ROCKED ME... MY LEGS FEEL LIKE RUBBER...
I LOST TOO MUCH BLOOD AGAINST IKKAKU...
WOBBLE
STOP SWAY-ING, DARN IT!!
SHOOT!!
GASP...
TMP
YOU TALK BIG, BUT...
...YOU CAN BARELY STAND.
OOM
SH

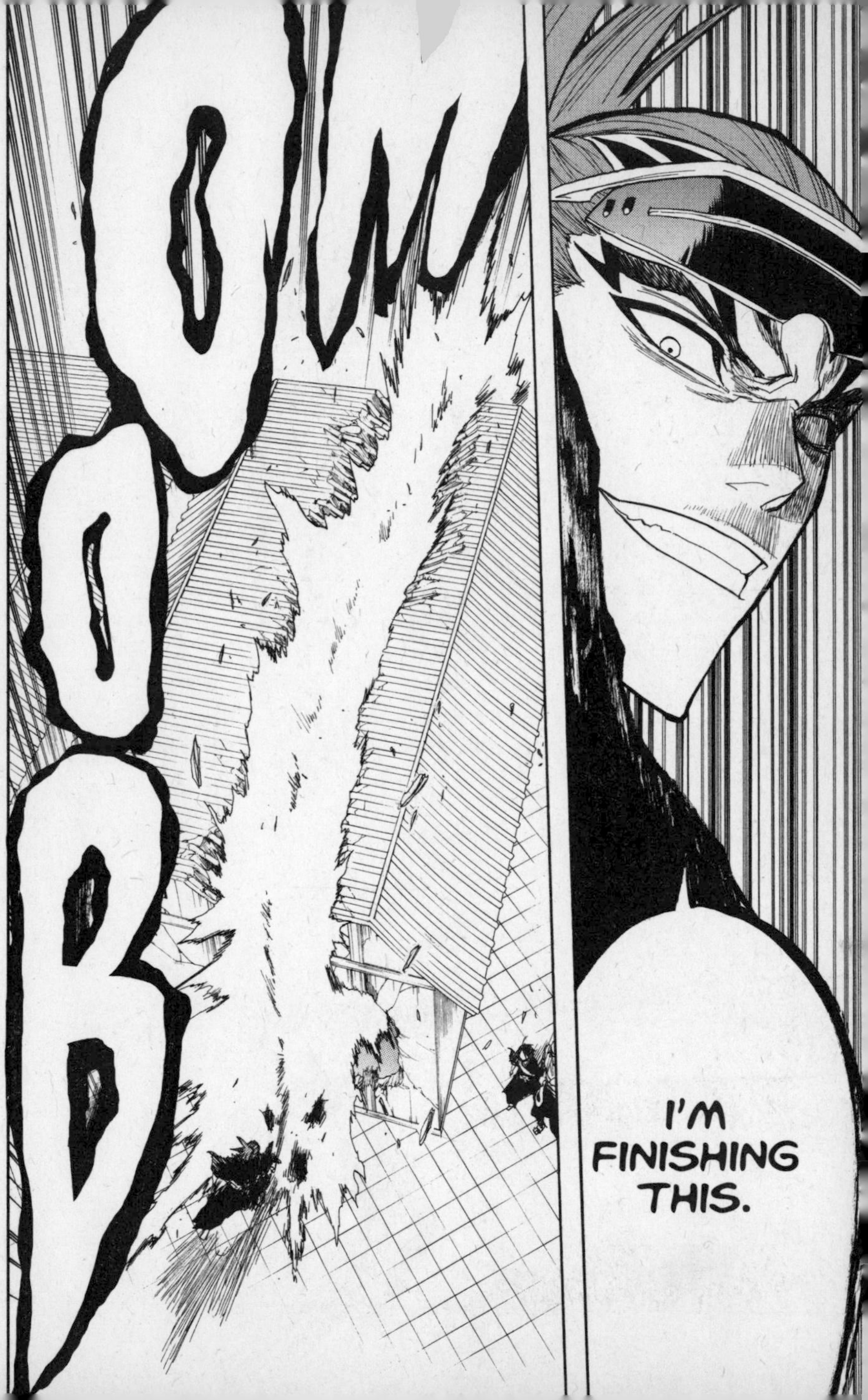
I'M FINISHING THIS.
BOOM

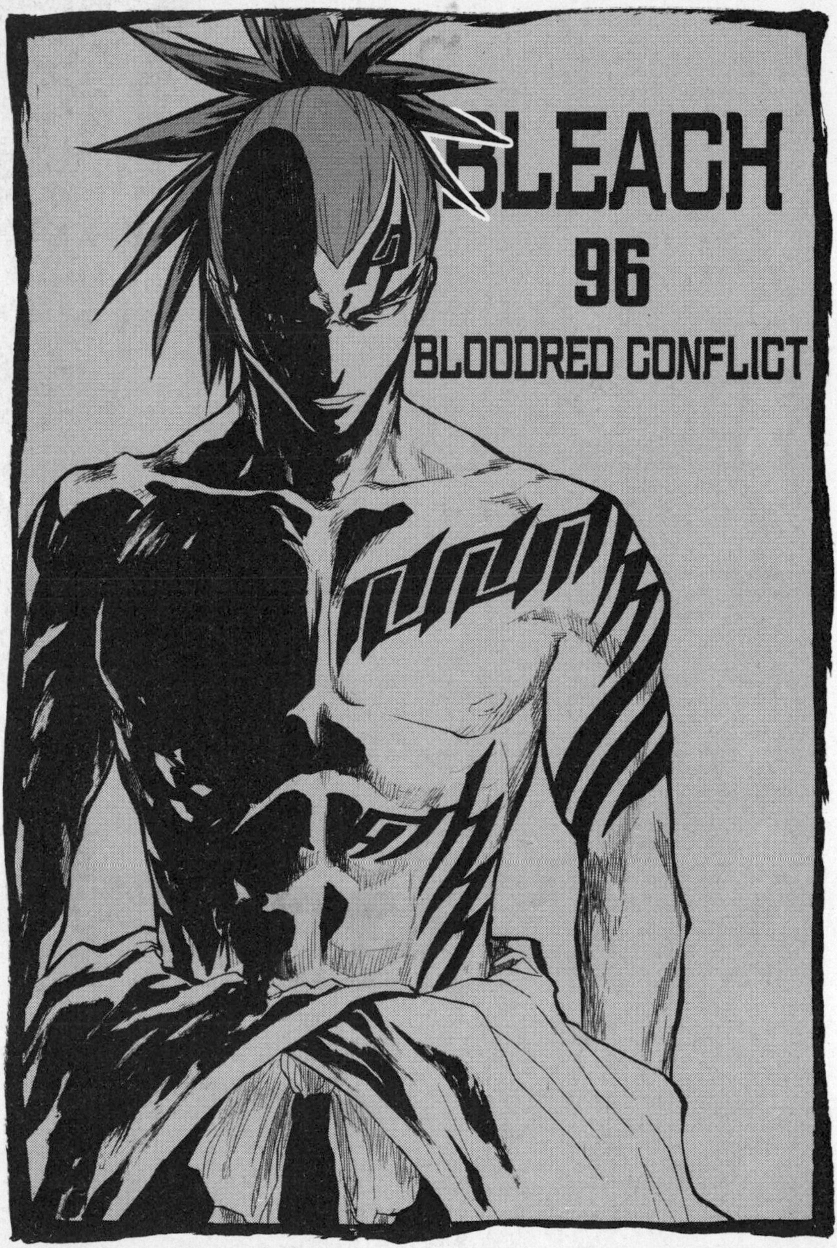
BLEACH
96
BLOODRED CONFLICT

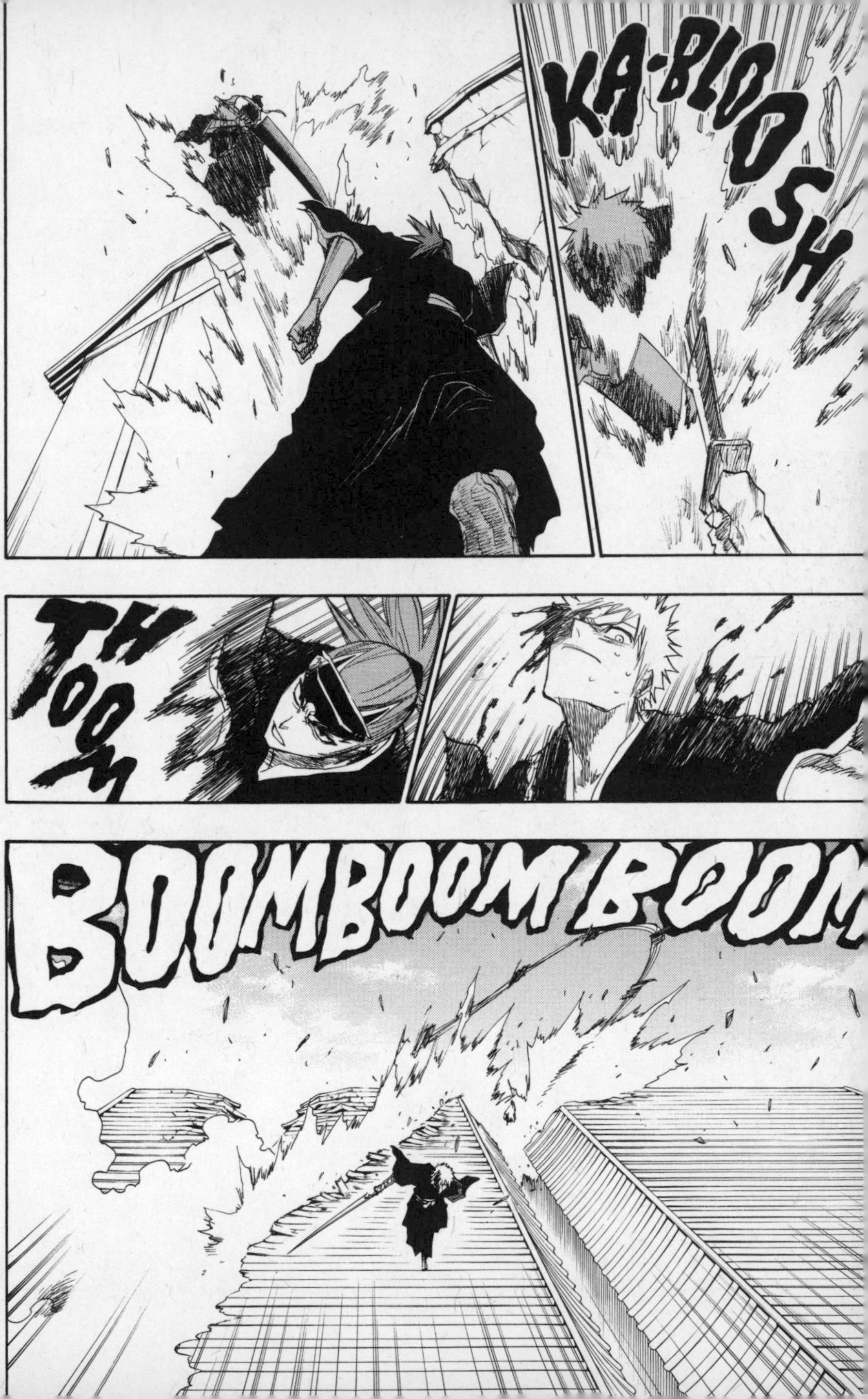
KA-BLOOSH
THOOM
BOOMBOOMBOOM

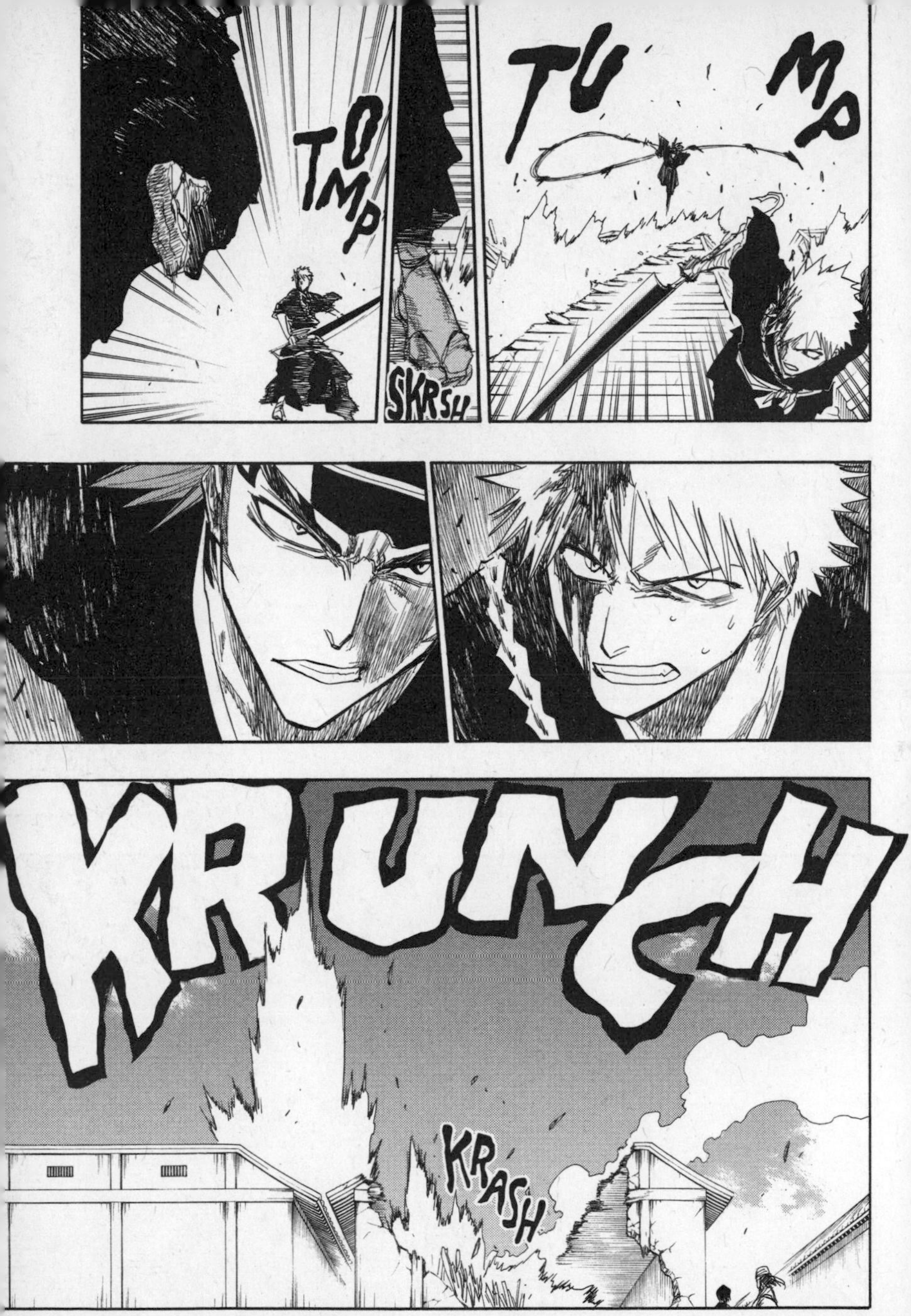

TU MP
SKRSH
TOMP
KRUNCH
KRASH

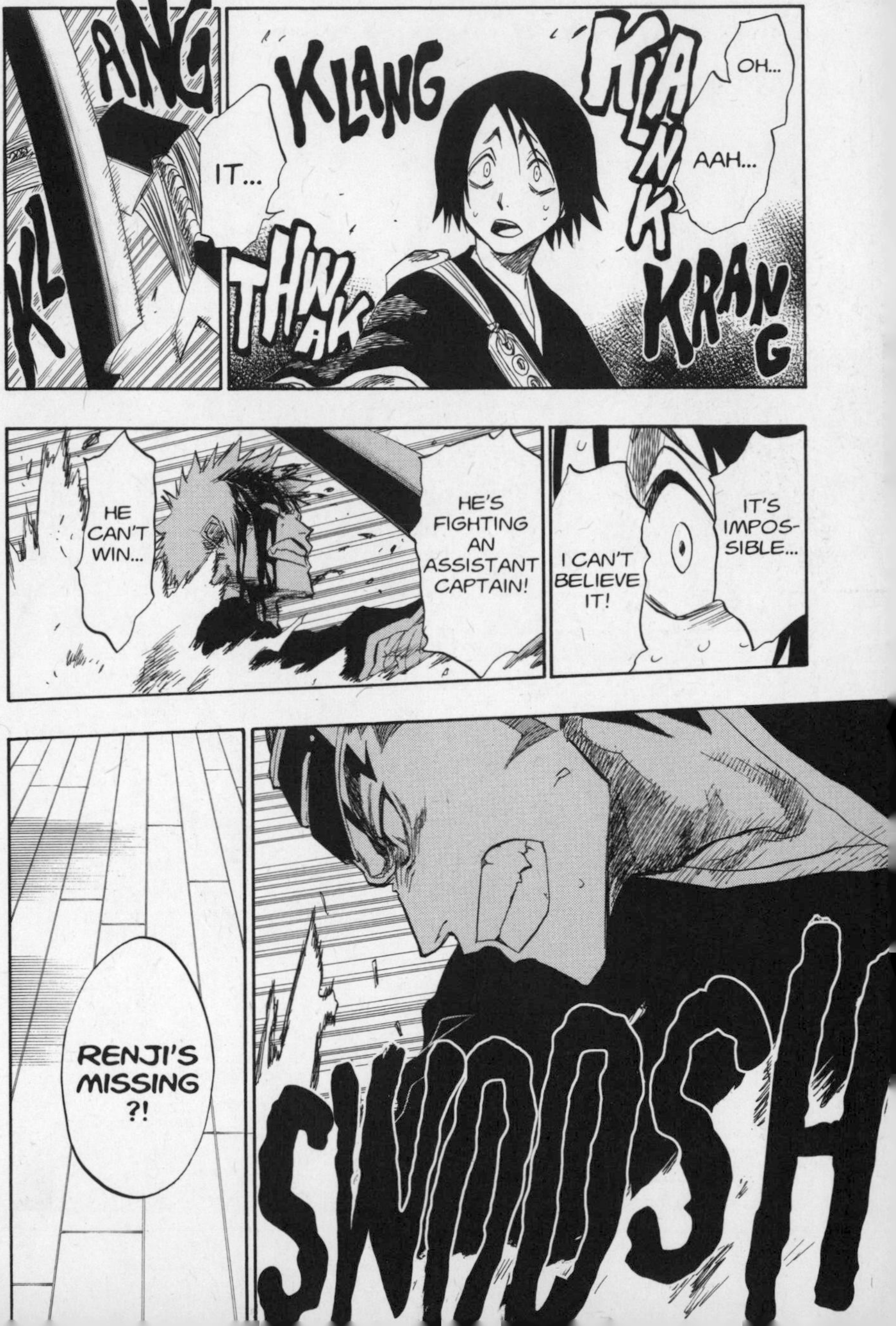
OH...
KLANK
AAH...
KLANG
IT...
KRANG
THWAK
KLANG
IT'S IMPOSSIBLE...
I CAN'T BELIEVE IT!
HE'S FIGHTING AN ASSISTANT CAPTAIN!
HE CAN'T WIN...
SWOOSH
RENJI'S MISSING ?!

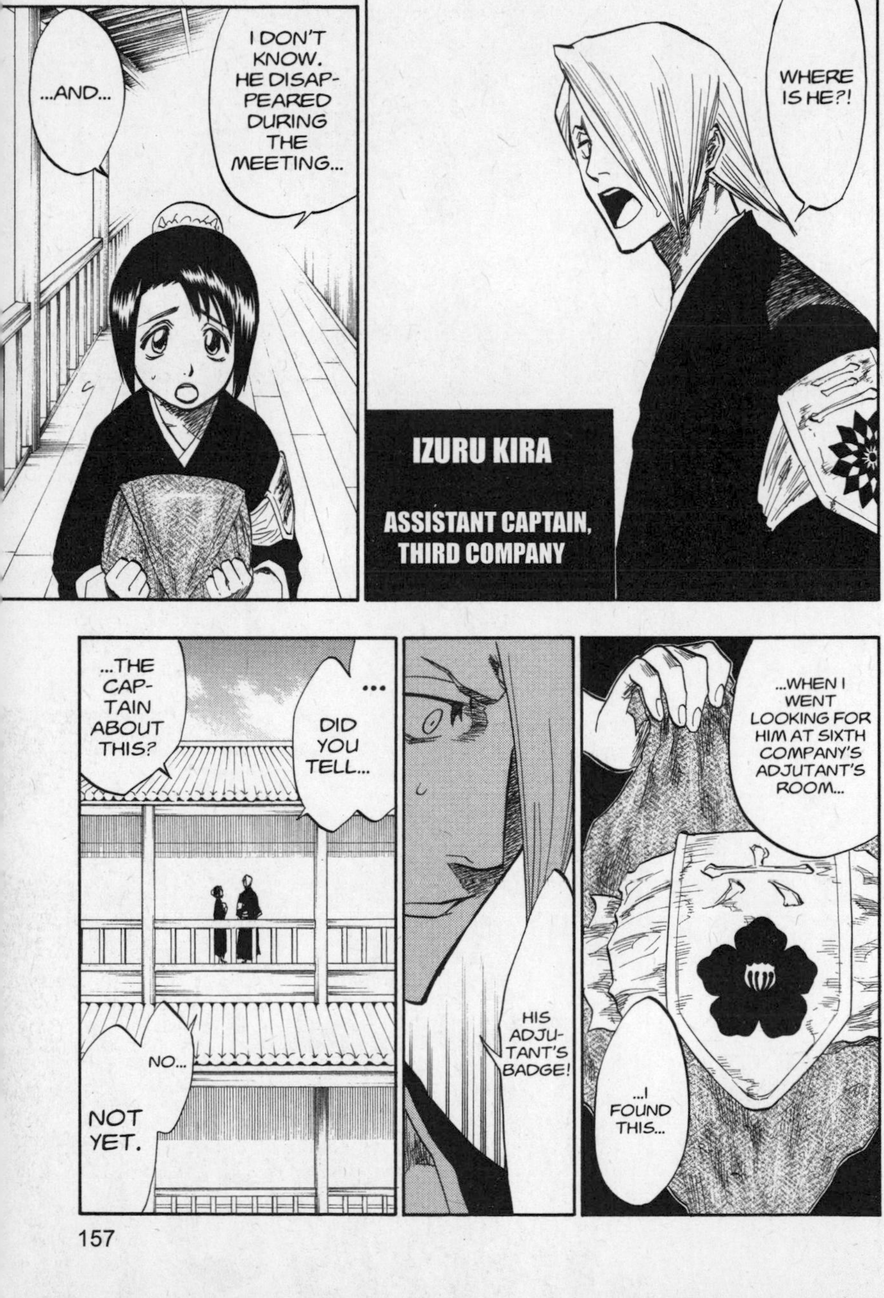
WHERE IS HE?!
IZURU KIRA
ASSISTANT CAPTAIN, THIRD COMPANY
I DON'T KNOW. HE DISAPPEARED DURING THE MEETING...
...AND...
...WHEN I WENT LOOKING FOR HIM AT SIXTH COMPANY'S ADJUTANT'S ROOM...
...I FOUND THIS...
HIS ADJUTANT'S BADGE!
... DID YOU TELL...
...THE CAPTAIN ABOUT THIS?
NO...
NOT YET.

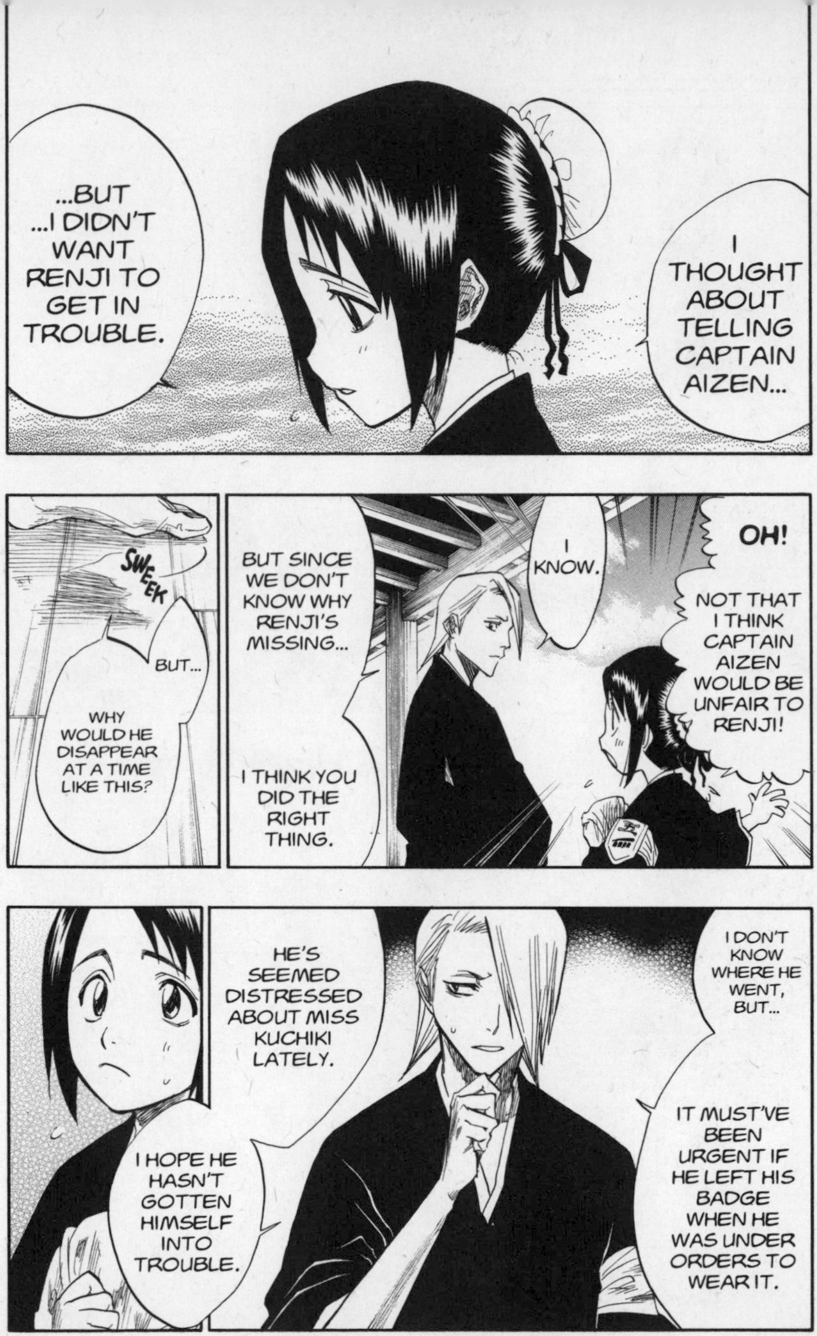
I THOUGHT ABOUT TELLING CAPTAIN AIZEN...
...BUT ...I DIDN'T WANT RENJI TO GET IN TROUBLE.
OH!
NOT THAT I THINK CAPTAIN AIZEN WOULD BE UNFAIR TO RENJI!
I KNOW.
BUT SINCE WE DON'T KNOW WHY RENJI'S MISSING...
I THINK YOU DID THE RIGHT THING.
SWEEK
BUT...
WHY WOULD HE DISAPPEAR AT A TIME LIKE THIS?
I DON'T KNOW WHERE HE WENT, BUT...
IT MUST'VE BEEN URGENT IF HE LEFT HIS BADGE WHEN HE WAS UNDER ORDERS TO WEAR IT.
HE'S SEEMED DISTRESSED ABOUT MISS KUCHIKI LATELY.
I HOPE HE HASN'T GOTTEN HIMSELF INTO TROUBLE.

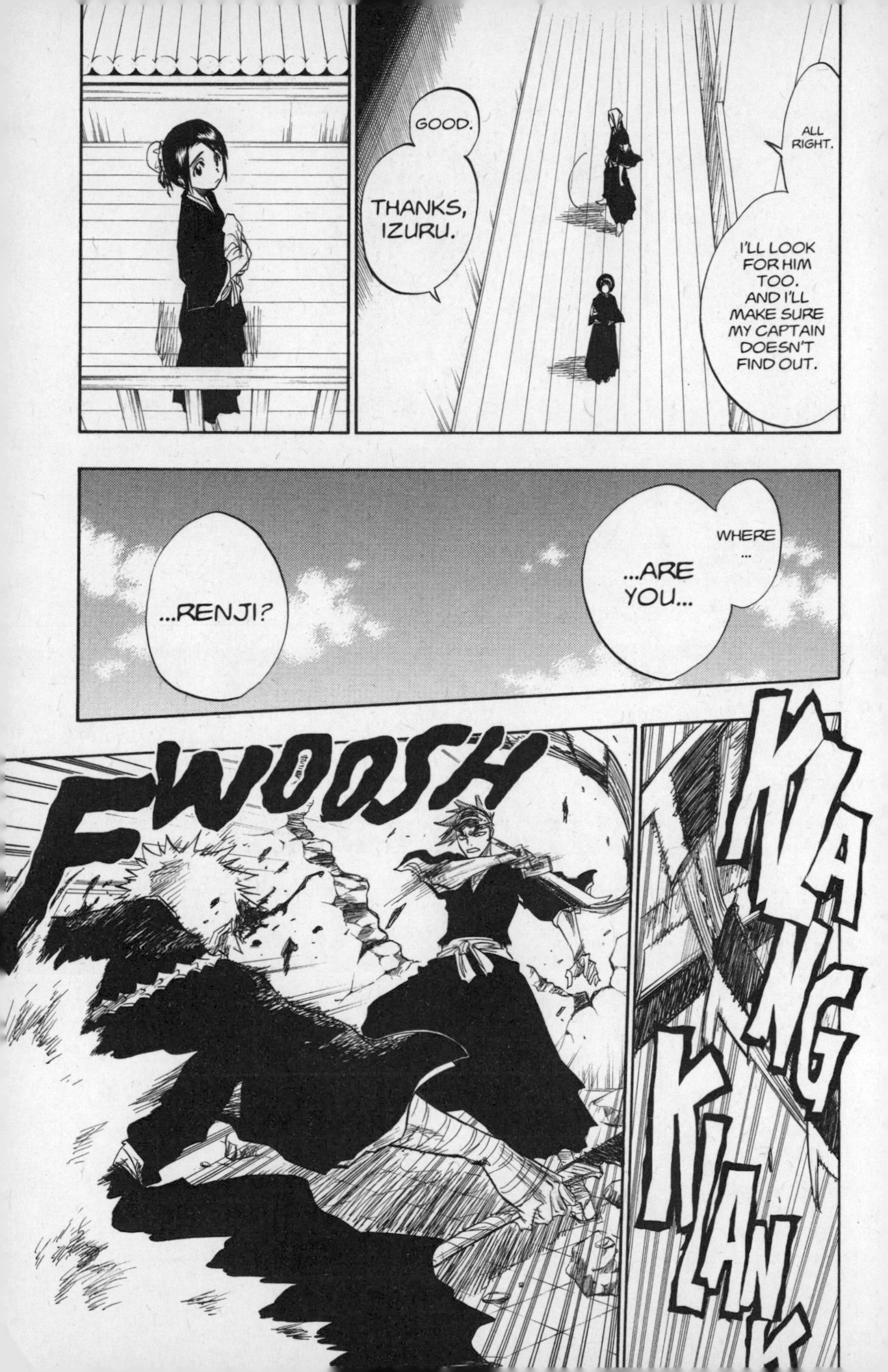
ALL RIGHT.
I'LL LOOK FOR HIM TOO. AND I'LL MAKE SURE MY CAPTAIN DOESN'T FIND OUT.
GOOD.
THANKS, IZURU.
WHERE ...
...ARE YOU...
...RENJI?
KANG
KLANK
FWOOSH

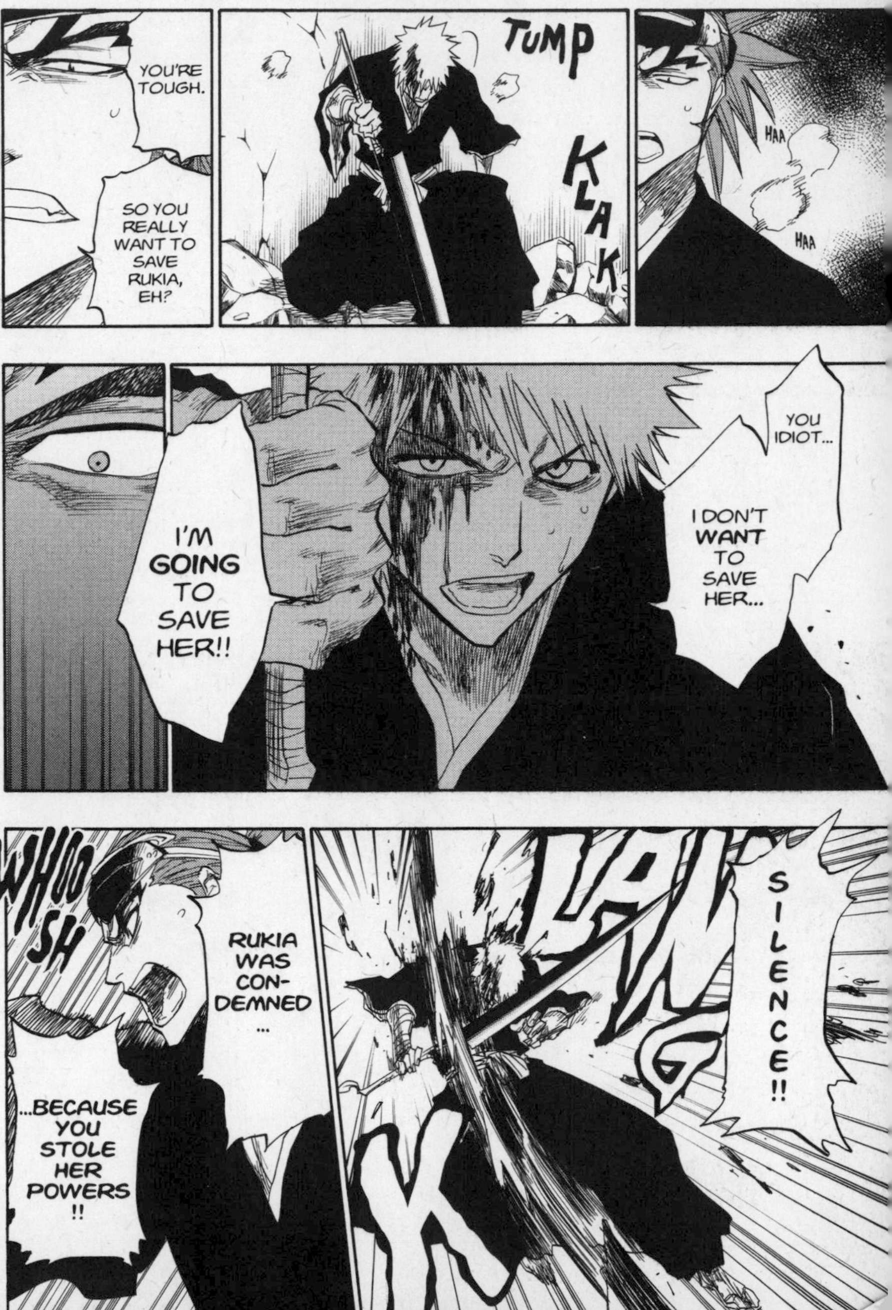
HAA
HAA
TUMP
KLAK
YOU'RE TOUGH.
SO YOU REALLY WANT TO SAVE RUKIA, EH?
YOU IDIOT...
I DON'T WANT TO SAVE HER...
I'M GOING TO SAVE HER!!
SILENCE!!
CLANG
WHOOSH
RUKIA WAS CONDEMNED...
...BECAUSE YOU STOLE HER POWERS!!

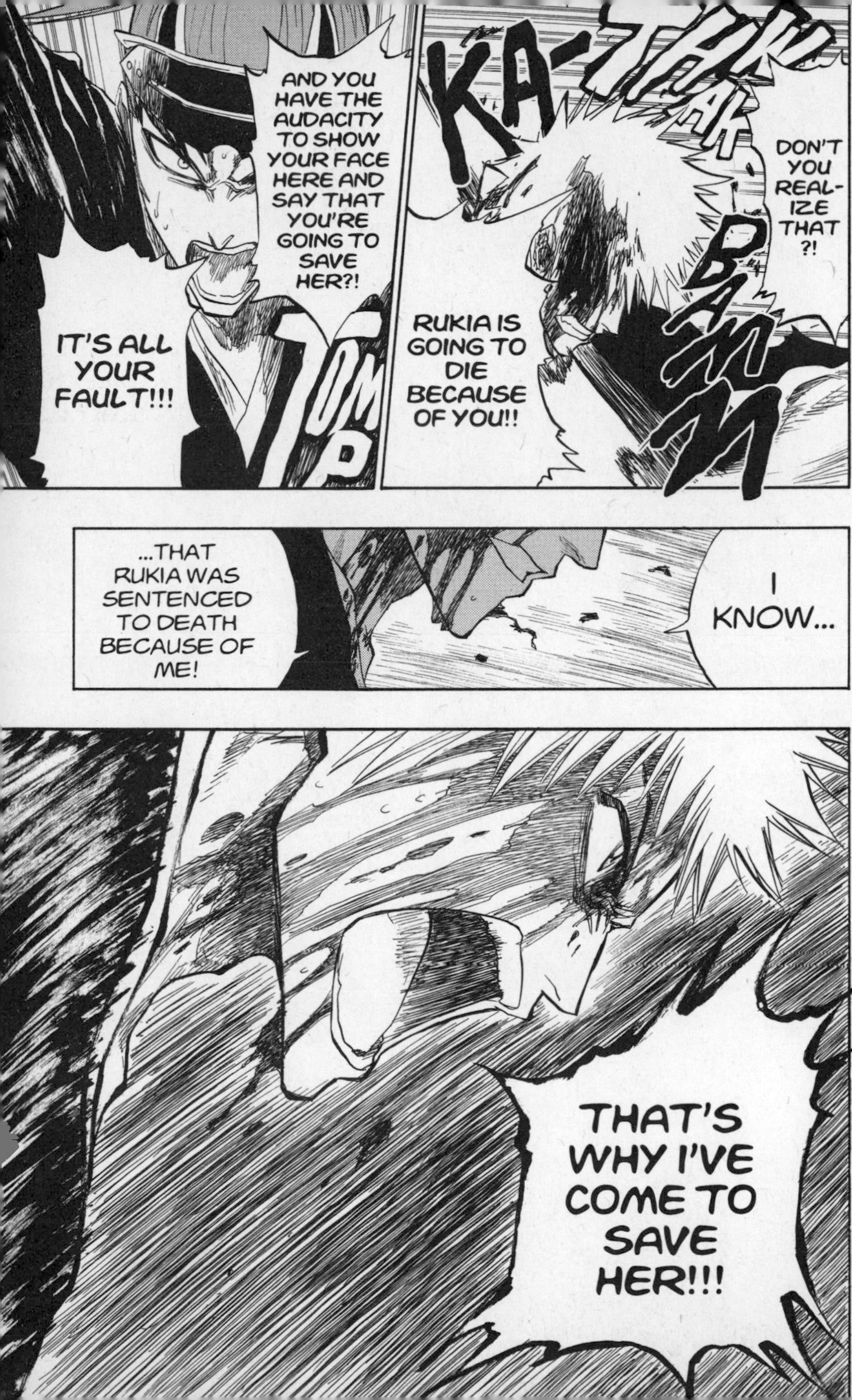
KA-THAK
DON'T YOU REALIZE THAT?!
BAMM
RUKIA IS GOING TO DIE BECAUSE OF YOU!!
AND YOU HAVE THE AUDACITY TO SHOW YOUR FACE HERE AND SAY THAT YOU'RE GOING TO SAVE HER?!
IT'S ALL YOUR FAULT!!!
I KNOW...
...THAT RUKIA WAS SENTENCED TO DEATH BECAUSE OF ME!
THAT'S WHY I'VE COME TO SAVE HER!!!

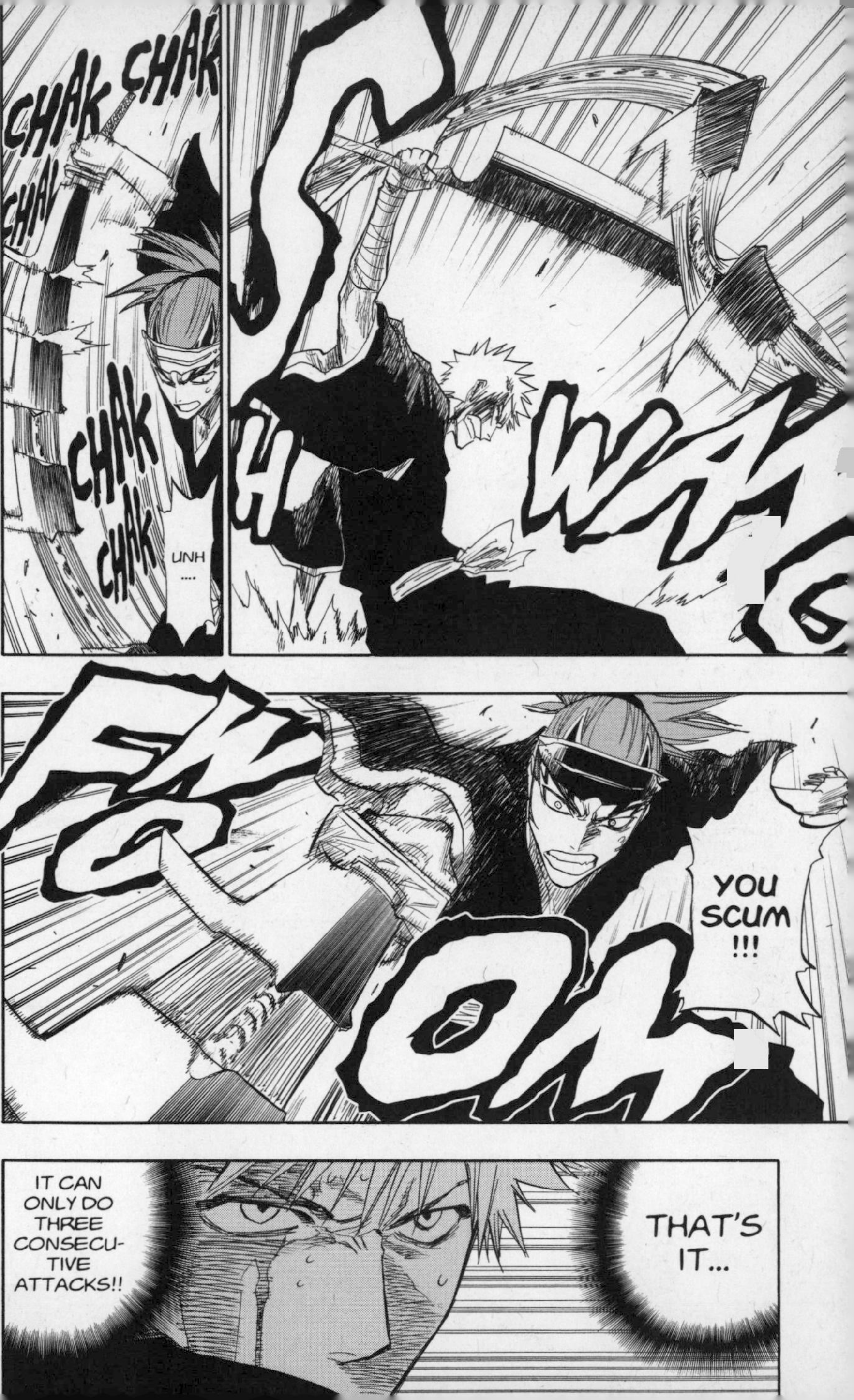
CHAK CHAK CHAK
CHAK CHAK CHAK
UNH ....
YOU SCUM !!!
THAT'S IT...
IT CAN ONLY DO THREE CONSECU-TIVE ATTACKS!!

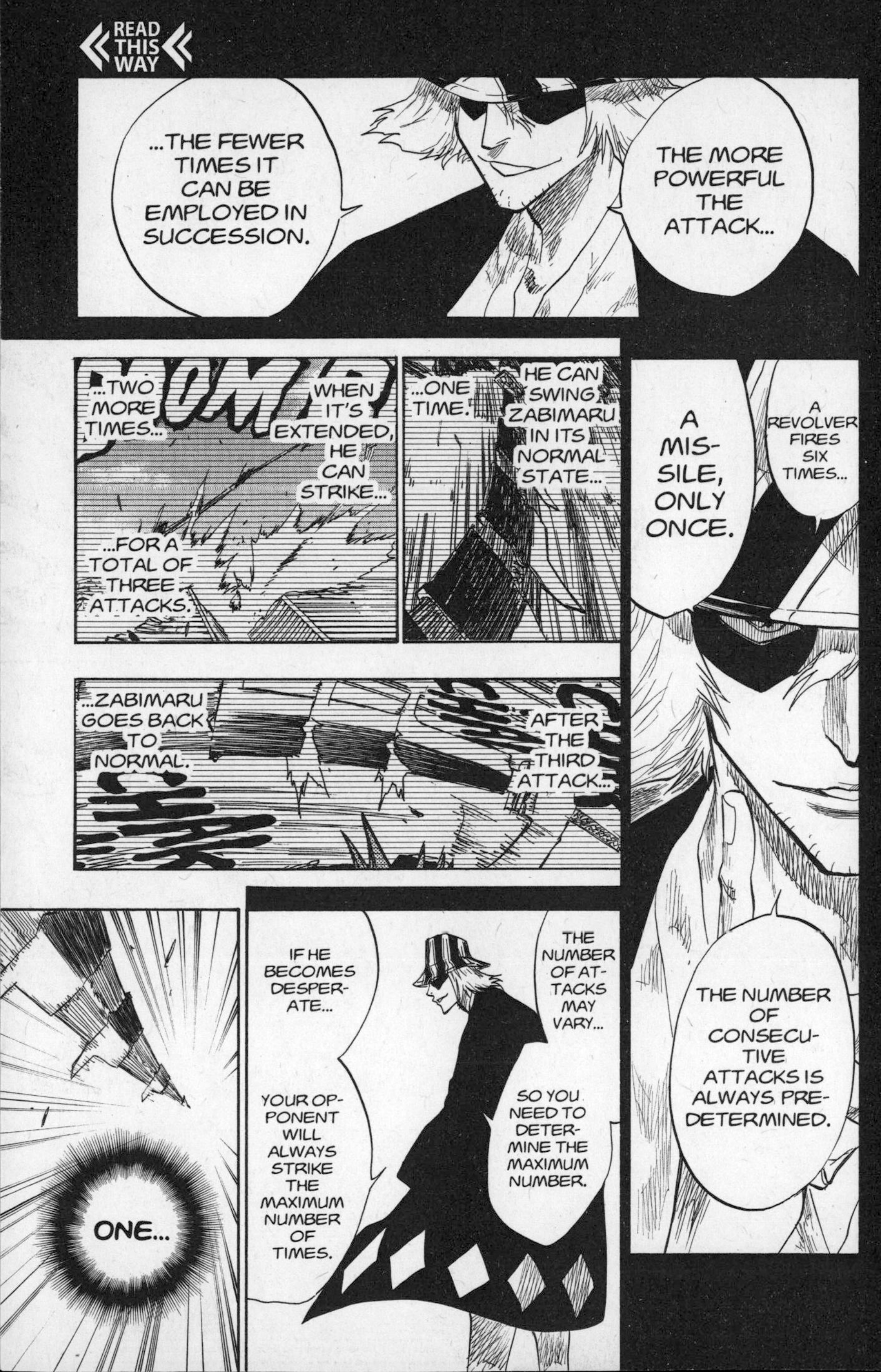
READ THIS WAY
THE MORE POWERFUL THE ATTACK...
...THE FEWER TIMES IT CAN BE EMPLOYED IN SUCCESSION.
A REVOLVER FIRES SIX TIMES...
A MISSILE, ONLY ONCE.
THE NUMBER OF CONSECUTIVE ATTACKS IS ALWAYS PREDETERMINED.
HE CAN SWING ZABIMARU IN ITS NORMAL STATE...
...ONE TIME.
WHEN IT'S EXTENDED, HE CAN STRIKE...
...TWO MORE TIMES...
...FOR A TOTAL OF THREE ATTACKS.
AFTER THE THIRD ATTACK...
...ZABIMARU GOES BACK TO NORMAL.
THE NUMBER OF ATTACKS MAY VARY...
IF HE BECOMES DESPERATE...
SO YOU NEED TO DETERMINE THE MAXIMUM NUMBER.
YOUR OPPONENT WILL ALWAYS STRIKE THE MAXIMUM NUMBER OF TIMES.
ONE...

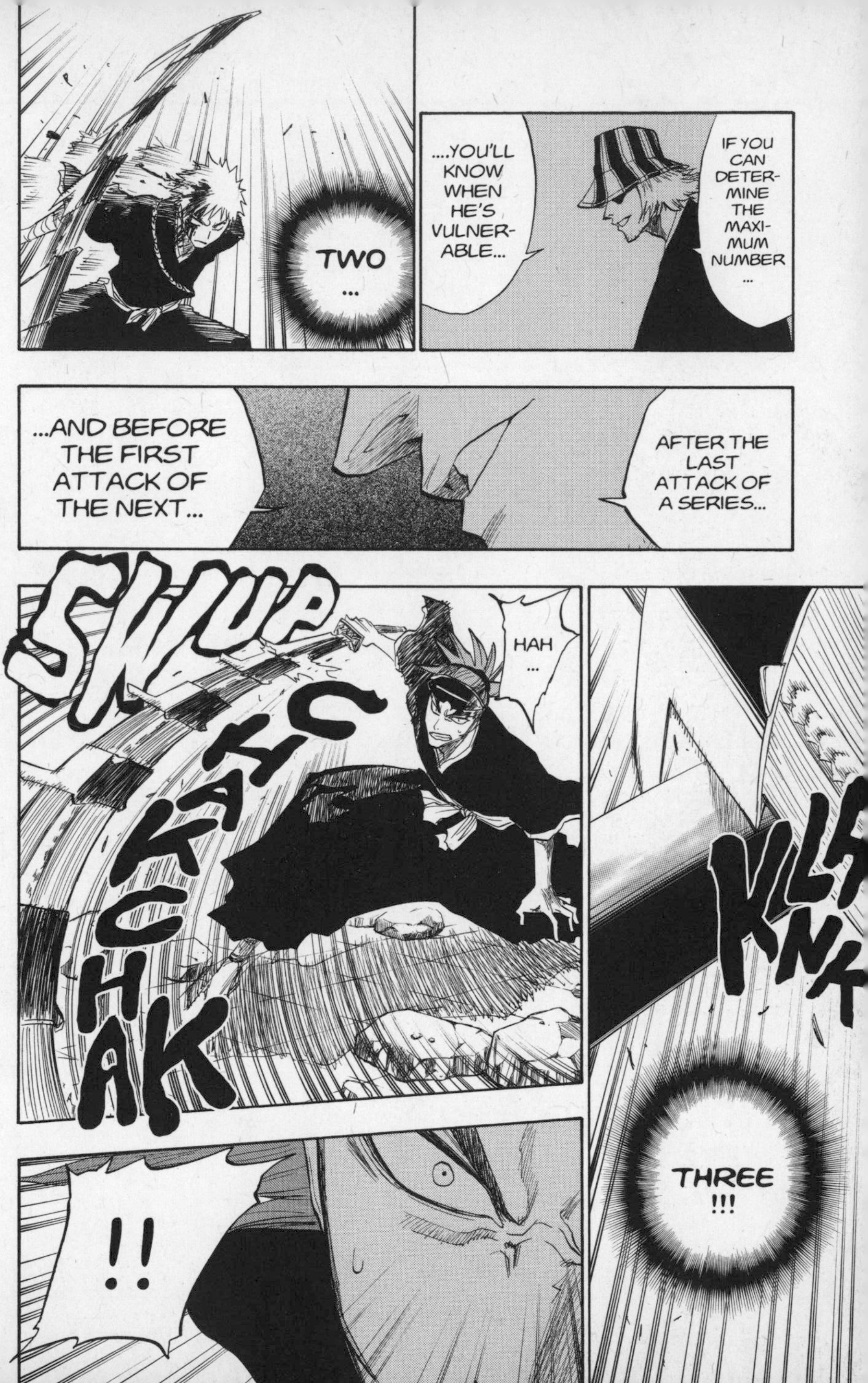
IF YOU CAN DETERMINE THE MAXIMUM NUMBER...
....YOU'LL KNOW WHEN HE'S VULNERABLE...
TWO ...
AFTER THE LAST ATTACK OF A SERIES...
...AND BEFORE THE FIRST ATTACK OF THE NEXT...
HAH ...
THREE !!!
!!

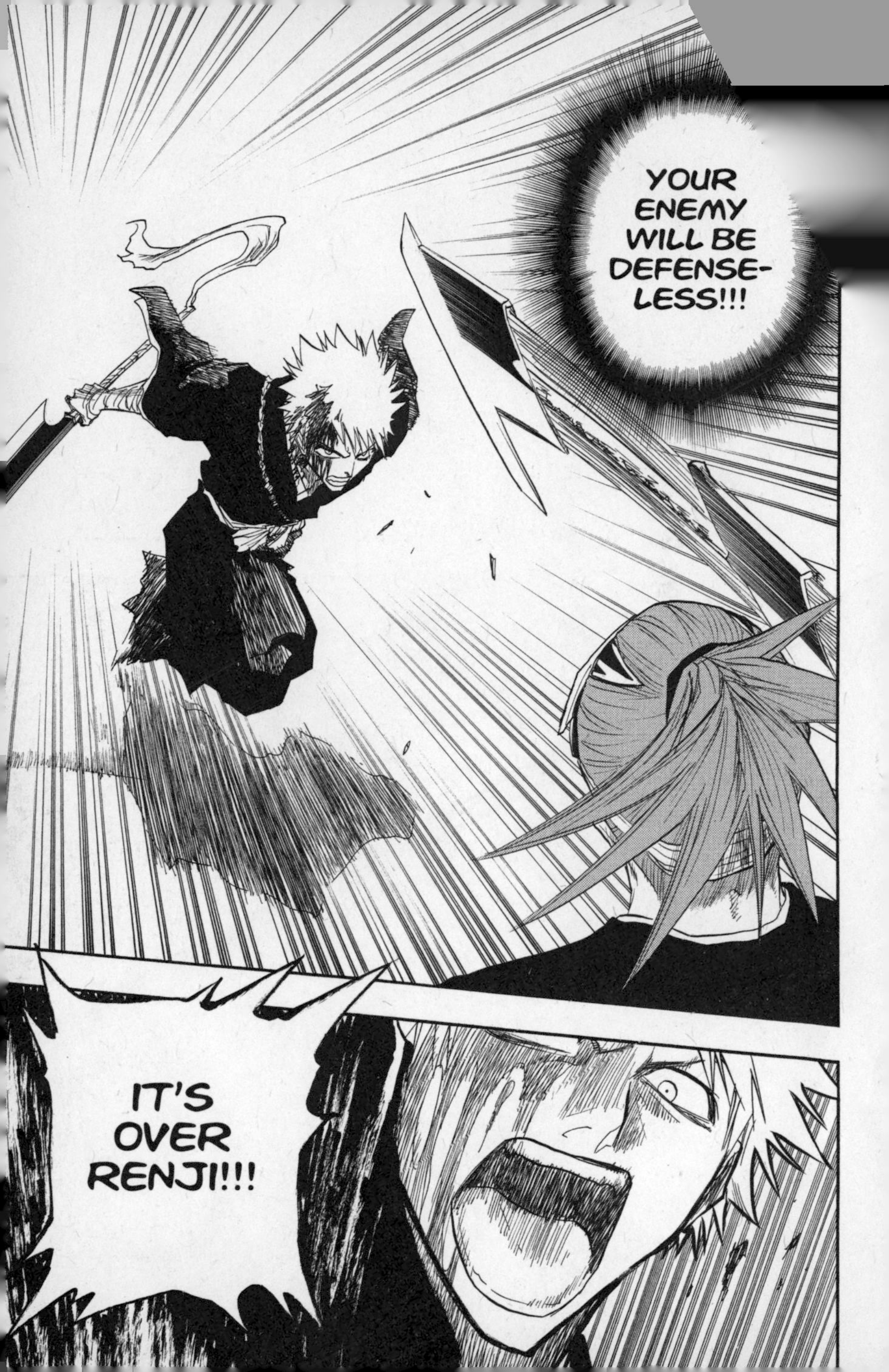
YOUR ENEMY WILL BE DEFENSE-LESS!!!
IT'S OVER RENJI!!!

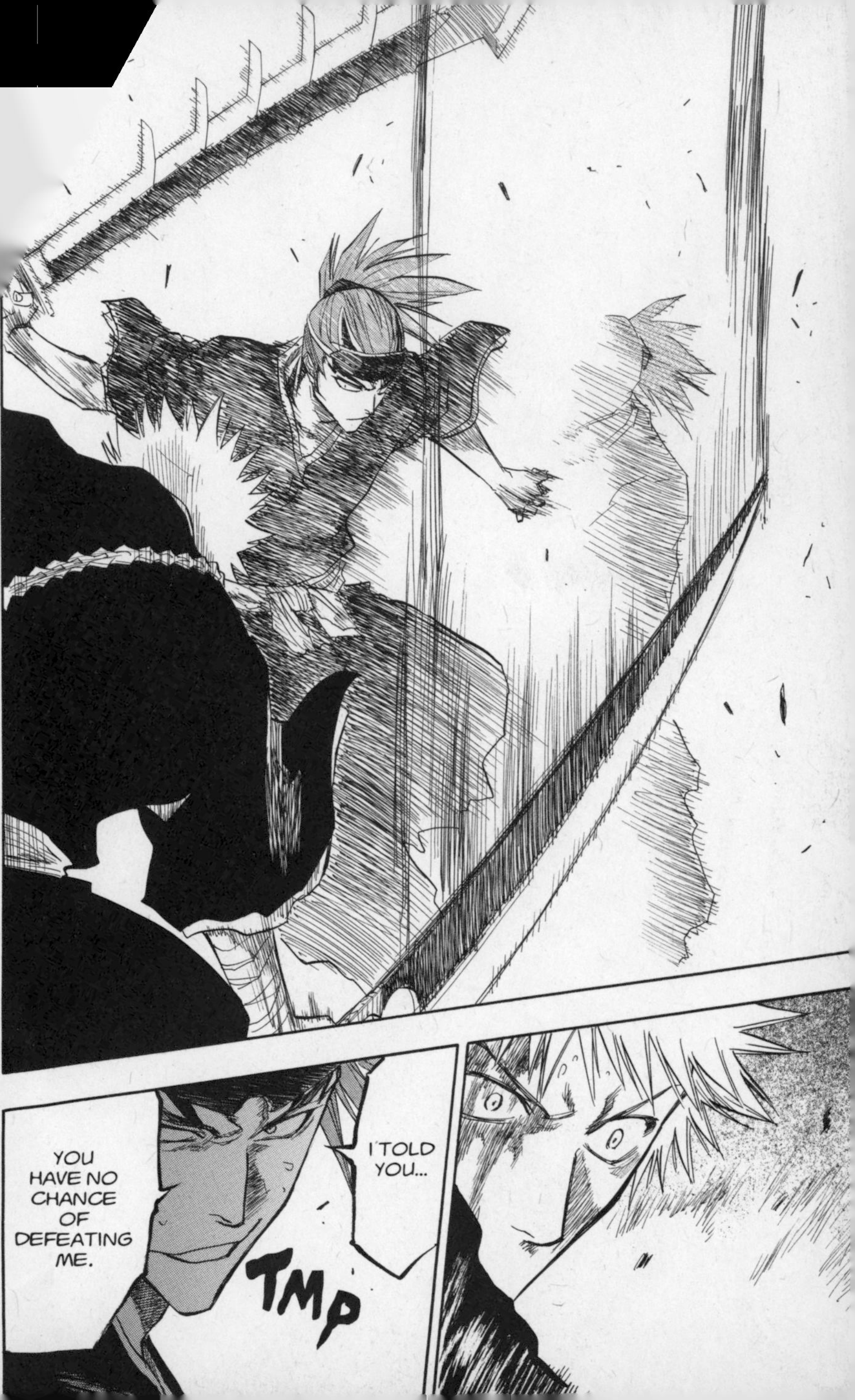
I TOLD YOU...
YOU HAVE NO CHANCE OF DEFEATING ME.
TMP

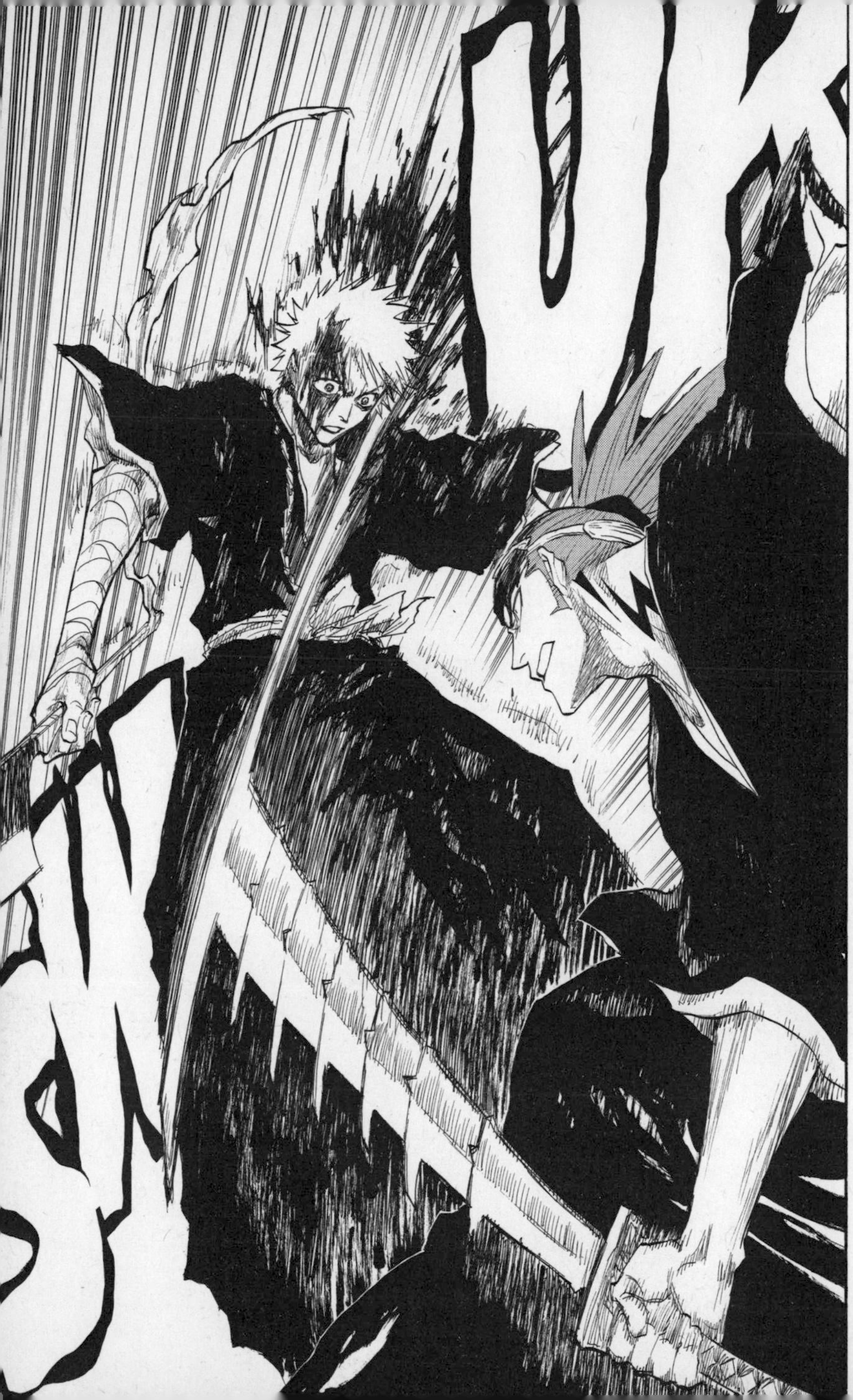

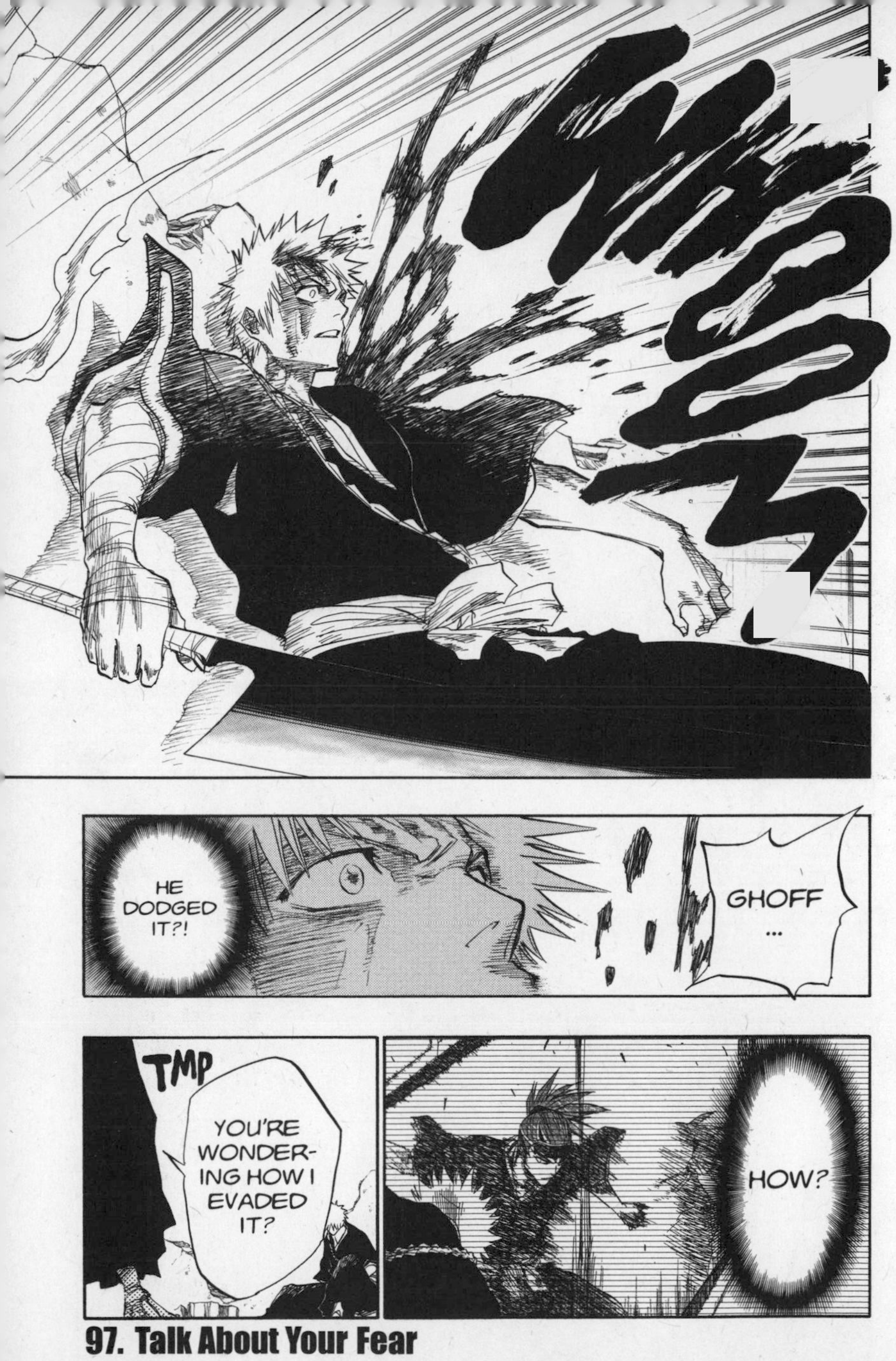
GHOFF
...
HE DODGED IT?!
HOW?
TMP
YOU'RE WONDER-ING HOW I EVADED IT?

97. Talk About Your Fear

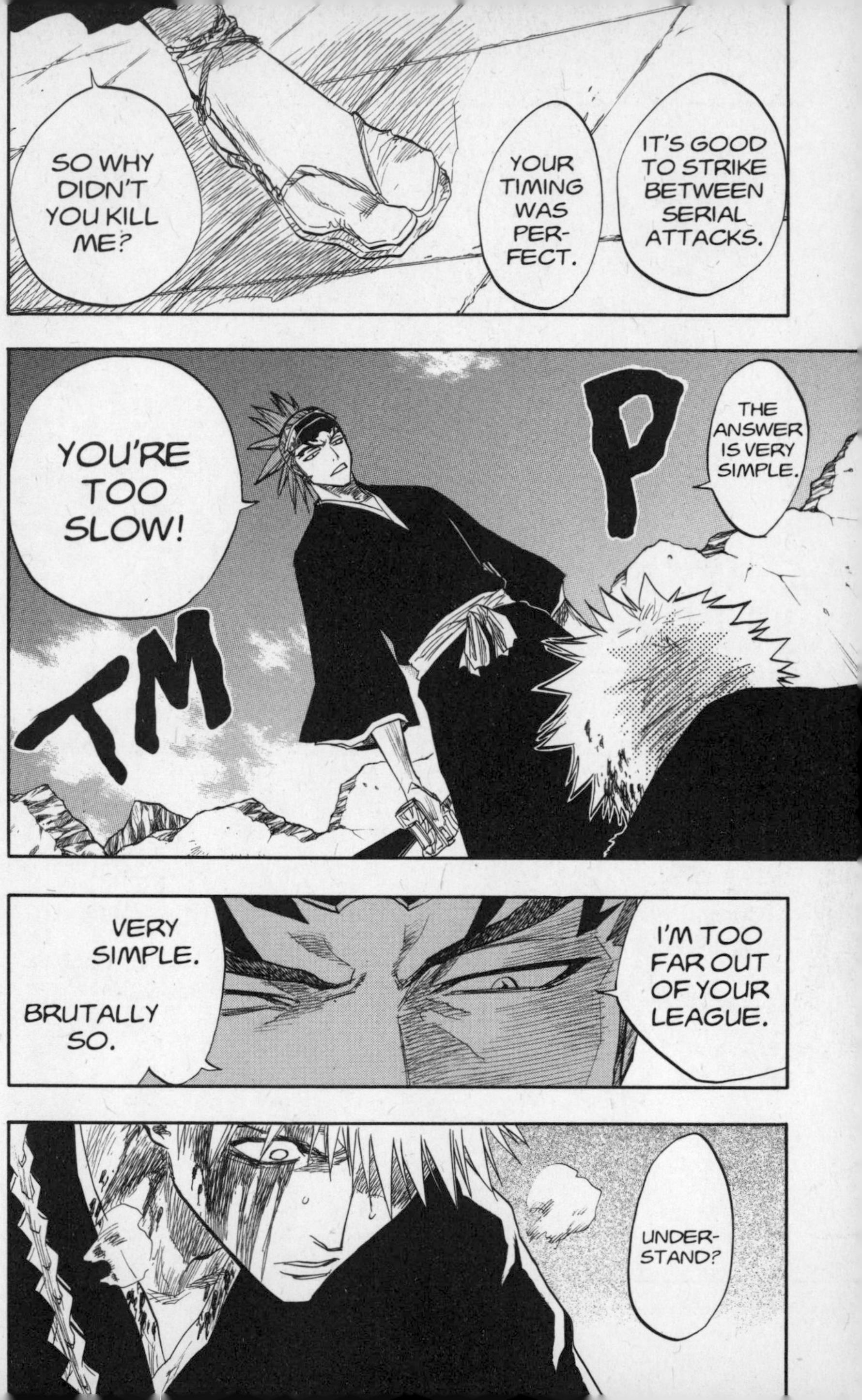
IT'S GOOD TO STRIKE BETWEEN SERIAL ATTACKS.
YOUR TIMING WAS PER-FECT.
SO WHY DIDN'T YOU KILL ME?
THE ANSWER IS VERY SIMPLE.
TMP
YOU'RE TOO SLOW!
I'M TOO FAR OUT OF YOUR LEAGUE.
VERY SIMPLE.
BRUTALLY SO.
UNDER-STAND?

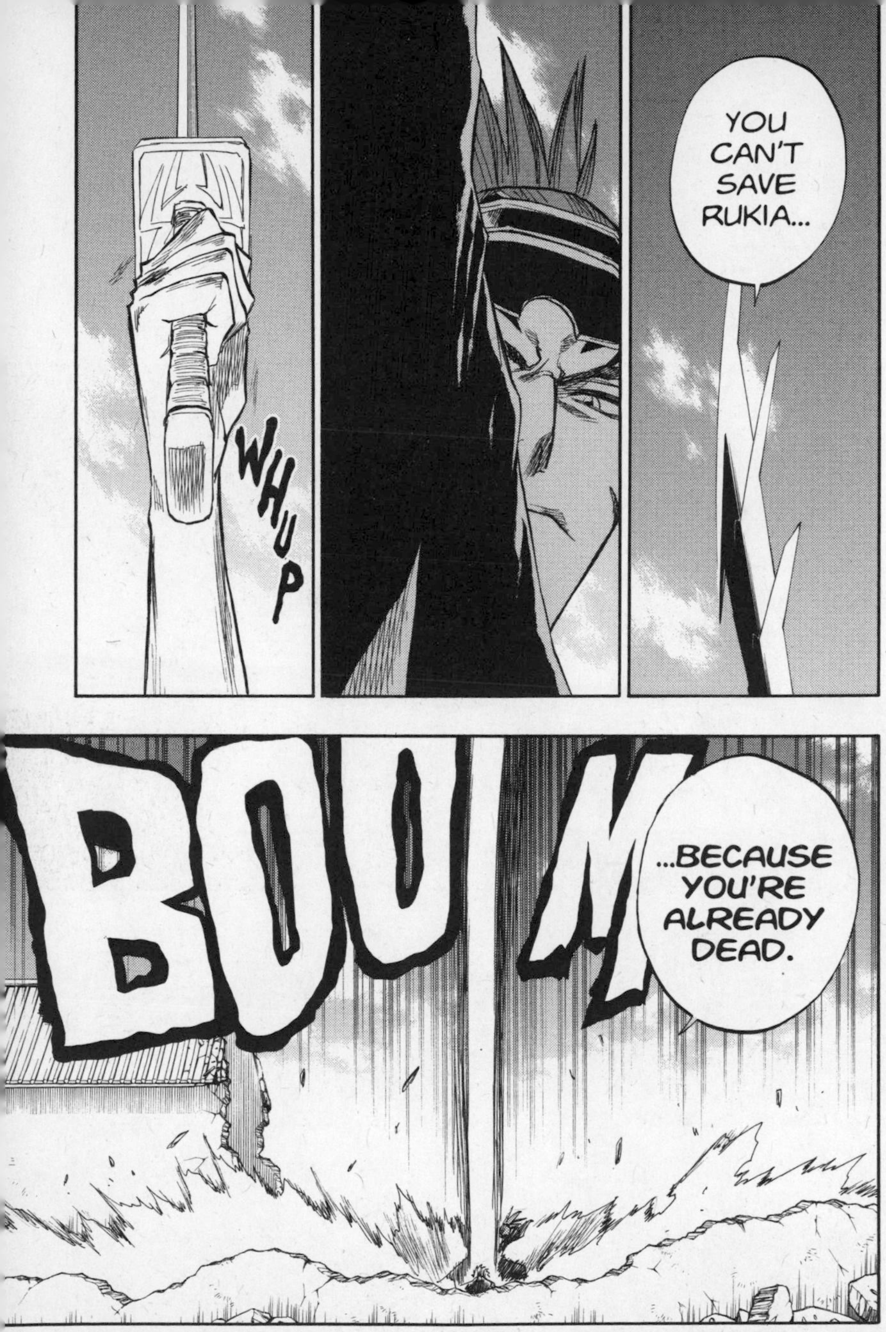
YOU CAN'T SAVE RUKIA...
WHUP
...BECAUSE YOU'RE ALREADY DEAD.
BOOM

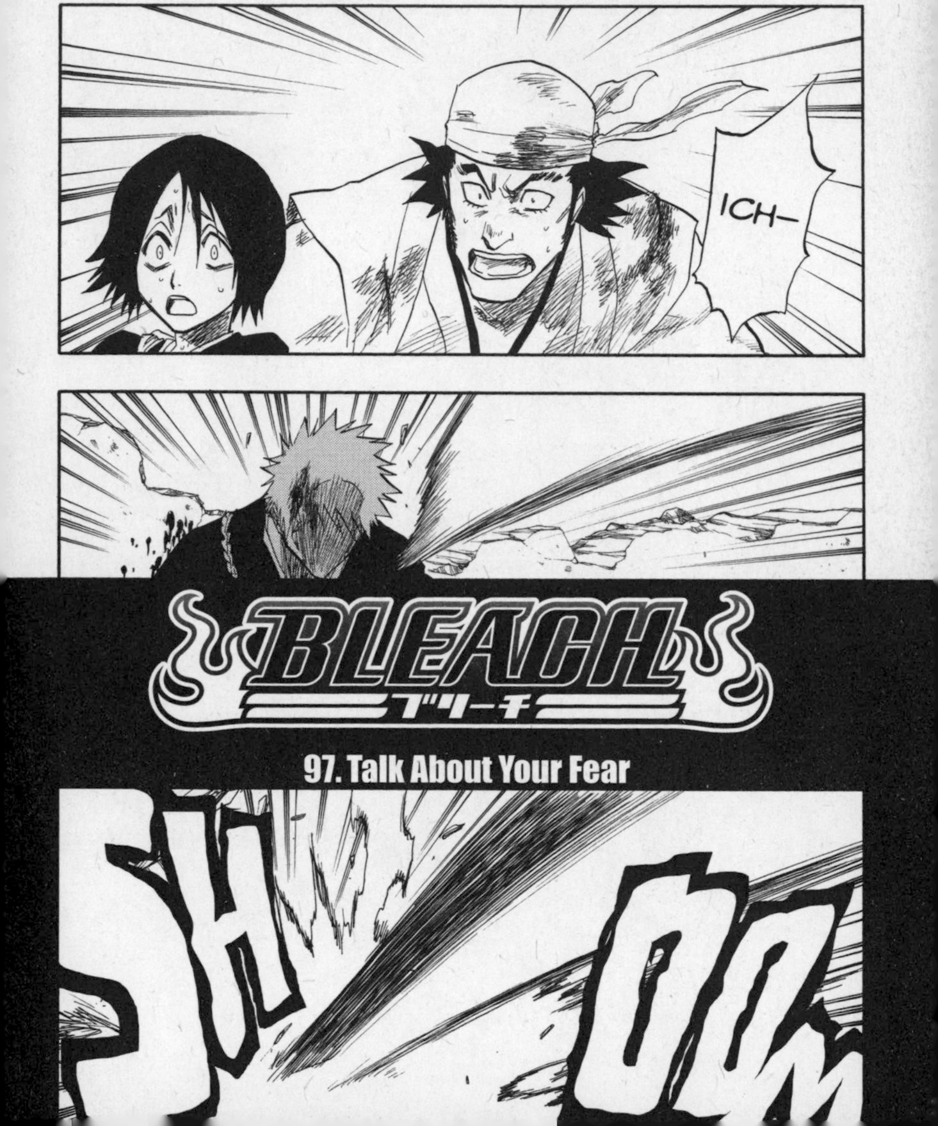
ICH—
BLEACH
ブリーチ
97. Talk About Your Fear

READ THIS WAY

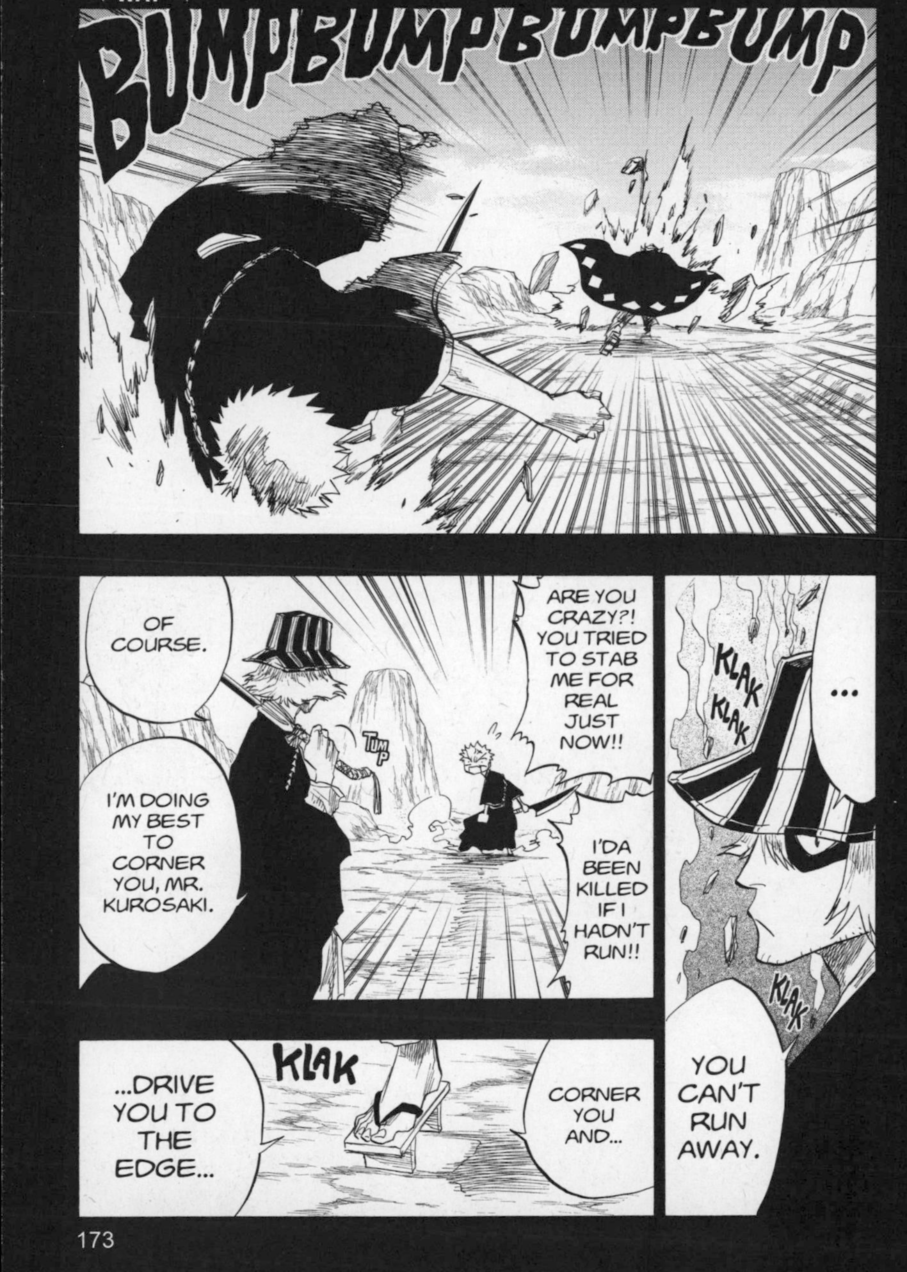
BUMPBUMPBUMPBUMP
...
KLAK
KLAK
KLAK
YOU CAN'T RUN AWAY.
ARE YOU CRAZY?! YOU TRIED TO STAB ME FOR REAL JUST NOW!!
I'DA BEEN KILLED IF I HADN'T RUN!!
TUMP
OF COURSE.
I'M DOING MY BEST TO CORNER YOU, MR. KUROSAKI.
CORNER YOU AND...
KLAK
...DRIVE YOU TO THE EDGE...

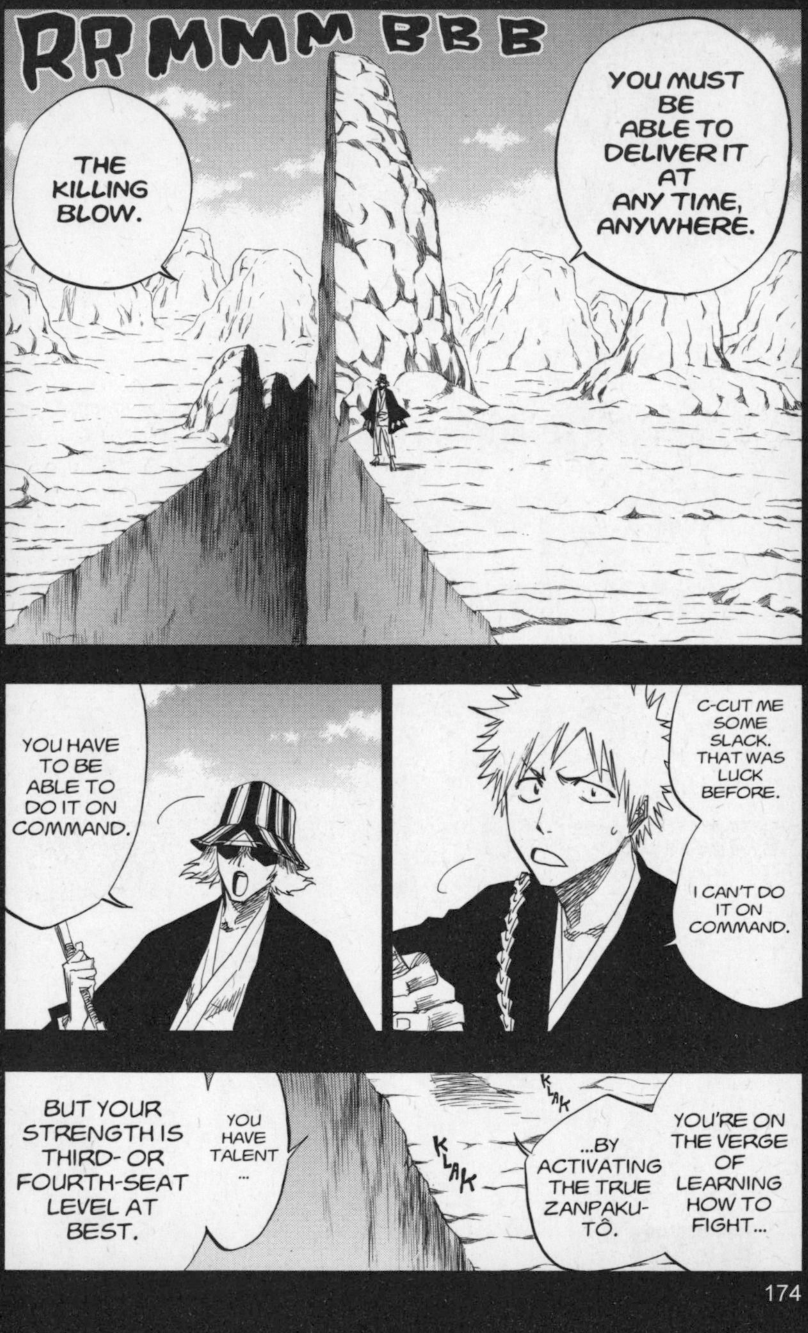
RRMMMBBB
THE KILLING BLOW.
YOU MUST BE ABLE TO DELIVER IT AT ANY TIME, ANYWHERE.
C-CUT ME SOME SLACK. THAT WAS LUCK BEFORE.
I CAN'T DO IT ON COMMAND.
YOU HAVE TO BE ABLE TO DO IT ON COMMAND.
YOU'RE ON THE VERGE OF LEARNING HOW TO FIGHT...
...BY ACTIVATING THE TRUE ZANPAKU-TÔ.
KLAK
KLAK
YOU HAVE TALENT...
BUT YOUR STRENGTH IS THIRD- OR FOURTH-SEAT LEVEL AT BEST.

READ THIS WAY

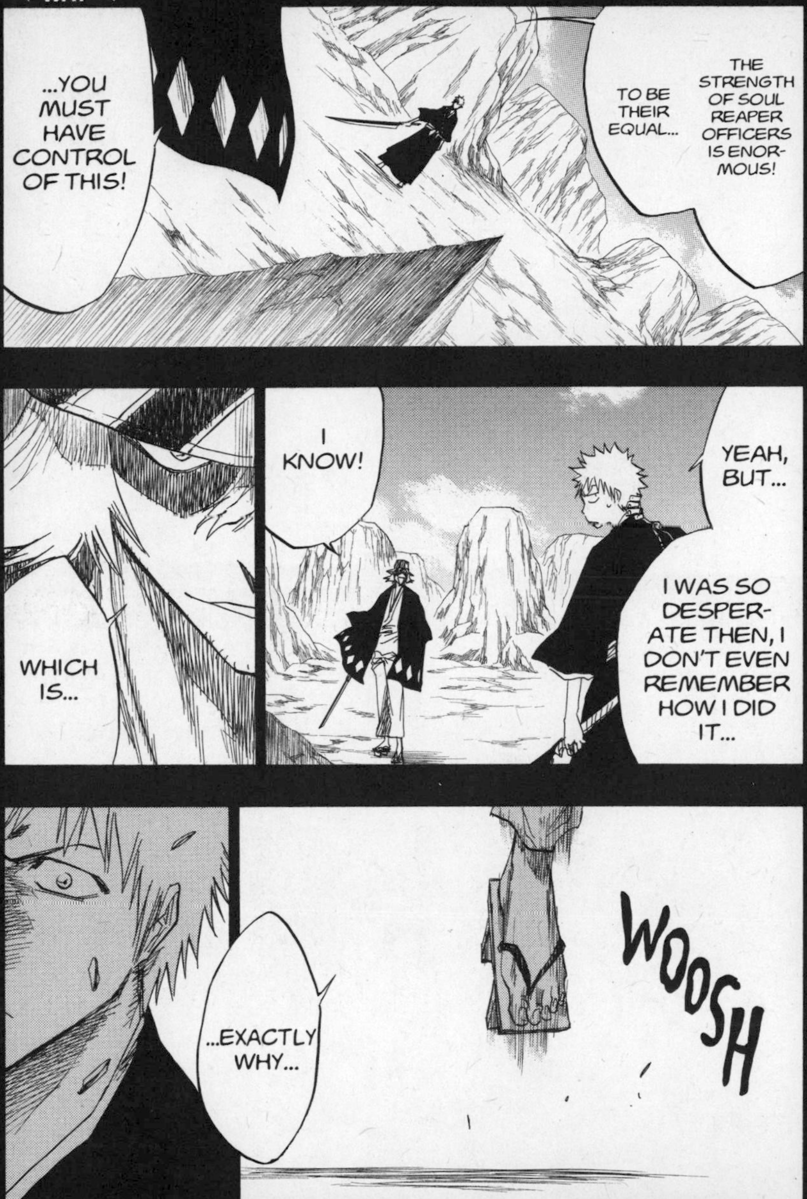
THE STRENGTH OF SOUL REAPER OFFICERS IS ENORMOUS!
TO BE THEIR EQUAL...
...YOU MUST HAVE CONTROL OF THIS!
YEAH, BUT...
I WAS SO DESPERATE THEN, I DON'T EVEN REMEMBER HOW I DID IT...
I KNOW!
WHICH IS...
WOOSH
...EXACTLY WHY...

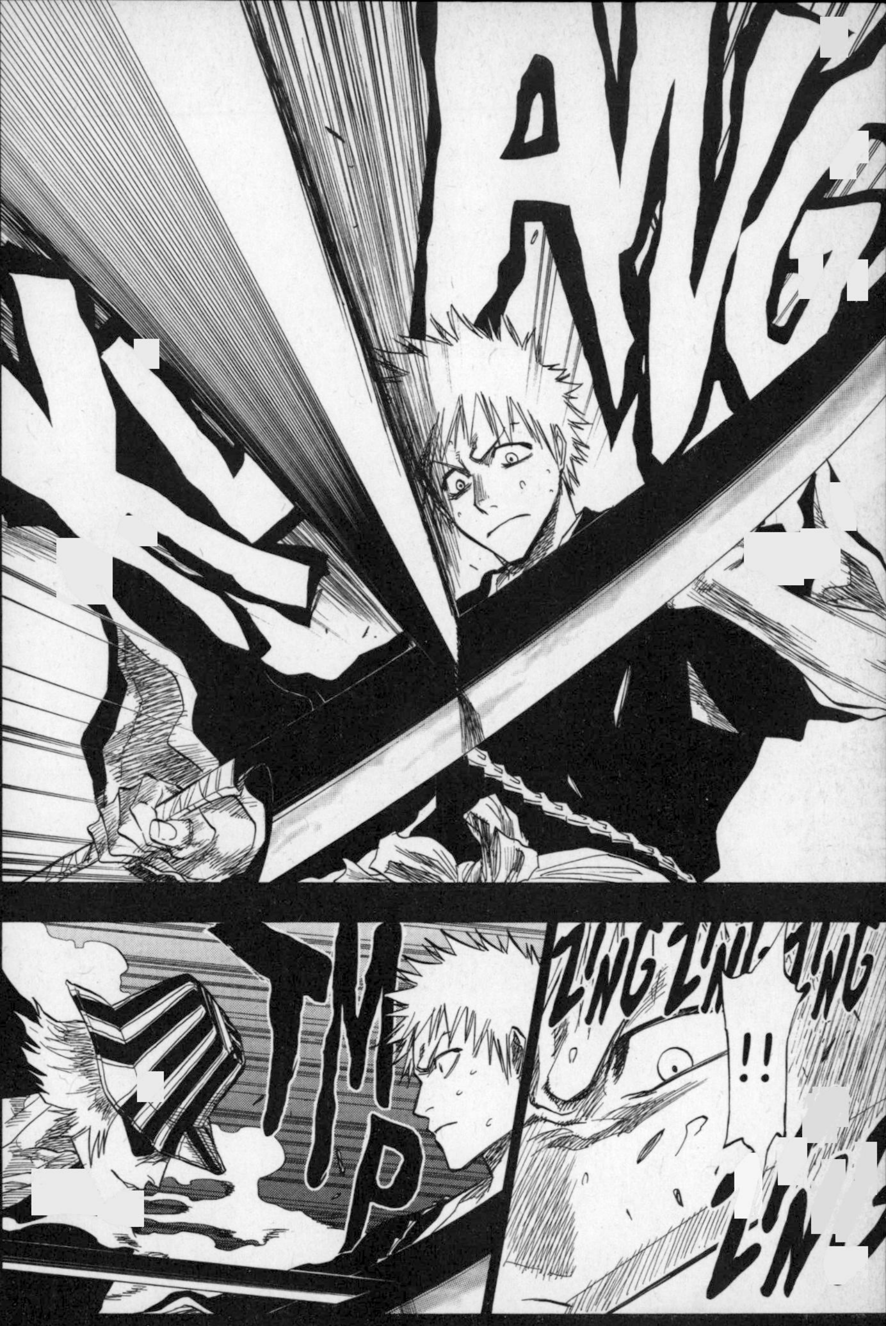
!!

READ THIS WAY

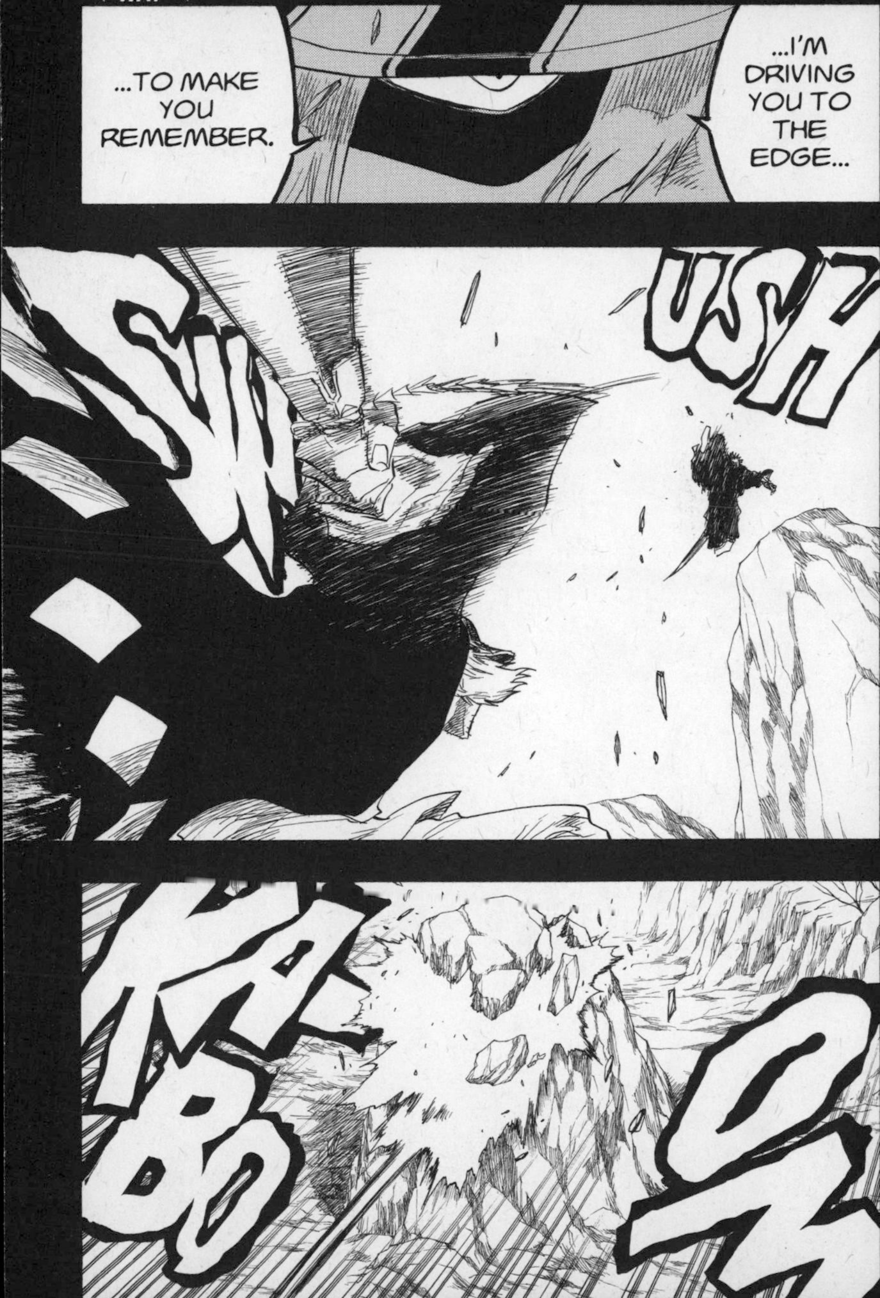

...I'M DRIVING YOU TO THE EDGE...
...TO MAKE YOU REMEMBER.

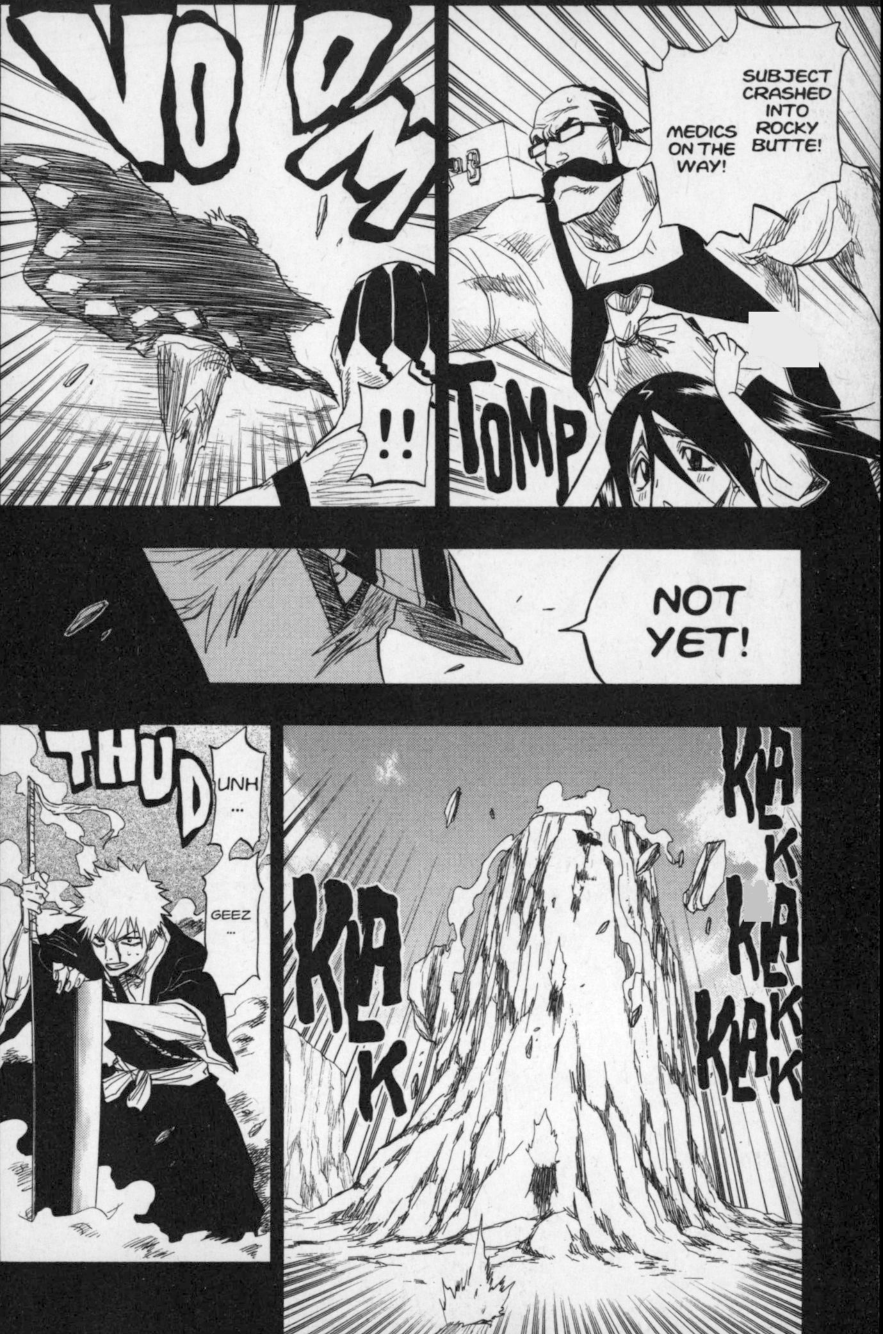
SUBJECT CRASHED INTO ROCKY BUTTE!
MEDICS ON THE WAY!
TOMP
VOOM
!!
NOT YET!
KLAK KLAK KLAK
KLAK
THUD
UNH ...
GEEZ ...

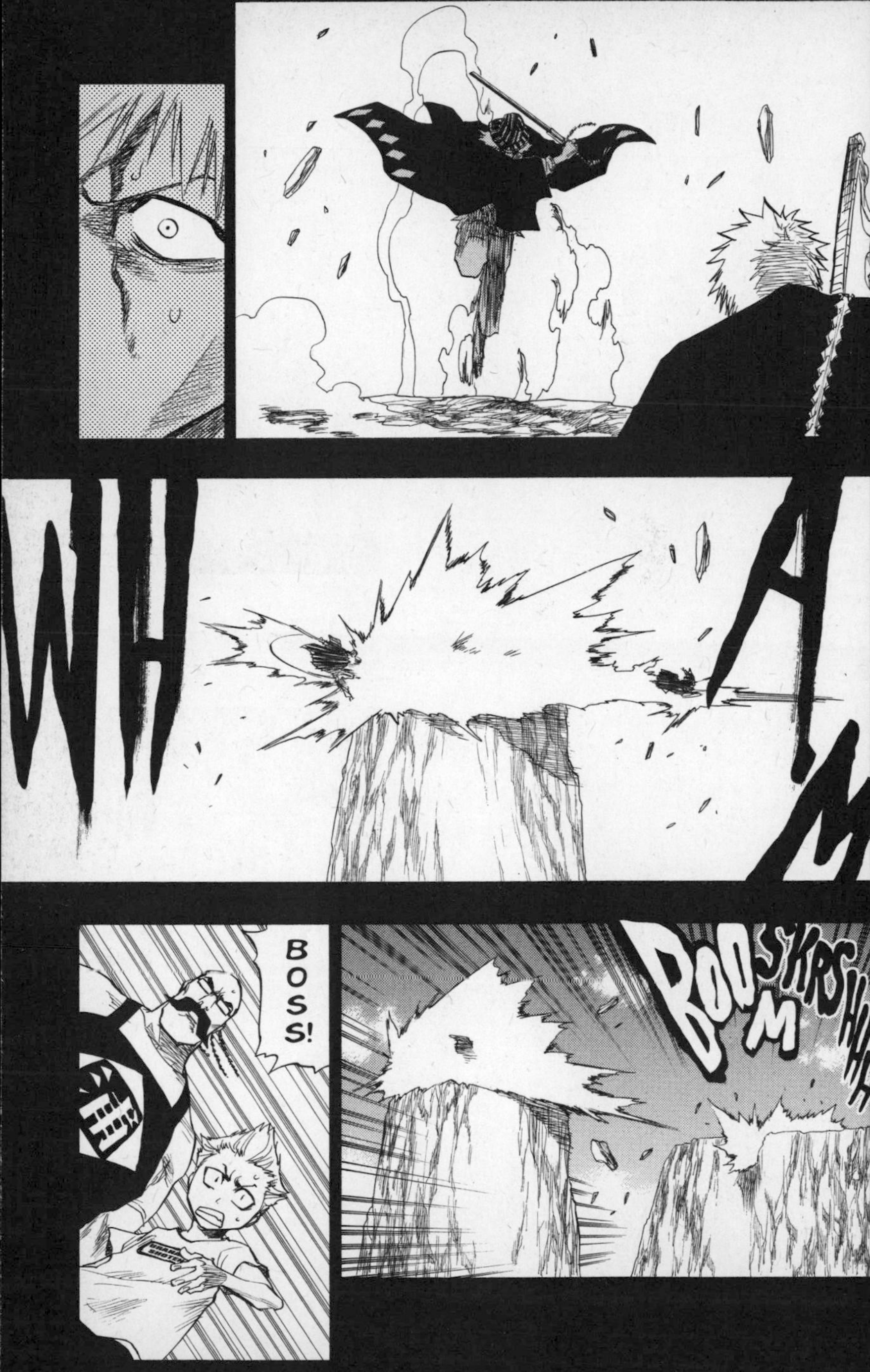
WHAM
BOOM
KRSHHH
BOSS!

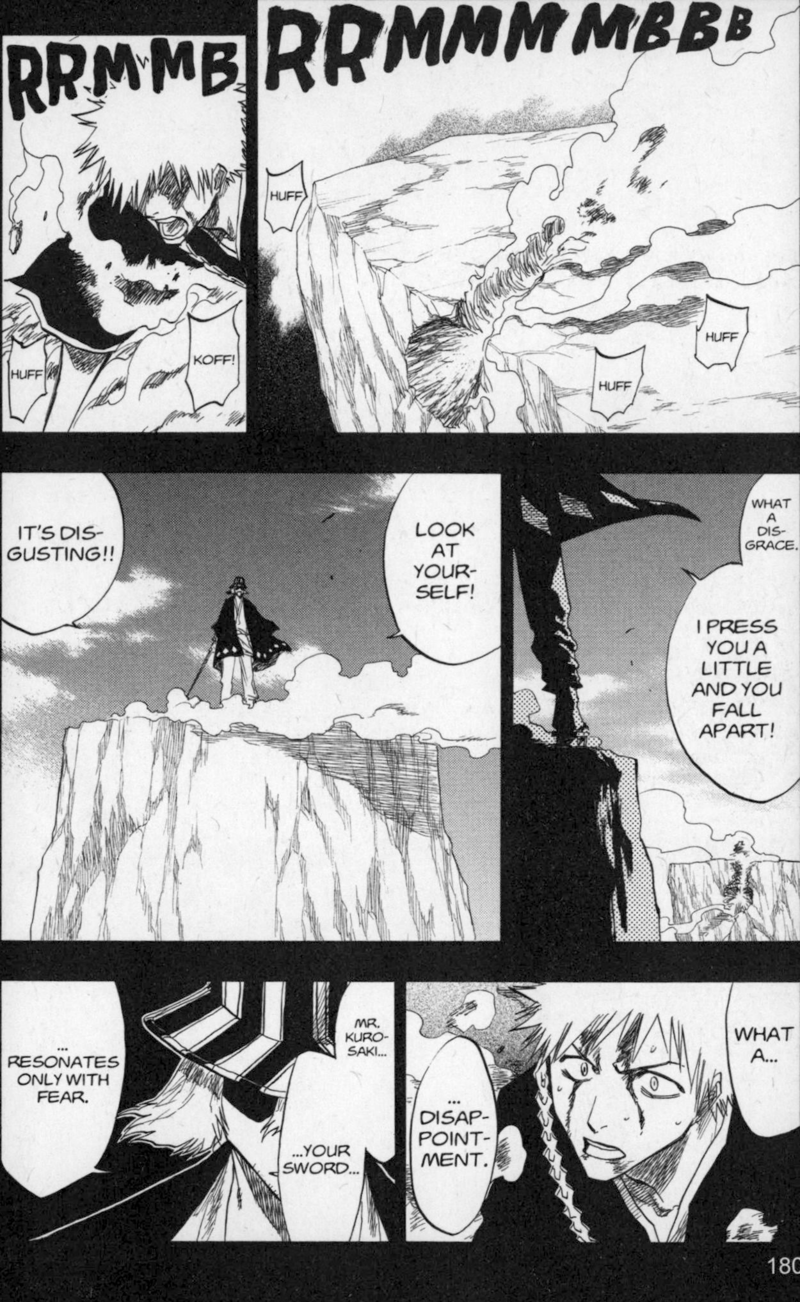
RRMMMMBBB
HUFF
HUFF
HUFF
RRMMB
KOFF!
HUFF
WHAT A DISGRACE.
I PRESS YOU A LITTLE AND YOU FALL APART!
LOOK AT YOURSELF!
IT'S DISGUSTING!!
WHAT A...
...DISAPPOINTMENT.
MR. KUROSAKI...
...YOUR SWORD...
...RESONATES ONLY WITH FEAR.

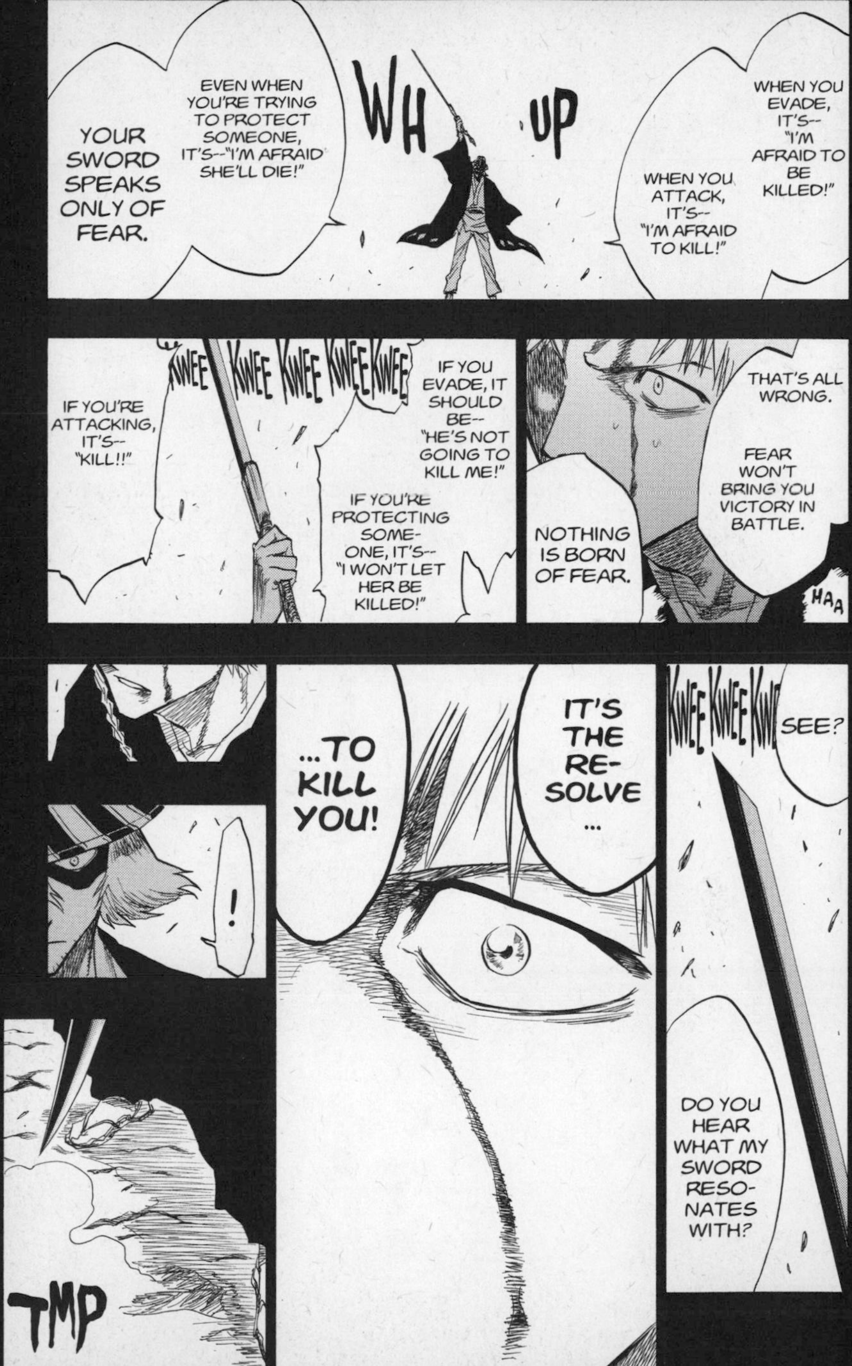
WHEN YOU EVADE, IT'S-- "I'M AFRAID TO BE KILLED!"
WHEN YOU ATTACK, IT'S-- "I'M AFRAID TO KILL!"
WH UP
EVEN WHEN YOU'RE TRYING TO PROTECT SOMEONE, IT'S--"I'M AFRAID SHE'LL DIE!"
YOUR SWORD SPEAKS ONLY OF FEAR.
THAT'S ALL WRONG.
FEAR WON'T BRING YOU VICTORY IN BATTLE.
NOTHING IS BORN OF FEAR.
HAA
IF YOU EVADE, IT SHOULD BE-- "HE'S NOT GOING TO KILL ME!"
KWEE KWEE KWEE KWEE KWEE
IF YOU'RE ATTACKING, IT'S-- "KILL!!"
IF YOU'RE PROTECTING SOME-ONE, IT'S-- "I WON'T LET HER BE KILLED!"
KWEE KWEE KWE
SEE?
DO YOU HEAR WHAT MY SWORD RESO-NATES WITH?
IT'S THE RE-SOLVE ...
...TO KILL YOU!
!
TMP

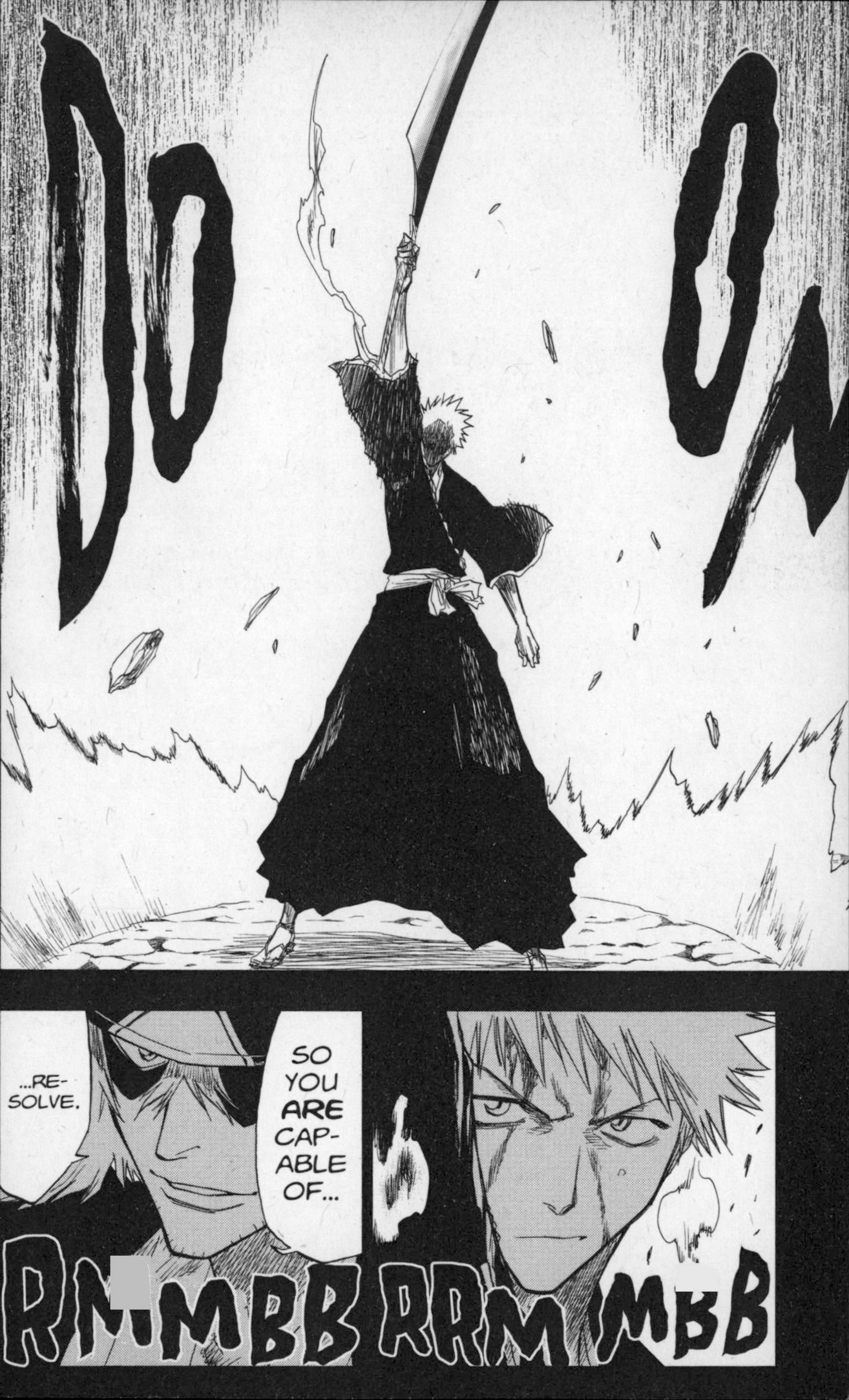
DOON
SO YOU ARE CAPABLE OF...
...RE-SOLVE.
RMMBB RRMMBB

READ THIS WAY

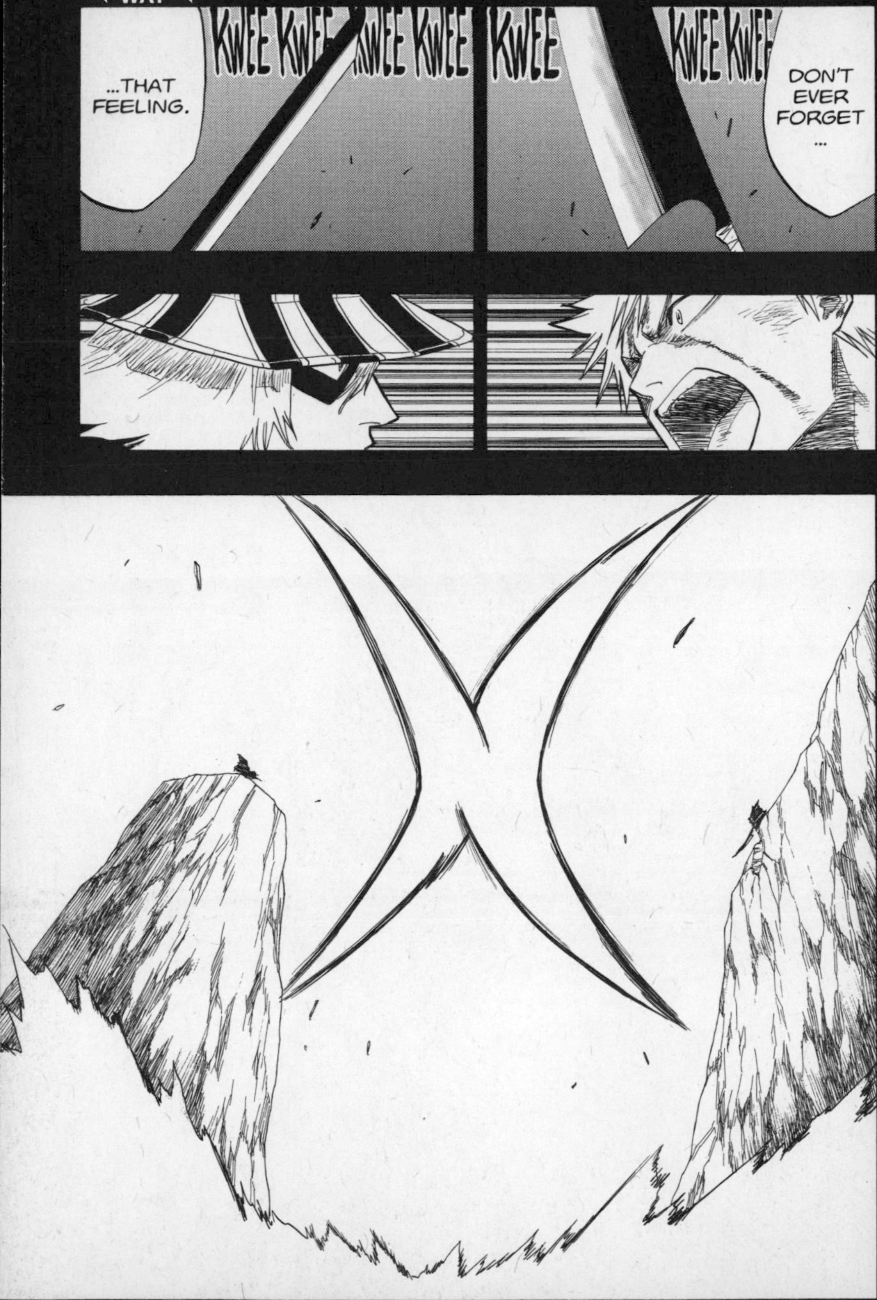
KWEE KWEE
KWEE
DON'T EVER FORGET ...
KWEE KWEE
KWEE KWEE
...THAT FEELING.

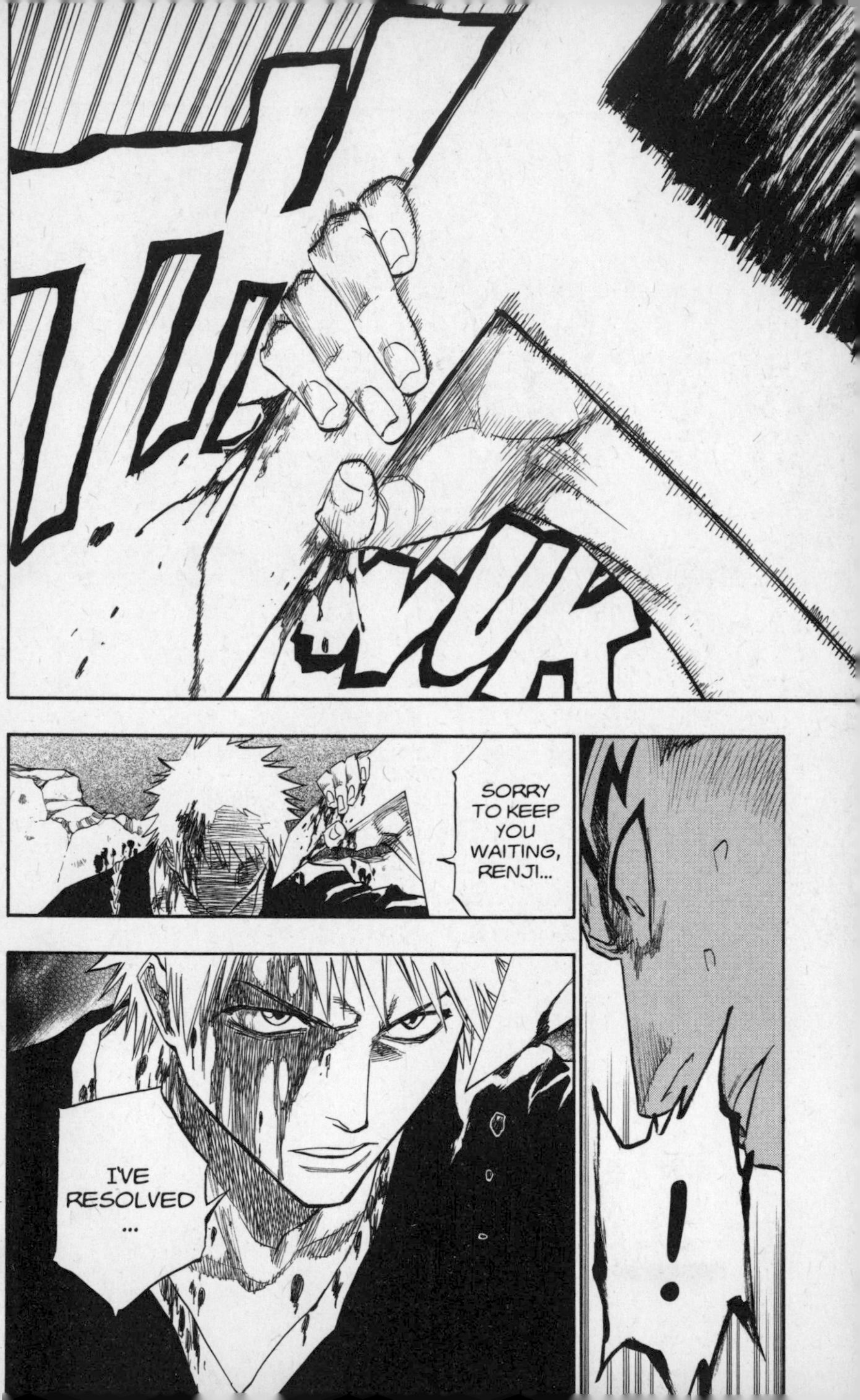
!
SORRY TO KEEP YOU WAITING, RENJI...
I'VE RESOLVED ...

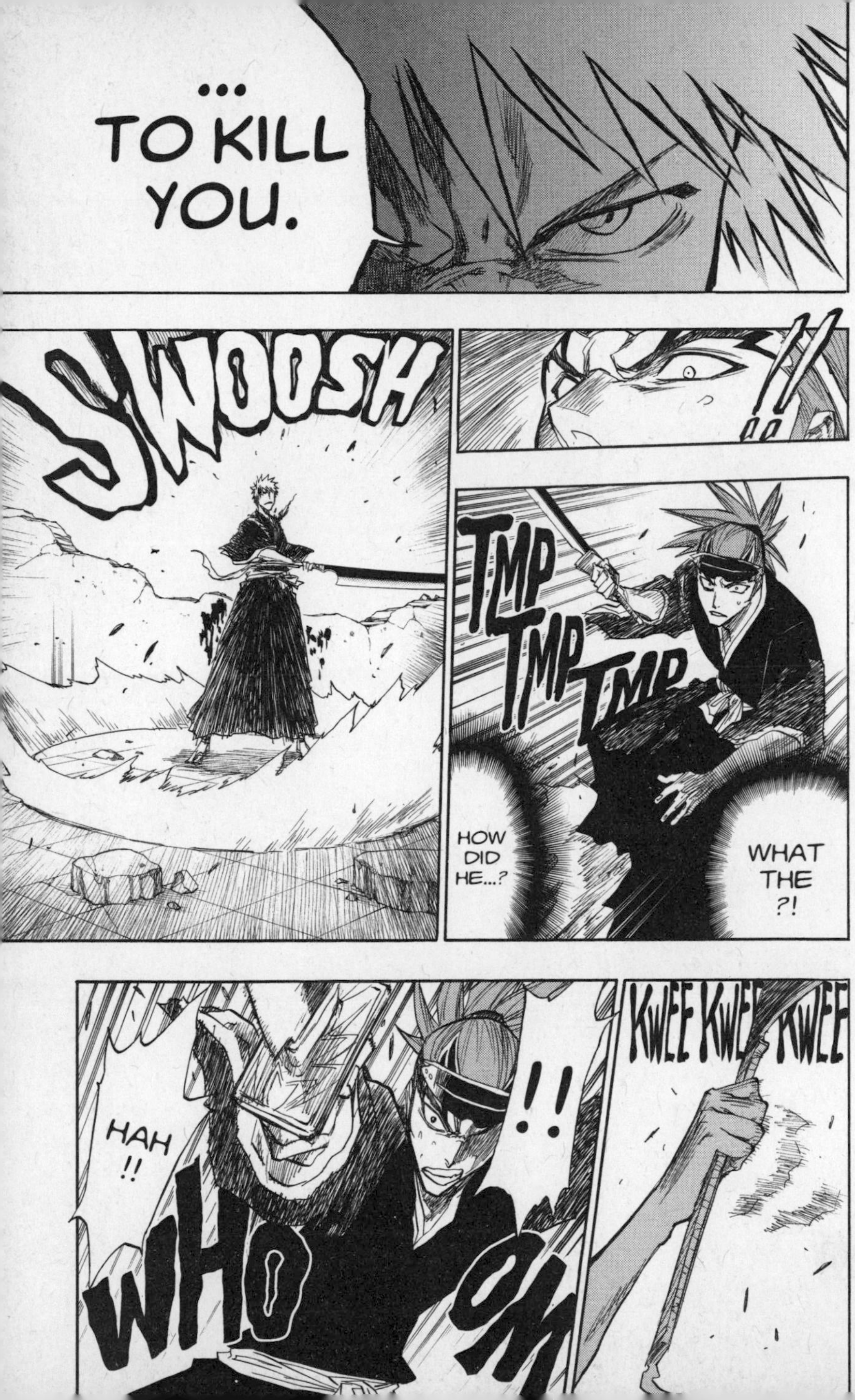

... TO KILL YOU.
!!
TMP TMP TMP
WHAT THE ?!
HOW DID HE...?
SWOOSH
KWEE KWEE KWEE
!!
HAH !!
WHOOM

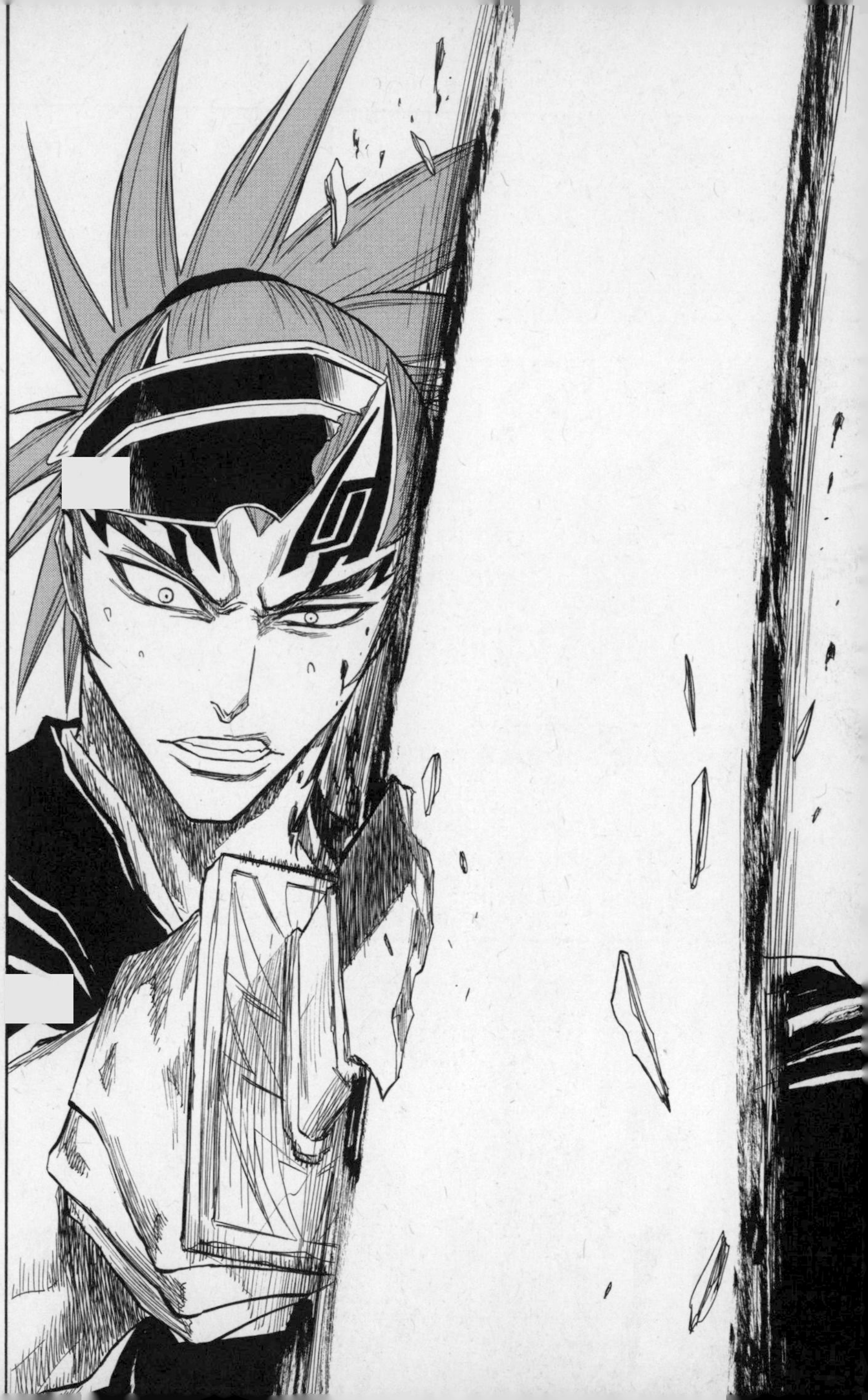

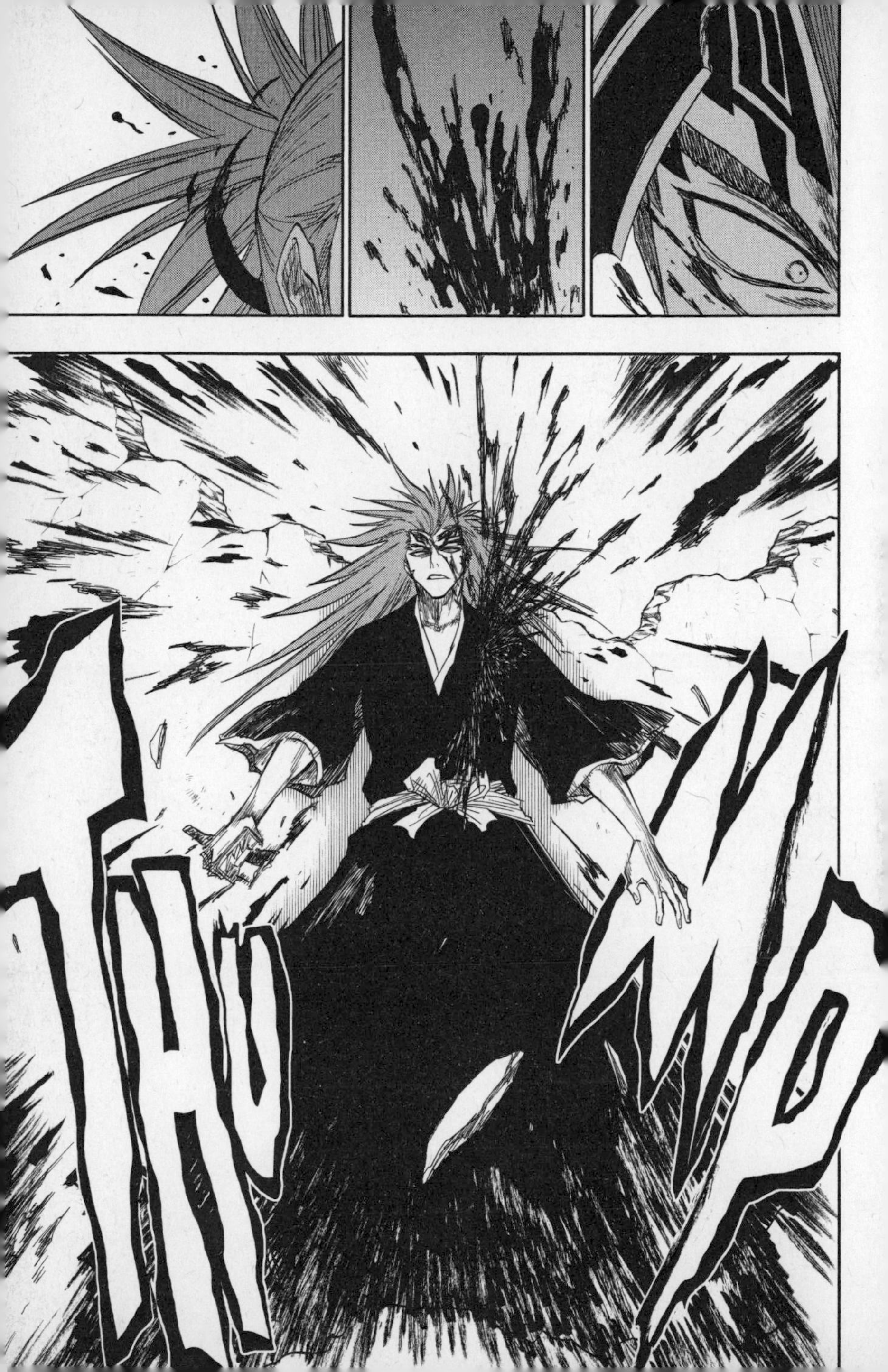

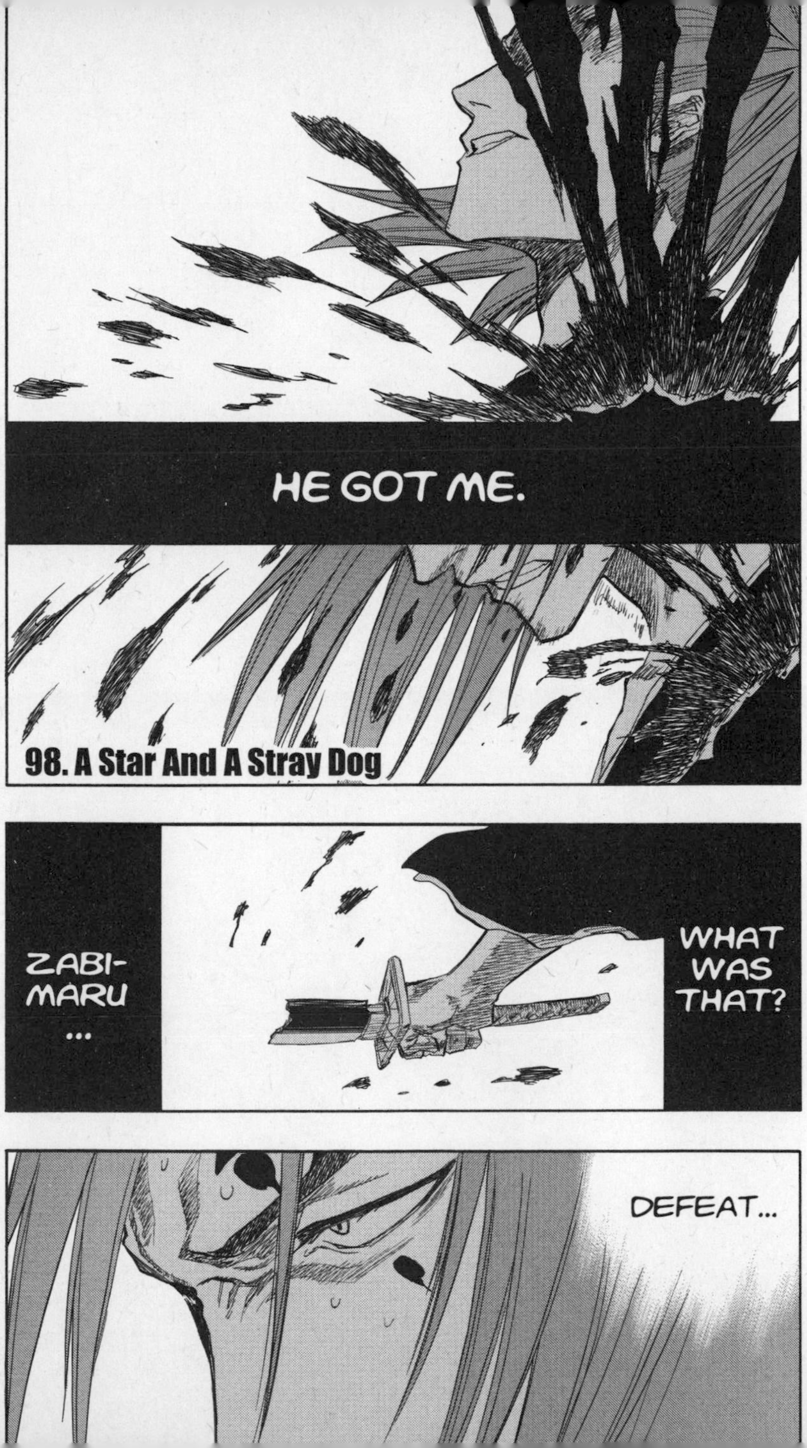
HE GOT ME.
98. A Star And A Stray Dog
WHAT WAS THAT?
ZABI-MARU...
DEFEAT...

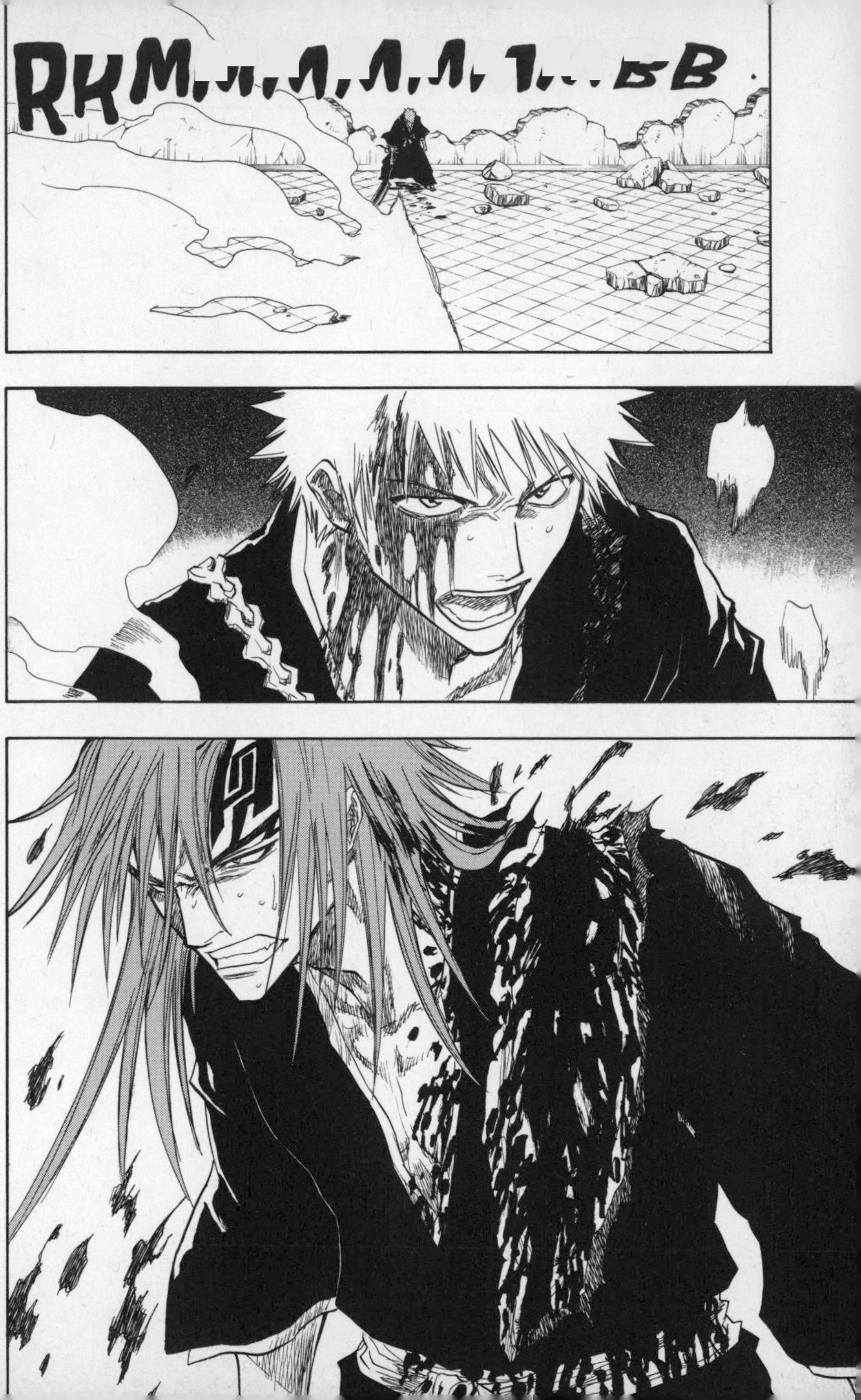

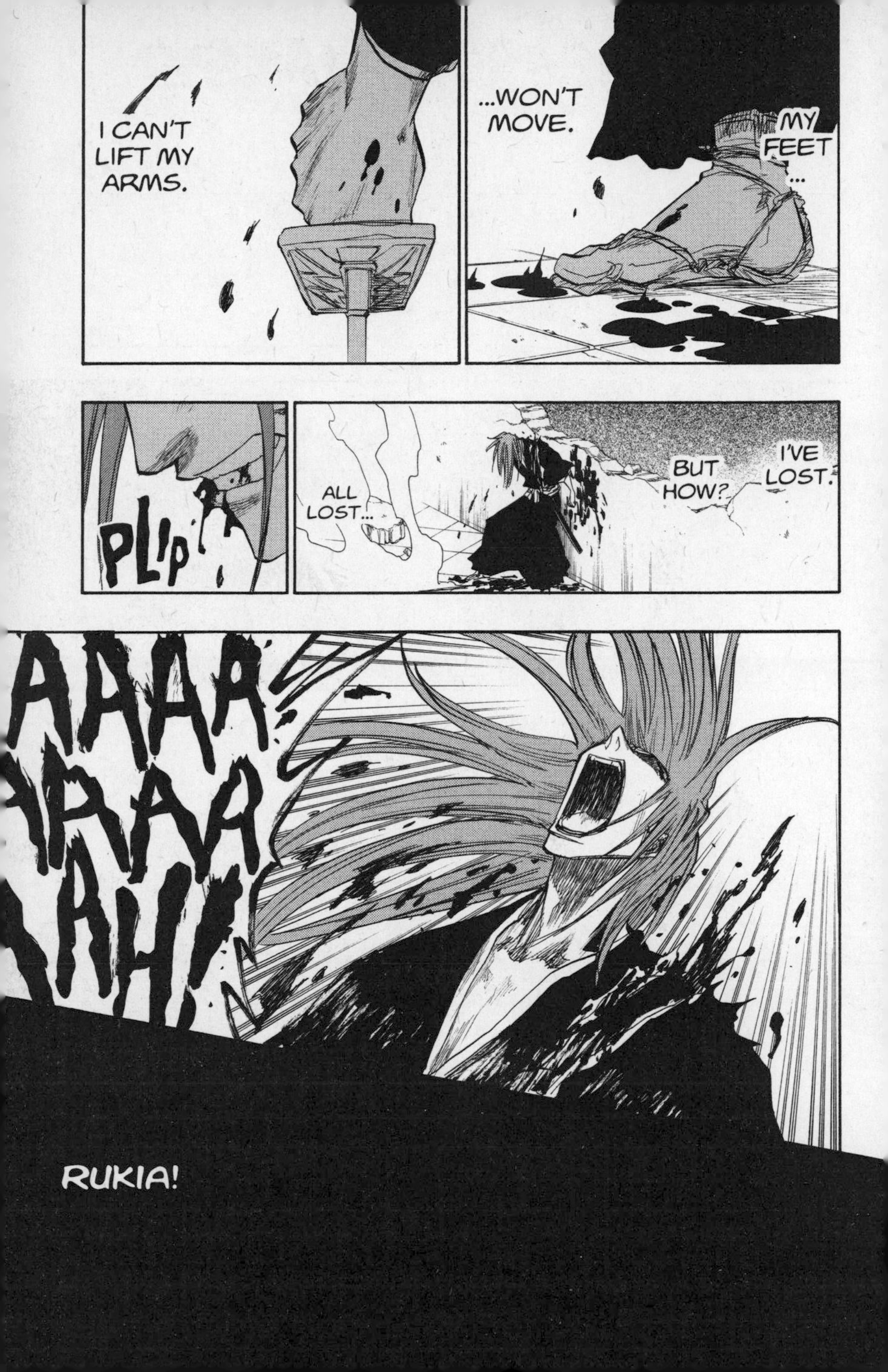
MY FEET...
...WON'T MOVE.
I CAN'T LIFT MY ARMS.
I'VE LOST.
BUT HOW?
ALL LOST...
PLIP
AAAARAAAH!
RUKIA!

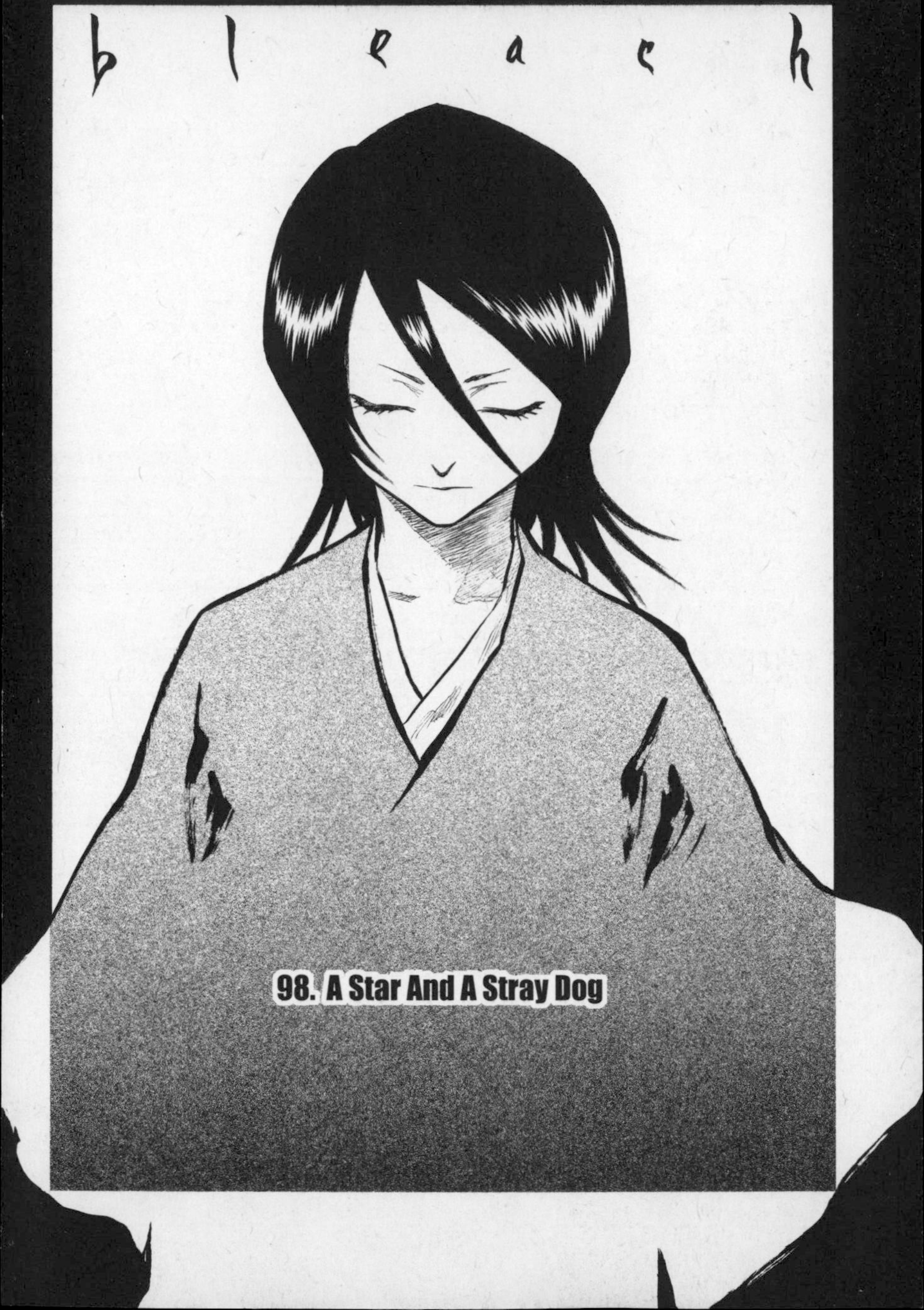
bleach
98. A Star And A Stray Dog

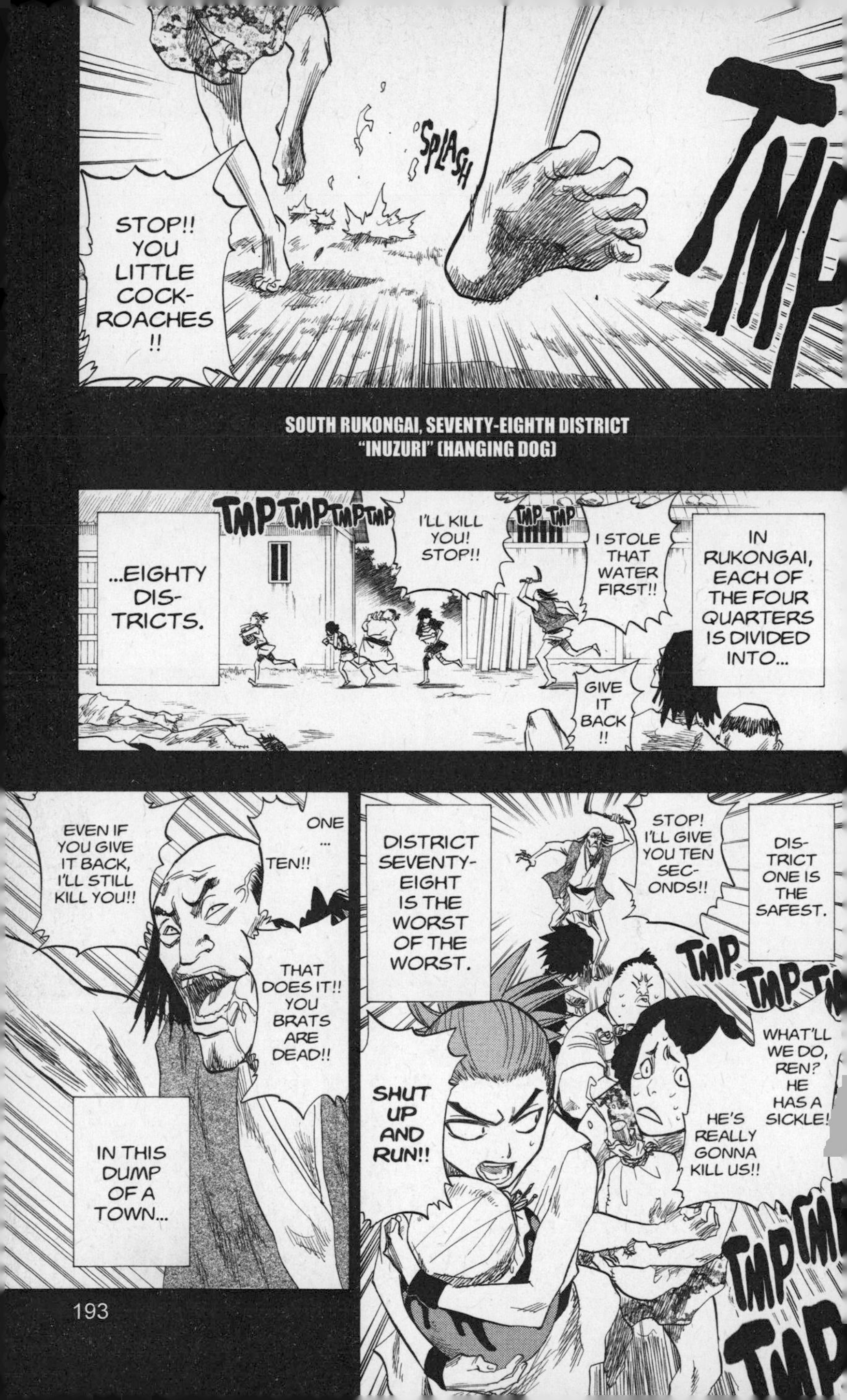
TMP
SPLASH
STOP!! YOU LITTLE COCK-ROACHES!!
SOUTH RUKONGAI, SEVENTY-EIGHTH DISTRICT
"INUZURI" (HANGING DOG)
IN RUKONGAI, EACH OF THE FOUR QUARTERS IS DIVIDED INTO...
I STOLE THAT WATER FIRST!!
GIVE IT BACK!!
TMP TMP
I'LL KILL YOU! STOP!!
TMP TMP TMP TMP
...EIGHTY DIS-TRICTS.
DIS-TRICT ONE IS THE SAFEST.
STOP! I'LL GIVE YOU TEN SEC-ONDS!!
DISTRICT SEVENTY-EIGHT IS THE WORST OF THE WORST.
TMP TMP TM
WHAT'LL WE DO, REN? HE HAS A SICKLE!
HE'S REALLY GONNA KILL US!!
SHUT UP AND RUN!!
TMP TMP TMP
ONE ... TEN!!
EVEN IF YOU GIVE IT BACK, I'LL STILL KILL YOU!!
THAT DOES IT!! YOU BRATS ARE DEAD!!
IN THIS DUMP OF A TOWN...

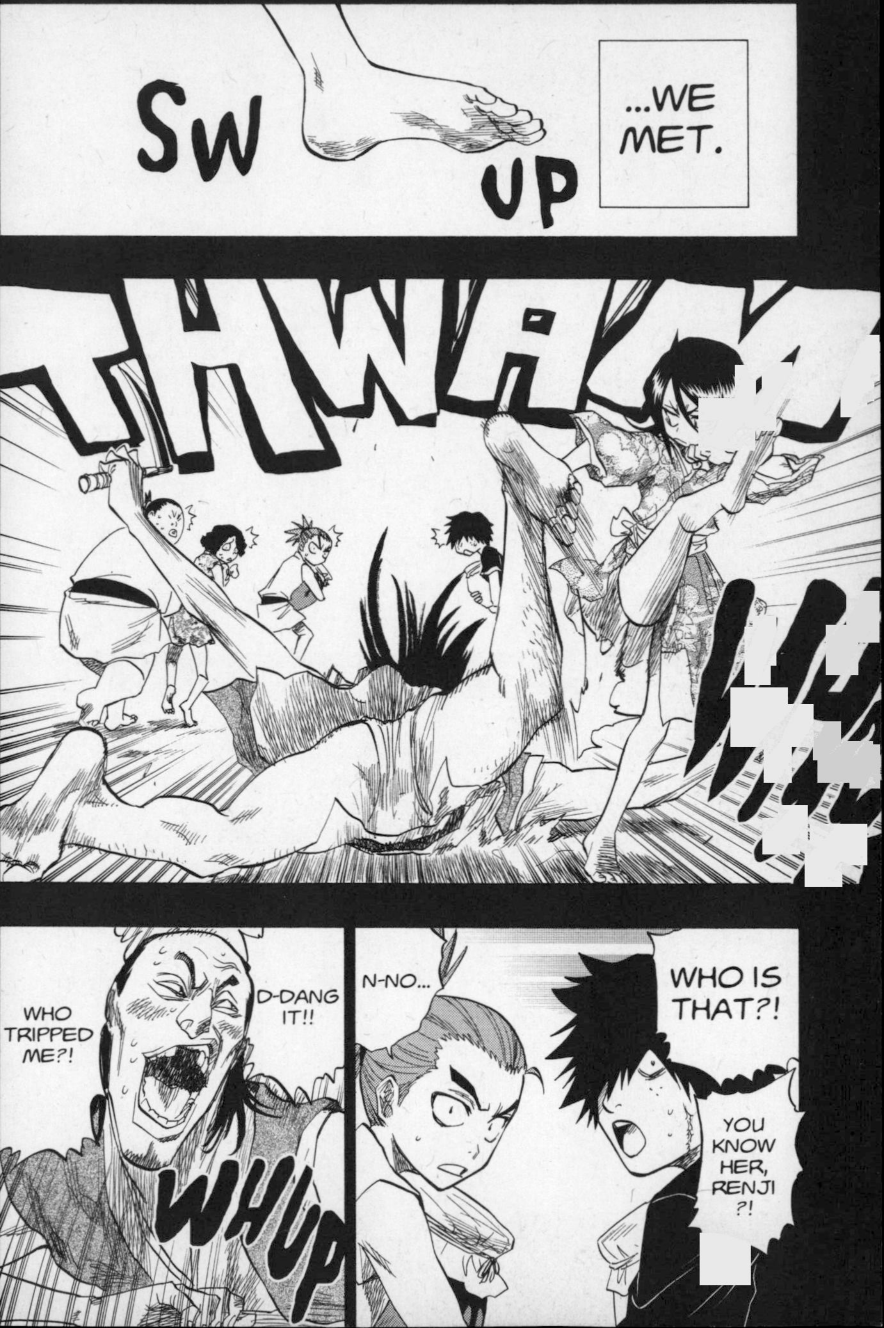
...WE MET.
SW
UP
WHO IS THAT?!
N-NO...
YOU KNOW HER, RENJI?!
D-DANG IT!!
WHO TRIPPED ME?!
WHUP

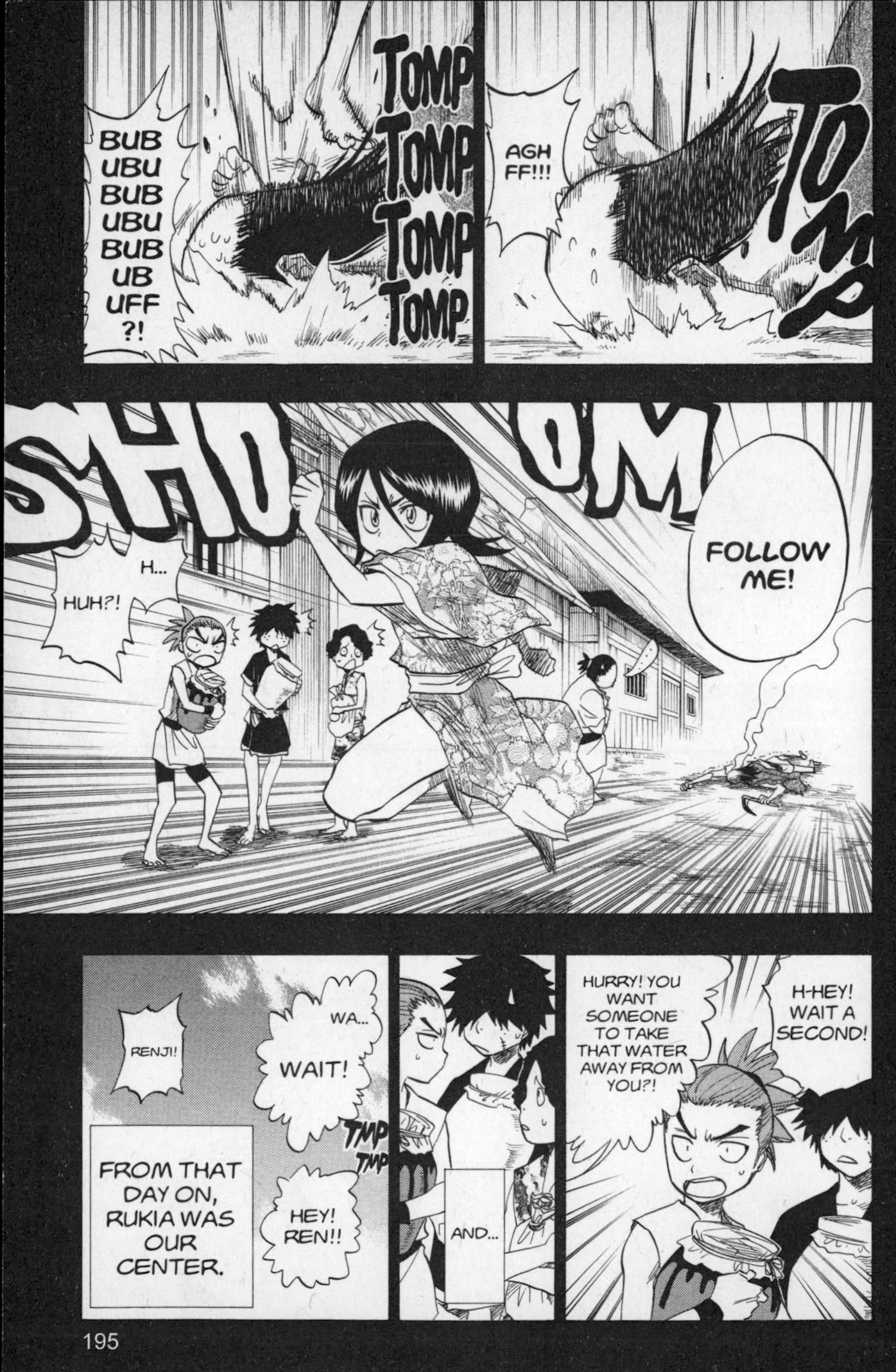
TOMP
AGH FF!!!
TOMP TOMP TOMP TOMP
BUB UBU BUB UBU BUB UB UFF ?!
FOLLOW ME!
SHO
OM
H...
HUH?!
H-HEY! WAIT A SECOND!
HURRY! YOU WANT SOMEONE TO TAKE THAT WATER AWAY FROM YOU?!
TMP TMP
AND...
WA...
WAIT!
RENJI!
HEY! REN!!
FROM THAT DAY ON, RUKIA WAS OUR CENTER.

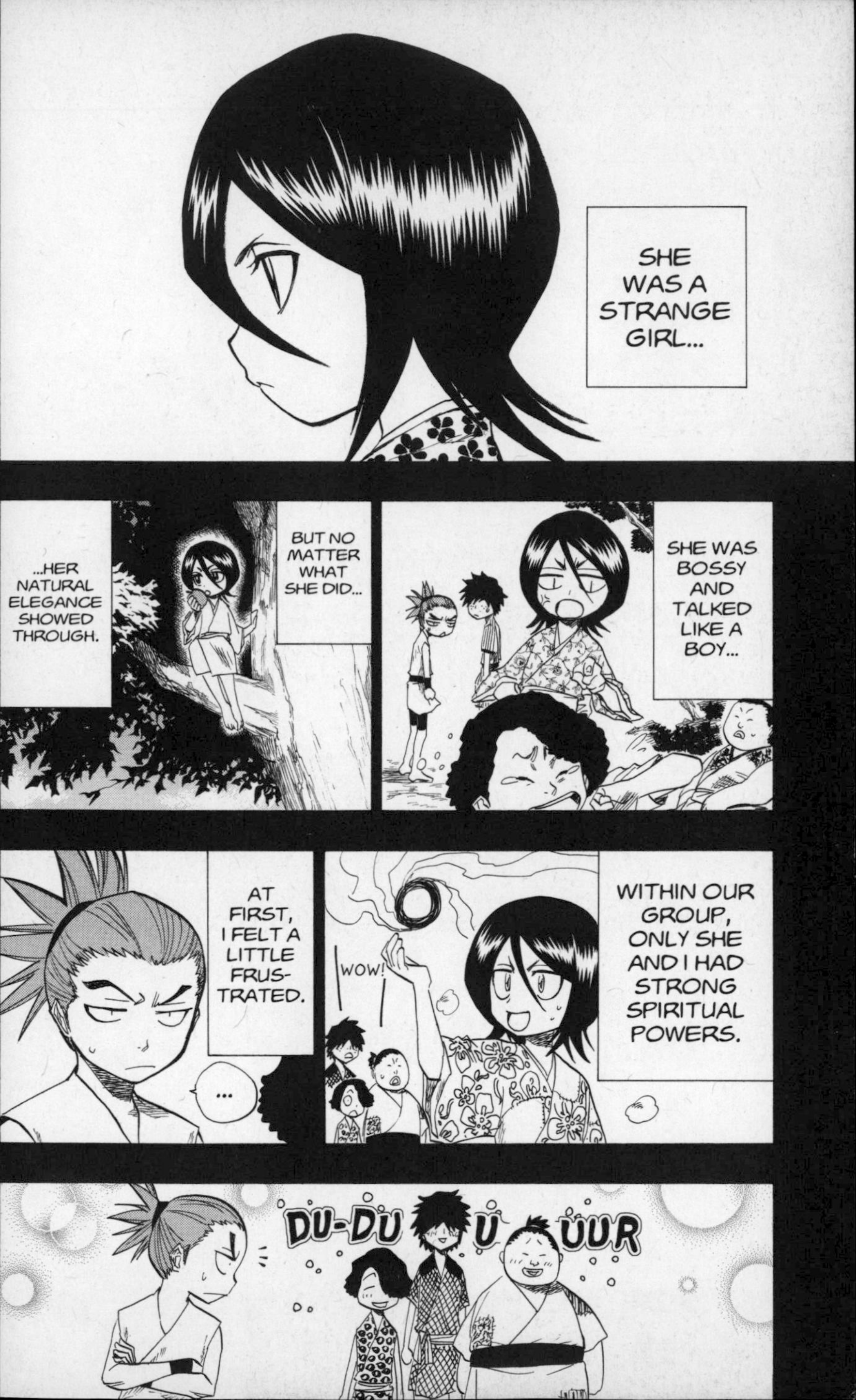
SHE WAS A STRANGE GIRL...
SHE WAS BOSSY AND TALKED LIKE A BOY...
BUT NO MATTER WHAT SHE DID...
...HER NATURAL ELEGANCE SHOWED THROUGH.
WITHIN OUR GROUP, ONLY SHE AND I HAD STRONG SPIRITUAL POWERS.
WOW!
AT FIRST, I FELT A LITTLE FRUS-TRATED.
...
DU-DU U UUR

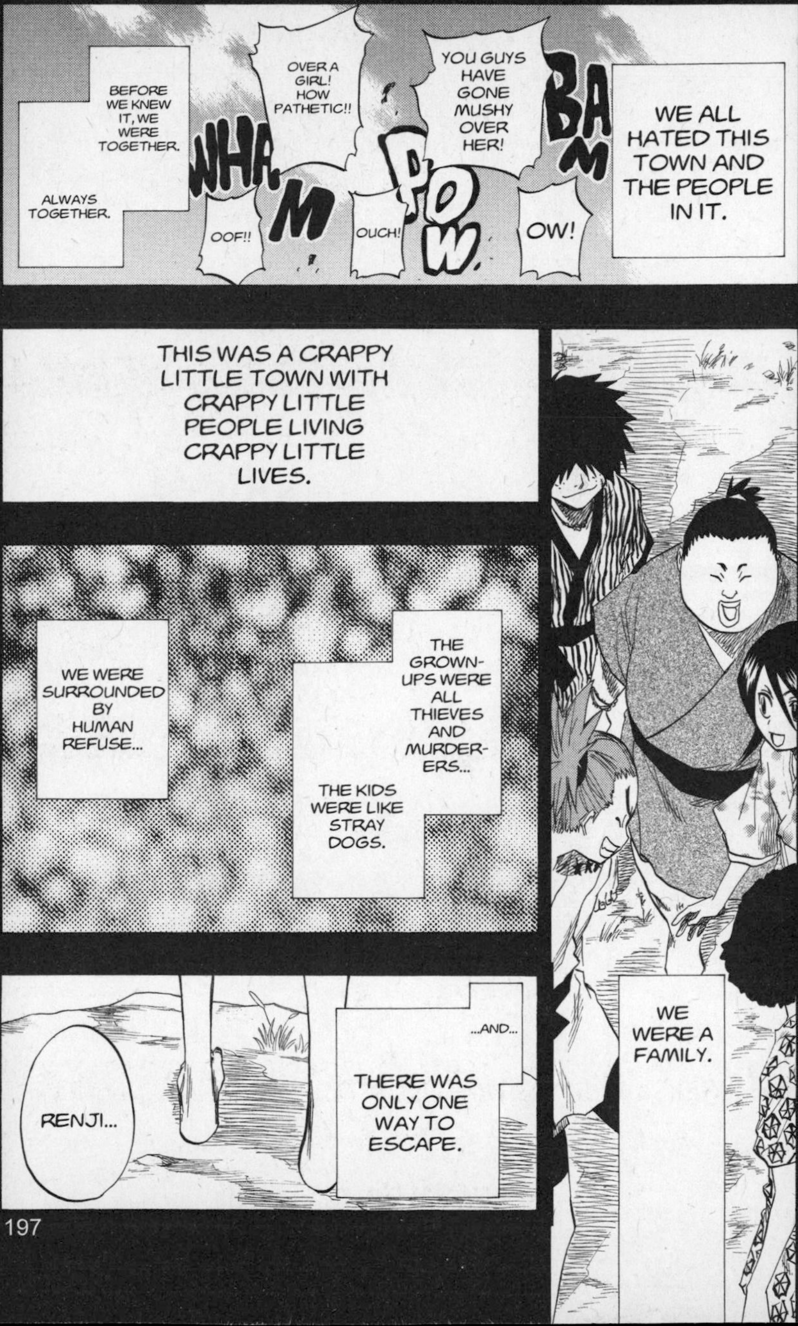
WE ALL HATED THIS TOWN AND THE PEOPLE IN IT.
BAM
YOU GUYS HAVE GONE MUSHY OVER HER!
OW!
POW.
OUCH!
OVER A GIRL! HOW PATHETIC!!
WHAM
OOF!!
BEFORE WE KNEW IT, WE WERE TOGETHER.
ALWAYS TOGETHER.
WE WERE A FAMILY.
THIS WAS A CRAPPY LITTLE TOWN WITH CRAPPY LITTLE PEOPLE LIVING CRAPPY LITTLE LIVES.
THE GROWN-UPS WERE ALL THIEVES AND MURDERERS...
THE KIDS WERE LIKE STRAY DOGS.
WE WERE SURROUNDED BY HUMAN REFUSE...
...AND...
THERE WAS ONLY ONE WAY TO ESCAPE.
RENJI...

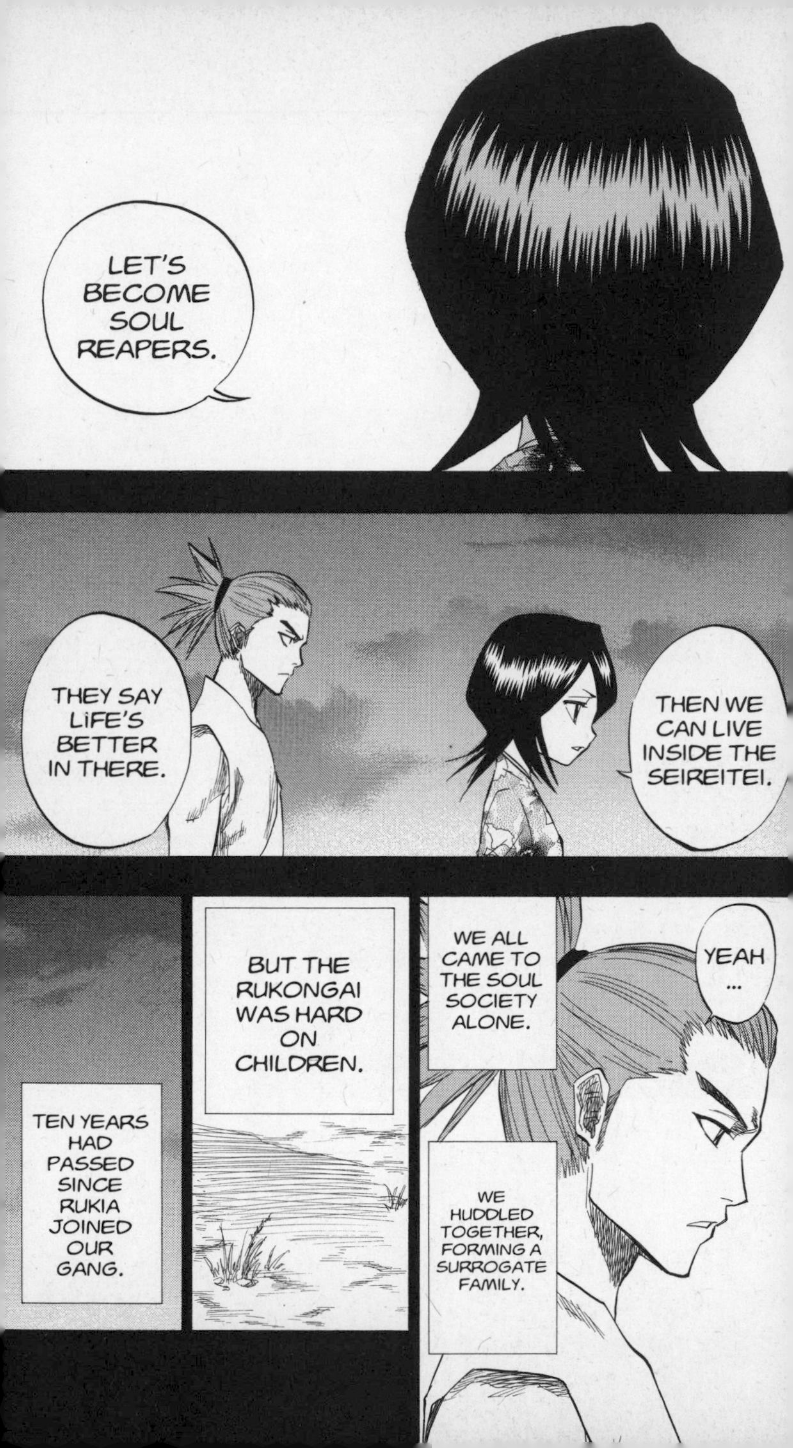
LET'S BECOME SOUL REAPERS.
THEN WE CAN LIVE INSIDE THE SEIREITEI.
THEY SAY LIFE'S BETTER IN THERE.
YEAH ...
WE ALL CAME TO THE SOUL SOCIETY ALONE.
WE HUDDLED TOGETHER, FORMING A SURROGATE FAMILY.
BUT THE RUKONGAI WAS HARD ON CHILDREN.
TEN YEARS HAD PASSED SINCE RUKIA JOINED OUR GANG.

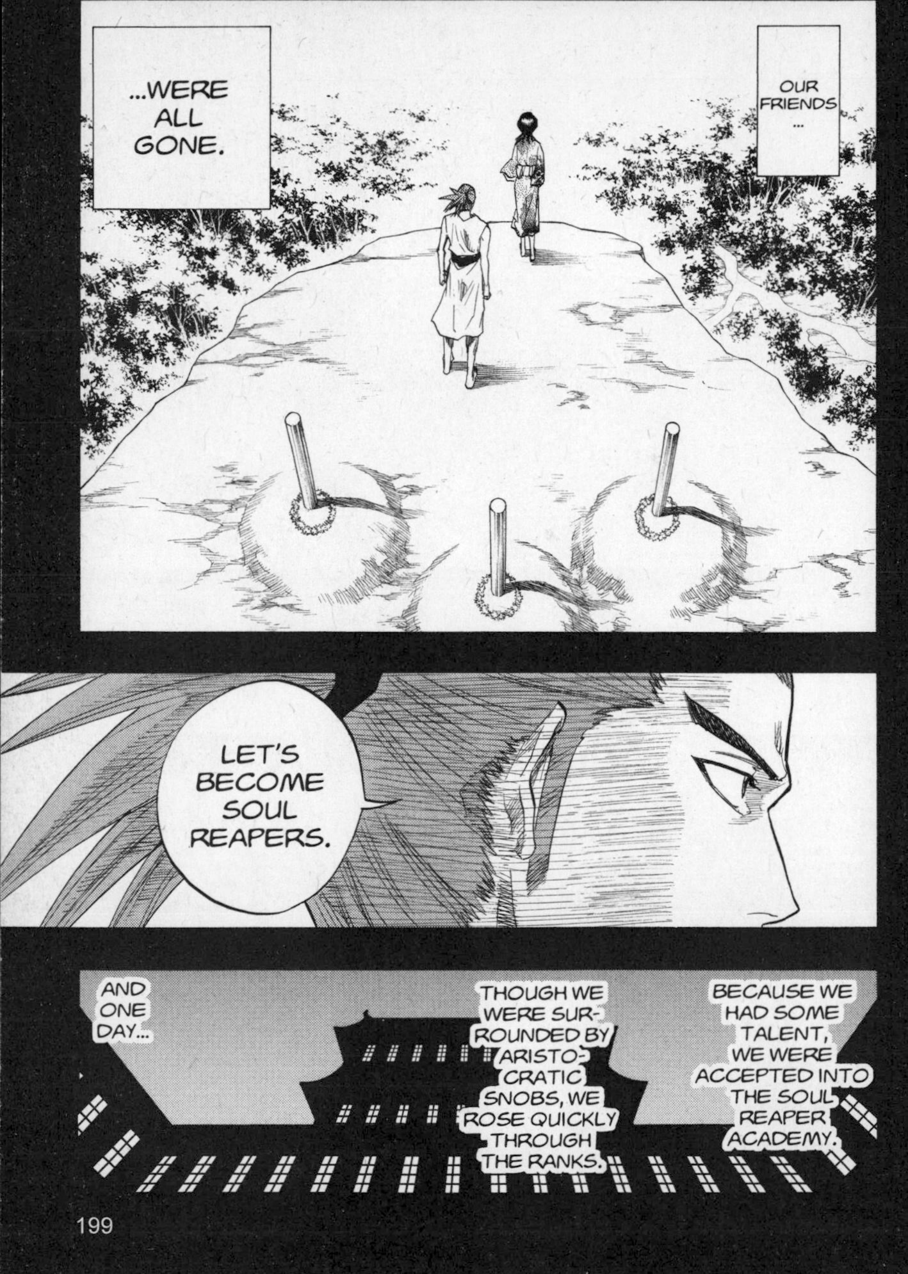
OUR FRIENDS ...
...WERE ALL GONE.
LET'S BECOME SOUL REAPERS.
BECAUSE WE HAD SOME TALENT, WE WERE ACCEPTED INTO THE SOUL REAPER ACADEMY.
THOUGH WE WERE SUR-ROUNDED BY ARISTO-CRATIC SNOBS, WE ROSE QUICKLY THROUGH THE RANKS.
AND ONE DAY...

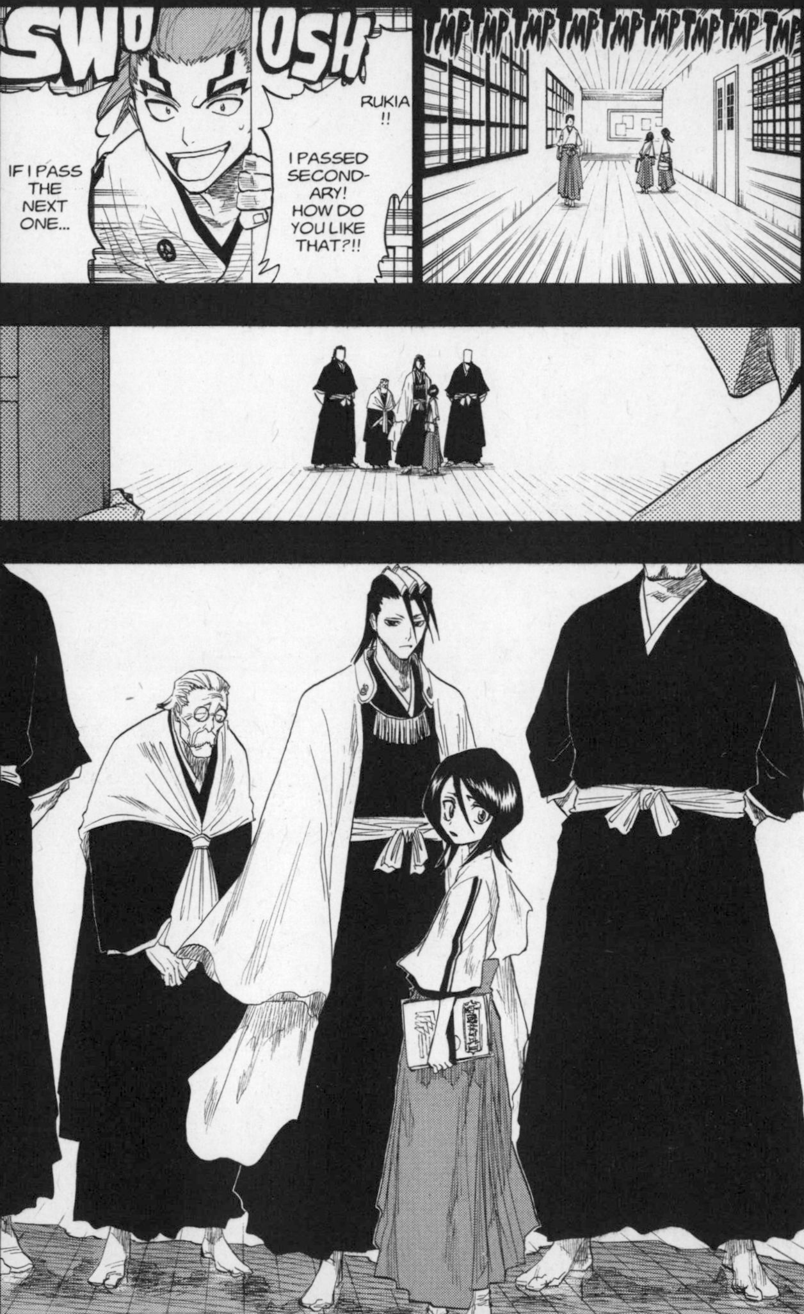
TMP TMP TMP TMP TMP TMP TMP TMP TMP
SWOOSH
RUKIA!!
I PASSED SECONDARY! HOW DO YOU LIKE THAT?!!
IF I PASS THE NEXT ONE...

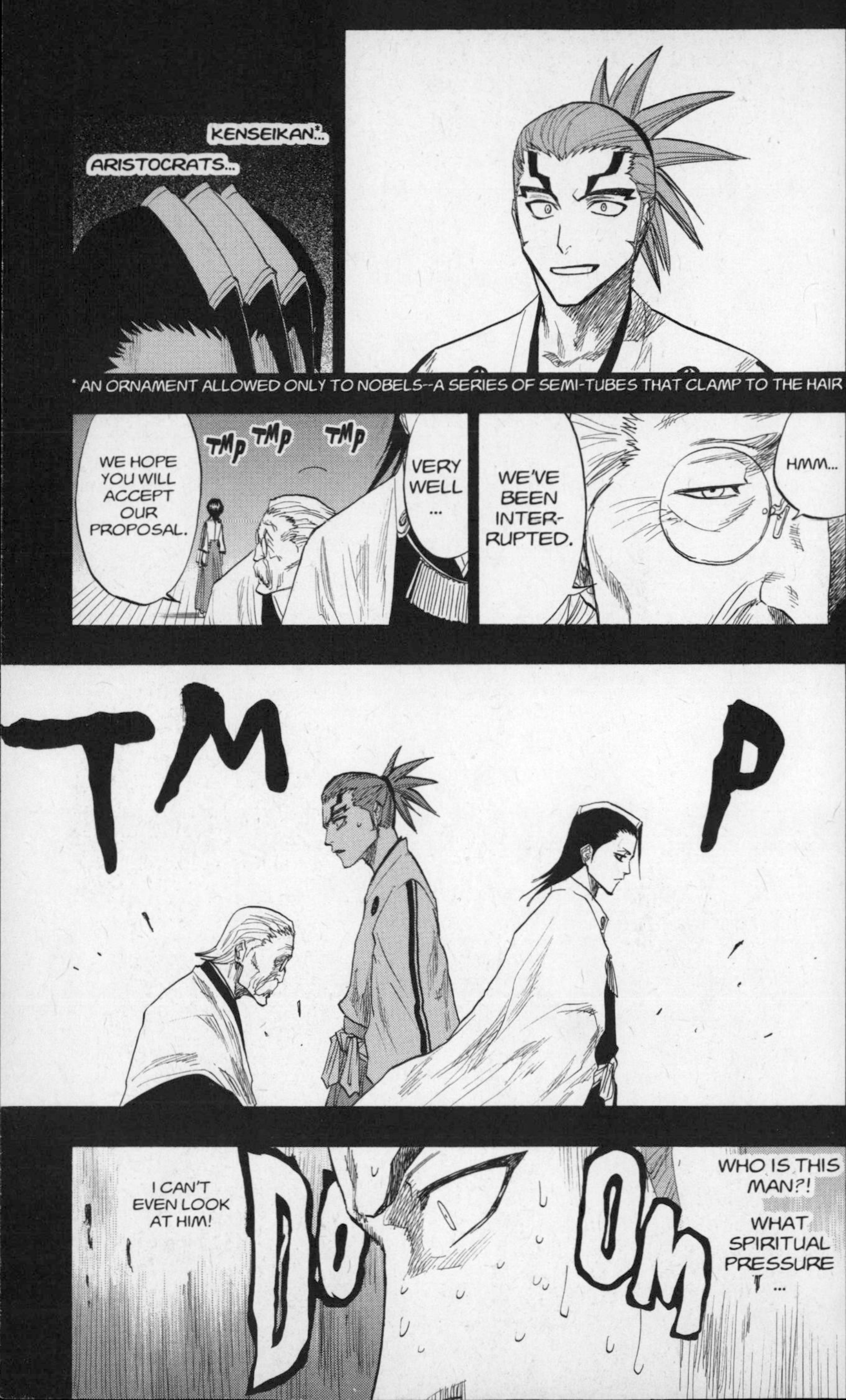
KENSEIKAN*...
ARISTOCRATS...
* AN ORNAMENT ALLOWED ONLY TO NOBELS--A SERIES OF SEMI-TUBES THAT CLAMP TO THE HAIR
HMM...
WE'VE BEEN INTER-RUPTED.
VERY WELL ...
TMP TMP TMP
WE HOPE YOU WILL ACCEPT OUR PROPOSAL.
TMP
WHO IS THIS MAN?!
WHAT SPIRITUAL PRESSURE ...
DOOM
I CAN'T EVEN LOOK AT HIM!

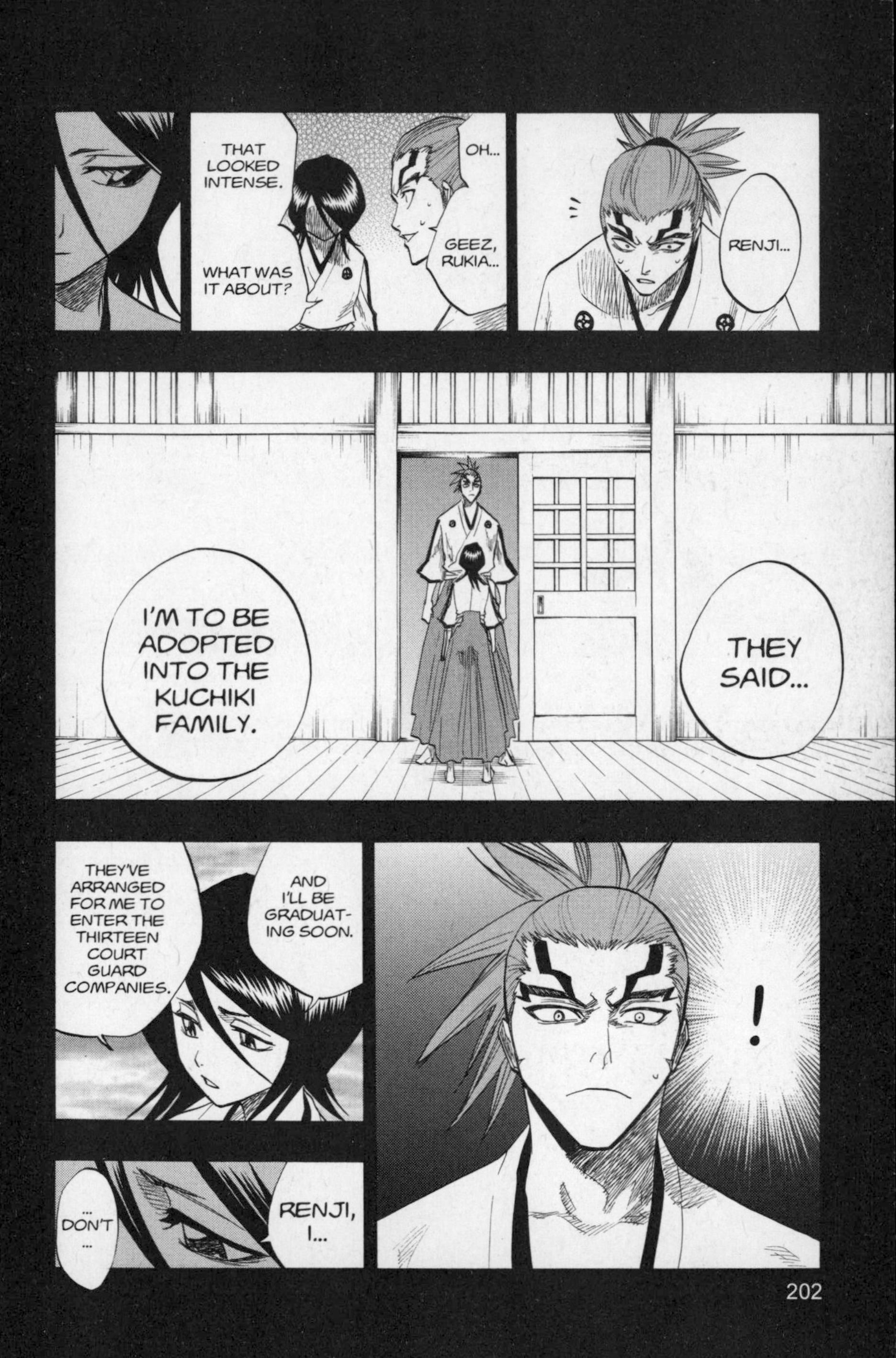
RENJI...
OH...
THAT LOOKED INTENSE.
GEEZ, RUKIA...
WHAT WAS IT ABOUT?
THEY SAID...
I'M TO BE ADOPTED INTO THE KUCHIKI FAMILY.
!
AND I'LL BE GRADUATING SOON.
THEY'VE ARRANGED FOR ME TO ENTER THE THIRTEEN COURT GUARD COMPANIES.
RENJI, I...
... DON'T ...

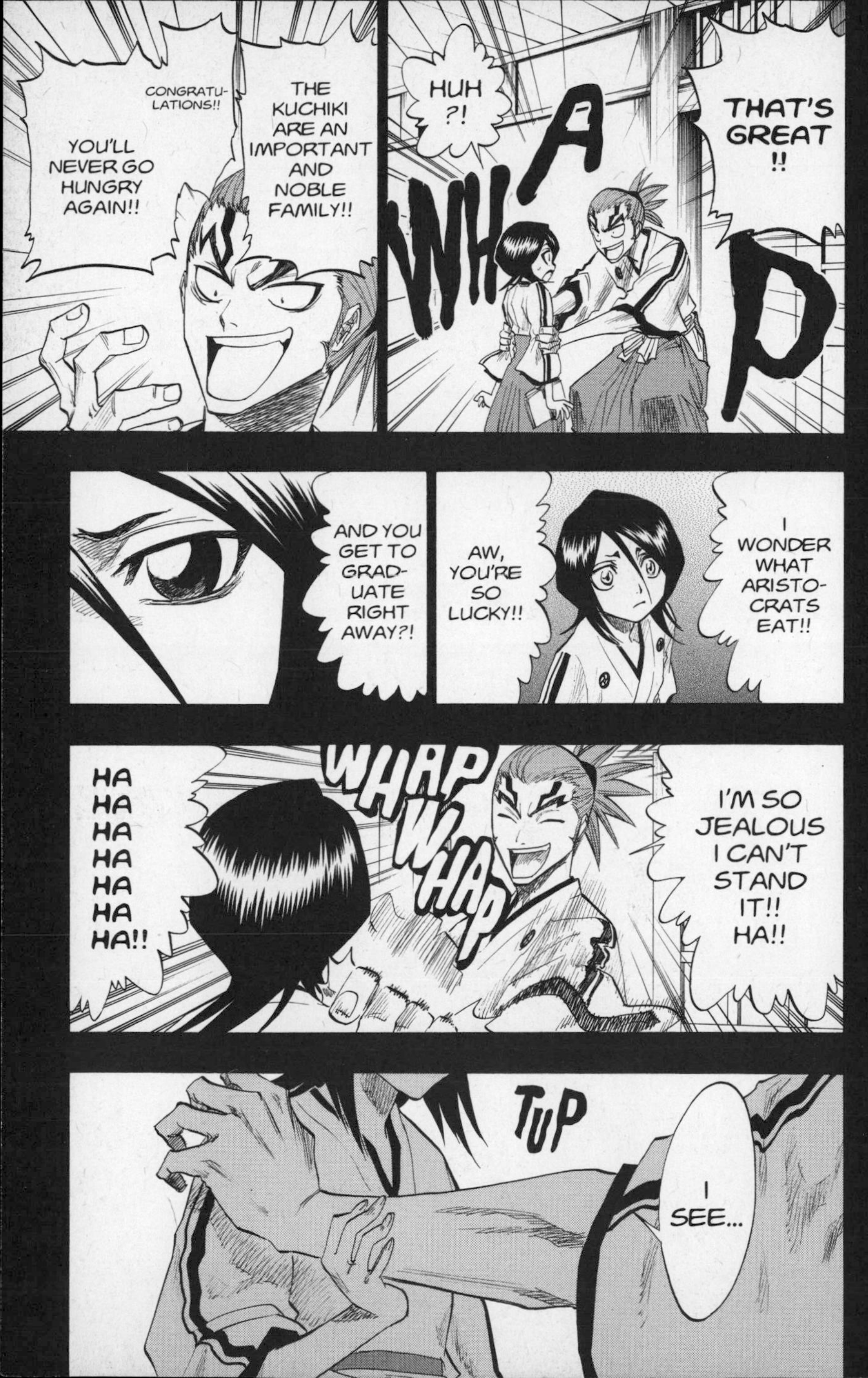
THAT'S GREAT!!
HUH?!
WHAP
THE KUCHIKI ARE AN IMPORTANT AND NOBLE FAMILY!!
CONGRATULATIONS!!
YOU'LL NEVER GO HUNGRY AGAIN!!
I WONDER WHAT ARISTOCRATS EAT!!
AW, YOU'RE SO LUCKY!!
AND YOU GET TO GRADUATE RIGHT AWAY?!
I'M SO JEALOUS I CAN'T STAND IT!! HA!!
WHAP
WHAP
WHAP
HA HA HA HA HA HA HA!!
I SEE...
TUP

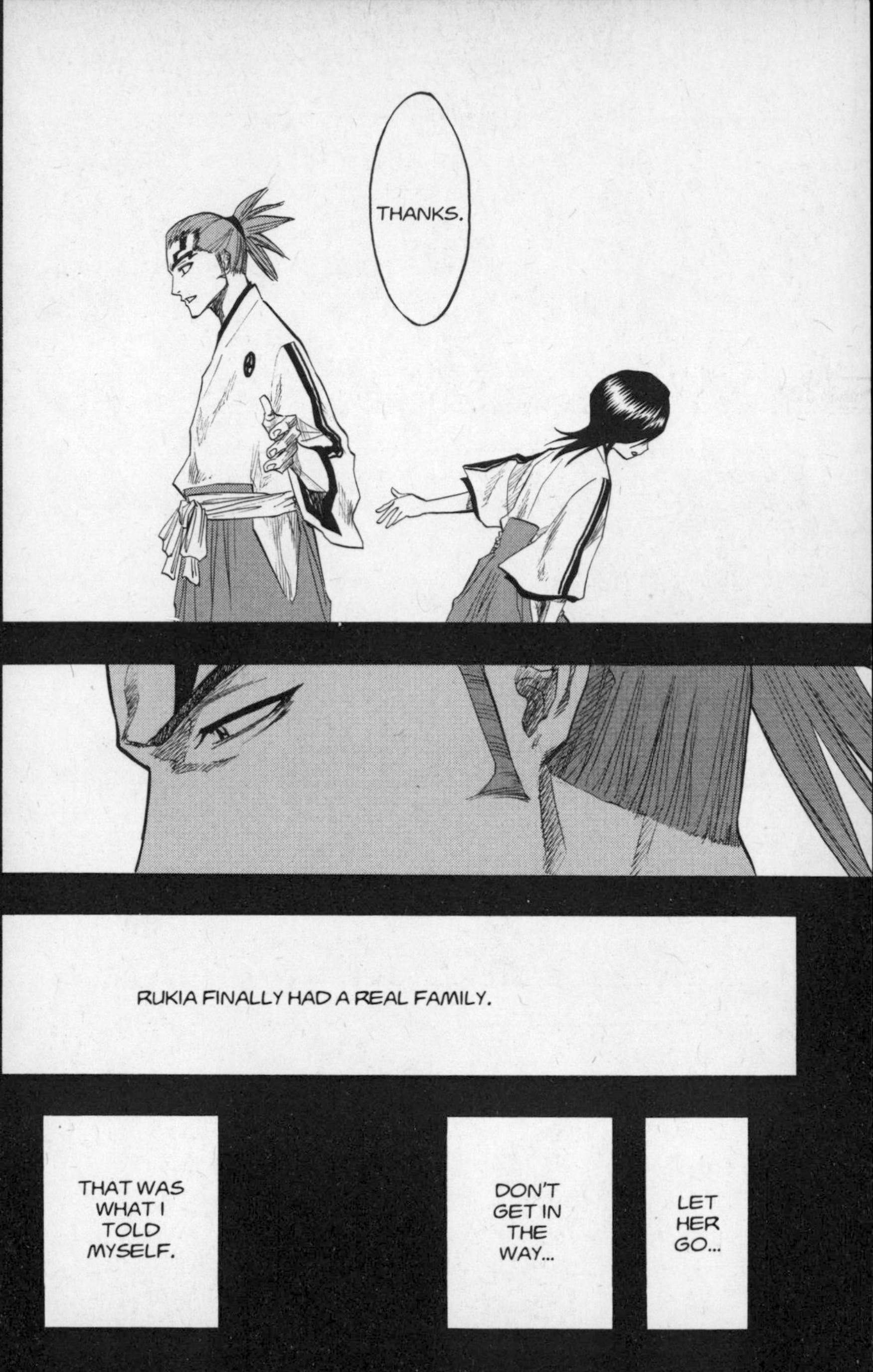
THANKS.
RUKIA FINALLY HAD A REAL FAMILY.
LET HER GO...
DON'T GET IN THE WAY...
THAT WAS WHAT I TOLD MYSELF.

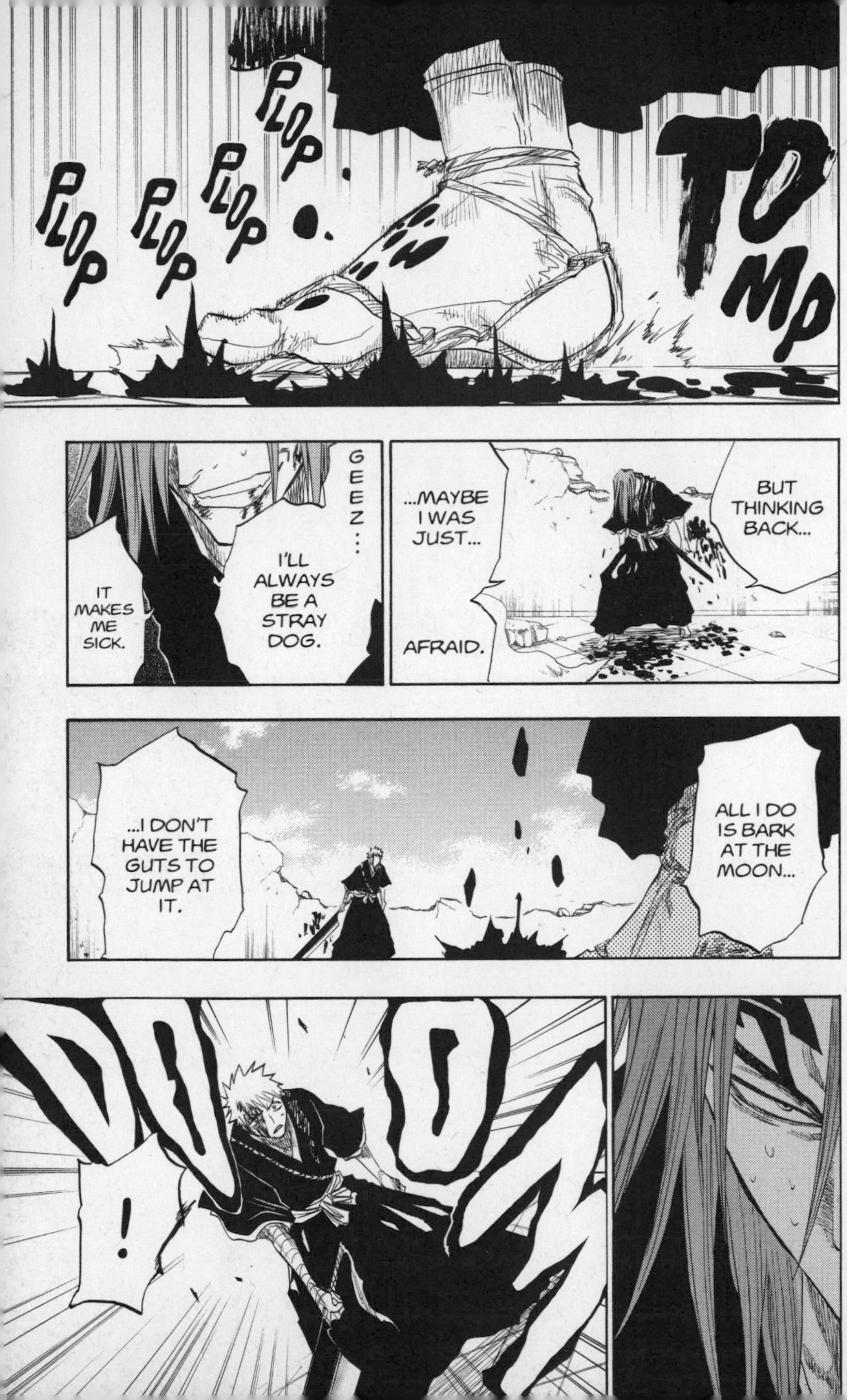
TOMP
PLOP
PLOP
PLOP
PLOP
BUT THINKING BACK...
...MAYBE I WAS JUST...
AFRAID.
GEEZ...
I'LL ALWAYS BE A STRAY DOG.
IT MAKES ME SICK.
ALL I DO IS BARK AT THE MOON...
...I DON'T HAVE THE GUTS TO JUMP AT IT.
!

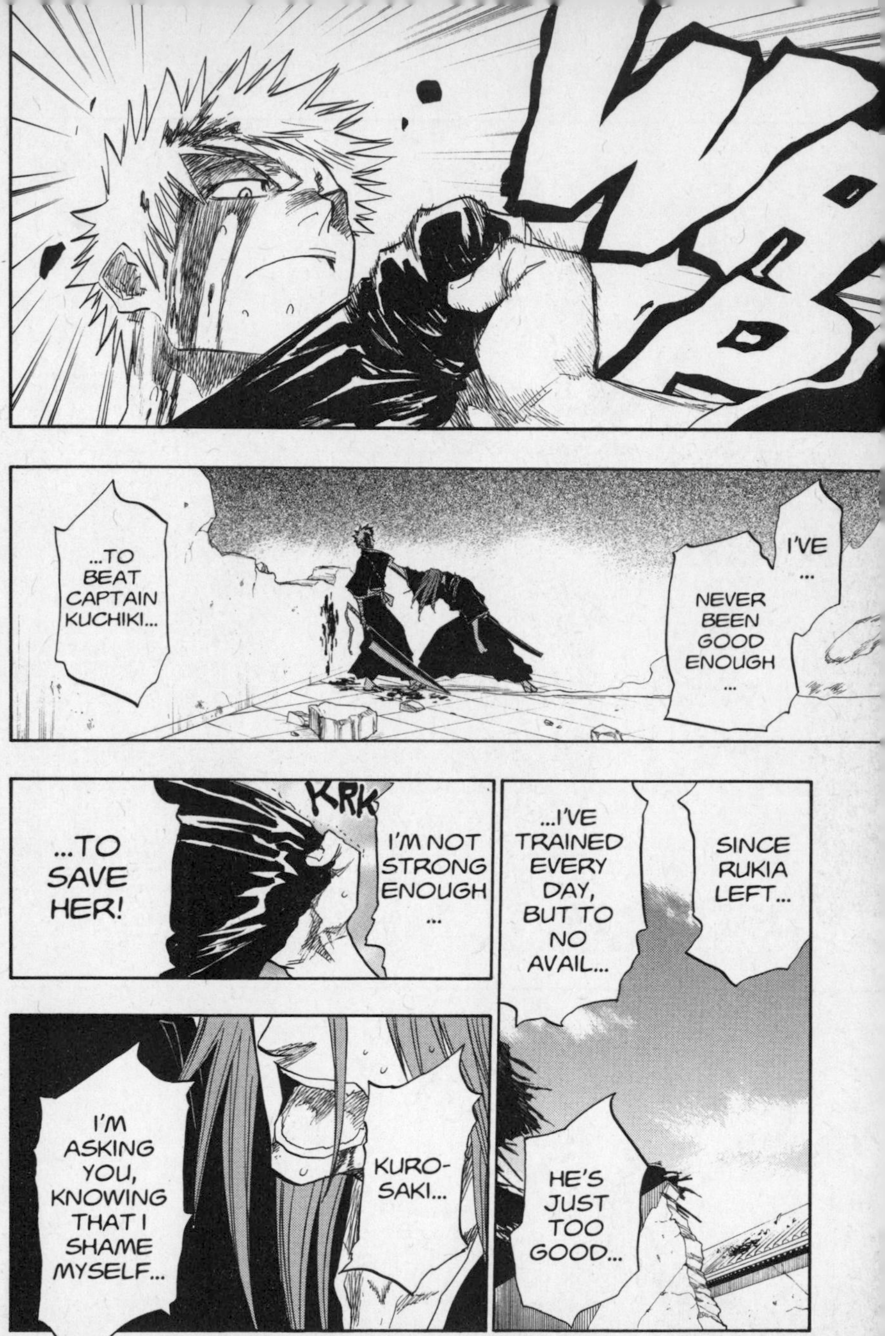
I'VE ... NEVER BEEN GOOD ENOUGH ...
...TO BEAT CAPTAIN KUCHIKI...
SINCE RUKIA LEFT...
...I'VE TRAINED EVERY DAY, BUT TO NO AVAIL...
HE'S JUST TOO GOOD...
KRK
I'M NOT STRONG ENOUGH ...
...TO SAVE HER!
KURO-SAKI...
I'M ASKING YOU, KNOWING THAT I SHAME MYSELF...

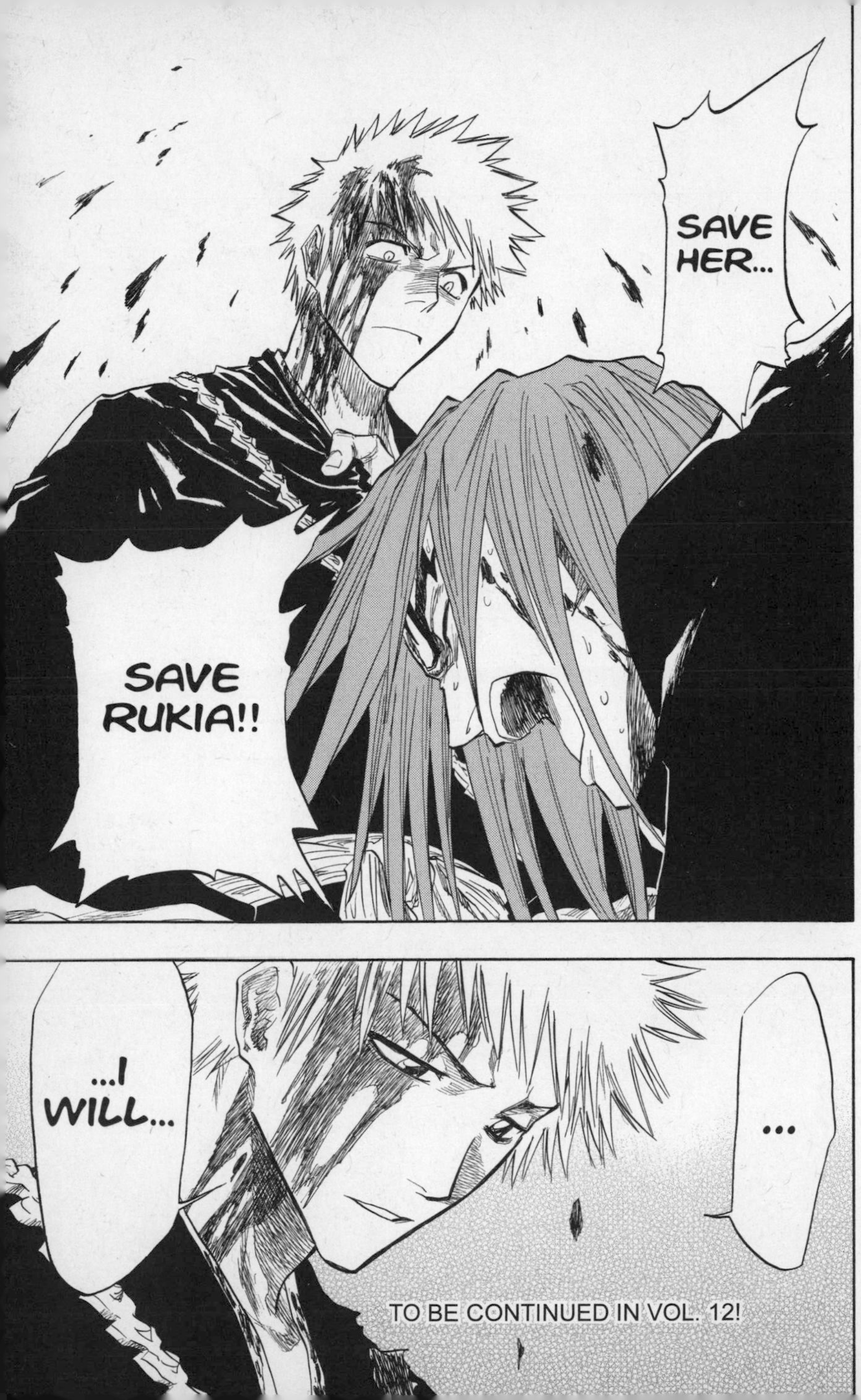
SAVE HER...
SAVE RUKIA!!
...
...I WILL...
TO BE CONTINUED IN VOL. 12!

Next Volume Preview

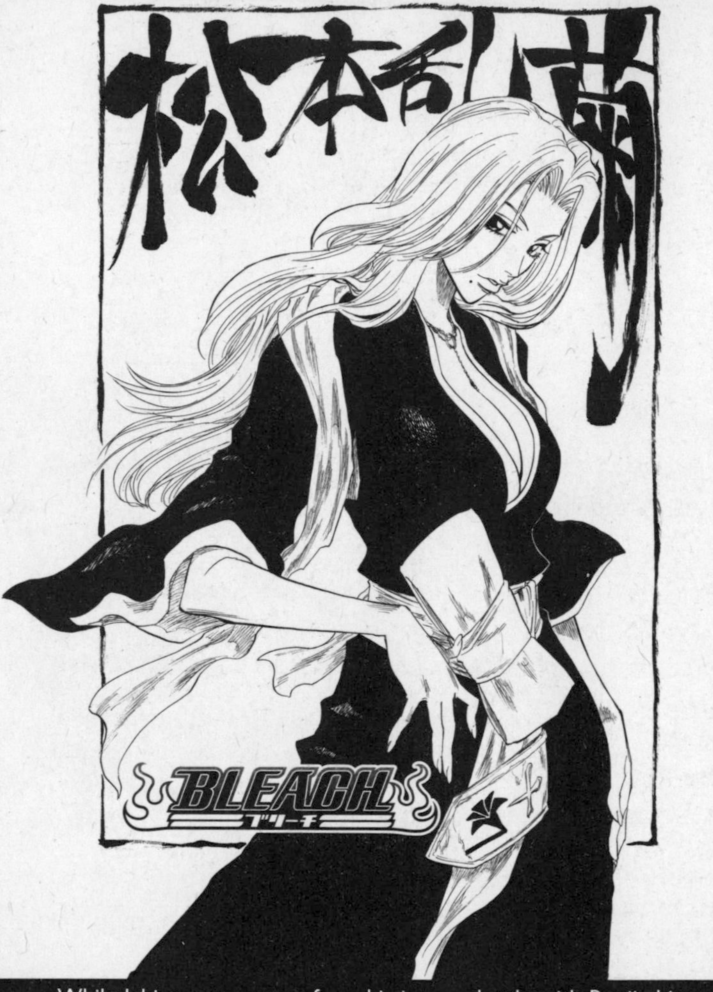
松本乱菊
BLEACH
ブリーチ

While Ichigo recuperates from his intense battle with Renji, things get really intense at Soul Reaper HQ. Now in a state of full alert, all Soul Reaper officers, including assistant captains, are allowed to carry–and use–their Zanpaku-tô. Rumor has it, though, that something untoward is brewing in Third Company, and all eyes are on its enigmatic captain, Gin Ichimaru. Just what is Gin planning, and how will this affect the Soul Reapers' war against Ichigo?!

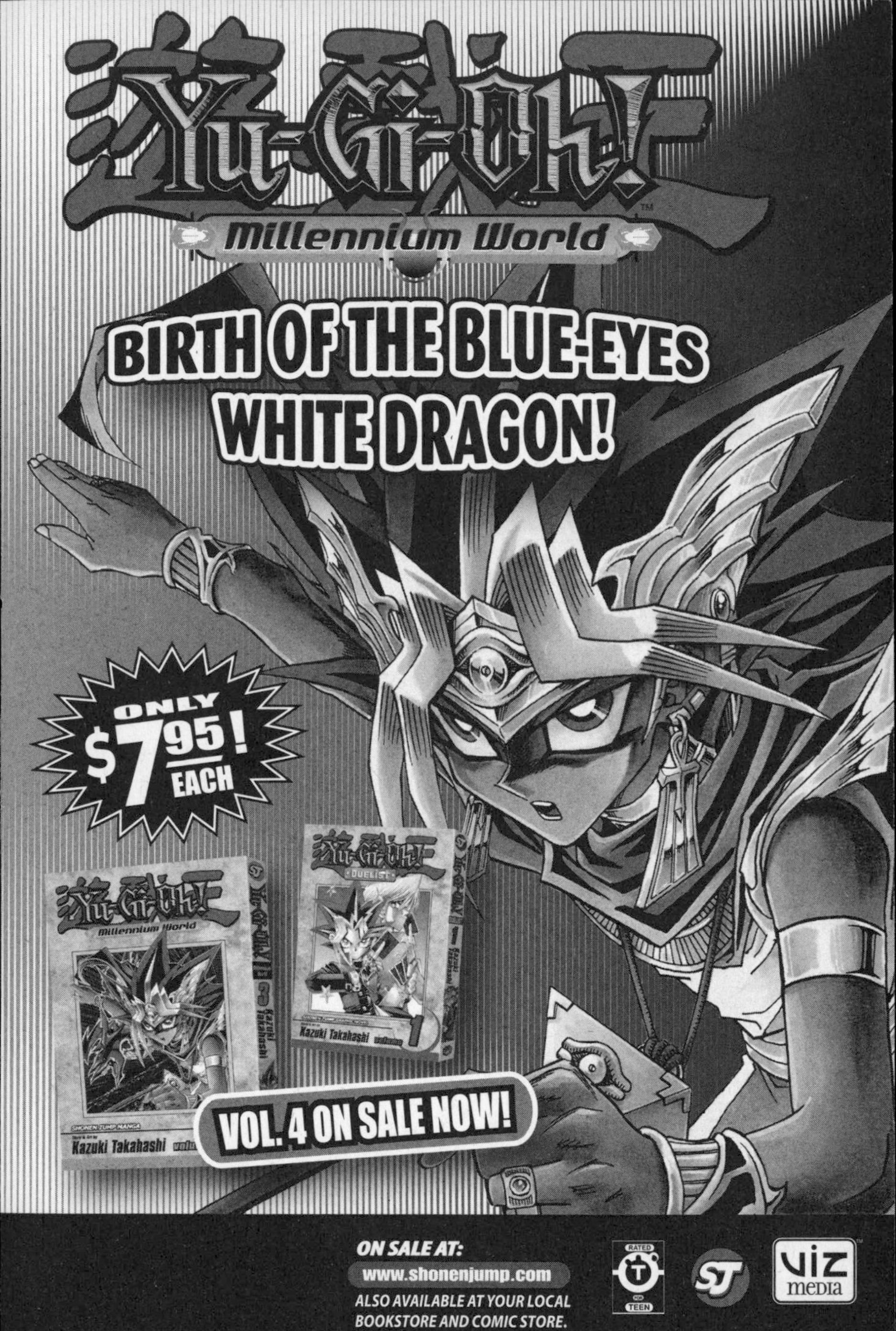
Yu-Gi-Oh!™
Millennium World
BIRTH OF THE BLUE-EYES WHITE DRAGON!
ONLY $7.95! EACH
Yu-Gi-Oh!
Millennium World
SHONEN JUMP MANGA
Kazuki Takahashi
Yu-Gi-Oh!
DUELIST
Kazuki Takahashi
VOL. 4 ON SALE NOW!
ON SALE AT:
www.shonenjump.com
ALSO AVAILABLE AT YOUR LOCAL BOOKSTORE AND COMIC STORE.
RATED T FOR TEEN
SJ
VIZ media

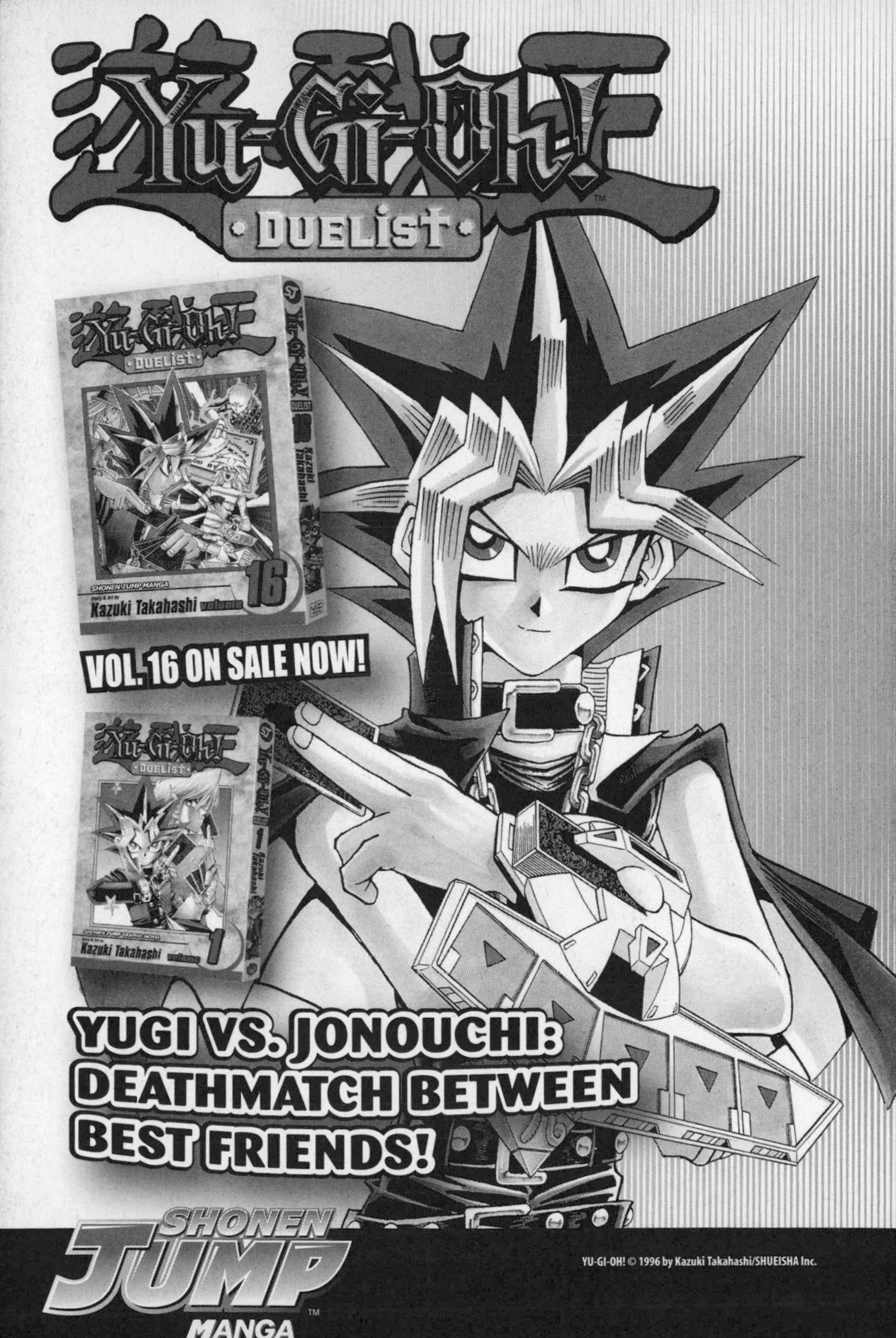
YU-GI-OH! DUELIST
VOL. 16 ON SALE NOW!
YUGI VS. JONOUCHI: DEATHMATCH BETWEEN BEST FRIENDS!
SHONEN JUMP MANGA
YU-GI-OH! © 1996 by Kazuki Takahashi/SHUEISHA Inc.

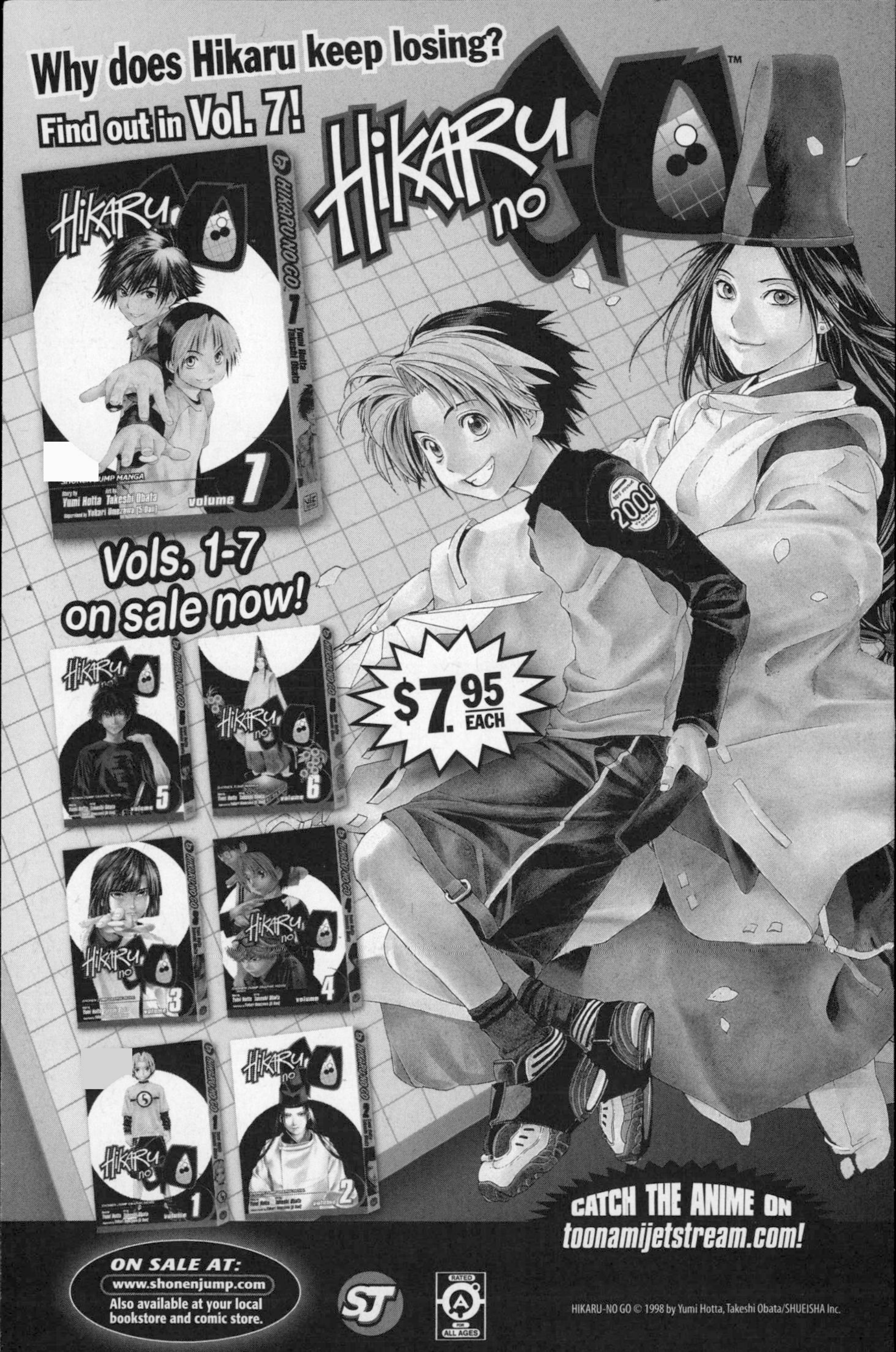
Why does Hikaru keep losing?
Find out in Vol. 7!
HIKARU no GO™
Vols. 1-7
on sale now!
$7.95 EACH
CATCH THE ANIME ON
toonamijetstream.com!
ON SALE AT:
www.shonenjump.com
Also available at your local bookstore and comic store.
RATED A FOR ALL AGES
HIKARU-NO GO © 1998 by Yumi Hotta, Takeshi Obata/SHUEISHA Inc.

Tell us what you think about
SHONEN JUMP manga!

Our survey is now available online.
Go to: www.*SHONENJUMP*.com/*mangasurvey*

Help us make our product
offering better!

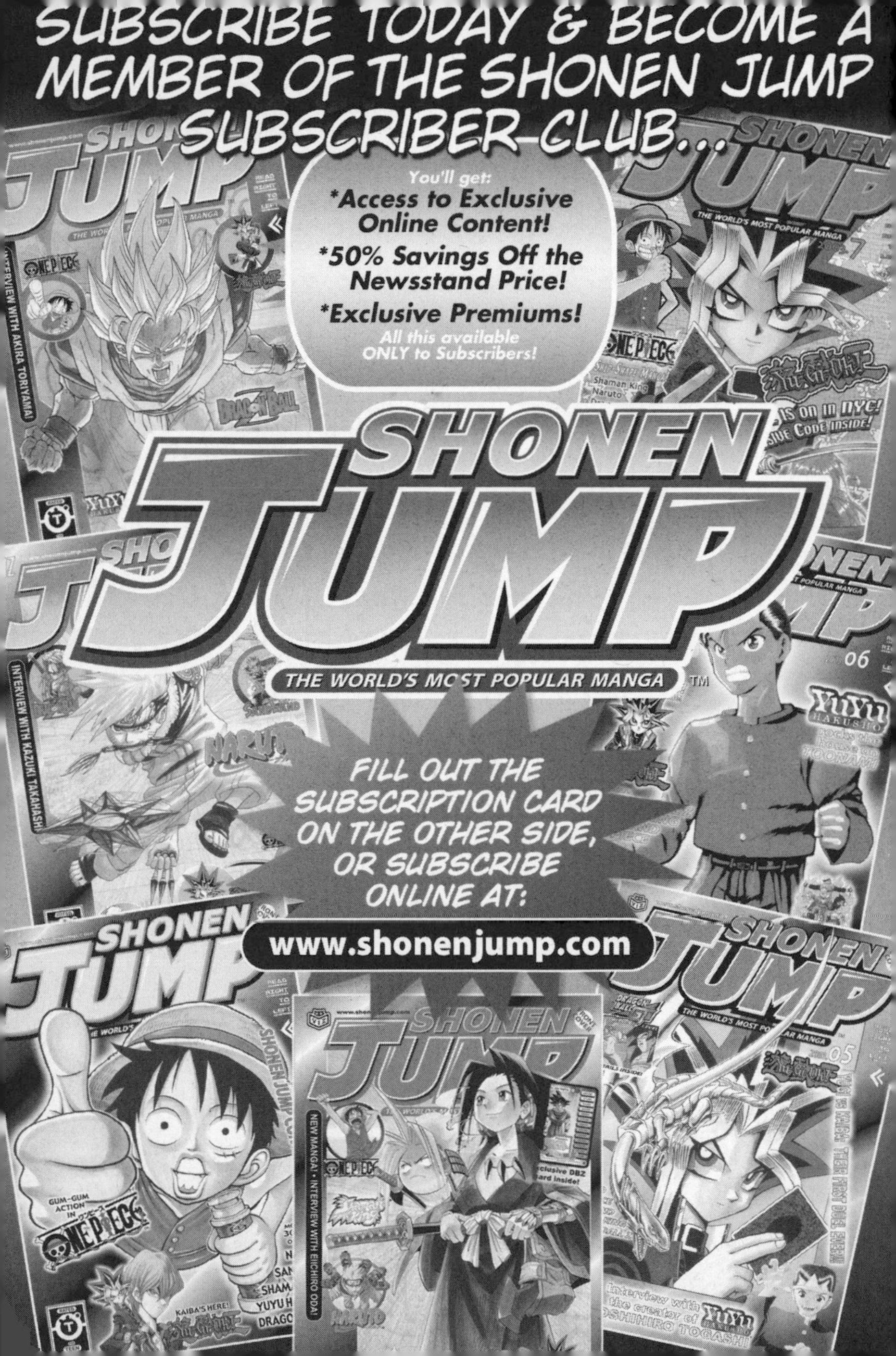
SUBSCRIBE TODAY & BECOME A MEMBER OF THE SHONEN JUMP SUBSCRIBER CLUB...
You'll get:
*Access to Exclusive Online Content!
*50% Savings Off the Newsstand Price!
*Exclusive Premiums!
All this available ONLY to Subscribers!
SHONEN JUMP
THE WORLD'S MOST POPULAR MANGA ™
FILL OUT THE SUBSCRIPTION CARD ON THE OTHER SIDE, OR SUBSCRIBE ONLINE AT:
www.shonenjump.com